THE REVOLUTION IN ANTHROPOLOGY

INTERNATIONAL LIBRARY OF SOCIOLOGY
AND SOCIAL RECONSTRUCTION

Founded by Karl Mannheim
Editor: W. J. H. Sprott

A catalogue of the books available in the INTERNATIONAL LIBRARY OF SOCIOLOGY AND SOCIAL RECONSTRUCTION, and new books in preparation for the Library, will be found at the end of this volume.

THE REVOLUTION
IN ANTHROPOLOGY

by

I. C. JARVIE

*Associate Professor of Philosophy
at York University, Toronto*

with a Foreword by

ERNEST GELLNER

*Professor of Sociology,
London School of Economics*

LONDON

ROUTLEDGE & KEGAN PAUL

First published 1964
by Routledge & Kegan Paul Ltd
Broadway House, 68–74 Carter Lane
London, E.C.4

Reprinted (with corrections and additions) 1967
Reprinted 1970

Reproduced and Printed in Great Britain by
Redwood Press Limited
Trowbridge & London

ISBN 0 7100 3440 7

FOREWORD

TWO teachers, amongst the many who have taught at the London School of Economics, are unlikely to be forgotten: Bronislaw Malinowski and Karl Popper. As thinkers, they are both complementary and contrasted. As teachers, they have certain characteristics in common, as far as I can judge (though I have never met Malinowski); they inspire as well as teach. Their seminars are (in Malinowski's case, were) electric and absorbing; they are not something 'on the syllabus' and the time-table that has to be given by the teacher and attended by the student; they are, on the contrary, parts of the history of the School and of their respective subjects, places where minds are (or were) formed or fertilised, where a life's work could be given its form and direction; they are objects of strong feeling. The list of the participants in Malinowski's seminars between the wars is very close to the list of present leaders in his subject. The importance of the ideas of these two thinkers is proportionate to the inspiration and feeling which they generate.

Their contributions to thought are of course not similar. Malinowski was the founder (or co-founder, with the late Professor Radcliffe-Brown) of modern style social anthropology. In substance, this consists of a shift of attention *from* speculative genetic theories of human society, and the associated attempt to use contemporary simple societies as surrogate time-machines, *to* intensive, thorough and accurate field-work, and a style of explanation which concentrates on exploring the interrelations of activities and institutions at any one given time, and refrains from invoking the passage of time as a facile and often vacuous deus ex machina. To paraphrase a remark of Dr. Zhivago's, the life of societies is something which has point in itself—it is not made up of left-overs of which they have somehow forgotten to divest themselves, or, for that matter, of anticipations of the future. Properly understood, this approach involves a disregard neither of history nor of change.

The achievements of this school are by now very considerable. Malinowski was most fortunate in his successor and successors. As a result of their work, our knowledge and our understanding of 'primitive' society are incomparably greater, in kind and extent, than they were before. If this—the recording of the simpler forms of life, before they disappear—were all, the contribution of 'functionalist' anthropology would already be of utmost importance. In fact, however, the anthropologist's characteristic approach, now centred on the valuable if hard-to-define notion of 'structure', is as fertile when applied to small communities anywhere, irrespective of the level of their technology, and may well prove as valuable when employed in the study of large societies.

The contribution of Karl Popper, primarily a philosopher, is not easy to summarise. From the viewpoint of those concerned with human society, however, his role was not unlike that of Malinowski: at a time when so much was dull, he was exciting. The hero of Thomas Mann's *Death in Venice* was described as having taught a grateful generation that it was possible to plumb the depths of knowledge without losing firmness of moral conviction: Popper taught some grateful members of another generation that it was possible to use the most razor-sharp and ruthless tools of philosophy and logic, and yet be deeply interesting and relevant to moral and social issues. The original centre of Popper's concern and work was epistemology, logic, methodology: the problem of the delimitation of science and the understanding of its progress. But when, in *The Open Society and Its Enemies*, he turned to politics, the thing which gave that work its appeal was the intimate interdependence in its argument of logical and epistemological issues on the one hand, and political and social ones on the other. He showed that there was no opposition between clarity and importance.

If we turn to the actual substance of the preoccupations and doctrines of the two thinkers and their schools, contrasts and oppositions are at least as striking as similarities. The most obvious similarity concerns the notion of *time*: Malinowski and Popper are probably the two most important influences that have undermined the facile invocation of the flow of time, and their viewpoints on this subject are similar. Malinowski's influence was, I suspect, the greater in destroying misguided uses of the past in social explanation, and it worked mainly through the example of his actual work, and that of his followers, rather than through the formal arguments; Popper's influence, on the other hand, has been far more important in demolishing the moral invocation of time, the ethical arguments from alleged directions of historic development, etc.

In other spheres, however, the two traditions appear destined for violent opposition. The Malinowskian image of society would seem to stress 'organic' interdependence, and its ethical suggestiveness is in the same direction: at the centre of Popper's ethics is the rejection of the cosy social womb. On method, the Malinowskian cult of field-work would seem, at least superficially, to be in conflict with the high Popperian valuation of intellectual daring, and the view of observation merely as a check on the truth of theories, rather than as the gateway to truth itself. (A witty follower of Popper once observed to me: 'For us Popperites, all facts are really falsifications.') For purposes of contrast with the commended Open Society, Popper operates with a model of tribal society which is a kind of Brave New World retro-jected into the past, a stable order without moral ambiguity—a picture which modern anthropology has in fact done much to destroy. No doubt there are other points of potential disagreement as well.

It is curious that two such stirring systems of thought, natural allies on at least one important point and perhaps natural opponents on a number of others, housed under the same roof (even if the two founder-teachers were not there at the same time), should so far have interacted relatively little. Some sparks have flown: but we were entitled to expect fireworks.

Part of the very considerable significance and interest of Mr. Jarvie's book, *The Revolution in Anthropology*, is that he has assembled a good number of the available fireworks; he has applied a match to the blue paper and, following the instruction in one of Mr. Searle's cartoons, he is now standing close. It is my desire to wish him the very best of luck, cordially if somewhat hurriedly, before I remove myself.

His vigorous book really does three things simultaneously: it is a study of the anthropological tradition; it is the working out of the implications of Popper's philosophy of science for the study of society; and it is a discussion of the problem of 'Cargo Cults' and a critical survey of the literature on this fascinating phenomenon. 'Cargo Cults' are messianic movements arising amongst primitive peoples, suddenly confronted with the marvels of modern technology and its riches, 'Cargo', often as a result of the Pacific war—movements which aim at obtaining for their participants the white man's 'Cargo' by magical means.

Mr. Jarvie does not, unfortunately, explore the cross-implications in the other direction, so to speak—the implications *of* anthropological work *for* Popper's notion of a 'closed society'. His claim that Popper really only means 'acephalous' tribes, when he speaks of the closed society, shows that Jarvie is aware of the problems involved here: but the remark itself seems to me ill-founded, and moreover if true, it would still not obviate the problem in question.

The three themes which he does so vigorously explore are closely interdependent. Mr. Jarvie's own field-work is of the anthropological community itself. (There is an irony about this, for Mr. Jarvie attacks the cult of field-work as a necessary precondition—

but in fact his superiority to those other philosophers, who graciously offer advice to becalmed social scientists as from a passing liner, is precisely that he really is familiar with the content and rules of anthropological discussion, that he has been to the region which concerns him.) He would however be untrue to his own principles if he were merely to discuss a *field*, rather than a *problem*. But Cargo Cults do constitute a crucial problem for anthropology. The subject of anthropology has tended to be simple and stable communities: Cargo Cults occur amongst simpler people, but they are the very opposite of stable. They are a phenomenon which, at the very least, presents a stumbling block to conventional anthropology.

Anthropology is facing a crisis in any case (Cargo Cults or not). This crisis arises, roughly, from the fact that Malinowskian anthropology has brought forth a very rich harvest in the form of knowledge and understanding of individual societies; it has not been as fertile as some have hoped in providing general or comparative theories. This crisis is connected not only with the methodological doctrines of anthropologists, but also, as Mr. Jarvie points out, with the internal organisation of the subject. The cures which Mr. Jarvie finds in philosophy are intended for this general crisis, as well as for the specific problem of Cargo Cults which highlights it and provides it with concrete, and inherently fascinating, illustration. Mr. Jarvie's title, *The Revolution in Anthropology*, is (no doubt deliberately) ambiguous: he describes one revolution which occurred a generation ago, and he is also anxious to be an assistant midwife for another one which is about to take place. He is somewhat harsh on those who would not move in the same direction: but then, revolutions are not periods of consensus. In any case, these are no fragile plants, and one need not fear for their fate.

Thus the rich triple bill which he offers has at the same time a complete organic unity (if he will forgive me the expression). It is bound to be of outstanding interest to anthropologists, philosophers, and those interested in Cargo Cults. They will not be able to avoid at the same time learning a very great deal about the other two subjects.

ERNEST GELLNER

CONTENTS

FOREWORD   *page* v

PREFACE   xiii
  1. The Problem of too much Methodology   xiii
  2. Summary of the Structure of the Argument   xvi
  3. The Problems to be Solved   xvii
  4. The Material to be Used   xviii
  5. Qualification: Philosophical Anthropology   xix

ACKNOWLEDGEMENTS   xxi

1. METAPHYSICS AND METHOD IN SOCIAL
   ANTHROPOLOGY   1
  1. Sobriety in the Scientific Attitude   3
  2. Metaphysical Interest in Human Society   7
  3. Malinowski's Critique: True *versus* Satisfactory
     Explanation   16
  4. Method, Induction and Theory   18
  5. Fact Worship in the Social Structure of Social Anthropology   28
  6. Candidate Explanation Frameworks: Situational Logic
     and Structural Functionalism   34
  7. The Slogans of the Revolution   42
  8. The Problem of Method Formulated   44
  9. Cargo Cults and the Problem of Method   47
 10. Method   48
 11. Background to the Case-study   49

2. AN EMPIRICAL CASE-STUDY: THE PROBLEM OF
   CARGO CULTS   55
  1. The Problem of Preliminary Descriptions   55
  2. General Description of Cargo Cults   56
  3. The Vailala Madness   59
  4. The Cult of John Frum   61
  5. Cults among the Garia   63
  6. Summary of the Distinctive Features of Cargo Cults   64
  7. A Theory of Cargo Cults   66
  8. The Problems of Cargo Cults   68

3. A SURVEY OF EXPLANATIONS OF CARGO CULTS   74
  1. Introduction: The Limitations and Value of Surveys   74
  2. The Prophet Dun It   83

Contents

3. It was All their Own Fault   *page* 87
4. Circumstances are to Blame   88
5. Prophets, Followers and Circumstances   92
6. Three Authors and their Theories   93
    (A) C. S. Belshaw   93
    (B) H. Ian Hogbin   97
    (C) K. O. L. Burridge   99
7. Conclusion   105

4. EXPLANATION AND EXPLAINING THE CULTS   106
1. Criteria of Explanation   106
2. Meeting the Criteria   107
3. Stating the Problems   109
4. How to Explain Social Change   111
5. An Explanation of Cargo Cults   114
    (A.1) Millenarianism in general   116
    (A.2) Cargo Cults in particular   117
    (B)   Cult doctrine   123
    (C)   Similarities of the Cults   125
    (D)   The apocalyptic aspect   127
6. Conclusion   128

5. METHODOLOGICAL DISCUSSION OF THE THEORIES   131
1. Religion is not Rational   131
2. The Rationality of Ignorance   142
3. All Historical Events are Unique   144
4. People aren't Rational   146
5. Belief does not explain Action   149
6. The Lack of a Structural-Functional Explanation   152
7. Structural-Functionalism's Difficulties with Social
    Change   154
8. The Failure to Find a Structural-Functional Explana-
    tion of Cargo Cults   156
9. Can there be a Structural-Functional Explanation of
    Social Change?   157
10. Other Faults of the Theories and their Presentation   159
11. How far have the Theories Solved the Problems they
    were Intended to Solve?   162
12. Conclusion   168

6. THE AIMS AND METHODS OF SOCIAL ANTHROPOLOGY   170
1. Back to Frazer   170
2. Remarks on the History of the Revolution in Social
    Anthropology   176
3. Functionalism   182
4. Structural-Functionalism   189
5. Anthropology as History: Evans-Pritchard and Worsley   198
6. Social Anthropology as the Science of Man   207
    (i) Contemporary Social Anthropology as Science   208

Contents

(ii) The Logic of the Situation and the Unintended Consequences of our Actions   *page* 216
    (iii) The Value of a Method   224

APPENDIX I
Eisler: Christianity as Millenarian Cult   225

APPENDIX II
Millennial Dreams in Action   229
    1. Thrupp's Report on the Conference   229
    2. Cohn on the Middle Ages   230
    3. Shepperson on the Comparative Study of the Movements   230
    4. Guiart on the Cargo Cults   231
    5. Eliade on Cosmic Regeneration   232
    6. Aberle on Relative Deprivation   232
    7. Kaminsky on Explanation   233
    8. Conclusion   233

APPENDIX III
Lawrence on the Explanation of Cargo Cults   234

BIBLIOGRAPHY   243

INDEX OF NAMES   251

INDEX OF SUBJECTS   254

PREFACE

1. *The Problem of too much Methodology*

PEOPLE complain that too much is written on the methods of the social sciences. Rightly they urge that sociologists and social anthropologists should spend more time on their work and on producing results than on talking about how they are going to do it. But what if they can't get on with their work? What if they are blocked? Is then the resort to methodology so surprising?

It should not be forgotten that present-day sociology, usually (and mistakenly) dated from Comte, grew up under the shadow of a vigorous and successful tradition of natural science, founded by Galileo and Newton. Scientific success, like all success, tends to have its worshippers. This worshipping was attacked by Bacon who said very early on that there was nothing mysterious or magical about science. Its methods were, Bacon argued, the key to its success. Once you understood these methods you would be able to duplicate science's achievements and see how unmysterious it was. Bacon argued that there should be no worship of the success of science, merely a patient application of those methods which had led to success and would no doubt do so again.

Naturally Bacon was misunderstood; many would-be social scientists took it that he was saying 'worship not the false god of science but the True God of Scientific Method which grants success in all fields of inquiry.' He was misunderstood because although he had denounced worship he had announced a new ritual: true scientific method. Ritual has a fascination for sociologists; they tend to take it seriously independent of the beliefs which back it. Bacon's ritual was taken seriously and his reasons for proposing it (which anyhow were very shaky) were not bothered with. Thus it was that scientific method became the object of a cult among social scientists —a cargo cult. Nearly all religions promise to deliver one or another sort of goods; they will save your soul or bring you to nirvana. A cargo cult is a religion which promises literally to deliver goods—like the cargo in a ship's hold. If the cultists carry out their religious performances properly some desirable goods will, it is believed, be delivered to them. In this case the deity was scientific method, the ritual was unprejudiced observation and patient induction, and the cargo the deity would deliver if worshipped by means of the correct ritual would be a science of society comparable in vigour and success to natural science.

This cargo cult religion, which F. A. Hayek nicknamed scientism, like most cargo cults, never produced the cargo. Consequently the cultists have tried to find out why. The most popular explanation has been that scientific method was not worshipped properly; its rituals were not properly carried out. A huge and barren literature on what the true rituals are was produced by those who accepted this explanation. Considerable comfort was to be found in an equally huge and barren literature which had been produced by philosophers and philosophers of science who had gone into Bacon's reasons for his new ritual and had found them unsound. Hayek has a better suggestion as to why the cargo has not come. He argues simply that scientism is a false religion because it is based in false ideas about science and scientific method, and in a false belief that the social sciences should ape the natural sciences.

My excuse for writing this book is that I have another explanation to suggest of the failure to produce the goods. A worshipping attitude is misplaced in these matters, certainly; but more important, the object of worship—true scientific method—does not exist in the form which Bacon claimed, and thus worship of it is ineffective. There does not exist, I believe, a 'scientific method' which can be mechanically applied and will produce results. But I think social scientists can learn from the natural sciences. They cannot learn from the false prophet of the natural sciences, Bacon. His ideas, and especially misinterpretations of his ideas, are a barrier to a vigorous and successful social science. In arguing all this I am simply working out for social science some ideas of K. R. Popper. In particular his thesis that scientific success is a product of being critical and having an incredible amount of luck.

So much for the history of the interest in method in the social sciences. I think to explain the continuing interest today another factor has to be brought in. My suggestion is this. People often turn to religion when they find themselves in a crisis or under stress. I believe that social scientists turn to the religion of scientific method when they find themselves in the intellectual situation of seeming to be unable to get to grips with, or to see any way to solve, some problem. Of course occasionally the problem makes them uneasy just because it is not genuine, i.e. they are puzzled not because they have a question which they do not know how to answer, but because they confuse, e.g. questions concerning functions of institutions with questions concerning the origins of institutions; and they sense this but cannot put a finger to what is wrong. But given an intractable and genuine problem their resort to a discussion of how to solve it seems reasonable. A discussion of how to solve a problem is a meta-discussion, a methodological discussion.

In common with Malinowski, Nadel and Worsley,[1] I hold that certain problems remain unsolved in social anthropology purely because the discussion of them became methodological and then got bogged down in the prevalent faulty methodology. I believe the problems involved are by and large genuine, but not formulated sharply enough to show the way to their solution; the theories put forward to solve them are interesting, but rarely satisfactory; the critical attitude to problems and theories is present, but not severely enough applied. All these faults are, I believe, closely connected with the revolution in anthropology initiated by Malinowski himself.

Social anthropologists—like most working scientists—are apt to be suspicious of those who suggest that more, not less, attention should be paid to methodological problems. After all, they could say to me, you yourself have already said the object of worship doesn't exist. But I would say their deeper reasons for this suspicion are perhaps a relic of the baconian ritual of observation and induction. Their empiricists' prejudice against armchair speculation from study or verandah dies hard; the working anthropologist approves of people who get down to practical questions, or who disappear to the ends of the earth for a couple of years and return with some real 'finds', rather than of those who philosophise and speculate on the sidelines or who make purely 'programmatic' remarks. I shared this attitude to the extent that I was forced into the study of methodology —in spite of myself—by the character of my problem-situation. Anthropological problems were interesting, but the solutions to them presented by anthropologists, especially structural-functionalists, seemed unconvincing—*as solutions*. I was able to discover the reason for this feeling of unsatisfactoriness only after going back into the story of the development of anthropology until I understood what was going on, and then beginning to work forward until I could really pinpoint where I got stuck. This point was at the revolution in anthropology.

So my reply to the argument that I am perpetuating the great disease which afflicts the social sciences, namely an excessive methodological self-consciousness, is that to see methodological preoccupations as a disease in themselves—rather than as the symptom of some genuine malady within the sciences themselves—is similar to

[1] See my 1961 paper, parts 1 and 4. All references are to the bibliography at the end of the volume.

interpreting a high suicide rate as a social disease rather than as the symptom of social disease.

Although I believe scientific method does not exist and should not therefore be worshipped by observation and induction or any other means, I still believe in methodology. This in the following sense: when we are stuck with a problem we should move to a meta-discussion to explore its structure and the sorts of solutions that are acceptable and possible. Methodology cannot do much more than this, and add the general advice that we make sure the problems are genuine ones, and that we remember to criticise any tentative solutions as severely as possible. This book then, while an attack on current methodological preoccupations, is not against methodological preoccupation as such. Until it is realised that there is no scientific method in Bacon's sense—all there is is being critical—methodological discussion is even a necessity.

If my view is correct then methodological inquiry should intersperse scientific inquiry—any scientific inquiry—quite regularly. It has often been denied that this is the case in physics; yet a glance at the methodological and epistemological discussion within the scientific works of leading physicists, past and present, should convince anyone that the picture of hard-working, philosophically-blinkered physicists is mythical.[1]

This book is largely organised round a methodological discussion of a problem with which anthropologists seem to have got stuck. It thus provides both an illustration of what can be done with a meta-discussion, and what sort of methodological discussion is pointless, and helps us to see the sort of case where method is needed and, by implication, where it is irrelevant. To understand how, we must look at the structure of my argument.

2. *Summary of the Structure of the Argument*

Since the revolution in anthropology social anthropologists say they do two things: ethnography and comparative (or theoretical) sociology, where 'ethnography' means the collection of facts about societies and 'comparative sociology' means the body of theories which are designed to explain these facts and which were arrived at by comparing societies. The generally accepted framework within which explanatory theories have been embedded since the revolution is called 'structural-functionalism'. The aim of these theories is to explain social life in terms of the functioning of institutions within their given social structure. Two questions arise immediately: (i) are any explanations embedded within this framework satisfactory; and

[1] For some material on this problem see Buchdahl and Agassi, 1959.

(ii) is it possible satisfactorily to solve all kinds of social anthropological problems within the framework of structural-functionalism?

The answer to (i) is twofold. (*a*) Structural hypotheses in the conditional form ('if *a* then *b*') are often alleged to explain their antecedents by their consequents (*a* by *b*); such explanations are unsatisfactory because they are based on a logical mistake. (*b*) In so far as structural-functionalism permits satisfactory explanation it is a special case of the more general theories that people act according to how they see the logic of the situation, and that many events are unintended consequences of other actions.

The answer to (ii) is 'no'; problems of social change, for example, cannot be solved within this framework. This will be illustrated by a case-study in the recurrent bouts of millenarian religion in Melanesia which have come to be known as cargo cults. The absence of any structural-functional explanation of cargo cults will be explained as being consequent on the impossibility of a structural-functional explanation of any social change. And this impossibility will be put down to the fact that structural-functional explanation presupposes essentially an unchanging structure.

After this examination of the present-day explanatory framework its origins in the revolution will be gone into. This will result in the very distinction it is based upon, between ethnography and comparative sociology, being rejected, on the ground that the ethnographic material is impregnated with interpretations and theories and cannot therefore be considered independent of the framework. A reinterpretation of the two kinds of material will show ethnography to be solutions to problems in one locality using situational logic, as distinct from comparative sociology which is the attempt, by whatever means, to solve wider problems.

3. *The Problems to be Solved*

I felt uneasy about the revolution in anthropology and the structuralist framework even before I could say why. I was told by my teachers of anthropology to press on with my studies so that I would come to appreciate the framework better. Then I would better understand the revolution. I did so, to no avail, and with unfortunate consequences in my finals. To pursue my studies in my own way I had to transfer to philosophy; the result of this is the present work, a much earlier version of which was my doctor's thesis. The two problems of the Summary amount to asking: is the structural-functional framework at present adopted in social anthropology adequate to the task of realising its aim of explaining human society? Another theme, not mentioned in the Summary, runs throughout the book. It is the question: if the present framework will not do, what alternative framework should be adopted?[1]

These problems are methodological. That is, they are remote and abstract, perhaps more abstract than at first sight. I should make it clear that strictly speaking this is not a book of methodology, it is *about* methodology, and this puts it at a third level of abstraction. In general whenever we assert, in an object language, statements *a* and *b*, we can produce arguments against either *c*, *d*, *e* . . . in the same object language. But when I say 'I disagree', or '*a* and *b* are alternatives' or '*c* contradicts *a*' I am in a meta-language; thus object *debates* are largely *meta*-linguistic and debates about method are mostly meta-meta-linguistic. We may call a science a first-order study because it is about substantive issues, and asserts *a*, *b*, *c* . . . We may call methodology, which is about science and the relations or status of *a*, *b*, *c* . . . a second-order study (or a meta-science). This book, which is about methodology, may be called a third-order study. It was in an attempt to minimise the effects of this degree of abstraction from substantive assertions that I resolved to present the argument, so far as possible, with constant reference to a concrete, first-order problem.

Thus the meta-methodological problems are to be tackled by way of a case-study in the first-order, empirical problem of cargo cults. The fact that social anthropologists have, working within their usual framework, got stuck with this problem of cargo cults will help us to show that the present framework is inadequate. This will give rise to a discussion about what alternative frameworks are available and which should be adopted.

4. *The Material to be Used*

The empirical material on cargo cults is fully surveyed in P. Worsley's monograph (1957); in discussing it I shall try to follow the methodological proposals of K. R. Popper.[2] I shall, however, try to write for the reader unacquainted with either. I shall try in fact, to write for the reader with no knowledge of social anthropology and only a very general interest in society. I shall try to give enough information to make the book understandable and self-sufficient. The subject of the empirical case-study, Melanesian cargo cults, is not a particularly difficult or peculiar phenomenon and should therefore present no

---

[1] The book is complemented by my paper on Nadel (1961) in which some of the more abstract issues are taken up. I am no longer satisfied with it but there is some useful material there.

[2] As developed in his books 1945, 1957, 1963 and especially 1959.

special difficulties to the non-anthropologist. Anthropologists have found it especially difficult.

A great many social anthropologists have tried to explain cargo cults, yet none has succeeded. I chose the problem of cargo cults for a case-study precisely because it was one that looked straightforward yet social anthropologists had got stuck with it. It transpired that the reason social anthropologists got stuck with it is because they get stuck with all problems of social change. Cargo cults are phenomena of social change, and social change raises acute difficulties for the structural-functional framework of social anthropology. In discussing social anthropologists' efforts with this particular problem of social change we may be able to form some idea of why they failed with it in general.

Worsley, in the monograph mentioned, also seems to hold that the problem of cargo cults is so intractable that it is necessary to go beyond the present framework of social anthropology. This is as far as any agreement between us goes. He resorts to the marxist method[1] and adds an appendix justifying this move. While it is good to see methodological argument arising from difficulties with empirical material,[2] I cannot see my way to accepting Worsley's marxism[3] so I shall try to offer another framework.

5. Qualification: Philosophical Anthropology

There are a number of things this book is not. It is not a full-fledged treatise on the cargo cult. It is not a guide to metaphysics or to sociological method although both are discussed. It is a philosophical discussion of certain problems of social anthropology, especially its explanatory framework—the metaphysics behind and the methods

[1] Or, more precisely, the Vulgar Marxist Method. See Popper, 1946, vol. ii, p. 100; and Mair, 1958.

[2] While it may even be the case (as Professor Gellner has suggested to me) that people turn to methodology because they find it easier than actual empirical work, I find it more rewarding and more rational to see the source of methodological interest in intellectual difficulties. For example, it is my conjecture that Malinowski's 'functionalist' revolution came about because of his struggles with a difficult problem: the *kula*. This extraordinary pattern of trade patently baffled Malinowski when first he came across it. By 1922, when his book appeared, little of this bafflement is any longer evident. Nevertheless, I conjecture that initial failure to solve this problem was what led him to abandon evolutionism (see Chapter 1, sections 3 and 6).

[3] In addition to its marxism Worsley's book suffers from another methodological fault, the use of the inductive style: presentation of the empirical facts *before* stating the problems which make the facts interesting and relevant. Only if an author *starts* by telling you his problem can you have any guide as to the relevance of such information as is offered and thus avoid being overwhelmed with information for information's sake. See Chapter 2, section 1.

entailed by that framework. Of course I hope it will interest those who have studied social anthropology or philosophy. But it is essentially an inter-disciplinary study, and a rebellious one at that. I hope no one will criticise it for falling between two stools and not trying to be a standard work in either.

Perhaps it seems odd that a philosopher should write a book on anthropology. Put in a historical context this could well be reversed: isn't it odd that anthropologists should do philosophy. 'Philosophical anthropology' is not much discussed these days, but the phrase itself should provide clues to both questions. Kant put philosophical anthropology well in his *Introduction to Logic* when he said that philosophy tried to answer four questions: what can I know (metaphysics); what ought I to do (morals); what may I hope (religion); and what is man (anthropology).

In reality, however, all these questions might be reckoned under anthropology, since the first three questions refer to the last.
—Kant, 1885, p. 15.

Anthropology, then, as the philosophical study of man, is one of the most far-reaching of subjects, in a way it even incorporates philosophy. Perhaps this historical link between the subjects explains how easily I, as a student, was diverted from social anthropology to philosophy and why what a philosopher may have to say about anthropology can be of some interest. It is mainly of some interest because much that anthropologists have to say about man interests philosophers greatly (see Chapter 1, section 1, footnote 1).

Anthropology was once upon a time, then, a philosopher's province, yet most sociologists and anthropologists date their subject from Comte. I believe this to be a mistake. I believe the Study of Man is as old as philosophy and that there is no useful historical distinction to be made between that early speculation and present-day science. Differences there are; but I believe I am right as a philosopher to stress that the links and the continuity are more important than the discontinuity. Detailed discussion of this whole question and especially of the growth of anthropology out of philosophy I hope to take up in a later work.

ACKNOWLEDGEMENTS

THIS book, which has grown out of a thesis accepted for the Ph.D. degree of the University of London in November 1961, owes a lot to a lot of people. It owes its existence to my parents who supported and encouraged me during the first two years of research. It owes any merit it may have to my teachers. Dr. Maurice Freedman taught me social anthropology in a critical spirit which stimulated me to pursue, not evade, the problems I was worried about. He also read and commented on a late draft of the thesis. Professor Karl Popper accepted me as his research student when I had little to offer, and taught me more than I can acknowledge. In addition, for eighteen months I was his research assistant with especially valuable opportunities for close intellectual contact and friendship with him. With my other supervisor and friend J. W. N. Watkins I had many long and fruitful discussions during the course of the research which helped considerably to crystallise my ideas, and he read the first draft and made a large number of shrewd criticisms and annotations. My friend Ernest Gellner read a late draft and gave me a sheaf of valuable comments. My external examiner Dr. H. Ian Hogbin also put at my disposal his critical notes on the work. Some incisive comments of the editor of this series, Professor W. J. H. Sprott, have resulted in substantial changes, especially in Chapter 3, which was completely rewritten. Professor Raymond Firth also sent me some criticisms which I have done my best to meet. To all these I owe a large debt of gratitude. Finally, the last version of the book was radically rewritten after I had received splendid critical comments from my friend Joseph Agassi of this university. For working over it with me in great detail and showing me how to improve it so very much at such a late stage I am very grateful to him. None of these people is committed, of course, to any opinion in this book.

I am indebted to Random House Inc., and the author, for permission to quote from *Sociological Theory: Its Nature and Growth* by N. S. Timasheff; to Watts and Co., and the author, for permission to quote from *Social Change* by H. I. Hogbin; and to Messrs. Methuen, for permission to quote from *The Messiah Jesus and John the Baptist* by the late R. Eisler.

There is one typographical eccentricity I should mention. Through-

Acknowledgements

out the book I have used small letters at the beginning of nouns and adjectives constructed from proper names. In this I am following the usage of Morton White in his *Towards Reunion in Philosophy*. I think the reform is sensible because it removes worry as to whether, for example, machiavellian should or should not have a capital 'M'.

Hong Kong,   I.C.J.
August 1963

For this reprint I have corrected some misprints and added several items missing from the bibliography. Appendix III, 'Social Anthropology and the Closed Society: A Comment', came to seem unsatisfactory and has been deleted. I have replaced it with a discussion of Lawrence's book *Road Belong Cargo* (1964) which brings the cult material up to date.

                                                               I.C.J.

London,
November 1966

1
METAPHYSICS AND METHOD
IN SOCIAL ANTHROPOLOGY

ABOUT fifty years ago the subject of anthropology began to undergo, in this country at least, considerable change. A number of thinkers in the nineteenth century—Morgan in America, Durkheim and van Gennep on the Continent, Maine, McLennan, Pitt-Rivers, Tylor, Robertson Smith and the incomparable Frazer in this country—had, without ever being members of a school, increasingly interested themselves in the diversity of human custom and society. Some of these were lawyers, some classicists, some just learned men; only their endeavour to explain aspects of human society as found all over the world did they share. This gave them affinities with sociology, but their scope was wider. They were said to be anthropologists rather than sociologists because they studied the social works of man everywhere, even in his most primitive manifestations. But unlike other anthropologists they did not study physical characteristics, blood types, race, etc. At first the tradition of study they had built had no name. Then, in 1908 Frazer, by far the most well-known of them, was given an honorary professorship at Liverpool in 'social anthropology'. Frazer's successors in social anthropology trace their descent to him and to the independent tradition behind him, they pay very little attention to other kinds of anthropology. Indeed they hold their ties of affinity with sociology to be stronger than their kin ties to other kinds of anthropology. Frazer, while not the intellectual father of social anthropology, was certainly the father of institutionalised academic social anthropology.

The academic lineage of which Frazer was the head was soon blessed with two distinguished sons, B. Malinowski and A. R. Radcliffe-Brown. Freud's theory was much in vogue at the time (the 'twenties), and the sons indulged in the fashionable pursuit of father killing: they tried to overthrow the influence of clever dons like Frazer, who spent their time concocting theories in comfortable armchairs in studies in Oxford and Cambridge. The weapon the sons used for the assassination was the accusation that their father had

1

never directly observed all the savage customs he wrote so much about.[1] They borrowed this weapon from other sons who had pioneered it—Haddon, Rivers, Seligman and Spencer and Gillen—and utilised it in their palace revolution. And a very successful palace revolution it was; for quite a long time now the Presidents of the Royal Anthropological Institute and most of the Professors of Anthropology in Great Britain have been social (rather than physical) anthropologists. This success was attributed to the weapon, the demand for direct observation, which weapon Malinowski and Radcliffe-Brown treated with religious awe, rapidly raising it into a totem, worship of which was a *rite de passage* for entry to the club of social anthropology. Malinowski died in 1942, Radcliffe-Brown in 1955; during their lifetimes they saw their palace revolution come to fruition in the intellectual and social success of their brilliant and well-trained pupils. While the subject as left by Malinowski and Radcliffe-Brown still has a certain on-going academic impetus of its own, there is already a detectable stagnation. It is this stagnation that has brought about the writing of this book.

In this chapter I want to outline what it is in social anthropology that has brought about the stagnation, to show what the book is trying to do about it, and, especially, to show how the central case-study will advance this aim.

Let me return, now, to the period of vigour in the teens and 'twenties of this century when the revolution in the history of anthropology came with the idea of fieldwork or direct observation. Here is the manifesto of the revolution in the words of its prime mover, Bronislaw Malinowski:

> The anthropologist must relinquish his comfortable position in the long chair on the verandah of the missionary compound, Government station, or Planter's bungalow, where, armed with pencil and notebook and at times with a whisky and soda, he has been accustomed to collect statements from informants, write down stories, and fill out sheets of paper with savage texts. He must go out into the villages, and see the natives at work in gardens, on the beach, in the jungle; he must sail with them to distant sandbanks and to foreign tribes; and observe them in fishing, trading, and

[1] 'Nevertheless it became apparent that if the study of social anthropology was to advance, anthropologists would have to make their own observations. It is indeed surprising that, with the exception of Morgan's study of the Iroquois [1851], not a single anthropologist conducted field studies till the end of the nineteenth century. It is even more remarkable that it does not seem to have occurred to them that a writer on anthropological topics might at least have a look, if only a glimpse, at one or two specimens of what he spent his life writing about. William James tells us that when he asked Sir James Frazer about natives he had known, Frazer exclaimed, "But Heaven forbid!" ' A double irony from the arch-anthropologist, arch-atheist Frazer. The quotation is from Evans-Pritchard, 1951, pp. 71–2.

ceremonial overseas expeditions. Information must come to him full-flavoured from his own observations of native life, and not be squeezed out of reluctant informants as a trickle of talk ... Open-air anthropology, as opposed to hearsay note-taking, is hard work, but it is also great fun.
—(1926, pp. 126–7).

This passage is subtle and very revealing; I shall take it for the *motif* of my chapter. Obviously Malinowski does not intend to make proximity to the savage as such the mark of scientific anthropology. He claims, to begin with, that you can be amongst the tribes and yet treat them as quaint savages. Being in the laboratory is, so to speak, not enough; participation is also required. An anthropologist has to approach the phenomenon of his fellow man carefully and soberly. If he comes in search of bizarre savagery, he will distort native life. He must get down off the verandah and live it. Only by living a way of life can he give a sober and considered account of it without falsification.

Two things are simultaneously and diffusedly advocated, I think, in the suggestion that the way of life of a people deserves to be lived; to live it is a gesture of scientific seriousness *and* a gesture of human respect, as opposed to the superficial and condescending gazing down at specimens from the verandah. Living a way of life (*a*) is useful for the scientific purpose of presenting the truth without distortion, and (*b*) has a metaphysical-cum-moral origin. This origin is an underlying belief that these are human beings, not merely specimens, and must be treated properly as such. This latter is a metaphysical view similar to that of the Enlightenment that all men are brothers, have the same rights, and deserve to be treated with the same respect.

These two impulses—the scientific quest for the truth, about human society as about anything else, and a humanitarian respect for and interest in the diversities of man's attempts to organise his social life—strike me as being at the root of all social anthropology, old-fashioned as well as contemporary. My theme in this book is that both impulses are admirable but that mistakes connected with the former have caused the latter to be neglected and that some way out of this difficulty must be found. Such is my chapter in a nutshell.

1. Sobriety in the Scientific Attitude

Social anthropology is, and is widely acknowledged to be, one of the most exciting and fruitful branches of social studies. The experience of learning it is very similar to that of learning economics; analytical clarity is suddenly introduced into a field where our pre-existing prejudices are plentiful, and counter-intuitive results very quickly show themselves. Recently a number of philosophers have paid tribute to the subject by taking the trouble to learn it and then use it in their own work.[1] Despite theirs being a prevailing opinion, statements made by certain social anthropologists run curiously counter to any claim to it being exciting or interesting. Here is Bronislaw Malinowski (in 1929*a*):

> Social anthropology really begins with a pre-scientific interest in the strange customs and beliefs of distant peoples, and in this form it is as old, at least, as the Father of History (p. 862).

Pre-scientific or not, there is certainly a good deal of interest in the 'strange' doings of 'distant peoples', guarded though these terms are. He continues:

> we have not yet succeeded in eliminating this cruder curiosity in 'Ye Beastly Devices of Ye Heathen' from modern anthropology, where the thirst for the romantic, the sensational and the thrilling still plays some havoc with the sober scientific attitude (p. 862).

This confession of failure to expunge the cruder curiosity is very interesting. While no one wants a drunken scientific attitude, it might be thought that there is nothing wrong with curiosity, crude or otherwise, and it is to be expected that people see romance, sensation and thrills in the findings of any vigorous, and especially new, science. Consider, one might say, how thrilling it must be to be probing the edges of the visible universe or the secret of life; and consider especially the number of young people who took to science precisely because they were thrilled by the thought of being able to study these things. Yet Malinowski is not isolated in his attitude; in fact I would go so far as to say that the prevailing atmosphere among social anthropologists is that we want to be scientists and if we want to be scientists we must be cold, sober, and careful. Witness Evans-Pritchard discussing (1951) the work of his students:

> You will note in the first place that there is nothing very exciting about the subject of these theses, no searching after the strange or colourful, no appeal to antiquarian or romantic interests. All are matter of fact enquiries into one or other type of social institution (p. 13).

I think it may be interesting to ask why such things are said. Why should a new and vigorously successful science be characterised in such a way that solid dullness is suggested if not advocated? This is one of the questions the present book sets out to answer. In brief the answer is as follows. There came a time when social anthropologists wanted to discuss their subject. To explain and characterise a subject

---

[1] See A. Macbeath, 1952; D. Emmett, 1958; E. Gellner, 1959.

you have to dabble in methodology, which is a branch of philosophy. My suggestion is that while social anthropologists are often very good social scientists they are usually not very good philosophers.

Why should they want to talk about their subject in the first place? Several answers can be given. It was new, and had to be explained to students and even to themselves. It was vigorous and exciting but they felt that if their scientific claims were to be sustained they must discipline this excitement. Finally, perhaps the best reason of all. The first flush of vigour soon wore off and attempts at a consolidation got under way. These went well until two facts came up. A failure of the subject to make theoretical progress, and the obvious cause of this in shaky theory.

Social anthropology began as a promise. Fieldwork was, like Bacon's induction, to produce the cargo of a science. But science is a little more than Bacon, or the fieldworker, imagines. The breakdown of Bacon's programme yielded the problem of induction. Natural science, however, was progressing nicely in the (mistaken) belief that it was following Bacon, and so the problems of taking induction literally were left to social scientists and philosophers. Social anthropology was not progressing and so the fieldwork programme was methodologically examined by the anthropologists to see why there was no progress. Since social anthropologists were not very good philosophers they explained their lack of progress by a failure properly to apply the inductive method. This came out as the prescription that fieldwork must be supplemented with comparative studies, because they did not know that the inductive method itself was highly problematic. Thus their philosophising had poor results. Worse than that, they were results that were likely if anything to stultify and do damage to their science when they consciously tried to apply them to it. The inadequacy of their philosophy and its bad effects will be exemplified in this book by the fact that certain well-known methodological or philosophical criticisms of social anthropology, because of the baneful influence of bad philosophy, have never been taken seriously with the result that the study is in serious danger of stagnation. A whole field of problems urgently requiring study—social change—has been treated, but with a conspicuous lack of success. Previously social anthropologists had success without special benefit of philosophy; the study of social change is now being impeded because the official philosophising has been taken seriously. The difficulties presented by problems of social change were discussed on the methodological level and, because the official methodology was inadequate, the difficulties remained intractable. It is my hope to show that if the official philosophy should ever allow the methodological criticisms of social anthropology and its methods to

5

be taken seriously then social change will become a more amenable phenomenon.

The fundamental idea of the official methodology, I have contended, is that we shouldn't get excited about strange peoples because this 'plays havoc' with our scientific endeavours. Now the source of this doctrine is Francis Bacon's philosophy of science. He it was who said we could either pursue the alluring but uncertain paths of imagination and insight, or we could be patient, careful and certain of our small measure of success. His philosophy was designed to escape the demon of error—leaps of imagination were uncertain and almost sure to lead to error. Were anthropologists, and everyone else imprisoned by Bacon's horror of error—like Oxford philosophers,[1] and indeed most scientists and philosophers of science who believe in the theory of induction (which claims to show how to avoid error, or irrational belief)—to overcome their fear and let their imaginations run riot the subject could be still more exciting: progress would be made. The thing is not to inhibit your imagination, but to be very critical of its products; the scientist perhaps should be drunk the night before and stone cold sober the morning after.

But if we assume with the bulk of methodologists that excitement is bad, the quotations from Malinowski and Evans-Pritchard are clear enough, except perhaps for these mentions of 'strange customs' and 'Beastly Devices' of 'Ye Heathen': why are these so exciting? Why indeed? They are so exciting that the mere usage of similar words already heats the atmosphere so much that Raymond Firth, writing in 1956, has to warn us:

> For convenience I have used the terms 'primitive' and 'primitive society' freely throughout the book. This does not mean to imply that there is a unitary character in such societies all over the world, but merely that they present certain broad differences of technology, social structure and organisation from the types of society which we ordinarily think of as 'civilised' (p. iv).

It may be merely my impression, yet I cannot help observing that Firth seems to feel a pang over using the words 'primitive' and 'primitive society'; that he is at pains to explain that he uses them 'merely' for convenience (and not in their usual way as the opposites of 'civilised'). It is a slightly puzzling situation. His explanation shows he thinks the words might be misunderstood or distorted. But if he might be misunderstood he could have used other words. 'Convenience', he says, prompts him to use 'primitive'. Does the convenience outweigh the possible misunderstandings? Apparently. In

---

[1] 'I do not want to laud present [philosophical] fashions but there surely is a real advance in trying to go a little way certainly rather than a long way uncertainly.' Jon Wheatley, 1962, p. 436.

6

what, then, does the convenience consist? My guess, and it is only a guess, is this. Ordinary people do operate fairly uncritically with the notions of primitive and civilised. Firth's book is designed for the general reader. Clearly his strategy is to use the common words 'primitive' and 'civilised' and gradually to divest them of all their invidious connotations. He perhaps intends that in this way he remains easy to understand while he argues his theme. Where, then, lies the source of the possible misunderstandings? Perhaps in the more sophisticated reader; perhaps in the racialist who can say that even anthropologists' usage follows his theories; perhaps in the anthropological colleague who would read the wrong attitude into Firth's mode of expression. Firth, in common with most of his anthropological colleagues, does not want to be mixed up with those repugnant racialist attitudes towards other peoples. He does not want to stand in judgment on the societies he discusses. And why should this be so dangerous and unpleasant? Aren't there primitive and civilised societies; aren't some better than others? The answer to this is 'no', such ideas generate too much heat. These repugnant ideas have been refuted and rejected by modern anthropologists. To show how this came about and the source of this heat we must make a brief excursus into the origins of social anthropology. This takes me to Ancient Greece. I ask for the reader's indulgence in this move and promise to dwell there no longer than is necessary.

2. *Metaphysical Interest in Human Society*

Plato and Aristotle strike me as having had the self-same seminal influence on the study of human society that they have had on much else. Both wrote a good deal about man and his society and they took it as a fundamental fact that men differ. I think most of us would agree that they are right; men do differ and especially from society to society. Men from different societies very often look different— are a different size or colour—behave differently and sometimes even seem to think differently. These *prima facie* differences raise a problem: are they merely *prima facie*? Plato and Aristotle incorporated these differences into their metaphysics by saying that men were really very different at a fundamental level of analysis as well as *prima facie*, and that men's *prima facie* differences were explained as a product of these deeper differences. Plato's and Aristotle's theories of man could be fairly said, I think, to be designed to show that barbarians *were* inferior, they were barbarians *in their souls*. But if the *prima facie* differences are real what made Plato and Aristotle bother with the deeper level? Obviously, from the logic of it, they were explicitly combating views which said that the *prima facie*

7

differences were *merely prima facie* and, somewhere deeper, unity lay. Unless it had been suggested that the differences were only *prima facie* I do not see that they need have bothered to provide a theory that the *prima facie* differences were real differences.[1]

Plato and Aristotle were not afraid to argue that slaves and barbarians and even the mob were inferior sorts of men. Indeed Plato went so far as to provide a theory which said it was 'just' that they be so, while Aristotle said slaves were not humans—because they have no souls—but are simply man-like machines. If those ideas heated the atmosphere in their times they appear not to have worried about it. Slaves, and the barbarian peoples they were usually drawn from, were savages. More modern synonyms are 'primitive', 'backward', etc. The theory founded by Plato and Aristotle was that savages, or whatever you care to call them, *are* inferior and that this justified their inferior status and treatment. Basically the theory is racialist: men are different, some are better than others. The theory is very powerful and convincing and it would be optimistic to say that it no longer exists in 1964. Like many primitive ideas it seems obvious; also like many primitive ideas it is false. The primitive idea, then, is that every superficial difference between men of different societies is nature's difference; the sophisticated idea is that the differences are artificial or accidental or humanly explainable diversities and the underlying reality is the same. The primitive idea is that the differences are fundamental and have to be explained (by the quality of souls or whatever). The sophisticated idea is that the differences are superficial appearances which have to be explained (away).

Between Plato and Aristotle and the Enlightenment social studies didn't make much headway. However, certain ideas which Plato and Aristotle had fought violently against were embodied in the liberal interpretation of Pauline Christianity. These were that all men were brothers in the eyes of God and entitled therefore to equal treatment. We are all children of God was the theme. A conservative stress was also possible. This emphasised that some people knew God and

[1] This suggestion deliberately ignores the fact that Plato had a theory that in general reality was a heaven lying beyond appearances, where the Ideas or Forms of things dwelt. Thus it might be argued that in saying social appearances overlaid a more basic reality of differences he was only working out some consequences of his philosophy. He was indeed doing this but there are independent reasons for believing he was concerned with differentiating men from slaves and barbarians, in other words for challenging the belief that all men are equal and their differences merely *prima facie*. (See below.) These reasons will be found set out in Popper, 1946, chs. 4, notes 18 and 29, and 6, note 14, in connection with the Athenian movement for the abolition of slaves and Plato's attack on equalitarianism.

others were still in heathen and savage darkness. Both interpretations have coexisted for a long time and have from time to time held sway over those who studied or had truck with savages. In some cases lack of God reduced the image of the savage to an animal; and his disgusting customs and childish ways made him a tiresome bother.

The Tasmanians, many of the Australian aborigines and the Red Indians were decimated because of such theories. It was true enough that some of the customs of savages were horrible and disgusting; it was true that they often did odd or even unreasonable things; it was true that they were often hostile. This is only to catalogue the differences which we agree exist. The problem remains: how are these differences to be explained? Already Plato and Aristotle seem to have faced movements which believed in the unity of mankind and which demanded equality and the freeing of slaves. Moral demands like these were met by Plato and Aristotle with a naturalistic theory of human differences between group and group which was used to support the morality of different treatment. Faced with advocates of the unity of all Athenians, Plato and Aristotle had argued for inherent superiorities and inferiorities. On the separateness of barbarians they had not been seriously challenged until Christ (under one interpretation of his teaching—the liberal).

Social studies revived in the seventeenth, eighteenth and nineteenth centuries in Europe, a time when the fundamental metaphysics of man had changed completely despite the influence of Plato and Aristotle. Now the theory was that in their souls (Christianity played a great role here), or fundamentally, all men were equal and their differences were superficial; *prima facie* divisions among men really were only *prima facie*. But this rationalist metaphysics didn't fit the facts nearly as well as Plato's and Aristotle's did. Rationalist metaphysics was counter-intuitive; it claimed that perfectly obvious, straightforward differences weren't real, or weren't fundamental, or weren't morally relevant. This metaphysics was argued religiously and morally; all men are equal in the eyes of god, all men are entitled to the same fundamental rights and freedoms because they are morally equal. Enlightenment metaphysics ignored the racialist and other theories of difference; indeed it might even be said flatly to assert that whatever the factual differences were, they were not relevant to the moral equality.

As more and more exploration of the world took place and greater depths of complexity, primitivity and barbarism were revealed, and the *prima facie* differences got bigger and bigger, this sweeping aside of differences seemed less and less reasonable. Rationalists were liberals, of course, but some of them also tended towards positivism. The positivists were the ones who rethought the Enlightenment belief that men were religiously or morally on a par. When they got down to it, what did words like 'God' and 'moral' denote; nothing that they could *see*, a damning remark for a positivist. How could a positivist base scientific studies of man in such ineffables?

Happily for those positivists who might have come round to asking that awkward question, Darwin entered this situation with a wonderful panacea: the theory of evolution. Applied to the problem of the unity of mankind and his *prima facie* differences this theory allows us to say that both man's equality is real *and* his differences are real, because his differences are simply stages of development: i.e. his equality consists in his potential: all men are capable of the same amount of development: differences consist in different groups having reached different stages of development. Thus, the potential development remains equal.

The only trouble with this theory was that it might explain far too much, that it was too easy to apply. Evolutionists were at first *simpliste*: they thought that the evolution of society must have been monodirectional; no two systems could be equally viable and the weaker would inevitably get pushed to the wall; *ergo* the system we have now must be the best ever. But unfortunately there are 'primitives', or very different peoples, alive and kicking today; if they are not equally as advanced as we are what are they doing there, how is it they haven't died out or evolved like us? Answer: they have unfortunately been frozen at some previous stage; alternatively, they have a smaller rate of progress. Problem: how can we test these ideas of the evolutionists? Answer: by working out a map of evolution such that, by means of their customs and institutions, we can tell whereabouts on the evolutionary tree any of the societies of our 'living ancestors' which exist today got themselves frozen. (The mechanism of how societies got frozen or retarded was never, to my knowledge, gone into. Morgan's theory of the miraculousness of inventions and the dependence of progress on inventions would, though, solve this problem.[1] It would do so by saying it is progress (namely inventions), not freezing that has to be explained. If all this is true the theory still remains a freak. The marxists, for example, who claim to base themselves on Morgan, reject his theory that ideas lead to progress. In fact they entirely refuse to discuss the question of the rate of progress. Their certainty that there is progress satisfies them. Perhaps theirs is a possible position, I think not. That every society will *eventually* progress to socialism is a fatal elasticity in their theory which renders it untestable. Of course their justification is to hand: while we know progress will come, because of the operation of historical laws, as scientists we do not want to be involved in

---

[1] As was pointed out to me by Dr. Agassi.

10

utopian predictions about the what and when of socialism.) The theory that societies evolved gradually degenerated into the idea that any anomalous or hard-to-understand institution in any society was to be accounted for as an element which had been frozen at an earlier stage while the rest progressed to a later stage. At this point the reaction to evolutionism set in.

Diffusionism, the name by which the reaction was known, was an equally simple idea. Customs didn't evolve and get frozen, but their diversity was a product of their being invented at one place and being passed on to some places but not to others. This process of passing on was known as diffusion. From a metaphysical point of view diffusionism was closely linked with evolutionism. But it was more complicated. Still the idea was that the unity of mankind was real. The diffusionist however postulated cultural 'centres' at which things had been invented before being passed on. Thus 'centres' were more advanced than borrowers; they, after all, invented things. Borrowing societies' development was less real than that of inventing societies. The development of both the inventing centre and the borrower was greater than that of the area untouched.

Into the quarrel between these two schools of thought stepped Malinowski. 'You both sit on the verandah spinning your theories and empty disputes', he seems to have said. Societies, he argued, are to be explained neither by evolution from earlier stages nor by borrowing from other societies but as working sets of institutions. All existing societies, he argued, exist, live, and function. They are peopled with individuals who *survive*: our job is to find out how these societies manage things so that their members survive. To do that would, he thought, be explanation enough. Evolutionism won't do because it says the present is a product of the past; but the present sustains itself on something. Not the past! Then what? Societies are living systems of people, not the diffusionist's rock-beds composed of layers of customs which have silted out of the cultural seas; our job is to find out how the parts work with each other, not where they came from.

Malinowski's idea may sound obvious, we all know that societies work, or function; but our task is to find out how they do, says Malinowski. This was excellent advice, and far from obvious, not only because it provided the programme of fieldwork, but because it provided the elaborate programme of fieldwork using no more than the very simple premiss: any system which works must in some way be satisfactory to those human beings who live in it. This indeed, is obvious in a sense because if it were otherwise the societies wouldn't have survived as they wouldn't have been able to fulfil the basic human needs of their members. (The idea is indeed so simple that anyone must share a variant of it; even the evolutionists who Malinowski attacked.) But Malinowski's variant of the obvious view is, in a way, so striking as not to be considered too trite after all. All surviving societies must be viable, and Malinoswki even goes further: they are equally viable, equally good; equal in fact. The wheel has come round full circle; *prima facie* differences aren't even real now: *there are no differences*. Any social system good enough for man to live in is as good as any other; there are no savages, no differences, only human social diversity. Plato and Aristotle said, 'All men are unequal.' The rationalists said, 'All men are really equal but some *appear* more equal than others.' The evolutionists said, 'All men are potentially equal but some are actually more equal than others.' Malinowski said, 'All men are equal but diverse and all diversities are equal.' And it is this striking feature of Malinowski's theory that led to his programme of fieldwork: the programme to collect and catalogue the diversity.

My interpretation of Malinowski is that he started from the very sensible and obvious idea that men are physically the same and have similar biological needs, and used it in an original way. To satisfy these needs men had built a variety of social systems whose existence was an earnest of their ability to satisfy these needs. Rejecting racialist naturalism and substituting a conventionalism in this way is fine, but what, I would argue, happens next, is not. What happens next is the introduction of what philosophers call relativism. Since men are morally as well as physically equal the societies they are pleased to live in must be equal too. The only criterion was: did a social system function? And the only criterion of whether it functioned was whether it led a viable existence. No other standard could be applied to societies, and this standard said that all extant societies must be equal or they wouldn't have survived. It followed from this that all functioning social systems are perfect. It may be noted that a moral code of one kind of society, namely egalitarianism, thus leads one to accept the idea that all moral codes are equally good if they survive, namely relativism. This is certainly a *tour de force*. Moreover, anti-evolutionism is similarly twisted round on itself. Since, according to Malinowski, societies are working organisms, if a part of any one of them persists from period t to period $t+1$, it either retained the function it had or gained a new one, or otherwise it would have disappeared: having no value it would be discarded. Thus the theory of evolution reappears and Malinowski is a naturalist after all; societies are perfect because of the law of natural selection: they discard the useless otherwise they die out.

The important fact is, however, that Malinowski by his relativism changed the whole metaphysical background to social anthropology.

12

The basic problem was, 'how do we explain man's differences?' The Greeks said because they are fundamental, the rationalists said because they are superficial, the evolutionists said by development, the diffusionist said by the accidents of contact and borrowing. Malinowski (in my interpretation) says, 'Bosh! There are no differences to be explained: there is only the miraculous diversity of mankind and his works. The problem of anthropology is now simply observing, describing and cataloguing this diversity.'

Malinowski's view may, paradoxically, be seen either as a metaphysics of equality or as an antimetaphysical (positivist) methodology, Either our job is to describe and generalise about what exists because everything that exists is equally valuable and interesting and only comparisons, not comparative judgments, can be made; or our job is to get on with description and generalisation because this is science and we don't want any truck with metaphysical speculations. Malinowski seems to be having it both ways: he provides two separate and contradictory arguments for his fieldwork programme. The first argument is that since all men are equal their social works are equal and demand equal study. 'Come down from the verandah of western society and look at men everywhere,' he says. The argument rests on the metaphysical idea that all men are equal. The second argument says that speculation on the verandah is not science, science is observation and description. This argument rests on the premiss that metaphysical speculation is not part of what the scientist does.

In this book I am, in a way, sitting on the verandah. Indeed, to be frank, it contains my apology for not yet having left the verandah. Now Malinowski (or the ghost of him I have created) and Radcliffe-Brown and my teachers urge me to come down off the verandah and muck in with the fieldwork programme. But when I resist and say that I do not yet feel sure that the descent would be a good thing they deploy arguments. Unfortunately one argument appeals to my metaphysical bias; the other appeals to my antimetaphysical bias. Now having it both ways like this is a bit hard on the person like myself who is worrying about these problems. I can answer one argument at a time but not both together.

Confessing for a moment that I am an equalitarian, liberal humanist, what shall I say to the cry that I should muck in with the others; experience the stuff of life as it is lived among my fellow creatures? My first reply might be that I don't need confirmation for my metaphysical beliefs: they are moral not scientific (although they have factual consequences). The conﬁrmation would be spurious and irrelevant. Another reply would be that I may find it easier to preserve my metaphysics by not doing fieldwork. This is not obscurantism but the simple knowledge that life in the raw can be too much for some people and that they have to be very strong not to take it out on their human brothers. For example it is hard to teach alien people; it is so hard that one is inclined to believe it is their fault, there is something wrong with them. Funny things go wrong in far-away places and it is tempting to attribute them to the 'natives'. For my metaphysics sake I'd rather not do fieldwork.

I cannot pretend that I am an antimetaphysician, but I must answer the argument which appeals to this bias. Professor Schapera and others have said it is time for some anthropologists to go back on the verandah and do comparative work. I think it better not to get down if one wants to do comparative work. If one descends to the field such a slice of one's life is gone that no one has yet had the strength to climb back up. For these reasons I reject the thesis that to be a scientist I must go in for observation and description, however reasonable and modern such a characterisation sounds. I believe it is nothing of the sort in fact. It entails an impossible methodology (inductivism) and it conceals another sort of metaphysical beliefs. Positivists have their metaphysics as well as anyone else; their metaphysics is however usually inferior to everyone else's. To take seriously only what can be observed, to deny clear differences between men and between societies, is almost an irrational metaphysics. By all means resist the smug judgments of Christian missionaries sent out to convert the poor savage. But because *those* differences aren't real it doesn't follow that there are *no* genuine differences between societies and that *any* society is as good as any other. Certainly primitive societies have their good and interesting sides, and they have things to teach us.[1] That doesn't at all affect the fact that man has made objective progress in improving his society and that we in the West seem at this stage to have the best society in recorded history.

Clearly here I am pushing a metaphysics very different from that of Malinowski's relativism and naturalism. I am saying there are objective differences, and that these can be '*made*' by man: I assume objectivism and conventionalism. Society is a human convention: partially made and partially controlled by man.

Let me briefly review the gist of what I have been saying, starting with a definition of social anthropology. Social anthropology is the subject studied by social anthropologists. Social anthropologists are the members of the Association of Social Anthropologists of the British Commonwealth, academics holding teaching posts in social anthropology, and other people the members of the first two groups

[1] See, for example, my article 1963*a*.

14

recognise as fellow social anthropologists. How, then, do social anthropologists define their activity? They say that they are students of human society. This raises the question not, I think, very often raised, why people should be interested in human society. The answer might be because what we lump under the single name of 'human society' is many interestingly different societies; there is infinite richness and diversity there. But this is not enough. Interest in something usually stems from a problem; it is problems intellectuals usually get interested in. What sort of problem could induce people to be interested in human society? I think the answer has to be a metaphysical problem, no less. A problem, that is, which goes beyond the bounds of ordinary scientific inquiry and undergirds the intellectual curiosity about human society. Metaphysics can be characterised as nontestable attempts to interpret the world; world views, or frameworks within which scientific inquiry can be carried on. In general a problem, something requiring an explanation, is the product of some information or theory or belief we are inclined to take seriously clashing with some other theory or belief we hold. In the case under discussion some metaphysical belief about man in society must have run into some awkward fact or other belief and the need to reconcile the two resulted in the problem.

The conjecture I offer as to what clashed with what is that doctrines about the unity of mankind ('all men are brothers under the skin', and so on) clashed with the *prima facie* differences between men in different societies. The problem arises, are these differences merely diversity among brothers or are they real differences and are thus some men more brothers than others?

'All men are brothers', the doctrine of the unity of mankind, is metaphysical. This says nothing against it; indeed whether you believe it or not will have a considerable effect on your scientific study of man in society. Depending on whether you believe men are the same or different you will take very different views of the myriad diversity of his social works. If you believe in the unity of mankind you will have the programme of explaining that all evidence which seems to show man differs is merely contingent or circumstantial and the essential unity remains unchanged, If you believe men are different, and some are better than others, you will try to explain all facts which point to the unity of mankind as deceptive or non-essential concealments of the fundamental cleavages which really exist. The relevance of all this is very simple: modern social anthropologists are mostly rationalists and humanists. They take it for granted that all men are equal. In accord with this they assume that all man's social systems must be equal in some sense, and that their task must be to show that they are so.

I believe that the positivist metaphysics, the relativist metaphysics, apparent in Malinowski's work clashes fundamentally with the overtly humane and liberal values which most anthropologists, including Malinowski, have adopted. The two cannot be reconciled. In this book I want to replace positivism and relativism by conventionalism and objectivism. These metaphysical ideas, and the method which, I shall claim, goes with them, would have interesting consequences for social anthropology. We would be free to say: that in some ways some people are morally and socially more advanced than others; that curiosity about explanations of these differences can legitimately be consuming and exciting; and that genuine scientific method is applicable to anthropology.

3. *Malinowski's Critique: True* versus *Satisfactory Explanation*

I feel that I have not yet made my last point sharply enough. Let us look more closely at my conjecture as to how Malinowski's view evolved. I would formulate the evolutionists' thesis like this: 'societies evolved, therefore everything in society is explained by its past'. This is, of course, a *non-sequitur*—(of my formulation; whether Malinowski's formulation suffers from the same defect does not matter here). I would formulate Malinowski's thesis as, 'societies are living things and cannot be explained by their past: therefore the belief that in explaining any social thing we have to refer to its past is false'—this is, again, an obvious *non-sequitur*—and, 'since things cannot be explained by their past, evolutionism is false and all societies are equal'—a *non-sequitur* again, if not a double *non-sequitur*.

Now, these *non-sequiturs* in my formulation of Malinowski's thesis could be easily eradicated by mastering a simple distinction between whether an explanation is satisfactory or whether it is true.

It is, I believe, very important to distinguish true from satisfactory explanations. We normally demand that an explanation be satisfactory, namely that it solve the problem it sets out to solve in a *non-ad hoc* fashion; normally it is unreasonable in science to demand, at least in the first instance, a true explanation; for we can never prove informative propositions, at least not at once. For my part, I think the demand for truth is one that is never satisfiable. This is one good reason for not demanding it. At the same time I am not against truth, indeed I am convinced it is an indispensable regulative idea. We must assume that there is such a thing as truth and aim at it if we are to have a progressive science. We should not worry that we can never know for certain when we have truth. Worry is unnecessary because there is something like a criterion which tells us that we are approaching it. This criterion is the discovery, and thereby the elimination, of some of our past errors. Although our ignorance is infinite, it is some achievement that we have detected and eliminated such quantities of errors in our theories. So although we should search for truth we should not demand it of our theories; what we should demand is that they not be known to be false. The only way of implementing this demand that I am aware of is for us to do our level best to test our theories for error: to check them against the facts. But first comes the demand of satisfactoriness, which I should now elucidate.

An explanation, I take it, consists in deriving a statement describing what is to be explained from another statement. The satisfactoriness of the explanation consists in several things: the testability of the explaining statement or theory; its power to enlighten; and the validity of the derivation. To illustrate: the easiest explanation to give of a statement is that statement itself. So easy is this that we are barely prepared to call it an explanation. Traditionally it has a special name: circular explanation. If a child asks 'why does the moon shine' and a bored parent replies 'because it does' that explanation is circular. The derivation is strict (provided we read 'because the moon shines' for 'because it does') but hardly enlightening. Similarly our freedom to invent explanations must be limited by this derivation procedure. If the child asks 'why does the moon shine?' and the parent replies 'because it is made of green cheese' the child has other logical grounds of complaint. He may complain that this is no explanation at all since the statement 'the moon shines' does not follow from 'the moon is made of green cheese'. This *non-sequitur* may be corrected by adding the false premiss 'green cheese shines'; the explanation will then be satisfactory but not acceptable on the ground that it is known to be false. Alternatively we can add the premiss 'If the moon is made of green cheese then it shines'. Now the explanation is *ad hoc*: it leads us no further than doing strictly what was demanded, namely explaining the shining of the moon; as it does nothing else, we can only take it or leave it. At a later stage we may discover that we can examine statements about what the moon is made of, either astronomically or by space travel, and then the status of the explanation would be altered.

The relevance of this discussion is very simple. 'Societies evolved. Therefore societies (and all their parts) are to be explained by their pasts from which they evolved.' This mode of explanation is satisfactory in the sense that if I ask why the kinship of a society is as it is this explanation allows me to say it is what it is because of what it was. Malinowski, while accepting that evolutionism had some truth in it, maintained that evolutionist explanations were unsatisfactory.

17

To me it is clear that they are satisfactory but sometimes false. This needs some explanation. Malinowski simply said that evolutionism does not explain the hows and whys of a society flourishing at this time. If we ask what the significance is of the *kula*, why people do it, it will be unsatisfactory to give an account of how the *kula* developed. To explain the workings of Parliament it is not satisfactory to give an account of its evolution. Its present role and workings must be discussed. Malinowski, however, has won an empty victory. The fact is that the evolutionists were not answering questions about the workings and significance of the *kula* or of Parliament. They were, rather, discussing *why* the *kula* or Parliament is as it is. By doing this, it was felt, the institutions would seem less strange, more understandable.

Evolutionists were answering different questions to those Malinowski was interested in, but theirs were satisfactory answers to the questions they had posed themselves.

They were sometimes false answers for precisely the reasons Malinowski gave: they were conjectural. More than that they were uncritically conjectural, their authors simply guessed what the *kula* or Parliament came from, even when it was not possible to check what they said, and they presented it as obviously true. They also neglected 'created' institutions with no past. Not all things can be explained by their past; but some things can be. This does not make explanations with reference to the past unsatisfactory; some things, it is true, are here today and not tomorrow because of the emergence of new functions, but others here today are still explained by assuming that they existed yesterday and that they survived; although their survival from yesterday to today is not yet explained by this. Malinowski however did conclude that any explanation referring to the past was unsatisfactory and urged jettisoning such modes of explanation altogether. Evolutionism is sometimes false but satisfactory, I have said. It is, however, an unsatisfactory answer to the sorts of questions Malinowski wanted to ask. Malinowski seems not to have seen that he was asking different questions from the evolutionists and castigating them for giving unsatisfactory answers to questions they had never asked. Both sets of questions should, I believe, be asked, but just as Malinowski's predecessors were blind to his kind of questions, he, because the shift was surreptitious, has been blinded to some of theirs.

4. *Method, Induction and Theory*

Malinowski's positivist and relativist view is bad metaphysics. As a methodological rule (look for the function which an institution has), it is often quite useful. Both his positivist methodology and his egalitarian metaphysics prevent fruitful study of one of the major problems of the study of society: social change. Now evolutionism (and, in its crude way, diffusionism too) could apply to social change. Societies evolved; new situations would have to be dealt with, new institutions would appear to handle it and if they didn't the society would perish; old institutions would change their function or disappear or cause the society to perish. Malinowski's theory cannot apply to social change, as I shall explain later. What is required is a view which will allow us to say men's differences are real, to say also that men are fundamentally equal, that will not explain everything by reference to the past, and will not break down over social change. I believe such a view has been put forward by Karl Popper under the name situational logic.

To repeat: Malinowski's positivist metaphysics is inferior because it is implicit not explicit and therefore not exposed to criticism; the inductivist methodology entailed by Malinowski's positivist functionalism is impossible, although a good methodological rule can be extracted from it; Malinowski's functionalism cannot apply to social change; and I have claimed there is an alternative method due to Karl Popper, which can incorporate all that is best in previous methods and supersede them. Now, this is a lot of claim-staking, and obviously I have to try to make these claims good, and as soon as possible. So I shall now make the *prima facie* presentation of my case, and, of course, make it more fully in my conclusion.

This book is not the place to substantiate attacks on positivist metaphysics. I have to rest my case on the fact that metaphysics is inescapable: all positions have metaphysical backing, including Malinowski's. So, if I can show Malinowski's metaphysics has all sorts of unhelpful consequences, like methodological impossibility and failure to handle social change, I shall have some case for demanding a revision of even the most fundamental parts of his view, i.e. his metaphysics. The impossibility of the method I will try to show in this section; the need for an alternative method in the next section; the value of situational logic in the next but one. Functionalism's difficulties with social change is the major theme of the whole work. I shall argue it abstractly (section 6 below, also in Chapters 4, 5 and 6) and concretely (Chapter 3). My strategy is two-sided; I want both to show that social change cannot be handled by functionalism and to take a problem which many people have written about and show how they persistently fail with it because of this abstract situation.

To provide an account of why malinowskian methods are impossible I shall have to go into them in a little more detail, beginning with the problems anthropologists set themselves. The problems which characterise British social anthropology are connected with fieldwork and comparative studies. 'Fieldwork' is the name of the empirical research; the empirical procedure adopted by anthropologists differs from, say, criminological statistics; it connotes a long-drawn-out and very detailed observation of a society which yields a mass of reports on 'ethnographic facts' concerning a variety of institutions, customs, cultural traditions, etc. The 'official' view is that it is possible to weld out of this vast mass of factual reports large-scale generalisations which will bring out the similarities and differences between divers societies.

Social anthropologists, then, are concerned with collecting factual data, with surveying human society by means of these data, and with attempts to formulate the results of this survey as general theories. This, at least, is how social anthropologists present their problems and aims. We come now to their methods of problem-solving. It is probably better at first to become more specific for a while and examine a particular anthropological topic. As they say, anthropologists want to collect factual data on human society in all its aspects. Let us take one tiny aspect: the fact that in all human societies the language contains general names for kin, like 'father', or 'uncle', which are in addition to the proper names, like 'Joe Smith', of the persons concerned. In the English language we have the names 'mother', 'father', 'brother', 'sister' which are usually unambiguous (although they might be ambiguous where there is plural marriage) and others, like 'aunt', 'uncle', and 'cousin' which, some may claim, are ambiguous since they do not distinguish whether the person is on father's side or mother's side. The idea that we may bother to distinguish maternal and paternal relatives will surprise an Englishman. Yet there are many societies in the world where maternal and paternal relatives are differently called, differences which we blur together with the names 'aunt', 'uncle' and 'cousin'. Anthropologists have come across societies where you call your mother's brother, and his father, 'father'. They were puzzled; and they were more puzzled by societies where everyone who was in the same group called each other 'brother' and 'sister'.

Anthropologists, according to their own lights, will first of all collect plenty of factual data on this phenomenon. Also they will probably give it a name—here 'classificatory kinship terminology'— and then classify their data into 'a reasoned comparative analysis of how people behave in social circumstances' (Firth, 1951, p. 1). They now have their generalisations and comparisons. Societies X, Y and Z are in group A, societies P, Q, R in group B, and so on. But they do not stop there. Indeed, it is when they reach that stage that their work has just begun. For now they turn to the problem of *explaining*.

First, you must catch the rabbit; you must have some facts to explain; you must have a problem. What problems activate social anthropologists? Basically they are of two kinds, functional problems and comparative problems. On the one hand they can ask for an explanation of custom *x* in society *Y*; on the other hand they can ask for a general account of custom *x* wherever it occurs. The one problem confines itself to a small local area—society *Y*—the other doesn't. I call these two kinds of problems *local* problems and *comparative* problems. Local problems are what Malinowski would solve by functionalism; comparative problems remain problematic for him.

Local problems seem to be clearly enough characterised and any good fieldwork monograph contains attempts to solve some. This is because certain aspects of a strange society are much more immediately intelligible than others. They will be so obvious the fieldworker will not bother with them. But he may find other aspects more intractable and will have to spend time explaining them in his monograph. For example, the problem of the leopard-skin chief in Nuerland was solved by Evans-Pritchard (1940, *passim*). Let me explain. Evans-Pritchard explored a society without chiefs and without central organisation of any kind. Their main principle of organisation was kinship; strong agnatic lineages. Yet dotted around the place were men whose title Evans-Pritchard could only translate approximately as 'leopard-skin prophets' or 'leopard-skin chiefs'. But strictly speaking Nuer society left no room for either prophets or chiefs: when Evans-Pritchard got down to examining these individuals he found they had no power and made no prophecies. Yet they were widely respected and looked up to. Soon he found out why: the principal function of the leopard-skin chief is to settle feuds between Nuer. To a murderer the house of a leopard-skin chief is sanctuary. There he can be absolved of the spilt blood, and the 'chief' can negotiate with the aggrieved party the price that shall be paid for the misdeed. The significance and horror of the feud is well brought out by Evans-Pritchard who is also therefore able to explain the importance of the 'chief'.

Such is a typical local problem and its functional solution.

Whereas local problems are straightforward, comparative problems are problematic: what is the aim of comparative studies? Has the aim of a theoretical or comparative sociology been achieved? If not, can it be achieved with present methods? Considering that comparative works like Steiner's (1956) on the problem of taboo, and Homans' and Schneider's (1955) on preferential marriage exist, it

21

may look as though there is no difficulty here. To show that there is a need to enter a little more deeply into the distinction between local and comparative problems.

(i) *Local Problems.* Attempts to explain actions within of a particular society I have called local problems. But this is to define them in terms of subject-matter; let us now look instead at method.

What is to be explained, and in what way is it to be explained, on the local level? The answer seems to be this: we explain what we cannot immediately see to be rational. Thus, the problem of why a person is referred to as a leopard-skin chief is answered by Evans-Pritchard; any society, even one without chiefs, needs an institutionalised means of dealing with murderers, and the leopard-skin chief is that means in Nuerland. The example we are using here harbours two problems: first, why is there a chief in a chiefless society; second, how does a chiefless society work? And Evans-Pritchard answers the first by saying that although the leopard-skin chief is not a 'chief' in the sense that the society is without chiefs, he does perform a function which a chief would perform were there one and which any society really cannot do without; and he answers the other by saying there are means of co-ordinating a society other than centralised political power, such as the leopard-skin chief. To put the point more generally, an anthropological problem may involve two aspects at least: the explicability of the social set-up, and the explicability, especially the explicability as rationality, of an action within the set-up. At first sight, it might seem that the set-up has simply to be described; it is given; it is not for us to explain. This is not so. As Malinowski already suggested, since a set-up is sustained by people we cannot get away without giving an account of why it should be sustained. He himself offered the highly pragmatic general theory that any set-up is there in order to serve human needs, so that if it were sustained that must be because it is *useful* in satisfying some of these needs. I shall later disagree with Malinowski over his specific theory to explain sustenance, but not as to the fact that such a theory has to be provided.

Given, then, that we have to explain the set-up, and that we have managed to do it, there may still remain something in need of explanation. For example, although we may have managed to explain how the set-up of a chiefless society works this does not necessarily explain something like the leopard-skin chief because there are chiefless societies without leopard-skin chiefs. Also, the very same society may have an institution like mother-in-law avoidance. This too cannot be explained in the same breath with the set-up because there are societies which have this institution which are not chiefless.

22

How then do we explain the custom of avoiding the mother-in-law? Again, take the custom of preferential first-cousin marriage which is prevalent among desert Arabs. This custom puzzles us; but might not our custom of frowning on first-cousin marriage (although not actually forbidding it in the Church of England's 'prohibited degrees') puzzle the desert Arabs just as much? It appears that what is a problem depends upon which society one comes from. But this is only the case because our background knowledge of the society we come from allows us to account for its customs; they seem natural and right. On the other hand, the study of social anthropology can cause us to question our understanding of things we had taken for granted in our own society. It has become a problem now to explain why the English kinship system is so 'shallow'; why, that is, few Englishmen are able to trace their kin ties back more than a couple of generations, and why they quickly lose track of relatives beyond first cousins. Previously we had taken this to be a 'natural' state of affairs. The problem turns out to be quite a difficult one. An anthropologist would not get very far by questioning Englishmen about why they do not bother to remember their kin ties: probably, if asked, most Englishmen would allow that they would quite like to know who their relatives and ancestors were. The explanation eventually produced might be quite subtle.

We would have to begin with a simple distinction between face-to-face societies, and abstract societies. 'Face-to-face societies' is an attempt to characterise a society where individual, person-to-person relations are all-important to the running of that society. An alternative name is a concrete society; the relations between its members are concrete meetings. An abstract society is one which is characterised by the fact that it largely ignores persons and considers only abstracts like the role or status of a person. As Popper, who invented the distinction,[1] put it in lectures, sociologists have an interesting idea with their role theory. But it is a terrible idea, for what they don't see is that although we do have abstract dealings with people it verges an immorality for us to do so because it amounts to treating people as a means. While to some extent we cannot escape it in modern society, we ought constantly to strive to. For sociologists to produce a theory which is interested only in these abstractions is unpleasant.

In a semi-abstract society like modern Britain we do not depend on our kin for very much so we have little incentive to go to the trouble of remembering or maintaining kin ties. Whether this theory is true I don't know, but it accommodates the fact that people going abroad will call on quite remote kin they would have ignored in the home country. In a situation where we do need our kin—for aid and

[1] See also note 1 to section 3 of Chapter 6.

comfort among strangers—ties are maintained. And why do we need our kin in such a situation? Precisely, I suggest, because we have moved from one semi-abstract society which we understand, to another with which we are unfamiliar. We must call on the help of relatives to help us find our way around the abstractions of the new society. Why do we call on kin? Perhaps because we misunderstand kin to be biological kin, and we instinctively expect biological kin to want to help each other. Thus in facing a new semi-abstract society we conquer it by calling on the reserves of a convenient concrete society of kin which we can understand easily and use as a bridge to the wider and more abstract society. This should be contrasted with a concrete or face-to-face society where the bonds of kinship are strong and remembered *all* the time because so many social rights and duties are organised by means of kinship. If the society is such that you depend for food on your share of everything one uncle kills, and all the wealth you inherit will come from another relative, and your bride will be provided by a third then you have certain obvious reasons for maintaining close kin ties. Should you forget about these relatives and they do not know where you are, you cannot receive your due from them. Moreover your dependence on them for so many things puts you in a special relationship with them.

(ii) *Comparative Problems.* In a concealed way I have introduced a comparative problem here. On the one hand there is an explanation of the Englishman's neglect of kinship. On the other hand there is the primitive's great interest in kinship and his investing it with special significance. But we are only able to talk of 'neglect' and 'great interest' in our context because we *compare* the situations in different societies. Both explanations given are functional and they seem to be based on the premiss that the maintenance of kin ties has a function and to the degree that kin fulfil certain functions to that degree will ties be maintained. Thus the comparative neglect of kinship in English society can be rendered understandable within the set-up of our somewhat abstract society, where we depend on kin for relatively little, and it can perhaps be seen as an unintended consequence of the transition from the previous, more concrete, stage of social organisation when we did keep track of kin ties.[1] So our explanation of the local problem was based on a comparison and the very existence of the local problem was only noticed because of the availability of

[1] I should add a factual point: it is by no means clear that the inhabitants of Northern Europe ever did keep elaborate kinship records (of the type which is very common in unilineal societies). Thus the alleged transition may never have occurred and will not therefore be in need of explanation. One must avoid over-compensating one's ethnocentric prejudices. See L. Lancaster, 1958, Part 1, section II and *passim.*

comparative material. It is in this way that social anthropology, by casting new light on the familiar, is a rewarding study.

Everyone knows that science contains facts and theories. We have already seen that the gathering of factual data on society is a declared aim of social anthropology, and that somehow out of this mass of facts theories are alleged to emerge. How are they to emerge? The official view is that comparisons will be made and generalisations of the facts will result: these comparative generalisations will be theories. Now this methodology does not appeal to me at all. I do not see that generalisations would explain anything, or even be amenable to tests: they would contain only as much information as the facts of which they were compounded and would be as reliable as those same facts. Leaving aside the question of how the theories are generated, I think I can account for the comparative nature of anthropological theory otherwise. Principally my discussion will turn on how anthropological theories can be tested. Two ways present themselves: first, to derive from the theory a prediction about other societies unexamined on this aspect and see if it is true; second, to derive a prediction about how this society will change and see if it turns out right.

Various difficulties interfere with the second procedure. For one thing, the society may be fairly static; for another the aspects we are interested in may be static; for a third the reaction against evolutionism disinclined many social anthropologists to involve themselves in predictions about social change. Social change is anyway somewhat problematic since evolutionism was abandoned. Let us, therefore, stick to contemporary materials; this means comparisons. Comparisons cannot just be made out of the blue: there are far more things to compare than time to compare them, and we must therefore choose what to compare and what to ignore. Comparisons, therefore, are made on the basis of hunches or guesses that something might show up there; and these hunches are general theories. 'Comparative problems' then, are not tied down to any one society. They are unexplained events or customs in separate societies which we believe, whether by a hunch or on some more general theoretical grounds, may have a common explanation. For example, taboos; what is the explanation of taboos? Various theories explaining taboos in terms of anything from psycho-analytic theory to social value and social dysvalue have been proposed at one time or another.[1] Another

[1] For the first see Freud, *Totem and Taboo*; for the second Steiner, *op. cit.*
Popper suggests that they are survivals left over from the closed society, where the distinction between the natural and the conventional is not always drawn. (This does not explain why some survive and some do not and we still do not know how they got into the closed society in the first place.) See Popper, 1946, i, ch. 5; and Chapter 4, section 5, below.

example would be the practice of encouraging marriage between cross-cousins, a uniformity peculiarly difficult to explain. A last example is cargo cults (or millenarianism in general).

In asking comparative or theoretical questions it is not necessary to assume that answers to them exist, or even, if they exist, that they will be found. The invention of hypotheses is a matter of intelligence, imagination and luck, and cannot be programmed. But we can advance a methodological proposal to the effect that because such common factors might have a common explanation it is reasonable to look for one. We can 'test' such proposals only in practice by seeing whether they bear fruit.

So much for the distinction between local problems and comparative problems. Now I want to discuss them. That there are genuine comparative problems is clear enough. Whether they must be answered on a special comparative level, where the explanatory framework used on local problems is not sufficient, is the central methodological problem of this book.

The reason I have replaced the old ethnography/comparative sociology distinction by that of the two levels of problems is that I believe the aim of science to be the solving of problems not the collection and synthesising of facts. And this means the 'ethnography'/'comparative sociology' terminology may be dropped with benefit, because it is misleading. For the notion of 'ethnographic fact' conceals the evident theory-impregnation of ethnography and encourages the naïve view that theories can or should somehow be 'synthesised' from this ethnographic fact.[1] We should not allow ourselves to be blinded to the theoretical content of ethnographic statements by the low level of the theories (e.g. theoretical terms like 'marriage', 'descent', 'religion', 'chief', and so on, should not be disguised as interpretation-free (or theory-free) 'facts').[2] We only *decide* to treat low level theories such as 'these two people are married' as unproblematic facts. And we only do so in order to explain[3] them or to use them as a base from which to test higher level theories;

[1] Naïve because it is a very crude solution to the problem of induction, unanswered arguments against which have been known at least since Hume. See Popper, 1959, appendix *10, and the references to Hume there given.

[2] Indeed anthropologists have themselves found these universals to be shifting sand when they tried to build their generalisations upon them. They therefore resorted to definitions, apparently not seeing that these terms are theoretical interpretations of our experience, not essences which can be sought by definitions. Beattie, 1959, pp. 48–9, points to the theoretical content of 'the most matter-of-fact descriptions'. Also Firth, 1936, Intro.

[3] I want to avoid here the important point raised by Agassi (1966) that we explain the fact that the statement of fact was made rather than the statement of fact. This is because we often find theories which show the statement of fact they explain to be false.

that is to say, as long as we consider them true, they can be used as statements which may contradict and thus refute more problematic theories.

In summary it might be said that ethnography is a dangerously misleading notion when used uncritically. The rescuable part of it consists, I would say, of trying to solve local problems, i.e. of elucidating the logic of the society in question (see section 6, below). No one asserts that we just go out into the field and write down everything which takes our attention. That would be useless, absurd, and need never have a stop. As everyone knows, the fieldworker selects. Selection, however, presupposes a point of view, a basis for selection against which one can decide what is relevant and interesting—interesting from a theoretical point of view which was possibly absorbed while studying social anthropology. Certain imprecisely formulated problems and hypotheses about society are picked up then and it is these which are semi-consciously used to sift out what is relevant. This interpretation of fieldwork is a consequence of my anti-inductivist view that the 'facts' are full of theory, even if that theory is on a low level and comparatively well tested. Since 'theory-free' fieldwork is a myth I reinterpret it as consisting of reconstructions of the social situation and of statements testing (often unarticulated) hypotheses about the society in question.

Sometimes fact-collection is defended on the grounds that anthropologists should record a society or a way of life before it dies out. This is not an argument for indiscriminate fact-collection,[1] but rather an expression of legitimate fear that a society which refutes some of our hypotheses might disappear without trace. Unless we have a pretty clear idea of the sorts of problems and hypotheses we are interested in, though, we might well 'selectively' record all societies and still not take down a point which later turned out to be vital. We can do our best to avoid some such oversight only by concentrating on sharpening our problems and articulating our conjectures. This is by far the most important methodological task facing anthropologists.

It is time, I suggest, that the intuitive approach to fieldwork was dropped and more attention was paid to telling the fieldworker *what* to look for, rather than *how* to look for it: the latter being what current preparation for fieldwork largely consists of. (On reading this Professor Gellner counter-suggested that current training for fieldwork *does* tell the anthropologist what to look for as well as how to

---

[1] Admittedly indiscriminate fact collection can provide relevant information, but only by accident, as it were. If we regard social anthropology as an explanatory science (not, to use Professor Schapera's simile, as a sort of ornithology of societies) then recording or 'surveying' (often cited as an aim) cannot be an end in itself.

look for it. Maybe I can make myself clearer and highlight our disagreement by further distinguishing between being told what to look for and being told what should be looked for. It is almost inevitable that in instructing people how to look for things what to look for will also be inculcated. Anthropologists are largely instructed in how to investigate social structures. This is a general sort of 'what'. Is it the 'what' they should be looking for? I would suggest that it is not. Their surveys of social structure are simply instances intended to confirm their structural-functionalist theory, whereas what they should be looking for is counter-examples to that theory. Of course the 'how' questions cannot be ignored but until the 'what' questions are answered, 'how' questions are a little premature. Indeed, when we examine current 'how' questions to see how they work, we find, first, their high degree of inefficiency, and, second, their conceding answers to 'what' questions which are dogmatically because subliminally absorbed. The How rather than What doctrine has been adopted in order to avoid prejudging issues; in order to avoid error, that is; but this is naïve. Preferably we might, with fruitful results, direct our conjectures and refutations more systematically by discussing what is genuinely problematic in sociology and what kinds of solutions are likely to work. More on this in Chapter 6, section 6 (i).)

5. *Fact Worship in the Social Structure of Social Anthropology*

I think I can now claim to have marshalled a pretty powerful array of arguments against the malinowskian method, especially that, being inductive, it is unselective. It is the method of simply piling up material to no specific purpose. But this is not strong enough to substantiate my claim that the malinowskian method is impossible. His views on method are really taken very seriously in social anthropology and I must provide this stronger objection to them. For, one may claim that unselective research, or research which is selective merely on intuitive grounds, may still develop and fruitfully so. To this my objection is simply that if malinowskian method is followed it takes so long there is no time for theorising or anything else. It is impossible because self-defeating not only as an abstract consideration may show but also in paralysing social anthropologists who try to follow it. I now deal with this point in detail, as it will be my last sally against Malinowski's positivism. From then on I shall regard him as an egalitarian metaphysician.

Nearly all working social anthropologists have done fieldwork; like analysis for a psycho-analyst fieldwork has become both a technical and an institutional qualification. Until you have done it you are not really qualified; until you do it your colleagues feel uneasy about appointing you.

Moreover, social anthropology is so organised that all aspirant professional social anthropologists *must* go through this arduous initiation ritual of fieldwork before they can become adults in the tribe;[1] they *must* learn to collect facts first. The sociology of the tribe or clan[2] is of some importance and interest for there would appear to be a number of aspects of its organisation which militate against my suggested modifications to its method. Why *must* they go through initiation before becoming adults? Induction may give the following rationale: because only with a basis of facts can you build theories. But this rationale is spurious: why collect your own? Is there any reason you shouldn't use each other's facts? This, the rank and file social anthropologist feels, somehow is not quite decent and perhaps a trifle dangerous. There is supposed to be something a little chastening about fieldwork; after undergoing the treatment sociology and fact-collection never look so simple and reliable again.

Now, it may well be that before speculating a student should indeed undergo this treatment, with all its disadvantages, because it also has advantages and the two are mixed up together. But one should notice, perhaps, that the advantages are social, not intellectual, in character. What are these (social) advantages?

Well the first is to the anthropological world. Initiation rituals are one way of keeping numbers down without having to bother with super-high entry standards. Most current social anthropologists are very good indeed, but that is not the only reason they were allowed to enter the profession. They also had to have stamina and luck. They had to have stamina persistently to ask for money for a field expedition, and luck to get it, and they had to have stamina to carry through a field expedition and luck to survive it.[3] There are far more bright young graduates who would eagerly enter the profession than there are jobs, and this rite is one way of thinning them out.

The second advantage is also to the anthropological world, although it is quasi-intellectual as well as social. This is that there are a finite number of societies on this globe and that some of them are being wiped out. Social anthropologists appreciate all the data they can get on diverse societies and therefore they want a survey of extant world societies completed as soon as possible. Now imposing the initiation ceremony of fieldwork may have this genuine

[1] The metaphor is E. Gellner's, see 1958, p. 182.

[2] See Macrae, 1961, p. 35.

[3] I don't mean 'survive' only in the literal sense. For disease, injury, lack of funds, or loss of interest can also take their casualties.

function of beating the clock. However, that they have to force the issue like that may suggest that fieldwork is not such fun that everyone is eagerly rushing out to do it. An element of coercion to overcome reluctance and to beat the clock seems to be needed. This element suggests that fieldwork may not be such fun as Malinowski in the quotation at the beginning of this chapter and Evans-Pritchard (1951, p. 79) in his discussion of sorrowful parting from it, suggest.

There is yet a third reason, also social, connected with the financial advantage of the anthropological world, and with the great foundations. Sending expeditions to remote parts of the globe is one way large foundations have of getting rid of their excess income. There is great prestige to be gained from relieving them of some of that money for social scientific research. If you submit a project which merely requires that you shut yourself up in (a verandah?) a mountain retreat for months simply in order to contemplate other people's observations and to think, your chances of an award are low. This is for the simple reason that the foundation knows as well as you do that you may fail, that nothing may come of your endeavours. To spend *n* thousand dollars and then have nothing to show for it that can be put in the annual report is discouraging and bad for prestige— a factor which foundations, like everyone else, have to take into account. Foundations like tangible results to show for their expenditure. Such is the inductivist climate of opinion that if you show evidence of having been a long way away for a long time and of having collected many new facts then your scientific pretensions are taken most seriously. This despite the fact that many natural scientists at institutes of advanced study never go into laboratories from one year's end to the other. The man who has once muddied his boats in New Guinea or who once got dysentery from the food served in the Amazon jungle, is already a more sober scientist less intoxicated by the bizarre; once and for all he is initiated since he is definitely thought to have been nearer to the stuff of life than those in the armchair on the verandah.

There is I think one genuine intellectual advantage in doing fieldwork; this advantage has been formulated in many ways by many authors. It is that fieldwork is an experience: an intellectual, emotional and even moral experience, invaluable for the student of man. First it is an intellectual shock to plunge into a totally alien social situation and make oneself entirely dependent on the native population. They do everything so differently you can never regard your own background as 'natural' or 'normal' again. Ethnocentric prejudice is dispelled. It is also an emotional shock because one has to overcome all sorts of emotional problems in order to live in another society. This teaches one that emotions are somewhat conventional and differ from society to society and should not therefore be introduced into the science of man. Here may lie an explanation of the social anthropologists' emphasis on emotional sobriety which I discussed in section one. While we may be repelled by killing, a sojourn among headhunters might help us to see things differently; while most of us would baulk at entering a slaughterhouse, constant contact with hunting, slaughtering and sacrificing among native peoples should harden us; while we may be emotional about cleanliness and hygiene, fieldwork can help us to understand that we shouldn't apply our own standards or emotions to other peoples. Finally, the very gesture of totally plunging in among this alien people helps one appreciate the deep human bonds that connect all men, even those separated by the intellectual and emotional barriers we have just mentioned. Despite these barriers we are all men living in workable, viable, valuable, social systems.

What, then, are the disadvantages of fieldwork? It is very prolonged, and the writing up, which most corporate sources of finance expect, takes even longer.[1] So, for a great deal of the time the anthropologist cannot step back to take a broader view, he is involved in the problems of the one area he has been to. Then, of course, there is the question of bias. To do fieldwork is a momentous experience which is likely to mark a man for life. Well and good, but what if he begins to see everything in terms of the one society he knows well?

> Malinowski ... is able to make the Trobriands a microcosm of the whole primitive world ... for Firth, Primitive Man is a Tikopian, for Fortes, he is a citizen of Ghana.
>
> —E. R. Leach, 1961, p. 1.

Exaggerated though this remark may be, it raises a real problem. Already the anthropologists have found the answer. Fieldwork in a second and even a third society! The result of this is that social anthropologists spend most of the rest of their active lives writing-up the material and notes they collected in the field in those societies and teaching students to do the same thing. As a result very little time or energy is left over for theoretical studies of comparative problems.[2]

Can the circle be broken? Professor Schapera has for years been

[1] See my discussion in Chapter 6, section 6(i). Evans-Pritchard's estimate of ten years on average spent on this task is a little conservative; spans of twenty or twenty-five years between fieldwork and publication are not uncommon, as the cases of Malinowski (1918 to his death in 1942) and Evans-Pritchard himself (1930 and 1936 to *Nuer Religion*, 1956) show.

[2] Titles which promise comparative study nearly always turn out merely to conceal a mass of facts about the society the author studied which vaguely bear on the problem, but whose relevance is rarely made clear by a discussion of the problems and theories.

advocating a genuine division of labour between field and theoretical anthropologists. Unfortunately, to use his own words, he seems to be a voice crying in the wilderness, especially as regards getting the initiation ceremony of fieldwork abolished. He attributes this state of affairs to the alleged desire of every young anthropologist to get into the field as soon as he can lay hold on sufficient money. For my part, I would guess that many students are well-disposed to his suggestions; the trouble is no one wants to forgo the really valuable experience of fieldwork, of immersing oneself entirely in a totally alien social situation, and thus counteracting ethnocentric prejudices and deepening the understanding of people and society. And while inertial reverence[1] for fieldwork has been a traditional attitude of the anthropological establishment since the days of Malinowski, it should not be forgotten that a naked curiosity about man and his ways is what often inspires people to do social anthropology. The literature is only a substitute gratification here. To contribute to the literature from one's own experience is the only real satisfaction.

But apart from that I think there is a confusion in the minds of social anthropologists as to what a comparative sociologist would be like. Consider for the moment: who can we take as an archetypal comparative sociologist? I am afraid the answer will rather disconcert social anthropologists: the dead father: Sir James George Frazer is the comparative sociologist *par excellence*. Frazer is by no means perfect. He is long-winded because of an inductive respect for confirming evidence. He was an evolutionist who never made his ideas on the subject explicit. To my knowledge, although he died in 1941, he never carried on an open controversy with his usurpers and intellectual assassins. Nevertheless Frazer had the intellectual capacity, the historical and classical training, and the absorbent memory which well fitted him for the job of comparison. Yet how do social anthropologists view him? Of course, despite their patricide, they all make lip-service obeisance in his direction. Now why do I say it is lip-service? Because he did precisely what they want the comparative sociologist to do and was still subject to severe attack. He was sneered at because he had never been in the field and expressed horror at the thought. Why shouldn't he stay in his study and think? Isn't that, after all, what a comparative sociologist must do? He was accused of accepting reports of customs uncritically. What else could he do but rely upon the literature; how could he possibly have personally checked all the facts in *The Golden Bough*? And anyway, why should

[1] Dr. M. Topley has pointed out to me that asking people to discuss fieldwork is rather like asking Christians to discuss the existence of God. Their lives centre on it to such an extent, to examine it would be so painful, that they prefer simply to go on without asking the question. Cf. pp. 171–2.

he? He was a great man with lots of ideas, even his errors were interesting and could be checked by others. Better that he should get on with creating ideas, checking them within reason, but leaving others to do the rest, than that he waste his time in the field.

I must say I find Frazer glorious and thrilling reading; there is an excitement to be found there which is sadly lacking in the work of the later generations and I am ashamed to have to report that he is not properly appreciated. My explanation for this would be that no one really knows how to appreciate him. They point out that his explanations were false because some of his facts were wrong. But to appreciate a man one must see whether, given his information, he gave satisfactory explanations. This Frazer's undoubtedly were. Credit where credit is due.

Minds must be made up. Do we want comparative sociology, and are we going to excuse its practitioners from the ritual of fieldwork or not? And if we do want this and we will let them off, let us be more careful how we treat those who we can count as precursors, especially when their problems were different from those we are now interested in. Frazer was a comparative sociologist and a great one; great because of his scope and explanatory power, his exhilarating anti-religiousness and his fine English style. That what he says is false does not detract from him at all.

Can we then increase the numbers of interesting and respectable studies of theoretical problems?[1] Methodological analysis, by showing the inescapability of theories can I believe help us. For the problem then becomes one of articulating and discussing these inescapable theories.

One can put this another way. The inductivist anthropologist, like all inductivists, takes a hard-headed, commonsense position. He believes above all in the reality of facts, not of theories; to him theories are simply generalisations or conjunctions built out of facts. On this view a lot of facts have to be available before the building of theories can begin. This result of the hard-headedness is less acceptable. Very few inductivists are ever prepared to say that we already have enough facts for the purpose of drawing firm theoretical conclusions from them. There are very few self-confessed theoretical anthropologists (or 'comparative sociologists'). I think this is a Bad Thing and my own view would help remedy it. My view is almost the reverse of the inductivists': instead of blurring the distinction between facts and theory in the inductivist direction, I blur it in the opposite direction. Whereas they are searching for theories as solid as facts, I see factual statements as almost as wobbly as theories. I do

[1] Examples are: Homans and Schneider, 1955; Steiner, 1956; Fortes, 1953; Firth, 1931; Schapera, 1956; Gluckman, 1955; Worsley, 1957; and so on.

not believe there is such a thing as a theory-free statement of fact; on the contrary I hold that all alleged statements of fact are theories or interpretations; thus *all* anthropologists (whether they know it or not) are theoreticians to this or that degree. They do not realise this, however, so progress is slow.

6. *Candidate Explanation Frameworks: Situational Logic and Structural Functionalism*

A critical reading of the previous section would turn up a number of points that could be made against it. I must deal with these before proceeding. There are, it may seem, some incongruities in my previous section. I begin by complaining that there is a lack of theories in social anthropology and I end up saying that willy-nilly social anthropologists are all theorists. Then I say they all do theorise and I mention the fact that they all want to theorise but have no time for it; how come they want to theorise when they are already theorising? And lastly, I, on the one hand make the technical down-to-earth complaint that too much time is spent between fieldwork and publication, and on the other hand I make the high-falutin' philosophical complaint that we all theorise without knowing it. Now which is it?

It could be said by an anthropologist that with the last point, a technical matter, we can easily deal. Perhaps, an opponent could say, we *should* provide more money for fieldworkers, enough to give them several years without academic duties in which they can more quickly write up their work, not just to Ph.D. standard but to book standard. We will think about it. This is a plain technical matter of organisation. The other point is a little more difficult, even philosophical. Look, it could be said, you say there is not enough theorising and that social anthropologists yearn to fill this gap, and you say we are theorising all the time. Now you can't have it both ways. How are we to answer you? You are saying that perfectly straightforward, uninterpreted ethnographic material is full of theories. Well, being a philosopher, perhaps we can give you the benefit of this doubt and say you are right. But we the anthropologists are clear that such theories are of no interest or importance to us. We therefore want to brush aside what you say as sophisticated philosophical irrelevancy. Perhaps functionalist theory is assumed but that doesn't matter to us; that is not really a theoretical bias, but a theoretical framework the better with which to organise our mass of facts when we write them up. That such a theory is not biassed, we argue, is shown by Worsley's reinterpretation of Fortes' material within the entirely different context of marxist theory (1956). If such a reinterpretation of Fortes' facts is possible his presentation utilising the functionalist framework couldn't have been all that seriously biassed.

My reply to this would be that Worsley had to reorder the facts to fit them into his theory. The functional ordering was a theoretical bias. There was no question of the facts naturally falling into a configuration which fits marxist or functionalist theory. It would be better if this were stated and the theories being used were discussed. What kind of theorising is it? According to social anthropologists it is functionalism (or structural-functionalism);[1] according to me it is logic of the situation. Let us go into this to see whether it is a philosophical irrelevancy. Why do I hold that social anthropologists use situational logic? When I began work on this book I was generally dissatisfied with what I took to be the myriad methodological faults of social anthropology. Although this dissatisfaction was rash, and although I have modified it since, it turned out that it did have a rational core: problems of explanation. That there were at least two levels of problems, local and comparative, in social anthropology strongly suggested that there might be at least two kinds of explanation: explanation of local problems in local terms and explanation of comparative problems on a higher theoretical level. All explanation uses theories, of course. The distinction I want to draw is really between explanations of local problems in terms of situational logic which uses only one hypothesis—why people acted in such and such a way can be rationally reconstructed; and comparative problems, explanations of which can use all sorts of other, macro-, theories, including those of sociology and economics.

First, then, local problems, I think the following example of a man from Mars is a paradigm of the way a social anthropologist proceeds in his local work.[2] It is intended to illustrate my contention that much of fieldwork consists simply of situational logic. Assume an extremely intelligent Martian scientist had landed in The Bible Belt during a severe drought. While he was being conducted around by a distinguished scientist of Earth he noticed that all the people of a town were crowded inside a hot, gloomy building. They alternately

[1] I shall try to keep these terms separate throughout the book although I shall only explain their different connotations in Chapter 6. The main difference is that Malinowski speaks of the function of a custom to culture and human needs, while Radcliffe-Brown speaks of the function of a custom within a social structure and the needs of societies. At the moment I intend 'functionalism' to refer to Malinowski and his revolution, 'structural-functionalism' to Radcliffe-Brown and his influence. Just occasionally I have used the former as a shorthand for it and the latter, but only when the context makes the usage quite clear.

[2] Another attempt to picture what the anthropologist does on the local level, using the metaphor of a parachuted spy, is made in Chapter 6, section 6 (ii).

fell on their knees muttering to themselves, and rose to their feet crying in unison.[1]

'Why', asks the puzzled Martian, 'are all these people behaving so peculiarly, so irrationally on such a hot day? Why do they waste their time in there when their crops are wilting in the fields? Why are they not busy dropping dry ice into the clouds or pumping water overland for irrigation? Don't they want crops?'

The Earth scientist smiles tolerantly and explains that of course they want crops. Then he explains that they all believe in, and act on, a theory that the world is the property, and under the exclusive control, of a Divine Being. They think that ultimately the drought is the work of the Divine Being and that the best, if not perhaps the quickest, way of ending it (but they are poor and cannot afford all these water-getting schemes) is to implore it of the Divine Being; it is this that they are doing in that building.

The Martian now sees that the earthlings have intelligible ends (they want crops) and have acted rationally faced with their situation, where 'their situation' includes their knowledge and beliefs.

This Martian example confronts us with a social situation in which what at first glance seems odd behaviour can be made perfectly intelligible without ever attributing bizarre aims to the actors. There is, notice, no use of functionalism here, no specification of the functional relations between institutions. Institutions come in only in so far as they, and beliefs about them, come into this particular social situation. No doubt this social situation indirectly connects up with all others and therefore with all institutions. You can choose any point in the social system and trace its connections with all others; social situations, like leibnizian monads, mirror the whole world. But we don't need to describe the whole world to explain a part of it. On the other hand this is a *very* small-scale local example and by no means typical of *all* the work of the social anthropologist.

There would seem to be problems of a much broader scope which require theoretically more sophisticated explanations, comparable to those in economics. Situational logic is nearly always an answer to the question: why are these people acting in this way? Some anthropologists conceive theoretical questions to be something like: why is this society like this (e.g. unilineal) and not like that (e.g. non-unilineal)? But (unless one believes the form social institutions take is determined by other, prior, social institutions, or by ecology) such

[1] Our Martian like Martians in most sociological discussions is a quasi-behaviourist. Since, however, I may assume that he is convertible from behaviourism to some other creed (he is no worse than his creators, the sociologists), I should perhaps call him a Saturnian to show how different he is from those other Martians.

questions require specific historical answers. With most of the societies social anthropologists study historical answers would be untestable, and for that reason social anthropologists do not find historical questions very interesting.

I do not accept the idea that because all the answers we can give to a question are as yet untestable it is an uninteresting question. It may be both fascinating and important. We can never know when empirical criticism may become possible and so it is better not to let testability be a millstone around the neck of imagination and critical power.

As I see it theoretical anthropology rather consists in questions like: 'what is the *explanation* of preferential cross-cousin marriage; ancestor worship; extended kinship terminologies; taboo?' or 'are there any combinations of social institutions which are incompatible or which, if combined in one society, will cause it to break down?' Despite their as yet vague formulations such questions strike me as a good first approximation to the problems of a theoretical social anthropology.

In the last century and for part of this, theoretical social anthropology consisted of the great evolutionary schemes of Maine, Morgan, Tylor, etc.; all customs were explained as integral parts of natural stages in the evolution of society. The great debate in theoretical studies was between these evolutionists and the diffusionists, who explained customs by cultural borrowing, a process which originally began at a centre or centres. The rivalry ended when the theories were combined. The theoretical questions I have endorsed are very similar to those tackled by these early anthropologists; they are very different from those tackled by most contemporary anthropologists, who ask: 'what is the *function* of preferential cross-cousin marriage; ancestor worship; extended kinship terms; taboo?' To understand this change in the focus of interest a little more history of the revolution in social anthropology, before and after, is necessary. Happily a version excellent for my present purposes has already been presented by Hogbin; here is the relevant passage:[1]

The social sciences, no less than the biological sciences, were for a long period dominated by the theory of evolution. Early anthropologists accepted the hypothesis that all societies were progressing upwards along the same line towards some final objective. The civilised peoples had made the greatest headway, they supposed, and the various primitive societies were placed at different points along the route, some near the bottom, others closer to ourselves. Students of this era referred to natives as 'our contemporary ancestors' and argued that the development of institutions

[1] Hogbin, 1958, pp. 15–18. I regret the length of the quotation, but I feel it justifies itself by the clarity with which it makes the point.

could be worked out by a survey of present-day customs, starting with the 'lowest' societies and climbing step by step to the groups 'higher' on the scale. Sallas, in a book dealing ostensibly with the prehistory of Europe, wrote that 'The Tasmanians, though recent, were at the same time a Paleolithic, or even . . . Eolithic, race, and they thus afford us an opportunity of interpreting the past by the present.' He follows his account of Eolithic remains in Europe with a description of the habits of the Tasmanians and inferred that this is how the ape-men who made the tools must have lived. Similarly, he concluded that because some of the implements of the mid-Paleolithic cultures resembled those of the Australian aborigines tribal life in Australia would provide information about the social organisation and beliefs of Neanderthal man. Morgan and McLennan, using methods of this kind, worked out an evolutionary sequence for the family. They suggested that the first stage was complete promiscuity and that then came group marriage, polygamy, and, finally, monogamy. Maine, Hartland, and Vinogradoff propounded corresponding sequences for law, and Tylor, Marett, and Frazer others for religion. All these writers were attracted by customs that differ markedly from our own. They regarded them as evidence for the prior existence of a less evolved type of society no longer visible in its pure form. So current examples of matrilineal inheritance were of interest as relics of promiscuity and group marriage. Paternity, so it was maintained, could never have been established until the stage of polygamy was reached, and patrilineal descent and patrilineal inheritance must necessarily belong solely to the higher forms of society. Except for Morgan, who had had first-hand experience of American Indians, these evolutionists relied for their material on travellers' tales and missionary accounts that were mostly prejudiced and always inadequate. Had they visited colonial territories they might even at that date have observed cases of matriliny gradually giving way before patriliny. But it was not till this decade that books and papers began to appear citing instances of such a change-over, with details of the causes and effects.

Anthropologists still believe in social evolution, but this crude unilinear theory has long since been abandoned. As a dominant theme it was replaced for a time by diffusion, the attempt to trace the spread of cultural items, mainly techniques and material objects, through past migrations. The diffusionists were equally indifferent to what was actually going on while they were spinning their theories. Perry, in *The Children of the Sun*, for instance, tried to prove that wherever such practices as mummifying the dead, building pyramids, and wearing gold and pearls as ornaments, were carried on they had been introduced by the ancient Egyptians or by peoples in contact with them. The Maya culture of Mexico, the Inca culture of Peru, and the island culture of the Torres Straits were all supposed to be derived from a civilisation which, after its creation on the Nile, travelled around the world. . . . Perry, and the members of several other diffusionist schools, assumed that each present-day culture was a sort of rubbish-heap of custom, the careful picking over of which would reveal a series of strata. Thus Rivers, in his *History of Melanesian Society*, said that he had reached the conclusion that Melanesian culture had come into existence as a result of a fusion of a number of peoples possessing different institutions. He maintained that waves of voyagers had blended with the original population and that the culture we now regard as typical of the area was a hotch-potch. He sorted out the betel-chewers from the kava-drinkers, the groups that cremated their dead from those that preserved them, and discussed the wanderings of each among the islands. His most spectacular triumphs were in convincing himself that the peculiar privileges of uterine nephews in relation to their maternal uncles, a feature of many societies following the principles of patrilineal descent, were derived from a state of affairs in which the elders were able to monopolize all the young women and that cross-cousin marriage became an established custom when the older men began giving their superfluous wives to their sisters' sons.

In England the reaction set in just before 1920, when the younger anthropologists at length realised that *the method of reconstructing history by conjecture was unscientific because the conclusions, even those that appeared to be reasonable, were incapable of proof* [italics mine].[1]

So much for the methodological state of affairs as 'the younger anthropologists' (i.e. Malinowski) saw it. But as to the 'younger anthropologists' realisation that their elders were being unscientific I do not think they realised any such thing. That charge seems to me a *post hoc* thing made only after an alternative had been thought of, and it was put forward more as a justification of the new alternative than as a serious criticism of the old. My supports for this contention are two. One is that functionalism was slightly prior to the charge and that charge was to increase in frequency as functionalism was consciously developed. The other is the story of how functionalism arose. No coherent account has ever been given of this so I offer mine to fill a gap. What social anthropologists of Malinowski's generation couldn't avoid noticing was the bankruptcy of evolutionism by that time and the fruitlessness of the evolutionism-diffusionism controversy. And yet, despite this, evolutionism continued as the reigning dogma until it was ousted by a powerful rival: Malinowski's functionalism. Apart from the fact that evolutionism seemed to be getting nowhere, slowly, Malinowski had come across in his fieldwork what he deemed to be a really tough problem: explaining the *kula*. The *kula* was a pattern of trade between Melanesian islands. They set out in boats to a neighbouring island and there exchanged necklaces for armbands with much ritual. Its explanation was to be two-sided: why should there be ritualised trading in useless ornaments,

---

[1] The younger anthropologists' criticism of their elders seems silly. Nothing but the propositions of logic and mathematics *are* even remotely capable of anything like proof. It would have been enough if the younger anthropologists had pointed out that their elders had a somewhat uncritical attitude to their own theories.

and why should the necklaces circulate round the islands one way and the armbands the other? Applying evolutionist techniques to this obviously struck Malinowski as useless. How could this immemorially old pattern of trade be explained by origins? In fact the problem with it was if anything that it seemed irrational. Since sensible savages do it Malinowski decided to find out why. Why expend all this effort to swap ornaments?

Once these questions were asked the rest was easy. The trading was a renewing of ties between communities, the ritual and effort reflected the importance of these ties; the ornaments functioned to express the ties. The theory was generalisable: all customs and institutions must have a function. Malinowski had thus developed a method of explanation he labelled functionalism.[1] My thesis, then, is that he developed the method of functionalism to handle a particular problem. It was successful. Successful methods are a temptation. There is a tendency in many fields for the practitioners to seize upon a successful method, forgetting the problems it was designed to solve, and to apply it elsewhere. The evolutionists, as well as the functionalists, are guilty of this. Darwin developed evolutionism to solve a particular problem: the relation of man to the animals and his environment. It was then applied to societies in order to explain the relations between them and their environments. However it was also and illegitimately used to explain why present customs were as they were. Popper (1962, p. 8) has remarked how this tendency to misapply methods is rife in philosophy. Functionalism was a solution to the problem of the *kula*, and of other institutions, but it was not a method appropriate to the evolutionists' problems. Once he had articulated and christened this new approach he was able to develop, with the help of functionalism, more abstract criticisms of the method of historical conjecture. Thus the history is not quite what Hogbin's official interpretation makes it seem: in fact the theoretical questions about the history of this or that institution which interested the evolutionists were *suppressed* in their original form and reformulated in very dubious ways after Malinowski; indeed there is at first an almost complete disappearance of theoretical problems, or indeed of problems, in the sense of things needing explanation, altogether. Instead of attacking, say, psychological explanation, Malinowski attacked other sociologists, namely those addicted to the historical

[1] The exact origin of the idea remains obscure. Malinowski *uses* it in his *Myth in Primitive Psychology* of 1926, and *says* it made its first appearance in the original of 1929a, written in 1926. He says this in his fascinating Special Foreword to the third edition (1932) of 1929b. In the course of this he confesses to abandoning traditional evolutionism and replacing it by functional evolutionism.

method. Deeply impressed by Cuvier, who had deduced whole skeletons from a single bone, Malinowski (1929*b*, p. xxv) foresaw a method almost as powerful in social anthropology. It should be possible to relate one institution to all the others in society. It would not be possible

in the science of culture to tear out a custom which belongs to a certain context, which is part of it, the very existence of which would determine all the work which it does within that context—to tear it out, to dote upon it in a collectioneering or curio-hunting spirit, leads nowhere (1929*b*, p. xxv).

Thus Malinowski's contextual functionalism provided him with a strong weapon against those evolutionists who discussed the evolution of details of custom. The evolution of societies, or social contexts, was all that was allowed. Societies being quasi-organic wholes we have to describe and classify them before we can do anything else. But empiricist revolutions are often followed by a counter-revolution on behalf of theoretical system-building. Having eliminated the dubious methods of their elders, the younger anthropologists began to ask themselves if their new methods could not be used to produce some work of larger scope. Few fieldworkers were content to describe the situational logic and institutional interconnections of a society. They were always posing disguised historical questions in semi-deterministic functional formulations. They interpreted questions like: 'why does society *y* have patriliny and not matriliny?' or 'why in society *x*, do they worship their male ancestor and not their female ancestor?' as 'what is the functional significance of patriliny rather than matriliny in society *y*?', 'what is the functional significance of male rather than female ancestor worship in society *x*?' Survival or evolutionary or historical hypotheses in these matters will not do. For one thing to say that matriliny is more primitive and that patriliny is a natural development out of it is an explanation in principle and not in detail. How and why does this natural development come about? As to ancestor worship one more step is required to reveal the complete unsatisfactoriness. Suppose some table of evolution has been constructed, how does it account for some things not changing while others do?

Behind the questions as they have been reformulated is the assumption that a society's institutions are adjusted to one another, and that examination will show why the one form fits in better than the other would; how the structure 'demands' it.[1] But these com-

[1] An interesting criticism of this argument as it is expressed by Fortes is given in Scheinfeld, 1960, preface. He also shows the difficulty of finding any sort of solution to these problems.

parative or theoretical questions began to be asked again only when a serious and misplaced anti-historical reaction had already set in. Not surprisingly, perhaps, still later there was a counter-reaction led by Evans-Pritchard which urged the reintroduction of the historical dimension. (See Chapter 6, section 5 (i).) I find it strange that Hogbin does not mention that the perhaps legitimate objection to historical conjectures had been with less reason broadened until the attitude could hardly be described as anything less than a dislike of history of any kind intruding into social anthropology. When the functional method was taken to extremes, it eliminated all conjectural notions of the origins of the customs and dictated that there *can be* no institutional survival from previous ages (i.e. that history can be neither a necessary nor a sufficient explanation of a custom). Whether this consequence was intended or not, consequence it seems to have been. The crucial question now faced by the functionalists who were forced into antihistorism was whether questions about the origins and causes of social change could be adequately handled despite it. And here, precisely, I would say that contemporary functionalist social anthropology breaks down. For antihistory tries to ignore the time element in social events, tries to take a snapshot of society at a point in time, seeks only 'the laws of process' as Malinowski calls them. The trouble is a snapshot is not a very good means of recording movement. Movie film, lots of snapshots taken at short intervals, and able to reproduce movement, is much better.

The problem of social change is how society x with institutions A, B, C, suddenly comes to have institutions A_1, B_1, C_1. No matter how much we know of A, B, C, we will not be helped here. Even should we say we have regularly observed that A, B and C give way to A_1, B_1 and C_1 that is no reason for assuming they will again. If we do assume that we have to assume something like 'past events are a guide to future events' and, as Hume pointed out, that statement can only be justified by appeal to itself so there is an infinite regress. The inductivist ideal of a pure description of a society, a snapshot, or a cross-section which will lead to correlations with other such is completely useless for explaining social change. This is mainly because correlations *simpliciter* have little *explanatory* power.

7. The Slogans of the Revolution

It is my thesis, then, that over the problem of explaining social change contemporary social anthropology proves inadequate. This means that the much-heralded 'revolution in anthropology' is also shown to be inadequate. The inadequacy is relative as well as absolute for the previous theories, evolutionism and diffusionism, were, as I have already noted, able to cope with social change. Post-revolutionary social anthropology cannot give so much as a satis-factory account of change, whereas the previous doctrines permitted satisfactory (but, perhaps, false) accounts. So far, I hope the main outline of my ideas is clear. To make doubly sure I want to state it again in brief.

Throughout this chapter I have operated, and throughout this book I shall operate, with three slogans which seem to me to sum up the revolution in anthropology as perpetrated by Malinowski. I strongly dissent from all three slogans and I shall discuss their different merits in the course of the book. So strongly do I dissent from them that they act rather like red flags to a bull. Whenever I can trace an idea back to them I get excited. In order to transform their effects into simple danger-warning red flags I want now to set them down and explain them.

The first battle-cry of the revolution is 'kill the chief-priest (or father) and his gang'. Translated this reads: 'overthrow the influence of Frazer and company; purge our new Science of Man of the influence of these victorian intellectualist evolutionists'. 'Why should we?' Malinowski was asked. 'Because all men are equal. There are no primitives. There is no place for such prejudiced thinking in a true Science of Man.' At first, of course, Malinowski's was a small voice. Yet with quite startling rapidity it began to be heard in the corridors of British anthropology. Before we know where we are there is a mob of Malinowski followers charging around tearing the place to pieces and rebuilding. The barricades set up by the establishment were hasty and scanty and easily overthrown. Soon the voices of the swelling mass of students could be heard demanding to know what they could do to join the cause. 'Accept the principle that all men are equal and deserve an unprejudiced science' they were told. 'Father we are willing to believe, but show us how we may come to do so', they beseeched Malinowski. Not at all disconcerted at being the new chief-priest, Malinowski heeded their plea.

Back came the reply, the second slogan: 'Come down off the verandah, come out of your studies and join the people.' Translated this reads: 'do not sit spinning theories like spider webs on the verandah of mission or government house, or at home in your library; go down among the people, get to know them, live with them as one of them, learn to appreciate their way of life as an orderly and satis-factory way, and then you will come to realise that the unity of mankind is a reality. This will kill the chief-priest.'

Fortified, the revolution began to be consolidated and institution-alised. But there were problems and uncertainties; life off the verandah was not easy. Bewildered the masses muttered among themselves and then demanded of Malinowski: 'Tell us, oh Father, how are we to know that men are equals? We have come off the verandah yet we can still see that our men produce science and technology while theirs dance around fires and intone.' Calmly and confidently Malinowski answered them: 'Verily I say unto you,' he said, 'study the ritual not the belief.' This was the third slogan. He went on, 'Pay no attention to what men say they are doing, only observe what they are doing and study the true objective social function of what they are doing. One set of men stand in laboratories in white coats and twiddle knobs and say they are doing science. Another set of men dance around a fire and chant and say they are doing magic. What is the truth: there is no similarity between the two at all. Only the dead father has misled you. The men doing the magic are strengthening ties, relieving social tension and so on; doing what we do in church. The men in white coats are doing what the natives do when they carve out a canoe: mixing ritual and technique. How do I know all this? Simply by studying the ritual not the belief. If the truth about the unity of mankind ye seek, study the ritual not the belief. Seek ye the truth there in the ritual and ye shall certainly find.'

For the facetious ring to this section I apologise. I want to dramatise the revolution and the crudity of the slogans it was based on. It was a great revolution which achieved many things. The purpose of my caricature is to throw emphasis on those things I shall later try to show to be mistaken. Let me note the slogans and the places where I contest each most fully. (1) Kill the chief-priest and his gang (Chapters 1 and 6). (2) Come down off the verandah (Chapters 1, 2 and 5). (3) Study the ritual, not the belief (Chapters 4 and 5).

Having recapitulated the revolution as I see it I can now sharpen the main thesis of the book concerning the post-revolutionary breakdown.

8. *The Problem of Method Formulated*

I can now formulate my central problem of method in such a way that it will help me present the layout of the rest of the book: as follows. British social anthropologists, since Malinowski's revolution, have adopted a framework of explanation which explains social happenings in terms of their function within the structure of social institutions. I ask: (*a*) is such explanation by structural analysis satisfactory explanation?; (*b*) in general, can this kind of explanation adequately cope with all the problems of social anthropology (both local and comparative) and, in particular, can it handle social change?

The answer to (*a*) is, 'in many cases yes; but occasionally no.' Question (*b*) is not difficult; at first sight it seems that a fairly straightforward answer can be given to it. The answer to (*b*) is 'no', for social change seems a *prima facie* counter-example. I try in this book to answer (*b*) by the following strategy. I take one particular problem of social anthropology which also happens to be a problem of social change—cargo cults (Chapter 2). I then survey the possible solutions to it and mention those which anthropologists have proposed (Chapter 3). What a satisfactory explanation of cargo cults might look like is then debated. An explanation within the framework of Karl Popper's situational logic is shown to be satisfactory (Chapter 4). I next discuss why there is no explanation of the problem within the framework of structural-functionalism in the survey and I try to argue that there *can be* no explanation of it within the limitations of the structural-functional framework (Chapter 5). This demands a return to the ideas of the revolution. Reviewing the detail of the revolution and finding that structural-functionalism is not always satisfactory explanation in general I discuss (Chapter 6) two other explanatory frameworks that have been suggested for social anthropology, namely those of history, and situational logic. Finally I discuss the implications the whole argument has for social anthropology.

My policy is to keep abstract methodological discussion to a minimum, so I shall now illustrate problem (*b*) by considering whether structural-functionalism copes with any of the problems of social anthropology.

Take the following problem.

In our society, children are sometimes taught to refer to close friends of their parents by the terms 'aunt' and 'uncle'—although no kinship relation exists between them. This is a curious thing; why should these terms be extended in this way? Many primitive peoples also extend such terms as those which we should translate as 'father' to a sizeable range of people whom the anthropologist knows (from the tribe's own kinship records) not to have the kin relationships designated by the term. This kind of extension of kinship terms presents a problem typical of social anthropology.

The problem of extended kinship terms provoked hot disputes, especially between Kroeber (1909, 1917) and Rivers (1914). One theory was that the custom was a remnant from a period of group-marriage or even 'primitive promiscuity' when people had little or no knowledge of their actual kin ties and so they used more generalised (or vague) kin terms than we do. A second theory was that it arose from the custom of marrying wife's brother's daughter. Another theory was that people who were given the same label, e.g. 'father', were people who were *psychologically associated in the mind* with the 'real' father.

The dispute was resolved in 1941 (in print, at least) by Radcliffe-Brown, the great structural-functionalist thinker, in a brilliant essay, 'The Study of Kinship Systems', where he showed, to transpose back to our own society again, that we want our children to call our friends 'uncle' and 'aunt' because we want our children to act towards, to behave as though, our friends were their aunts and uncles. In other words, the terms 'uncle' and 'aunt' designate a certain kind of social relationship with children and the extension of these terms is an attempt to extend these social relationships to people not strictly denoted by the term. Here the distinction between social and physical kinship was needed and came to be recognised as important.[1] The labels 'aunt' and 'uncle' even when not being used as courtesy-titles for family friends do not just signify genealogical relationships; they also define a person's sets of rights and duties towards other persons.

On the one hand the group-marriage theory did not explain the extended kinship in societies without group-marriage. Usually a 'survival' hypothesis was resorted to but this was *ad hoc*. Besides, Radcliffe-Brown questioned the assumption that marriage rules should determine kin terms: why should the language be so accommodating either to group-marriage or to wife's brother's daughter's marriage? Against psychologism it could simply be asked: why are the associations as they are?

Both hypotheses are thus immediately seen to be quite unsatisfactory. Radcliffe-Brown's hypothesis is satisfactory. It is that the language used by a society reflects the society it is used in. Clearly this is false, since it leaves no room for inertia and therefore survivals. But it is satisfactory (and, incidentally, could easily be modified to accommodate the survivals criticism).

The problem of extended kinship terms and other very interesting problems have been solved by what is virtually Radcliffe-Brown's method.

A list of interesting examples of other problems with which great progress has been made may be given here: the problem of how societies without centralised authority or government succeed in living orderly not anarchical lives[2] (by fragmentation and strict rules as to who is involved in any dispute and how it shall be settled); the problem of why mothers-in-law are avoided[3] (because of the necessity not to damage the marriage-alliance with a quarrel, and the respect which must be shown to the first ascending generation); the problem of why the mother's brother controls the upbringing of

---

[1] For a valuable discussion of this point, see Gellner, 1960.
[2] Evans-Pritchard, 1940; Fortes, 1945, 1949; Schapera, 1930; Gellner, 1958*a*.
[3] Radcliffe-Brown, 1952, chapter 4.

children in some societies[1] (because the father is not a member of the child's matrilineage); the problem of the social role of magic[2] (it invests important things with an aura and it gives a feeling of control over the unknown and vital forces); the problem of why marriage is more stable in some societies than in others[3] (the expense of repaying bride-price, the degree to which husband and wife separate roles); the problem of why unilineal (but not nonunilineal) societies often keep elaborate kinship records, and why they knowingly falsify and merge generations in them[4] (a pseudo-history which requires institutionalised adjustments to allow contraventions of the rules and yet preserve legitimacy); the problem of why murders between very close kin are sometimes not avenged[5] (because the vengeance-group is the same or overlaps with the bereaved).

These explanations are, without a doubt, functionalist and, perhaps, are essentially so. Functionalism is the doctrine that societies are evolved, harmonious wholes. All these explanations deal with ways in which societies try to avoid conflict, try to re-establish harmony: avoidance of anarchical conflict; avoidance of mothers-in-law; avoidance of conflict between lineages; avoidance of conflict with nature; the avoidance of marital conflict; the avoidance of legitimacy conflicts; the avoidance of inter-family feuding.

Such successes may to some extent explain the rapid acceptance of the framework of method of structural-functional analysis by British social anthropologists; some very tough problems are thus solved; it works, it delivers the cargo of a science of society! These are not arguments for uncritically accepting it as a panacea for all problems. My task is to show that there are many problems unamenable to structural-functional methods (especially the nodal problem of social change); and that, in some cases, to explain in that way is not to explain at all satisfactorily.

9. *Cargo Cults and the Problem of Method*

I have accounted for the dearth of theory by saying it is a consequence of certain peculiarities and disputes in the history of social anthropology which have given the subject an empiricist, or anti-theoretical, twist. The straightening out of this twist has been prevented—during the recent revival of interest in theoretical problems—by induction and structural-functionalism. The former was strengthened by, the

---

[1] Radcliffe-Brown, 1952, chapter 4.
[2] Evans-Pritchard, 1937; P. Mayer, 1954; R. Fortune, 1932.
[3] Mair, 1953; Gluckman, 1955; Bott, 1957.
[4] Evans-Pritchard, 1940; Radcliffe-Brown, 1950.
[5] Schapera, 1954.

latter introduced by, the revolution. Structural-functionalism explains an event or an institution by reference to a permanent or underlying structure of the social situation; so variations over time are assumed away in its models; consequently attempts to explain the happenings of social change with these models break down since change can hardly be divorced from time. I conclude that critical study of the post-revolutionary methods of social anthropology would do well to concentrate on this weak spot; the problem of explaining social change. This methodological weakness can be examined in some detail and the possibility of repairing it can be explored. Such a programme involves retracing the history of the methods of social anthropology to show just where in the revolution things begin to go wrong and how much will be involved in putting them right.

These considerations weighed heavily as I cast around for a suitable example of social change which could be fitted into my general discussion of the revolution, and used to exemplify my methodological suggestions. To be an adequate example it would have to be a theoretical as well as a situational (or historical) problem. There must needs be ample empirical and theoretical material available on it, and preferably it should be something sufficiently non-technical to interest non-anthropologists. I believe I found a problem fulfilling all these requirements in the millenarian religious phenomenon known as 'cargo cults'.

Before going into detail about these cults I want first to describe the methodology they are to be used to exemplify—having already outlined the point they will be used to make against the post-revolutionary methods—and second to give a brief background survey of millenarian religious movements. Thus equipped I shall proceed to the cults, the problems they raise, and the theoretical accounts that can be given of them.

10. *Method*

Karl Popper often begins his lecture course on scientific method with the categorical assertion that in an important sense scientific method does not exist. There is no scientific method, he says, which, if learned, will inevitably lead to success in science. Nevertheless there seems to be something peculiarly or rigorously rational about the way science proceeds. This feeling reflects the fact, Popper adds, that the (only) method of science is a systematic application of the rational method of *critical discussion*. Science, he says, aims at explaining the world. To this end it concentrates on isolating genuine problems and putting forward bold hypothetical solutions to them. The method of science consists in doing our utmost to criticise and to overthrow these tentative hypotheses, so as to make way for better ones.

This is virtually all that needs to be said about methodology for the purposes of the ensuing argument. The expansion and discussion of this view can be left until later in this book. All the criticisms I produce of other methodologies (Chapters 5 and 6) will be to the effect that we do not need more than this.

This outline of methodology is, however, deceptive in its simplicity. What Popper has done is to shift all the methodological stress from how we arrive at the hypotheses (theories, guesses) of science to what we do to, and with, them after we have attained them. For, his argument goes, however we obtain our theories, we are not absolved from the necessity of testing them; there is no method of reaching the truth which is so mechanically sure that we need not test the results; to believe otherwise is to accept the view that knowledge can be got from authoritative sources,[1] a view which Popper has decisively criticised. We can claim, then, that we are not (or ought not to be) *qua methodologists*, concerned with how we get our ideas, but only with criticising them and testing them once we have them. But this entails a serious criticism of the methods of contemporary British social anthropology. First because it means that we must be very clear as to exactly what our problems are. This, as I hope to show with the problem of cargo cults, is not always the case with British social anthropologists. Secondly, because anthropological methods centre on close, careful observation; slow, tentative comparative generalisation; sampling; limited area studies, and so on. Valuable though these methods are when applied to testing hypotheses, when applied to generating hypotheses by sticking to the verified facts, and to generalisations of the verified facts, they amount to the attempt to seek truth by shunning bold hypothetical ideas, and sticking to statements that are known to be true.[2] But the creative side of science *is* wild and undisciplined; not to allow it to be so is the quickest way to retard scientific progress. I shall in this book advocate the freedom to speculate, within the context of discussion of a clear problem, as the most fruitful method.

11. *Background to the Case-study*

In calling social studies 'sciences', and expecting from them explanations, we are assuming, at least as a methodological convention, that

[1] A view, that is, which asks where you got your information rather than is it true; see Popper, 1961, *passim*.
[2] Forgetting, of course, that the truest statements (tautologies, demonstrable statements) are also trivial.

such social explanations are possible; otherwise we would not look for them. This involves the broader assumption that human behaviour can to some extent be explained. An immediate test case for these assumptions is religion. In the sense that few men have no 'faith' of any kind, religion is a universal phenomenon (e.g. I have a faith in the rational attitude, atheists a faith that God is but a mythological being; baconian scientists a faith that the ritual correctly performed will bring them the cargo of science). And in speaking of 'faith' we seem to be calling religious feelings 'irrational' or inexplicable. But we are not labelling religious *actions*, inasmuch as they are based on these faiths, irrational or inexplicable. In fact we are counting religious feelings both as capable of affecting a person's aims and as being part of the situation within which he decides and acts.

This is how I view the sociology of religion. It would be natural for a westerner to envisage religion as a settled, comfortable institution, which has suffered only a few violent changes in its long history. When confronted with this astounding proliferation of chilisatic movements in the space of a few years in Melanesia he finds them in need of explanation. This is how the problem presented by the plethora of millenarian religious movements in Melanesia arises. We shall discuss what causes them; why they are so similar; why they are so short; what can and should be done once they occur; and so on. But before going into detail about the questions they raise and the answers which have been proposed, I want to describe the problem-situation, i.e. try to give some historical background against which the Melanesian cults can be seen. As I shall explain later, such information cannot but be biassed, filled with my own theoretical ideas both in what is selected for display and in how it is put. In one sense this need not be taken too seriously; the way I shall present the picture will not differ substantially from the way others have presented it. Still, my bias should not be forgotten. I have confessed to being a conventionalist, individualist and objectivist. Thus in presenting the problem I shall probably be somewhat unfair to my opponents. I ask critical indulgence.

One of the most remarkable things about apocalyptic millenarian movements is that, despite the fact that they crop up at all periods of history, in all parts of the world, and in all sorts of different social set-ups, we can find remarkable similarities between them. To emphasise this point my background examples of the general phenomenon of millenarianism will be taken from outside Melanesia and from the historical past.[1]

[1] I should stress that the descriptive literature on these phenomena is enormous; in English alone there have been many books and papers published since the last war. The scrappy background I shall provide on the universality

The main elements which I want to isolate as widespread are (*a*) the promise of heaven on earth—soon; (*b*) the brief life of the movements; (*c*) the overthrow or reversal of the present social order; and (*d*) the terrific release of emotional energy.

The first chiliastic movement to which I will refer is the Jewish doctrine of the Chosen People. For my description of this I use the excellent text of Professor Norman Cohn (1957, pp. 2–3), who describes the Jewish eschatology as follows:

Already in the Prophetical books there are passages—some of them dating from the eighth century—that foretell how, out of an universal cosmic catastrophe, there will arise a Palestine which will be nothing less than a new Eden, Paradise regained. Because of their neglect of Yahweh the Chosen People must indeed be punished by famine and pestilence, war and captivity, they must indeed be subjected to a sifting judgment so severe that it will effect a clean break with the guilty past. There must indeed be a Day of Yahweh, a Day of Wrath, when sun and moon and stars are darkened, when the heavens are rolled together and the earth is shaken. There must indeed be a Judgment when the misbelievers—those in Israel who have not trusted in the Lord and also Israel's enemies, the heathen nations—are judged and cast down, if not utterly destroyed. But this is not the end; a saving 'remnant' of Israel will survive these chastisements and through that remnant the divine purpose will be accomplished. When the nation is thus regenerated and reformed Yahweh will cease from vengeance and become the Deliverer. The righteous remnant—together, it was held latterly, with the righteous dead now resurrected—will be assembled once more in Palestine and Yahweh will dwell amongst them as a ruler and judge. . . . It will be a just world, where the poor are protected, and a harmonious and peaceful world, where wild and dangerous beasts have become tame and harmless. The moon will shine as the sun and the sun's light will be increased sevenfold. Deserts and waste lands will become fertile and beautiful. There will be abundance of water and provender for flocks and herds, for men there will be abundance of corn and wine, and fish and fruit; men and flocks and herds will multiply exceedingly. Freed from disease and sorrow of every kind, doing no more iniquity but living according to the law of Yahweh now written in their hearts, the Chosen People will live in joy and gladness.

This vision of the millennium bears startling similarities to the prophecies of the Melanesian cults we shall discuss. There is the

---

of the cults does not pretend to be adequate for any other task than making the point that these cults in Melanesia are not localised oddities either in the speed with which they appear, and disappear, or in the length of time they are drawn out, or in the structural characteristics of their organisation, or in the kinds of doctrine they propound. Of course, there are elements in them which make the Melanesian cults unique and thus give them added interest; but the important problems connected with them, including the problems of their widespreadness and homogeneity, are universal.

Chosen, the Day, the poor faithless, the regeneration, the resurrected spirits, the new world of justice, harmony, happiness, abundance and virtue.

After a few hundred years of these beliefs; after conquest and re-conquest; and after the appearance of various prophets who tried to lead the Chosen People on to a different path, a new, and in many ways sensationally influential, prophet rose up and presented a new case to the Jews. I mean, of course, Christ. Several scholars, among them R. Graves and J. Podro and R. Eisler[1] have suggested that Christianity was itself yet another millenarian movement, I have quoted the relevant sections from Eisler's learned and provocative book as an appendix;[2] here is the crucial passage:

> The people who listened to his preaching were attracted not so much by the narrow path he pointed out to them, as by the alluring hope of a golden age in which the first would be last and the last would be first, when those who hunger and thirst would be fed, whilst those who are satisfied now would then be hungry; and still more by the dark rumour that the despised sinners would partake of that kingdom before the righteous.

Clearly with cargo cults we are dealing with a special case of a very old and very typical form of religious movement.[3] A form which almost certainly dates back into prehistory, and which is certainly reduplicated on innumerable occasions in historical times. Indeed the whole of Eisler's chapter from which I have quoted is a chronicle of the recurring appearance and suppression over and over again in one small part of the Roman Empire of messianic religious revolts. Worsley (1957, concluding chapter) mentions Polynesia, Micronesia, Africa, the western hemisphere, China, Burma, Indonesia and even Siberia as other areas of notable chiliastic cult activity in historical times. But also in the history of Europe from the time of Christ to the present millenarian religious phenomena have cropped up.

I do not want to say that all these millenarian movements are cargo cults—I want to mention them merely in order to raise the question of just how different and just how common-or-garden cargo cults are.

[1] Graves and Podro, 1953; Eisler, 1931, pp. 567–71. I do not want to suggest that the theories these scholars propound are correct. But at least their contributions to the discussion of millenarianism are bold and speculative.

[2] I have given this longer quotation at the end of the book because the progress of this movement from religious sect to political threat, to eventual suppression by the powers that be, is a melodramatic paradigm for the progress of many of the cults we are interested in. We have here, in summary, a highly stimulating (if somewhat overwritten) interpretation of events by a diligent scholar, who sees it as a not-too-well documented but certainly as influential a messianic cult as has been seen so far in historical times.

[3] For a suggestion that most religious movements are of this character, see Wallace, 1956.

Another feature of millenarianism, also shared by cargo cults, besides millenarian prophecies and quasi-political risings, is a curious form of hysterical twitching or dancing which affects the cultists. H. Zinsser (1937, pp. 80–4) tells us of

> the dancing manias spoken of in medieval accounts variously as 'St. John's dance', 'St. Vitus' dance', and 'tarantism'. These strange seizures though not unheard of in earlier times, became common during and imme-diately after the dreadful miseries of the Black Death. . . . They seem . . . like mass hysterias, brought on by terror and despair in populations oppressed, famished, and wretched to a degree almost unimaginable today. To the miseries of constant war, political and social disintegration, there was added the dreadful affliction of inescapable, mysterious, and deadly disease. . . . For those who broke down under the strain there was no road of escape except to the inward refuge of mental derangement which, under the circumstances of the times, *took the direction of religious fanaticism.* In the earlier days of the Black Death mass aberrations became apparent in the sect of the flagellants, who joined in brotherhood and wandered by thousands from city to city. Later, for a time, it took the form of persecu-tion of the Jews, who were held guilty of the spread of the disease. . . . The most severe dancing mania began in 1374, in the wake of the Black Death, at first at Aix-la-Chapelle, soon in the Netherlands, at Liège, Utrecht, Tongres and Cologne. Men, women, and children all lost control, joined hands, and danced in the streets for hours until complete exhaustion caused them to fall to the ground. They shrieked, saw visions, and called upon God. The movement spread widely, and undoubtedly the numbers of the truly afflicted were enhanced by multitudes of the easily excited, in a manner not unlike that observed in modern camp meetings and evangelis-tic gatherings. [Italics mine.]

'St. Vitus' dance' illustrates another kind of millenarianism which shares features with cargo cults.

As a final example of the general phenomenon of millenarianism I may perhaps mention a quasi-religious prophecy of the millennium which is not usually treated as such. Here is Toynbee's interesting interpretation of marxism as religion.[1]

> The distinctively Jewish . . . inspiration of Marxism is the apocalyptic vision of a violent revolution which is inevitable because it is the decree . . . of God himself, and which is to invert the present roles of Proletariat and Dominant Minority in . . . a reversal of roles which is to carry the Chosen People, at one bound, from the lowest to the highest place in the Kingdom of the World. Marx has taken the Goddess 'Historical Neces-sity' in place of Yahweh for his omnipotent deity, and the internal pro-letariat of the modern Western World in place of Jewry; and his Messianic Kingdom is conceived as a Dictatorship of the Proletariat. But the salient

---

[1] As quoted by Popper, 1946, vol. ii, p. 253.

features of the traditional Jewish apocalypse protrude through this thread-bare disguise, and it is actually the pre-Rabbinical Maccabaean Judaism that our philosopher-impressario is presenting in modern Western costume.

Cargo cults are a special case, in a number of ways, despite their general resemblance to millenarianism.

2

AN EMPIRICAL CASE-STUDY:
THE PROBLEM OF CARGO CULTS

In the beginning, . . . God created Paradise, the bush, all animals and foodstuffs. He put Adam and Eve in Paradise, and He made and gave them cargo. The two copulated in the garden, so God threw them out into the bush where they existed without cargo. There was no cargo in the world until the time of Noah. At this time there was a Great Flood, which only Noah and his family survived. As Noah had obeyed the word of God, He was sorry for him and sent him cargo. Now the three sons of Noah had access to it as well. Shem and Japheth went to the land of the white men and to Israel, and as they and their descendants continued to obey God's word, they continued to get cargo. But Ham was arrogant before God, who was angry, threw him out and took from him his right to the cargo. Ham came to New Guinea. The people of New Guinea are the descendants of Ham, and as they have never obeyed the word of God as the result of his sin, they have no cargo.—*New Guinea Native Version of the Old Testament*,
—Lawrence, 1954, 12–13.

1. *The Problem of Preliminary Descriptions*

MY problem in the present section is that although scientific work should always start from a problem, the reader can hardly know what the problems of cargo cults are before he knows what cargo cults are. It seems as though we must know what cargo cults are before we can describe them, a description—of a preliminary character—must precede any study of them. Yet how can I do such a description without knowing the problem from which it must be angled? In Chapter 1 I argued that all description involves theory because all factual statements have theoretical content. This theoretical content can either be consciously centred on a problem, or unconsciously centred more or less well on a problem or problems. In accordance with this all authors who treat of cargo cults describe them from a particular problem-angle. Thus any individual description of the cults will be *biassed*. How can I possibly extract from such a welter of

55

biassed descriptions, and descriptions not, at that, all having the same bias, anything like an objective, factual account of the phenomena, which will not prejudice the reader?

Happily I am not in the impasse I may seem to be in because another argument of mine has been neglected—that science, to use Popper's expression, is a web of conjectures and refutations. There is, by this means, a way of getting at what the problems of cargo cult are before knowing what they are. This way is by guessing. We can conjecture the theory with which cargo cults clash and which thus makes them interesting, makes them a *problem*. My conjecture as to why they are interesting is that two factors—their apocalyptic and millenarian character—clash radically with our western ideas of religion. They come and go with revolutionary speed and they promise actual material things (nothing even as abstract as healing, as in some western religions). How, really, can a westerner credit their participants with rationality; how can they live with such things? Here is a first guess as to the problem of cargo cults.

Besides this surprising character of cargo cults which makes them so interesting and deserving explanation there is another route to their problems which I have followed. My theory was that structural-functionalism couldn't explain social change so I began to hunt for a circumscribed problem connected with social change. Cargo cults are connected with social change and are very difficult to explain, even as religion. This is why cargo cults are interesting to me.

Therefore the description I shall give of the cults cannot be ideally objective but I can do my best not to bias the case too much in my favour. I shall construct my description from the accounts of authors whose theories are far from my own (I would say furthest from my own except that it would be difficult to know in what sense this was meant). After this factual account I will sketch at once my own interpretation of them in order to bring out sharply my own bias and then try to formulate the problems of cargo cults which need to be explained.

2. *General Description of Cargo Cults*

Our case-study is in the apocalyptic millenarian religious movements of Melanesia known to social anthropologists as 'cargo cults'. These cults have the intrinsic interest of being: colourful and interesting, plentiful and widespread.[1] They have the extrinsic interest to a methodologist of: an extensive literature; requiring explanation both as bizarre occurrences in particular societies, and as surprisingly

[1] *Man*, February 1961, saw the first report of cargo cult activity in Polynesia. See Crocombe, 1961.

similar occurrences in diverse societies; having had a large number of not altogether compatible theories put forward to explain them.

*   *   *

Populated land areas in Melanesia range in size from the jungles and heights of New Guinea down to tiny coral atolls with only a few hundred people on them. All over this part of the world, in this century for the most part, but particularly since the two world wars, cargo cults have appeared and disappeared. These are cults recognisable as doctrinal offshoots, or modifications, of one or other brand of Christianity.

Usually a native prophet arises and announces that, provided certain conditions are fulfilled, the millennium will soon come on earth. Mostly they say it will be in the very near future, and they often name a specific date (some put it off into the remote future, or make it a spiritual millennium, but we shall not concern ourselves with that kind of cult). They are known as 'cargo cults' because a central tenet of their doctrines usually is that when the millennium comes it will largely consist of the arrival of ships and/or aeroplanes loaded up with cargo; a cargo consisting either of material goods the natives long for (and which are delivered to the whites in this manner), or of the ancestors, or of both.

Another frequently mentioned aspect of the millennium is that the order of society will be inverted; but that this inversion will in reality only be a return to the original state of society as it is described in 'the first page of the Bible' which is 'known' to have been torn out and kept from the natives by the (white) missionaries. It is thought that the missionaries wanted to suppress the fact that in the original state of affairs black people were God's chosen and He sent them rewards in the form of cargo, and that when the whites came they usurped the natural order of things by intercepting and misappropriating the shipments of cargo. When the millennium arrives things will return to their proper state: the blacks will rule the whites; the cargo will go to its rightful owners; the ancestors will return; and, sometimes, the skin of the blacks will grow whiter and that of the whites black.[1] A rule of peace and justice will be established for ever.

The conditions to be fulfilled if all this is to come about vary. Some prophets provoke states of religious ecstasy with dancing, writhing, twitching and general conditions of revivalist hysteria. Others proclaim that a complete break must be made with the past,

---

[1] Mr. Watkins has suggested that this belief might off-set the message of the missing page of the Bible in which the blacks are described as privileged. Perhaps in summary the doctrine becomes too explicit; or perhaps the skin-change idea never coexists with the missing page of the Bible theory.

as, for example, by a complete overthrow of all the old taboos. An overthrow in which either the old taboos are not to be replaced and a period of unprecedented licence is enjoined; or, a later doctrine, much stricter taboos are imposed as necessary to guide the unworthy along the way towards ascetic righteousness, a fit condition in which to enter the millennium. And in many cases it is held to show sinful disbelief in the coming to work or cultivate or even to continue to hold stocks of food. Therefore the movement often is accompanied by a rapid squandering, or even deliberate destruction, of stocks of food, goods, and money to demonstrate faith in, and to prepare for, the millennium.

In some cases the millennium will only be finally achieved, it is prophesied, after the whites have been driven out. Not unnaturally, therefore, white officialdom (already baffled and enraged by the seemingly wanton destruction of food and stocks) has not been particularly sympathetic to the movements, even where the 'drive-out-the-whites' doctrine was not actually propounded. There is thus a history of harsh and sometimes brutal oppression by the various European powers who at different times administered the area. And the Japanese invaders of world war II, whom the natives were at first sympathetic towards (the whites disliked them, and their ancestor cult was intriguing) acted in the end in the same way. Finally the American liberating forces of that war (with their astounding negro contingents) were seen as white hopes. But they too left, colonial rule returned, and the cults went on.

I have already briefly indicated how old and how widespread is the pursuit of the millennium. But in many ways the most homogeneous and theoretically interesting cults of the millennium are these which occur in the kin-based and often politically noncentralised societies of Melanesia.

The problems for our case-study, then, are, for example, what is the explanation of these cults; what causes them;[1] why are they so similar; what do they aim at; what is special about the places they occur which is not about the places they do not occur; and so on.

*   *   *

Having given this outline of cargo cults and the problems they present, I want in the next four sections to go into a little more detail about the former. As an introduction I can do no better than to quote Dr. Lucy Mair (1958, pp. 175-6).

[1] Here I diverge from the important work of Burridge: 'To answer the question "Why do cargo cults occur?" would entail raising profound metaphysical issues.' See Burridge, 1960, p. 246. The issues raised are sociological.

The Problem of Cargo Cults

Isolated examples of these movements in Papua have been reported from 1893 onwards, and there is one in the Schouten Islands, in Netherlands New Guinea, which dates back even earlier. They appeared sporadically in one place after another throughout the period between the wars, and at the end of the Second World War and shortly after they could almost have been said to be pandemic. . . . The characteristic feature of the New Guinea movements was the belief that the millennium would be accompanied by the return of the dead in some mechanical means of transport—ship, aeroplane, or lorry—which would be loaded with imported goods of all kinds. These goods, it was held, were made in heaven by the ancestors for the use of their descendants, but Europeans had diverted them from their rightful owners. Hence these movements have come to be collectively known as 'cargo cults'.

3. *The Vailala Madness*

Compare now the following extract from Hogbin's book (1958, pp. 208–9) in which he quotes from Mair (1948) and F. E. Williams in describing 'The Vailala Madness' of Papua.

'The first time this attracted the attention of the Australian authorities was in 1919, on the Vailala River in the Gulf Division of Papua.
'As this was described by the officer who investigated events at the time, reports spread among the natives that their ancestors were about to return in the guise of white men, by steamer, or, according to one version, by aeroplane, and would bring with them a large cargo of European goods of every kind. These goods, it was said, were actually the property of the natives, but were being withheld from them by the whites. The latter, however, would soon be driven out of the country. The leaders of the movement, who claimed to have received the messages to this effect from the spirits, ordered the people to suspend all work and prepare feasts of welcome. Platforms were built and loaded with presents of food. The leaders, and some of their followers, imitated European manners in various ways, some ludicrous or pathetic. The leaders drilled their own 'police boys'. At a certain time each day they would sit, dressed in their best clothes at tables, decorated, European fashion, with flowers in bottles, which had been set up to entertain the returning spirits. . . .
'A feature of the Vailala movement was a violent reaction against the native religion. The leaders ordered their followers to abandon all the traditional ceremonies and destroy the ritual objects associated with them, and they met with an enthusiastic response.'

As Hogbin says,

The anthropologist on the Papua Government staff [F. E. Williams] referred to the mass hysteria with which the movement was accompanied .

And, he quotes him,

'Great numbers were affected by a kind of giddiness; they lost or abandoned control of their limbs and reeled about the villages, one man following another until almost the whole population of a village might be affected at the same moment. While they indulged in their antics the leaders frequently poured forth utterances in "Djaman", or "German", a language composed mostly of nonsense syllables, and pidgin-English which was almost wholly unintelligible.'

Hogbin now allows Mair to take up the story again.

'By now the cargo cult has appeared in every administrative district (of Papua and New Guinea), and even in the highlands, which have only known the white men for fifteen years. . . . The common characteristic is the insistence on the cargo of European goods to be sent by the ancestors, and the disappearance of the white man and his rule. Underlying the cargo myth is the idea that all trade goods have been manufactured in the spirit world by the ancestors as gifts for their descendants, and are misappropriated by white men. . . . In every case, the leaders order economic activities to be suspended. No gardens need be made, since the ancestors will provide all the food required—but only to those who have shown their faith by not growing any themselves. The people spend their time preparing to welcome the ancestors; sometimes this involves special songs and dances. In the highlands, where it would be unrealistic and beyond the scope of the people's imagination to expect a ship, they make airstrips and decorate the borders. . . . On Karkar Island the root conception of the natives' entry into the kingdom from which the whites have debarred them was expressed in the belief that their whole island would be turned upside down, and those who survived would have white skins.

'Usually there was some attempt to set up a rival government. The leader of the movement would often be a village official, but if he was not he would disregard . . . authority. He drilled his own "police boys", sometimes with dummy rifles made of wood, and on some ccasions set up an "office", where he sat in imitation of the government official, pathetically surrounded by the paraphernalia of writing.'

Mair also relates (1948, p. 66) a delightful little story illustrating the belief that the trade goods were being misappropriated by the white men.

The prophet of one of these movements, who was named Batari, scored a strong point on one occasion when a crate marked 'battery' was unloaded from a ship—but not delivered to him.

The Vailala Madness is one of the most interesting of the cargo cults, and because it was one of the first to be adequately reported, tends to be looked on almost as a prototype; but there are many others. Worsley (1957) lists the following as the best-documented and most important of these movements. They start, more or less, with the Tuka movement of Fiji, which began in 1885, disappeared for a time and recurred after world war II (ch. 1). Next there was the

Milne Bay Prophet Movement of 1893 (ch. 3); followed by the Baigona Movement of 1912 (ch. 3) and the Taro Cult of Fiji in 1914 (ch. 3). After world war I there was the already mentioned Vailala Madness of 1919 (ch. 4). Between the two wars there was a large number of cults cropping up all the time, too numerous to mention. When the Japanese invaders swept across the Pacific a wave of cargo cults preceded them and continued after their arrival. Typical of these was the fantastic progress of the Mansren Myth in the west of Dutch New Guinea which is mentioned by Worsley (ch. 7). Beginning as early as 1867, prophecy and cult activity seem to have gone on intermittently in this area until in 1942, in a flurry of activity, a prophet organised whole villages in imitation of an army, with 'officers' and dummy equipment. Despite being massacred by the Japanese the Mansren cultists continued to be active. The impact upon them can be imagined of the transit base for 400,000 U.S. soldiers and equipment which was set up after the Japanese were ousted.

The other principal movements which occurred during and after world war II are the Naked Cult of Espiritu Santo (ch. 8); the John Frum Movement of Tanna (ch. 8); Masinga (or Marching) Rule of Malailu, Solomon Islands (ch. 9); and the Paliau Movement on Manus, Admiralty Islands (ch. 9).

Naturally there is no space to describe the many cults here listed and Worsley's detailed work has made this unnecessary. I have given a description of the Vailala Madness, the original report of which is due to Williams who believed the cults to be a form of psychological disturbance. This was one instance of using descriptive materials compiled by someone whose view of the cults is very different from my own. To complete my cross-section of typical cults I shall use accounts of Guiart (1952) and Lawrence. Guiart believes the cults to be incipient nationalism, which is very far from my view; Lawrence tries to construct an almost theory-free account, an intention I have already argued to be mistaken. Every description contains theory and Lawrence's theory is given in my review of the literature (Jarvie, 1964).

4. *The Cult of John Frum*

Tanna is an island in the New Hebrides group. There was some unrest there in 1940, and in 1941 a revolt broke out.

Associated with Mount Tukosmeru on the island was a god called 'kerapenmun'. One night he appeared to some people in an encampment calling himself 'John Frum'. He encouraged people to celebrate his appearance and criticised idleness. At a later appearance he began to say he would appear to everyone on Tanna and bring with

61

him, when he did, the material civilisation the whites had denied them. He prophesied that the whites would leave the island and John Frum would take power and pay the chiefs and teachers. The missionaries would leave too and John Frum schools would be set up. John Frum money, and coins struck in the image of the coconut tree, would replace gold, pounds and silver. There would no longer be any need to work. John Frum would provide metal houses, clothes, food, transport. He claimed that he was the master of the planes which flew overhead. The day of rest was to be Friday, not Sunday. All money in the natives' possession was to be returned to the whites or destroyed.[1] If this was carried out there would be no reason for the whites to continue to stay; but not one 3d. piece must be kept by the natives or this ousting plan would not work.

A number of messengers called 'ropes of John Frum' were sent to carry the doctrine all over the island.

The effects of this teaching were startling and swift. Churches of all denominations were deserted. Families left the villages built around the Christian Mission, to live on their own land. Dances and *kava* drinking were organised on Saturday evening (this gains significance if we remember the puritannical attitude the Presbyterian missionaries would have to such pleasures). The natives also began frenziedly to spend all their money in European shops and, in some cases, even threw it away.

By this time 'John Frum's' prophecies had gone even further. Perhaps Tanna would become flat and be joined with its neighbouring islands and then a new youthfulness and perfect health would come to all.

A very important point about the participants was that only the Christianised natives participated in this movement, the pagans placidly went on making *kava* to meet this sudden increase in demand.

Eventually the authorities clamped down and exposed 'John Frum' as a native called Mancheri who had duped the people by ingenious stage management. He had used tricks of make-up, lighting and suggestion, to give the impression he was not a mortal. He and his principal 'ropes' were shipped off into exile.

One of the leaders wrote home from their place of confinement (interpretations of the letter, which is in pidgin, vary). He either said that John Frum would send his son to the United States to see the King, or that John Frum was in America and would send his sons to

---

[1] Cp. the interpretation of the story of the tribute money (Matt. xxii, 15 sqq.) given by Eisler, 1931, pp. 331–5. He suggests that the story is properly understood as an attempt by Jesus to escape the power Caesar's money had, and also to avoid its polluting effect.

Tanna to prepare the way for his coming. Soon rumour had it that the sons of John Frum had landed and were communicating through a little girl of about twelve years of age who received the messages under a banyan tree. It was soon after this that the Americans began to arrive in the New Hebrides. One man thought Mt. Tukosmeru was full of soldiers and would open up, when the time came, letting them pour forth to help John Frum.

Now began what has been called the Second John Frum Movement. A native called Neloaig proclaimed himself John Frum, King of America and of Tanna. He surrounded himself with 'armed' police and organised the building of an airfield on which the Americans could land.

When the district agent (i.e. the representative of the government) arrested him there were threatening demonstrations. So, under cover of radioing for a boat to leave on, the agent sent for police reinforcements and an American liaison officer. When these arrived there were arrests and displays of force; this, and speeches by the American officer engendered calm, if not trust.

There was another outbreak in 1947—on a minor scale. Meanwhile some of the exiled leaders had success on other islands—one village being organised so like a military camp as to have three guarded entrances, halt signs and a register kept of those entering and leaving.

5. Cults among the Garia

For a third example of the cults which constitute our empirical case-study we turn to P. Lawrence (1954) who reports on the Garia, a people which had, between 1944 and 1949, at least ten outbursts of cargo cult. Without exception this series of cargo cults was based on a general belief current in the Madang area of New Guinea to the effect that all cargo was derived from a deity over whom the Europeans had some control. A description of three of the cults will suffice to illustrate both their common elements and the limited variations which were possible.

Cult number one came about like this. In 1947 a woman had a dream in which one of God's angels warned her that there was to be a second flood but that a ship would be sent to her village. She urged people to foregather there on pain of doom or being eaten by crocodiles. She had seen God, Jesus, angels and the spirits of the dead in the clouds above the mountains; she had seen there too a storehouse full of cargo which would be brought down by the spirits to the survivors. No flood appeared and the cult fizzled out.

The second cult among the Garia which I shall discuss centred around a native who was an ex-soldier of the second world war, named Yali. He had been to Australia during the war and had returned afterwards to help advance his people. The extent of his actual participation in the subsequent cult is rather vague. As a prominent man he was called away to Port Moresby, the capital of New Guinea and a long way away, for talks with the administration; whereupon several men calling themselves his 'lieutenants' began to spread the following tale. During the war Yali had been killed by the Japanese but had later returned to earth as a spirit. He had gone to Australia to see the King and then to Paradise to see God. God had asked him about conditions on New Guinea and had told him to go back to Australia and tell the King that God was sending him back to New Guinea, in the form of a man, to improve the country and run it for the natives. While Yali was doing this God would send the spirits to Sydney with cargo which the King was to put in a ship and keep until Yali sent for it, then send it to Madang under spirit guard.

Yali, his lieutenants alleged, had gone to Port Moresby to meet the ship which the King had personally escorted there, and Yali, in his new role as a district commissioner, would bring the ship on to Madang where he would distribute its cargo to his followers. Among the cargo would be war equipment with which to drive out the Europeans. But before distribution could be effected the people must organise themselves in larger villages or 'camps' and build there houses for Yali. The lieutenants appointed 'boss boys' to carry this out. The movement was eventually suppressed.

The third Garia cult I want to mention centres on a man called Kaum, a sort of professional cult founder, who returned from jail to claim that he had been killed there. He had been to Paradise and had seen the spirits making cargo. God had given him a new name and prescribed ritual which he now followed. The ritual contains an interesting prayer:

O Father Consel, you are sorry for us. You can help us. We have nothing—no aircraft, no ships, no jeeps, nothing at all. The Europeans steal it from us. You will be sorry for us and send us something.

6. *Summary of the Distinctive Features of Cargo Cults*

After these few examples of typical cargo cults, I want now to analyse out the main features of them. I shall do this by combining my own analysis of their principal characteristics with that of W. E. H. Stanner.[1]

(1) Cargo cults are usually founded and led by a single prophet,

---

[1] Stanner, 1953, ch. 5. I should mention that I stress different things from Stanner, and express them *very* differently.

who both receives the revelation and propagates it. He is often a 'charismatic personality'; this is meant descriptively; some authors (e.g. Worsley) explicitly reject 'charisma' as explaining anything.[1] It may also be noted, though it may or may not help us to explain these cults, that in all reported cases the prophet has no special social standing in the society prior to the cult.[2]

(2) Most of the prophets are, like everyone else in their society, hardly educated and often seriously misinformed about the workings of western society outside of Melanesia; if their ideas bear any relation to reality it will be shaky.

(3) All the cults borrow European rituals of one sort or another —both secular and religious. This may be a matter of definition in that we only recognise as cargo cults those which are borrowing from European rituals. For example, they will use mock radios, dummy telephones and rifles, fake messages, 'offices', set up 'governments' and train 'armies' as intrinsic parts of their rituals. Concomitantly with the introduction of such new elements they tend to stress the necessity for abandoning the old ways (i.e. precult ways). They frequently draw up lists of orders, or charters, which involve systematic instruction in the cult doctrine, the dangers of sin, the necessity of gifts as a token of belief or good faith, and so on. There is some, though not much, parody of European church rituals, possibly because most of the missions involved are pretty 'low church' and so do not go in for elaborate rituals.

(4) The new beliefs are grafted on to older local beliefs. For example, all these prophets claim some sort of contact with the spirit world, or the ancestors, or the gods, or the culture heroes, etc., of their locality.

(5) They all predict the coming of a millennium in the very near future, and in material form: a Paradise on Earth. Ships or aeroplanes, sometimes sent by spirit powers, sometimes manned by the ancestors, will appear with a welcome cargo of *non-traditional* (i.e. European) wealth, e.g. tinned foods, axes, horses, dogs, firearms, cloth,[3] etc. These beliefs are usually accompanied by some sort of other belief in, e.g. the end of the world, and/or the ejection of the Europeans, or some sort of cataclysm followed by a colour exchange whence the whites will become black and the blacks white and the

[1] Worsley, 1957, appendix, section (i), where he suggests that in some cases at least there is another very powerful figure behind the prophet, sometimes exercising considerable control over him.

[2] Although Melanesia is without real economic, political or social classes, some people, by reason of personal qualities, can attain a certain standing in the community.

[3] Horses and dogs are, of course, not native to Melanesia; and their bark cloths are not much like our machine-woven materials of the same name.

social and economic positions would change, giving them a different position in the power-structure.

(6) The cults are always characterised by some form of organised activity like instruction, communal gardening, the building of platforms, houses, warehouses, jetties and airstrips. Also associated with them are various kinds of collective hysteria: visions, dreams, swoons, fits, seizures, 'deaths', shaking fits, dancing manias, nonsense talk, and gibberish.

(7) They nearly always take place in colonised areas which are economically underdeveloped, highly isolated, politically acephalous and, on the whole, not given to violent resistance to white rule. (It is reported that in parts of the New Guinea Highlands cults have occurred among tribes *before* they have contacted the European. Since these may be explained by simple diffusion of ideas and behaviour, I shall not regard them as counterexamples to this characteristic of colonisation.)

(8) There have nearly always been attempts to Christianise the natives by missionaries.

7. A Theory of Cargo Cults

At this stage I want to sketch my own interpretation of cargo cults—for reasons already given in section 1. I intend to go into the theory in more detail in Chapter 5.

Religion, it seems to me, is a set of theories or myths. The function of all theories is to explain something. In the case of religion the problem to be solved is big: the world. Most religions claim to explain the origins, ground plan, building materials and working of the world; often they also prescribe conduct. Millenarian religion, I would contend, is most often an attempt to solve a more urgent problem, namely the felt need of what is promised. Cargo cults promise a material heaven on earth, this suggests that what Melanesians feel when confronted with the white man and his society is an endless material poverty which they want to alleviate. A paradise, a heaven, where all troubles are removed and all wishes satisfied, seems to be a common enough human yearning. But heaven, unfortunately, is not to be found on earth; perhaps this fact explains man's seemingly never-ending quest to discover how it might be made on earth. Heaven though, by definition, cannot be on earth; perhaps *this* explains why man's quest always ends in failure. People in Melanesia are no more and no less prone to yearnings for heaven than people anywhere and they have sometimes listened to those who promised to show them the way to heaven on earth; the way to the millennium.

The Problem of Cargo Cults

Cargo cults may be seen in this light as embodying in their doctrines attempts to explain the differences between the standard of living of affluent colonial administrators and settlers and that of the native peasant farmers. They are religious explanations or, more accurately, magico-religious explanations; and they are magico-religious explanations because that is the characteristic type of explanation which is current in that society; i.e. magico-religious explanations of the unknown or the unintelligible are still used there in an uncritical way. We can see the uncritical attitude at work when a prophecy fails to come true and the prophet, not his prophecy, is discredited. An animistic theory that error is humanly caused is employed; the prophet's lies are explained by a conspiracy theory of error—the failure is his fault (Popper, 1961, *passim*). The way remains open for another prophet to come forward with only a slightly modified version of the doctrine and teaching that he, not the previous impostor, is the True Messenger of God.

My theory of cargo cults is now obvious: the structure of their doctrines indicates what is wanted and they are attempts to provide an explanation of why they haven't got it and a religious prescription for how they can get it. Knowledge is power, so people flock to the man who says he knows how the whites get the cargo and that he too can lead them to it. It is only later that these explanations are found unsatisfactory, or that astute leaders come to realise that the best way to get the cargo is not by using the language of magic and religion, but by using the language of political demands on a harassed administration.

There is in my position a defence of Frazer's doctrine that there is the following close relationship between magic, science and religion. They are all attempts to explain and control the world. However, he takes the pragmatic view that science is accepted now because it rarely fails to deliver the goods. I think this doctrine too clever; it assumes, unwarrantedly, that we have a very sophisticated attitude towards ideas and select those with the highest utilitarian value. I modify Frazer and argue that the similarity between magic, science and religion consists in a methodological resemblance. They all try to solve problems, often the same problems; but they are dissimilar in the extent to which their solutions to these problems are testable.[1]

Frazer seems to me to stress a key resemblance when he argues that magic, science and religion all provide us with hypothetical knowledge. The difference is that their doctrines are held open to criticism in varying degrees. We in the West prefer the knowledge of science to that of magic or any other because it is more open to independent

[1] For this view (Popper's) see Watkins, 1957a, 1958b, and 1960, and the references to Popper there given.

67

critical test than is magic. The theory that the world is influenced by magical and religious forces or entities is hardly open to serious test since these are designated in a way which more or less rules testing out. Magic is preferable in this respect to religion.

Another difference is that magic tends to work over a selection of old problems but that with the critical attitude which produced science began an advance on ever-new problems; I believe new problems and new answers to them are a stimulus to social change; and I believe that we can see something like this going on with cargo cults.

This last thought was reinforced by a passage of Popper's *The Open Society and its Enemies* (vol. i, p. 172), where he speaks of the magical attitude towards social custom as a characteristic of 'tribal' life.[1] He suggests that changes in tribal life frequently take the form of 'religious conversions or repulsions, or of the introduction of new magical taboos', adding weight to the contention that cargo cults are phenomena of social change.

8. *The Problems of Cargo Cults*

Peaceful, hitherto quiet,[2] South Sea Islands suddenly erupt in a frenzy of cult activity which, despite the separation of the islands by hundreds and often thousands of miles of sea, is remarkably similar cult activity at that. In the previous section I have outlined a simple theory of the cults based on the logic of the situation that faced Melanesians. Now I want to go into the theory in a little detail and show how it raises hosts of simple factual problems which we cannot at the moment solve.

I will list the principal sub-problems that I can detect at the moment. The list does not pretend to completeness, and no particular significance should be read into their order of presentation. Moreover, it being based on a simple situational logic basis most of

[1] Nothing depends on words, of course, but in case anthropologists reading this out of context should be surprised I will explain that Popper uses 'tribal' in a way which suggests that what he means is societies for which the anthropological jargon is 'acephalous', i.e. without heads, without centralised polity. Popper also argues that it is not too misleading to speak of tribal societies as resembling something like social wholes (as opposed to abstract societies which stretch the metaphor much more). This kindness to holism requires careful circumscription of the notion of 'tribal'. There is, I think, some case for considering acephalous societies as in some respects resembling social wholes, but it is pointless to call nations like the Zulu or Sotho, with their huge scale, diversified populations, and considerable degree of social abstraction (in Popper's sense), social wholes.

[2] This has now become a disputed point. Dr. Mair (1959) has argued that there may be a *tradition* of similar messianic activity.

the questions will be 'common sense' to the sophisticated anthropologist, at least up to (*h*)

The situational logic of these cults can be split up into several sub-problems: who leads and who follows; how do we explain doctrine, behaviour and effects; how do we explain the remarkable similarity of the events in and the content of, cults in different places?

(*a*) Why do people join the cults?

In his proclamations the prophet makes certain promises and stipulates certain conditions which must be fulfilled if these promises are to be realised. We must ask whether the promises themselves explain the acquiescence in the conditions; whether the conditions strike the audience as reasonable (i.e. fulfillable and likely to bring about the promises, given their background knowledge); or whether other psychological or social factors enter in. Here we should try to isolate typical individual situations and aims and see how the promises and the conditions fit in with these. A person's aims may harmonise or conflict with the promised millennium; his situation may make the conditions arduous or easy to fulfil. Unless we know these things we cannot give a detailed explanation of cult membership, and the later loss (if any) of converts. We should consider whether different cults recruit from different types of people in different societies. For example, the hypothesis has been advanced that cults are always recruited among politically non-centralised peoples. Can we find any counter-examples to this? Is it possible to test whether economic deprivation is a necessary or non-necessary condition? Could we test whether people conceive of the cults as emotional or political outlets?

In short we ask the fieldworker to seek out the logic behind the actions of the typical cultist. How that typical cultist viewed the cult; what ends of his he thought it fulfilled; what peculiarities of his situation gave him the opportunity to join a radical and time-consuming new religion.

(*b*) is simply (*a*) with 'not' in all the questions. Who does not join the cults? Why not? Can any significance be read into non-participation? How, and in what ways does the situation of those who stay out differ from that of those who go in?

I can add here some questions about the sort of people among whom a typical cult recruits which could also be asked under (*a*). It is very difficult to discover in the literature the answers to simple questions like: does the cult sweep over the land absorbing all the people in an area? Or does it selectively attract only some people in a village and leave others unmoved? Or, perhaps, do the others follow suit later, on the line of least resistance? Is there a situation in the developments of cargo cults comparable to that in Kenya during the

Mau Mau emergency, when whole villages and even families were divided over the question of whether or not to join? The reason for asking such questions is that if all the people in an area are recruited, then that suggests that important elements of their situations are similar; if only some people join then interesting questions of the variation between the situations of these individuals in that one society are raised. We do not really know whether aims or situations differ. We do not even raise this question until we ask whether recruitment is selective. If an arbitrary half of a village joined a cult and the other half did not one might be suspicious of any too-sweeping attempts to generalise about the reasons for cult member-ship; but if the whole village had been swept along one would be less suspicious. The smaller the proportion of the population that has joined the cults the more involved and detailed must the ex-planations be.

We might also check whether the lines of selective recruiting follow social divisions. The aims and situations of, for example, christian-ised people, or westernised people or something of the sort, may be similar enough to explain the fact that these groups are or are not recruited *en bloc*. If, of course, they are not recruited *en bloc* but only selectively, then the assumption that the aims and situations of these groups of people are similar as regards cult activity comes into question.

(c) A study of the various prophets would enable us to see whether ideal-typical explanations of them (and possibly, therefore, their cults) can be constructed; or whether each cult is an historically unique event which requires a particularised historical explanation.

The importance of the individual qualities of the prophet starting and maintaining the cult requires investigation. Another point, purely on the factual level, is to ask whether the ostensible prophet is in fact the driving force behind the cult. In other words, we should test Worsley's conjecture that each prophet always has a sort of Machiavelli-figure behind him who is the real (i.e. political) force behind the cult (see Chapter 3, section 17). We should reconstruct the aims and the situation of the typical prophet and, by comparing these, see whether any common denominator emerges in order to find out whether they are entirely disparate figures, united only in expressing themselves through the common cultural form of the cargo cult. We might see whether a social explanation can be given of a person becoming a prophet—whether it was in fact the most reasonable thing to do in a certain situation. In this connection we might inquire about the effects a cult has on the social standing of a prophet. To what extent the ends of typical prophets differ will be interesting too. Various obvious hypotheses must be tested: those relating the prophet's behaviour to his education, to Christianity, and so on. And this in itself is a problem. Why did the prophet try to realise his aims by founding a cult? Why did he take the course of a cult rather than some other to try to realise his aims? What did he hope the cult would actually achieve (apart, that is, from his own personal aims)?

Having now looked at the membership and leadership of the cults we must turn our attention to somewhat less personalised questions about them. Let us now turn to the social happenings.

The start of a cargo cult is when the prophet begins to proclaim his message to the people. Generally speaking the question of where he got the doctrine, how the idea of a cult came to him, etc., in its early psychological form, can be set aside. We may even not be interested in why people listened to him. We may find if we ask about the social status of the prophet and the social make-up of his audience that he was a leader who had to be listened to. While Melanesian society has no chiefs on the African model, there are prominent men in every society. Of course if he is a nobody who relies on his oratorical powers then part of the explanation would have to be psychological.

(*d*) After personnel and recruitment we come to explain the idea behind the cult doctrine. We want to know where the peculiar myth of a material millennium filled with European consumer goods came from, and how it came to figure so large in native aims. We should not try to explain away ideas, but we can seek the inspiration of such ideas. We can test the widespread theory that the natives are only interested in the material goods because they associate them with the white man's power; and that it is the power they 'truly' covet. We can try to explain why the doctrine takes the form of a revealed truth and also its very peculiar mythological and ethical content.

(*e*) We have the problem of explaining the extraordinary speed at which the cults grow up and spread over their island homes. On top of this we have to try to explain why, after such lightning success, they so rapidly fold, despite or because of administrative discouragement; how in some areas they just fade out and in others they recur over and over again. The answers to these may possibly be sought in (*f*).

(*f*) is the problem of explaining the failure of the cults. At the risk of seeming to repeat the obvious I suggest that there are unsolved and even unposed problems here. It is too easy to be uncritical of our Advanced Scientific Knowledge and enlightened Rationalist Viewpoint, thinking *we* know why the cults failed: because the natives' millenarian theories were false and the predictions they derived from

71

their theories were also false. This does not go far enough by any means. For example, some cults recur, despite failure, in very similar form; other cults become what Worsley calls 'passivist' and put off the millennium into the remote (and possibly spiritual) future; and still other cults just fade away altogether. Each of these reactions has to be explained. One possible explanation of them is due to Popper. He argues that when we have over-optimistically high expectations of a doctrine and then it runs into a difficult point, the reaction often takes one of three typical forms. Either: the disputed doctrine is repetitively insisted upon—this is dogmatism; or one becomes sceptical of the possibility of any doctrines being secure—scepticism; or one talks vaguely about understanding of the doctrine transcending reason, etc.—this is mysticism. These reactions correspond very closely to what happens when a cult fails. Either: the cultists stubbornly go on believing and blame the failure on the individual prophet and his lies—dogmatism; or the whole thing fades out from lack of faith—scepticism; or the millennium becomes a vague, remote and even spiritual thing—mysticism.

How can a myth which has been refuted over and over again still have a grip on people? What determines whether a cult shall 'go passive' or disappear?

(g) We have to account, using all the above material, for the startling similarities between the cults although they are separated by the vast seas of Melanesia. These similarities consist, not only in doctrinal resemblances, but also in similar patterns of organisation, and in striking parallels of inception, development and decay.

We have here to weigh up diffusion against the at first glance unconvincing theory that over and over again history could repeat itself, by arranging that the same conditions should be present, *and arranging that* they should give rise to the same sort of happenings.

(h) After having looked at all these problems we can come to some final problems which will be more familiar to the anthropologist. We can ask questions like: what consequences did the cargo cult have for the native society, for the white society, for the administration, for the prophet, and so on. Only by investigating the aims and situations of the various persons involved can we understand them. But these actions, added up, may still not be sufficient to explain all the happenings which we have some reason to suspect were a result of the cargo cult activity. It is at this stage that we may make use of structural-functional analysis. By pointing to the functional connections between this institution and that institution in the society we are able, thanks to structural analysis, to explain otherwise puzzling events causally, as unintended consequences of antecedent changes in other institutions.

We may suspect, for instance, that the breakdown of a traditional marriage system which occurred in the wake of the cult was due to the cult. And we might be able to show this because we know there is a functional relationship between the marriage system and the economic or religious system. The cult having disrupted the latter, it is easy to explain the breakdown of traditional marriage patterns as consequent on this.

What we have so far looked at are the empirical problems connected with cargo cults. Before passing on I want to mention a general methodological problem raised by the cargo cults. Namely a sub-problem of the sociology of religion: to what extent must psychology be a factor in any explanation of religion?

The answer to this question will depend to a large extent upon how the questions about religion are framed; my own preference is for so framing sociological problems that sociological solutions are almost dictated to us. However, it also turns on how far we are prepared, in the sociology of religion, to undermine the methodological principle we have adopted, the rationality principle, and look at religion as a product of irrationality (perhaps as a consequence of guilt, fear, insecurity, or what not). Once we take this step we are plunged into the labyrinth of abnormal psychology and problems admittedly beyond our interest and competence. Further dangers in this way out are: that the explanation can so very easily become *ad hoc*; that it can be used to complete an otherwise incomplete explanation; and that it silences criticism because it is very hard to challenge, especially when it refers to the past, for it is then in principle untestable. In other words, if, in a reconstruction of the logic of someone's situation, you cannot quite explain his action, you can always say 'oh, he had guilt feelings which he wanted to assuage which, together with what I have already said, explains his decision to act that way'. Almost any difficulty can be evaded in this manner.

3

A SURVEY OF EXPLANATIONS
OF CARGO CULTS

1. *Introduction: The Limitations and Value of Surveys*

HIS chapter is a survey. In it I shall set out as systematically as I can all the possible explanations of the problems posed in Chapter 2, section 7, of which I can think. I shall survey these problems and their solutions in as logical a manner as I am capable of. But the function of the survey will not be to test my ingenuity in concocting explanations; my intention is to create a matrix or set of pigeon-holes into which those theories which have been published can be fitted. We shall then be able to read off at a glance what avenues or pigeon-holes have been explored, and what neglected, in the published literature. So, as I sketch my matrix of problems and theories I shall, *en passant*, indicate where actual writers have proposed one of the particular explanations I am discussing. This denies me the possibility of reviewing the literature[1] but enormously facilitates illustration of my theme: the peculiar value of methodology to the social sciences. Methodology can not only help one analyse one's problems, and discuss the satisfactoriness of the answers, it can also enable one to do surveys of the answers.

Surveys of all the possibilities should be distinguished from *histories* of those possibilities which have in fact been realised.

I have already discussed the role of theory and theoretical study in social anthropology. I want now to add one remark to that whole discussion: *surveys are theoretical work*. To do a survey of the theories about something is almost inevitably to contribute to those theories, either in formulation or in filling gaps not previously noticed. In case my own opinion is of any value I should confess I even believe that by far the best way to approach a fresh problem in science is by means of a survey of what has already been done with it.

Too much should never be expected of surveys, naturally; they are no substitute for original ideas. What are their other limitations?

---

[1] But anyway I have done this in my 1964 paper.

74

For one thing fields are amenable to surveys to a greater or lesser degree—some fields are too diffuse or confused to be adequately surveyable; for another there will always be more alternatives than are worth bothering about—one may well decide to stop a survey with the assertion that its purpose is completed, by a sort of *reductio* it has been shown not to be worth going on with. Another general limitation on surveys is that they do not lead to the truth; this is very simply because they do not concern themselves with truth; this is very simply because they cannot concern themselves with truth. There cannot be more than one wholly true answer to a question. Consequently if you survey the answers to a question, the solutions to a problem, the very use of the plural (answers, solutions) shows you do not mean the *true* answer or solution. If not the true one, then what? Here I may refer back to Chapter 1 and the distinction made there between true and satisfactory explanation. A survey is a survey of satisfactory theories; this makes things easy for we have a simple logical criterion for satisfactoriness but we have no criterion for truth. It may occur, of course, that a *prima facie* satisfactory theory turns out to be unsatisfactory and then it would go into the survey and reasons for its dismissal would be given. One may be forced to go into the vast proliferation of idiotic and unsatisfactory theories simply because they look, or are thought by others to be, satisfactory. These qualifications aside, our concern in this survey, as in most surveys, is to look at the possible range of satisfactory theories and *en passant* to note which of these possibilities has been realised in the published literature.

There are, too, some metaphysical limits set to surveys. Every survey is of the answers to a problem. All problems stand within a metaphysical framework, a metaphysical point of view which excludes metaphysical novelty (i.e. other points of view). Further, social science has a well-defined metaphysical tradition of problem-interests and methods of solution which are more constraining than might be thought; they make for a difference between the value of surveys to natural as opposed to social science. To take these points in turn.

Within the present century metaphysics has been routed by philosophers and then suddenly been discovered to be inescapable. By metaphysics I do not mean any untestable gibberish, or theology. I mean doctrines characterised by Popper (and later, following him, Watkins and Agassi), which are unfalsifiable, have no explanatory power, but which have consequences and thus are criticisable. Metaphysics can be characterised here as frameworks for scientific inquiry; frameworks which yield a programme for our inquiries. Examples are conventionalism and animism: the one the programme

75

to explain human society as man-made, man-changeable conventions; the other the programme to explain the behaviour of the physical world by means of animal spirits. Atomism is another metaphysical point of view and so is Faraday's field-view. Other metaphysics important in social science have been naturalism (behaviourism), psychologism, and historicism. I have claimed elsewhere in this book that equalitarianism is the fundamental metaphysical framework within which the tradition of social anthropology has arisen.

It seems obvious that in principle you can multiply metaphysics at will; consequently you cannot survey metaphysics you can only write a history of metaphysics; you can discuss what has been said, you can't cover everything that possibly could be said because these possibilities are infinite. Again, within a metaphysics it may not be possible for reasons given above to survey the field exhaustively—the silly and unsatisfactory possibilities may be too many, and some of them may turn out later on to be not so silly after all; who can foresee it? Some surveying is however possible within a point of view. So much for surveys having a metaphysical point of view, now we come to some differences between natural and social science.

Physical science has a tradition of being revolutionary; its revolutions are deepest when it changes its metaphysics. Animist metaphysics has given way to atomism; atomism to field metaphysics.

Social science, too, has had its revolutions, or attempted revolutions. Usually, however, these were not attempts to overthrow the egalitarian metaphysics but to specify the true egalitarian metaphysics. I use the idea of egalitarianism in such a way that it embraces those who have the programme to refute it as well as those who wish to build it. Racialists and evolutionists have attacked versions of egalitarianism. Proponents of the doctrine have said the essential unity of man lies in his nature, his physico-chemical nature, his moral nature, his rational nature, his irrational nature, his spiritual nature, his psychological nature, his machine-like nature. There is to my knowledge no tradition which ignores the problem, 'are men equal?' No doubt it is possible: happily for the surveyor in social science it is discountable. A possible reason may be that interest in man, more often than not, assumes man's humanity. While our moral progress to date could be better, we have perhaps discovered at least one thing. It is better to assume man is what he seems: human. To attempt to destroy our vision of man has grave moral consequences. Unless men are Men, that is to say, unless all men are assumed to possess the essential nature which makes them human, unless they are all created in the image of God, we cannot treat them properly with dignity. Most people interested in the science of man are on man's side, want to treat him with dignity, are appalled at inhumanity. They do not care for metaphysical problems which have connections with doubtful or repugnant moral attitudes. So the metaphysics of egalitarianism, of social science, has curiously significant connections with morality compared with the relative moral neutrality of metaphysical ideas in natural science.

Another reason why surveys and therefore methodology are perhaps more valuable in social than in natural science may be this. As Popper puts it: natural sciences like physics and chemistry explain the *known* world of experience (hard tables, colours of things, reactions between things) in terms of underlying and often unseen, or *unknown* worlds. Matter becomes in 'reality' a macro-effect of point charges in fields of force in empty space; reactions are explained as involving complex exchanges and reformations of minute bodies. Social science, on the other hand, more often explains peculiar or unintended or *unknown* aspects of the world of experience in terms of more ordinary, acceptable, known aspects of experience. That strange economist's entity, 'the market', is explained in terms of more familiar things like people's aim to get rich by buying and selling. Clearly it is easier to survey the known than the unknown, so it should be easier to survey the theories of social science which deal mainly in the known than those of natural science which are free to appeal to the most unknown—the as-yet-unthought-of metaphysics. What is this known and unknown? The known by means of which we explain in social science is the understandable or rational actions of individual people. The unknown in natural science is the appeal to entities circumscribed only by the limits of our metaphysical imagination. In social science complicated rules about who one can marry, as among Australian Aborigines, can be explained in terms of simple intentions framed within a structure of society that allows of certain moves only with regard to marriage. By appealing, more often than not, to a model of a man acting rationally to attain an end in a situation structured in a peculiar way, social science fulfils what explanatory functions it has. Social science constantly appeals back to an assumption of action taken to achieve an end (rational action) and to a basic layer of experience and concepts of the world which renders (or should if the explanation is successful) the puzzling action non-mysterious, non-puzzling or understandable. It would seem as though the starting-point of natural science is the perfectly well-known world; objects fall towards the earth, iron rusts; these well-known phenomena we try to explain. Similarly the starting-point for social science appears to be the unusual, unexpected, inexplicable. The perfectly well-known in the social world we can usually account for. We appeal to a common layer of experience, and thinking

77

modelled on our own rational ideal, and we find things become understandable.[1] Thus, as Percy Cohen[2] puts it, social science has a natural ceiling, a limit which, I may suggest, may be rooted in the egalitarian metaphysics of the tradition of social science discussed above.

A possible objection should be dealt with at once. True, someone could say, the social scientist will have some interest in the equality of man—either to affirm it or deny it. Should he take either position there is a positive moral commitment involved in his choice as well. But, the objector would continue, the idea that social scientists must appeal to a model of man acting rationally, does not follow because it is not the case that unless we follow that model of explaining behaviour rationally our explanations must be unintelligible. Surely, he could say, the historicist theories of Plato and Marx, and Freud's psycho-analysis, do not make that appeal and yet they explain men's actions quite intelligibly. Plato's (cyclical?) law of political decay, they could say, and Marx's historical materialism, and Freud's theory of the unconscious, undermine the rationality-type explanation and to that extent are alternatives which have even to some extent entered into the tradition of social science which has been significantly affected by these thinkers in a number of ways. In the first place, this attack could go on, scientific explanations in natural science do not appeal to any rationality principle and yet they make phenomena intelligible. So clearly what is intelligible is not coterminus with what can be explained rationally. Now we can press this even further, the critic could say. Plato, surely one of the world's greatest sociologists, shows very cogently that, however rationally people may act, timocracy, oligarchy and democracy must all decay into tyranny. Marx pointed out that even if capitalists and workers acted rationally the law of increasing misery would function and lead to the eventual explosion of a bloody revolution. Freud showed that even the rational man who wanted to escape his neurosis could not do so. These explanations show that not only is intelligibility not coterminous with what can be explained rationally, but that what can be explained rationally is not coterminous with social science.

[1] This argument borrows heavily from that of Hayek in his excellent *Counter Revolution of Science*, 1952. 'Not only man's action towards external objects but also all the relations between men and all the social institutions can be understood only in terms of what men think about them. Society as we know it is, as it were, built up from the concepts and ideas held by the people; and social phenomena can only be recognized by us and have meaning to us only as they are reflected in the minds of men' (p. 34).

[2] In a paper read to Popper's seminar some years ago which he has told me of in private conversation. He also discusses the idea in his review of *The Poverty of Historicism*, Cohen, 1964.

As a final sally the critic could point out that these explanations not only do away with my rationality principle, they do away with moral commitment too. In this sense they are much more like the explanations of natural science in being ethically neutral. Explanation is made simply by means of an appeal to discovered laws (of decay or of increasing misery) or to a discovery (the influence of the unconscious) about the structure of the mind.

Happily I think it is easy to rout this criticism, and to show that the very plausibility of these three examples which are thought to count against me turns on the fact that the authors employ the model of rational action to explain their discoveries.

Plato gives a very cogent account of how timocracy, oligarchy and democracy have structural weaknesses such that the logic of the situation of people acting rationally within such a structure will be such that the society will decay into the next type, because of what they do. Marx too gave a very rational account of why, for example, the law of increasing misery applied; he actually said it was an inevitable consequence of people acting rationally within the social set-up of capitalism. Freud, too, while more interested in mind than society, wrote a rational account of civilisation and its discontents, employing his theories, and indeed his general theory is an attempt to show that the seeming-irrationality of neuroses is based on a failure to see the situation as the person concerned saw it. Given that the person concerned sees it in the way he does his neurosis has its rational aspects. There thus seems to be little substance in the critics' counter-examples; his three great thinkers are as committed to rationality as anyone. Their alleged ethical neutrality also goes by the board. There remains the claim that these thinkers have influenced the tradition, or even created a sub-tradition of nonrational explanations. Here, I am afraid I have to yield to the critic. There is an element of nonrational explanation in social science—historicism and holism—and I believe much of it stems from misinterpretations of these thinkers who were thought not to adhere to the rationality principle.

So much about the three differences of lack of metaphysical freedom, value commitment, and the rationality principle, which mark off social science from natural science. Besides these there may be others of which I do not know; however many there may be these differences should not blind us to the similarities. To begin with, there is what Popper calls the unity of method, namely his thesis that all scientific explanation has the same (logical) structure. In his *Poverty of Historicism*[1] Popper argues that our idea of explanation can be

---

[1] There is also a useful discussion of Popper's idea, and its critics, to be found in Bartley, 1962*a*.

given a fairly precise logical meaning which amounts to deriving the fact to be explained from a universal law or laws, combined with a set of factual statements or 'initial conditions'. This similarity I will simply take for granted as a result. Now earlier I discussed another thesis of Popper's, that social science and natural science differ in that the one explains the unknown by the known, and the other explains the known by the unknown. It seems to me that right in this point of difference there also lies a similarity: both kinds of science begin from common sense, the known, the one to explain it, the other to use it in explanations. Although they rely on it in this way they both also have as an aim the revision or correction of common sense. Both natural science and social science try to revise our everyday conceptions of things and substitute better ones:

... the social sciences no less than the natural sciences aim at revising the popular concepts which men have formed about the objects of their study, and at replacing them by more appropriate ones (Hayek, 1952, p. 36).

This point may seem paradoxical and rather difficult. How can we start from common sense as a basis and then change it? No one quite knows how we do it, but we do. It may be common sense that a well-known optical illusion is the way it looks: the fact is that it is not. Although the oar in water looks bent, it is not. Although matter feels hard and solid it happens in fact to consist largely of empty space. To go into this in more philosophical detail would not, I think, be appropriate here and again I must take it as a result. But given that this revision of common sense is an aim, doubts may be legitimate as to how far our common sense ideas do manage to get revised. Copernicus certainly revolutionised our conceptions of things, but Mr. Koestler has written a book on our view of the world which stops at Newton because, he says:

in spite of more than two centruies that have passed since his death, our vision of the world is by and large still Newtonian (1959, p. 496).

In the social sciences the situation is much the same. Everyone who has done economics knows how hard one still has to work in this day and age to exorcise 'common-sense' economic ideas, which happen to be mistaken and to have been known to be so for many generations, before one can begin to make progress with the subject. One is in very much the same jam one would be if one started to study the earth and planets believing the former to be flat. As another example, I have written a paper on how ordinary conceptions of social class have been refuted by social science and even the social scientists haven't noticed it and yet got round to substituting something more 'appropriate'.[1]

[1] 'The Idea of Social Class' (forthcoming).

To sum up. Surveys should be more valuable in the social sciences because there is a metaphysical restriction there. In addition there is involved in this metaphysics a moral view of man as someone with human dignity and rationality. These further narrow down the range of possible explanations which are worth surveying. Those which appeal to irrationality or contingency needn't be bothered with because they go against this. And explanations which completely ignore the metaphysical egalitarian tradition of social science, like mechanism, cybernetics, theological determinism, or racism, can reasonably be ignored.

The value of surveys of the possible means of accounting for a problematic social phenomenon should emerge from our present survey of attempts to explain cargo cults. Before I come to it a brief warning may be in order. A peculiar difficulty of this survey was that single authors often subscribed to a number of theories. As a consequence their names may appear in more than one pigeon-hole of the survey. This strikes me as better than trying to fit each author into one single pigeon-hole. After all, some of the theories they hold are not mutually exclusive.

And now to the general outline of my survey. The chief theories are as follows. First, *the prophet is responsible for the cargo cult.* Why he was responsible, why he did it has to be gone into. The prophet theory, although true, can be shown to be unsatisfactory by pointing out that not only the prophet is involved: there are more prophets than cults, so the question of which prophets are followed and why has not been handled by the prophet theory. This lacuna can only be partly filled with further reference to the prophet; cognisance has also to be taken of why the followers followed if unsatisfactoriness is to be avoided. The second theory, then, evades this difficulty by saying that *the followers of the prophet are responsible for the cult.* Why they followed, why they did it, has to be gone into. The followers theory, although also true, can be shown to be unsatisfactory by pointing out that still more is involved: some prophets are followed by some people, but neither the prophets nor the followers operate in a vacuum, they are members of a society which has a particular structure and thus creates a certain social situation at a particular time. All action is constrained by this situation. This criticism hits both prophet and followers theories and thus any combination of them. The third theory, then, would be that *the cult is a product of the situation in which the followers and the prophet act.* Why the situation is such and such, how it got there, need not be gone into. Even this theory can be shown to be unsatisfactory by pointing out that other societies have had the cargo cults happen to

81

them and just because one cult was a product of one situation doesn't mean that every cult was a product of a similar situation. In fact *there may be as many different situations as cults*, or *there may only be one type*, or perhaps even *the cult diffused through from one 'source' society to spread over the whole of the Western Pacific.*

So much for the outline of the survey. I shall now refer briefly to the chief literature on the topic before beginning the survey in detail. Unfortunately, as the subsequent discussion will show, not all of this ground has been covered in the literature. In some cases I shall only sketch the explanation precisely because it hasn't been developed in the literature by anyone. After my attempt to state each theory I shall also indicate in square brackets into which pigeon-hole I think it should be allotted. Chronologically the theories which exist of which I have taken account are these. Mooney (1892) argued that such cults were caused by a nearby messiah cult which took root in propitious circumstances of deprivation and discontent [situation]. Haddon (1917) traced them to general social unrest, a state of affairs which frequently resulted in religious upheavals [situation]. Williams (1924, 1934) attributes them to disappointed expectations and failure to absorb western ideas [followers]. Barber (1941) also explains them as a product of unrest brought on by deprivation [situation]. Linton (1943) explains them as a form of escapism utilising magical means in an attempt to revive a golden age [followers]. Belshaw (1950, 1954) sees them as rational attempts to explain the white man, framed in a religious setting because everything is framed in a religious setting [situation]. Guiart (1951, 1952 and 1956) sees the cults as incipient nationalism [?]. Bodrogi (1951) sees them as the consequences of a developing but not yet sufficiently developed class-consciousness [followers]. Firth (1932, 1951, 1955) attributes the cults to deprivation, which is a consequence of the lack of the necessary technical knowledge needed to get coveted goods [situation]; a fantasy explanation of this is projected and combined with an attempt to assert moral equality or worth [followers]. Berndt (1952, 1954) explains them as a form of social change brought on by the traumatic effect [followers] of the white man [situation]. Stanner (1953, 1958) says the failure of the Melanesians to digest new ideas brings on a social crisis, which is also a striving for a new life, and that an appeal to the gods is simply the most rational means at their disposal [followers]; the new life is a materialist one because their culture is materialistic [situation]. Burridge (1954, 1960) says the Melanesians attempt, with the myth-dream, to become new men, with a new life in community with the whites [situation]. Lawrence (1954) also asserts their materialism and says they accepted the religion because they thought they would get the goods, but they didn't [followers]; inferiority feelings also played a role [followers]. Cohn (1957) talks of the strain of change, and the paranoia it engenders [followers]. Inglis (1957, 1959) speaks of a cultural disposition to messianism, which is a symbolic act [situation]. Hogbin (1958) explains the cult as logical within the social situation [situation]. Mair (1959) says the colonisation created new status differences and they made typically native attempts to overcome them [followers and situation]. Worsley (1957) says stateless and segmented societies used the cult to create unity from diversity, peasant societies to create unity from separation, and defeated societies to re-create unity from desolation [followers?].

2. *The Prophet Dun It*

This is a survey of possibilities, not of the literature. Therefore despite the discrediting and abandoning of straightforward theories which blame the cargo cult on the prophet, we shall now look at them. The fact that they have been neglected by social anthropologists may make their study very interesting (if they shouldn't have been neglected) or merely an exercise (if they should).

Mystery stories often turn on the question 'whodunit?' The most obvious answer of all to the mystery of why cargo cults occur is to blame it all on the butler, namely the prophet. History, it is sometimes said, the message of destiny, is carried by the leaders of men; it is the history of these men. We don't know to what extent the prophet is a great man but, this theory proposes, to the extent to which he was following, to the extent to which he is the causal agent in history, he is. Much can be said in favour of this theory. It is certainly the case, for example, that there are no cults without prophets,[1] although this may be a matter of definition. Prophets everyone agrees, found the cults, and, if the cult should live so long, it probably dies with them. The very shortness of cargo cults precludes dynasties of these prophets. By and large the cult collapses when the imminent millennium fails to come. This, however, only discredits the prophet, not the general cargo theory. Witness the way cults will again and again spring up in the same area—those people cannot have been disillusioned about the whole cargo mythology, only about the prophet. This recurrence of the rises and falls of cults and their correlation with the rise and fall of the prophet constitute as clear-cut evidence as one can ever expect that the prophet dun it.

[1] Burridge in his 1962 paper seems to disagree. He claims that the simple appearance of drawings in the sand, or a mood of unrest, can be called cult activities; but this is less of a disagreement than an attempt to stretch the concept of the cargo cult further than most people would consider desirable.

Even more significant is the fact that the lull between cults frequently occurs when the prophets are in gaol; and there is the fact we know from the John Frum case that from gaol and exile prophets can still provoke cults. At first sight, then, we must conclude that there is a good deal to be said for blaming or attributing the cults to the prophets. Yet we may ask for further elaboration of this prophet theme.

The crudest form in which this request could be met would be simply to add that there exists what amounts to a race of men in Melanesia who have personalities which express themselves in these types of prophecies. The structure of the cults could then be explained as the direct outcome of the way these particular men think. They are optimistic by nature and have a half-baked knowledge of the white man with which they try to help the even less enlightened members of their groups, namely their followers. Because they are truly unique people, because they do possess more imagination and knowledge, because they have charisma, they do succeed in getting the thing going.

The literature is not exactly filled with theories of this character. The nearest to the The Prophet Dun It theory is Margaret Mead. Yet even she, in her frankly hero-worshipping book about Paliau (*New Lives for Old*), only comes near this sort of explanation, not quite to it. She certainly argues that Paliau is a representative of change, and that much turns on his terrific personality and abilities. However she goes on to discuss other things as well.

Another expressionistic theory is that the prophets are expressing not themselves but their anti-Europeanism.[1]

A casual reading of Burridge's *Mambu* (the name of a prophet) may suggest that this is also a case of attributing the cult to the prophet. No so; Burridge would not deny that the prophet plays some role, but his theory is more sophisticated and appeals to situations and aims and not to personalities, as we shall see later.

So much for a crude The Prophet Dun It theory of expressionistic character. This is the nearest to an irrational explanation of the cargo cult. Cutting out the expressionistic element in the theory we must provide the prophet with a new motive. Now as the prophet dun it, his action was either intended, or it was unintended. (The third possibility, that he acted under duress, attributes the cult to a conspiracy, not to the prophet, and discussion of it belongs later.) Regrettably I have yet to come across, in the literature, an explana-
on of the cults as an unintended consequence of the actions of some prophet. After all, if a man gets to his feet and declares that he has suddenly seen the light about the white men, and that what must be

[1] See Bodrogi; Stanner, 1953, p. 63; and Burridge, 1954.

done is this and this, and he will show how, he could hardly be said
not to intend what subsequently happens.

So let us turn instead to the cases where the cult is intended (how
far it was intended to go exactly as it did is another question we can
leave aside; there is some reason for thinking that it would be miraculous if in any society things turned out exactly as men intended
them). Again we must distinguish between when the cult itself and
its expected consummation in the millennium is the only aim of the
prophet, and when the prophet undoubtedly is using the cult to
further some ulterior aim. Let us stick to the latter for the moment.
It is the conspiracy theory.

One theory to this effect is much favoured by the administrators
and starts from the notion that nearly all sorcerers are demagogues.
The prophet is said to be an exsorcerer seeking power by means of
this cult. The theory is discussed and dismissed by Belshaw (in 1950).
It must be obvious that all the possible ulterior purposes of the prophet cannot be surveyed. Suggestions have been made that the
prophets, being cunning, realised that they could get wealth and or
extra sexual opportunities, as well as power, from a cult. It would
then be said that these, or any combination of these, was the real
aim of the man, whose actions should be interpreted in this light.[1]
Another likelihood is that the conspiracy is not that of the prophet
but of others to whom the prophet is a mere tool. Worsley hints at
this with his theory that there is nearly always a powerful figure in
the shadow of the front man, a Nasser behind the Neguib. Others,
too, in claiming marxist conspiracy in Masinga rule, or in attributing
the cults to the pernicious influence of American troops, succumb
to this theory. Any adherent of conspiracy ideas has the responsibility of showing how the authors of these ingenious and demoniac
conspiracies succeeded in consummating them.

In all these cases founding the cult was a secondary aim to the
achievement of some ulterior purpose. Now we come back to the idea
that founding the cult was the only aim. As far as I can see, the only
possible explanation of this would be that the prophet thought what
he was saying was *true*. It seems utterly reasonable that, like any
convert, the prophet should think he suddenly has grasped something which he wants to tell other people about. But such a true doctrine doesn't come out of thin air; it must come to solve a problem,
resolve an issue over which he had been puzzling. Sure enough, those
authors who do more or less accept that the prophet believes what
he says and knows what he is doing, those authors all begin from a
fundamental problem or conflict in the society which needs explanation. The cult doctrine both provides that explanation—solves the

[1] Cf. Stanner's discussion of their 'standard motives' in 1953, p. 63.

problem—and provides a course of appropriate conduct—resolves their conflicts.

The problem which everyone thinks faces the Melanesian, is the problem of culture contact with the west and consequent social change. It is explained that the Melanesian both envies and resists the white man, and is involved in certain conflicts internal to the society because of him. There is some disagreement as to the nature and significance of the millennium. To some authors it is an attempt to adjust to the Europeans,[1] to others an attempt to revive or perpetuate their society,[2] to still others an attempt to gain a new life.[3] To put it bluntly, the psychologistic possibilities of explaining the prophets' actions, and the historicistic possibilities ('tool of history', etc.) have been ignored. Most of the authors I know of explain the prophets' actions by means of the logic of his situation.

Perhaps the reason why discussion of these individualistic paths of explanation we have been surveying is, to say the least, so thin on the ground in the literature is that the attribution of the cults solely to the prophet is open to such obvious criticism. Clearly the theory is true: there are no cults without prophets. Unfortunately it is also unsatisfactory because there happen to be more prophets than cults. Not every would-be prophet became one, and not every would-be cult-leading prophet succeeded in being one. The prophet doesn't operate in a vacuum; other individuals are involved in the cult and their actions must be explained as well. Moreover, as prophets are themselves to some extent products of their social environment, which may be different from the environment they operate in, some mention of the circumstances in the explanation is also necessary. The pure prophet explanation, then, is unsatisfactory. The obviousness of this kind of criticism, I suggest, is the principal reason for the lack of explicit prophet theories. So obvious is it, in fact, that no one bothers to state it; writers simply start talking about the prophet and continue talking about the circumstances in which he operates. Yet I have found it necessary to discuss this kind of theory for a few reasons. One, that prophet theories are at the back of a lot of writer's minds, as they write; they are Aunt Sallys to be knocked down. Worsley, for example, attacks The Prophet Dun It, i.e. charisma theories, which he must have got from somewhere. Secondly, the theories have been put forward by administrators and others and should be discussed. Third, elements of prophet theory are insinuated or interleaved in the writings of many people (Worsley's own theory of the shadowy figure behind the prophet is a prophet-conspiracy

[1] Firth, 1951; Burridge, 1960 (myth is their only truth).
[2] Linton, 1943, *passim*; Stanner, 1953 (p. 63, *en passant*).
[3] Stanner, 1958 (Cargo is a *motif*, p. 3); Burridge, 1960, *passim*.

view). Finally, it is a good thing, in my opinion, to bring out into the light of discussion even the most obviously inadequate theories, if they have life left in them. Carlyle and others invented the 'history is the history of great men' theory and nowadays it is discredited. Readers may even have become impatient at having to read such obvious nonsense. However, if it is taken as an analytical exercise in distinguishing theories from each other it may have some value.

3. *It was all their own Fault*

Since the prophet theory is unsatisfactory let us turn from it to another theory, that which blames it on the followers. Again, the crudest version of such a theory would be that the followers simply express themselves by means of such a cult. For one thing it could be suggested that in a culture like this, apocalyptic religion was one of the normal means of self-expression, or letting off steam.[1] Or, perhaps, the cult is a quite new form of expression because what the followers want to express is something quite new: say, frustration and bafflement with the white man, anti-Europeanism.[2] Such a followers theory hovers on the edge of rationality.

In parallel with our analysis of the prophet theories we can also consider a different kind of followers theory, which is rather more rational, by distinguishing cults which are intended by the followers from those which are unintended. It would be very difficult to construct a theory that the cargo cult was unintended by the followers, because the degree of participation by the followers is so great we can hardly believe their actions to be unintended.

As to an intended followers theory, we can differentiate those which allow that the cult is itself an aim, and those which insist that it is simply a means to a further end. Unlikely though it may seem, theories claiming the cult is an end in itself do exist. It has been argued that the airstrips and the warehouses are built as a symbolic gesture of moral rectitude.[3] Another author has suggested cult practices and ritual are very enjoyable and the opportunity to perform them is never passed up.[4] The cargo cult is simply the latest opportunity or fashion like the latest dance craze (Williams). Lastly, of course, there could be the simple and very ordinary theory that the

---

[1] 'Steam' being energy needing to be siphoned off in organisation (Sundkler), or football (Williams) or released (Worsley). Cp. Mair, 1959, and her discussion of this theory, with references.

[2] See Bodrogi; Stanner, 1953, p. 63; Burridge, 1954 (briefly).

[3] Firth, 1951 (pp. 111–13); Hogbin (p. 219); Burridge, 1960, *passim*; Mair, 1959 (p. 211).

[4] See the last paragraph of section 1 of Appendix II.

followers believed the cargo myth to be true and acted accordingly. Guiart, Belshaw and Hogbin came closest to this.

Most theories, however, do accept that there is an ulterior end in the desire to have a cult. Either: the followers, being in a religion-oriented culture,[1] were frustrated by the inadequacy of their present religion and were attempting to get a new one;[2] or there is a desire for European-type wealth (most authors); or a desire for moral community with the Europeans (Burridge); or a desire to explain and incorporate, to adjust to the experience of the European;[3] or an attempt to revive or perpetuate selected aspects of the society;[4] or a desire for a new life.[5] Generally speaking, then, the cult is a means to attain a more fundamental aim of the followers.

Clearly two accusations of unsatisfactoriness could be levelled against followers theories. (1) That they ignore the prophet. (2) That the followers do not act in a vacuum and that their circumstances are surely relevant to their aims and actions. Leaving aside (1) for the time being, we are led by (2) to a new theory.

4. Circumstances are to Blame

To know all may not be to forgive all, but it might well be to explain all. We are dealing now with suggestions that the circumstances produced the cult. We rule out the human circumstances as they have been covered in the two previous sections. But what kind of circumstances do we mean, then? A first suggestion might be about atmospheres: there was an atmosphere of unrest or cult and that this caused the cargo cult. Various suggestions have been made about atmospheres. Cohn suggests one of collective paranoia. Others suggest inferiority feelings.[6] For further suggestions we might leave such immaterial things as atmosphere and concentrate on material circumstances. It could be, for example, that the economic or the

---

[1] By a 'religion-oriented' culture I mean one in which religion in an organised and institutionalised form still plays its traditional role of dominating the thought of the culture, and makes claims to being knowledge. If in a culture events needing explanation are appealed to religious authorities (as in India, or the U.S.S.R., or the backwoods of the U.S. Bible Belt), then the culture is religion-oriented. I want to draw the contrast with societies in which the all-embracing character of any set of theories is mistrusted and subjected to criticism; and where progress in explanations is made.

[2] Haddon (p. 455); Firth, 1951; Bodrogi; Stanner, 1953 (religious crisis, p. 67); Cohn (means of expressing new aspirations); Mair (p. 119); Burridge.

[3] Cf. Firth, 1951; Stanner, 1953; Bodrogi; Hogbin; also Guiart, 1951 (they covet it, p. 85); Belshaw, 1950 (pp. 123–4, and later 1954, p. 83).

[4] Linton, *passim*; Stanner, 1953 (p. 63 *en passant*).

[5] Stanner, 1958 (Cargo is a *motif* of it, p. 3); Burridge, 1960 *passim*.

[6] Williams; Linton (*en passant*); Lawrence (1954, economic ones).

political circumstances were to blame for the cult. One suggestion is of a breakdown of economic or *political* authority.[1] Others are economic deprivation and hardship.[2] the oppression of colonial rule,[3] the rise of nationalist-political movements,[4] the materialism of the Melanesians,[5] their ignorance,[6] and their underdeveloped class consciousness.[7] Somehow or other the cult arose out of these.

All these answers are partial, they say that some part of the circumstances is responsible. Also possible is to say that any combination of these particular circumstances is responsible and, finally, that only the whole of the circumstances can be blamed. The whole social set-up, its material and its immaterial aspects, is to blame. What kind of specification of the circumstances would be satisfactory? You have here a society, with a world view, a morality, a social and political system. You also have a second society with those things, or at least its representatives. And finally you have the relations between these two societies.[8] Now the circumstances could be simply what the natives do in relation to the white men; or it could also be what they do within their society should it be disrupted by the white man's arrival. The white man is, after all, a challenge. He opens up new possibilities which seem attractive, especially when connected with such wealth, comfort and power. On the one hand it is obvious that envy may grow up and people desiring to get what the white man has will make certain gestures. On the other hand the white man actively interferes with native society, both as an administrator, and in the way his goods and customs influence natives. He introduces wage labour, leisure hours, individualistic morality (e.g. marry who you love), desks and paper as apparata of power rather than kinship, overwhelming new weapons. How shall native society and its customs accommodate this? Lastly there are dual problems facing the natives once they accept that the white men are men. Men for them are people you marry, have moral obligations towards, respect, and so on. How to achieve this decent relationship with men who are so

[1] (Cohn), Hogbin, Mair.

[2] Mooney; Barber (messianism is a reaction to it); Belshaw, 1954 (p. 83); Firth, 1955 (they were just without natural resources); Berndt, 1952 and 1954; Burridge, 1960; Lawrence; Cohn; Hogbin.

[3] Haddon (p. 455); Guiart, 1952, 1956 (exploitation); Bodrogi (colonialism); Cohn (subjection); Worsley (violent sanctions and failure create hysteria).

[4] Guiart, 1951; Bodrogi; Firth, 1955 (opposed political interests); Lawrence (cargo a power-symbol).

[5] Stanner, 1958 (pp. 4 and 23); Lawrence.

[6] Burridge, 1954 ('Bewildered'); Firth, 1955.

[7] Bodrogi.

[8] Mooney; Haddon (p. 455); Williams; Barber; Linton; Belshaw; Guiart; Bodrogi; Firth; Berndt; Stanner; Burridge; Lawrence; Cohn; Inglis; Hogbin; Mair; Worsley.

strange; whose customs are so different; whose morality, even, is different; who do not marry your girls?

(Clearly all these possibilities can with ease be combined with the theory that the prophet enters this situation with the conviction that he can resolve these dilemmas; with the conviction that he can make the logic of action clear.)

I think this is as far as we can go in this direction. For now the criticism of the satisfactoriness of this sort of solution comes up. It can be argued that, as the cults occur in many societies, do we know that circumstances are the same in all societies? Two answers are possible: that the cults are products of historically unique sets of circumstances; and that they are not: that their similarity can only be explained by the similar circumstances in all cases. Against circumstances-being-similar theories the objection could be urged that these cults have occurred in many societies which differ a good deal. The question of whether the cults had similar circumstances in different places or not has been begged in the previous theories.

The theory that the societies concerned have *not* had the same cult for the same reasons is a form of the theory that all historical events are unique and require particular explanations. The theory that particular events and organisations cause the cults, Mooney's theory of the diffusion of the Messiah cult, Inglis' theory of historical uniqueness, fit into this category.[1] There is really very little to say about it. Its proponents deny the possibility of there being *an* explanation of cargo cults. There can only be an explanation of the cult on islands *a*, *b*, or *c*. People who hold such a view are on the verge of denying the whole idea of cargo cults as an entity; of denying that their collective name suggests that there may be a general account of them. For this reason they are not appropriately discussed here. Their position is methodological, not theoretical. Having mentioned those theories which, while accepting any of the first three theories put forward, insisted that in different places there may be different causes, and a unified explanation of the cults was *a priori* to be ruled out, we can now deal with those theories which insist that similar events must have had similar circumstances, and similar circumstances similar causes. There falls under this rubric a number of theories: evolution, diffusion, function, historicism and irrationality. To deal with these in turn.

Nineteenth-century anthropology, with its cult of social darwinism,

---

[1] As do also Protestant Missionaries on Tanna (Belshaw, 1950; Guiart, 1952, 1962); the sale of liquor on Espiritu Santo; the marxism of the U.S. troops in the Solomons; the coming of the Americans and their generosity (Belshaw, 1954, p. 83); the administrative encouragement of politics (*ibid.*); European racialism (Guiart; Hogbin, 1958, pp. 221, 216).

explained every cultural event by giving it a position on the evolutionary tree and then referring vaguely to the survival of the fittest to explain the tree. This theory could presumably be applied to cargo cults: they could be seen as products of sets of circumstances which were inevitable stages in the evolution of societies which have suffered contact. Indeed I am sure that if the work of Cohn and Zinsser were extensively utilised this thesis could be defended as well as, say, Toynbee's about the decay of societies. Many facts fit in with it, especially its connection with change, whether or not the change be a product of contact. To some extent Guiart, Bodrogi, Worsley and perhaps even Inglis' thinking runs along these lines.

Diffusionism, the traditional rival to evolutionism, may more appropriately belong to the previous discussion since it does not accept that such events as cargo cults could be re-created over and over again in different places. Yet it does allow for only one explanation for all the cults, namely, that they began in circumstances somewhere and then spread or diffused to other places. Stanner and Mooney hint that there might be something in diffusion. Here one might also mention the view of Belshaw (Baigona, p. 124) and Burridge (1960, p. 20) that the cults are a local tradition being exploited by the cargo prophet, or even a 'cultural disposition' (Inglis, 1957).

Other possibilities in the direction of historicism needn't be too closely gone into. There's the theory that history is the inevitable march of economic forces, which are responsible for all 'objective' circumstances, or for the laws of growth and decay of civilisations. Cargo cults could easily be fitted into these views, which are so pitted with *ad hoc* adjustments anyway that adding in circumstances suitable for cargo cults wouldn't be noticed. Bodrogi suggests that the Melanesians are a proletariat in the making (from the stone age to a proletariat in one jump would have seemed quite something to Marx) and Worsley too sees them as the products of the economic forces acting on the Melanesians.

Some simple functional theories of how similar situations gave rise to such similar events could also be concocted. Religion, it could be said, sanctions the social order, it is a form of social control. When the social order, what is to be controlled, changes, the religion must change. I am at a loss to know quite how to develop this but Haddon, Firth, Stanner, Burridge, Cohn, Mair and Worsley all make moves along these lines. New aspirations are said to be sanctioned, and Stanner even goes so far as to suggest that the cult grows out of the revealed functional inadequacies of the traditional society; the cult prophecies misvalue key objects and the cult must die or else it would lead to social chaos.

As a last resort in this survey, I come to those theories which would assert that *the* fundamental similarity in the circumstances of the societies which have cargo cults is the irrationality of everyone.[1] This is not a followers or a prophet theory because it doesn't say the followers or prophets are mad, but that exposure to too many ideas, or to unintelligible happenings, and enviable goods, has been too much for them. So, although they have been trying to assimilate this experience, through no fault of their own, they have failed. Circumstances are to blame. Another reason for not putting this explanation in the followers or prophets sections is precisely because it appeals to irrationality. The nearest I have skated to irrationality-type explanations throughout this chapter is in sections two and three, where I discussed expressionistic prophet and follower theories. The trouble is that appeals to irrationality give up the possibility of any explanation at all. Instead of deriving the unknown or not understood from the known or understood, the irrational explanation says the unknown, not understood, event is not knowable or not understandable. When we have to resort to such theories we had better stop, because whether we know it or not, the resort to them is a defeat.

5. *Prophets, Followers and Circumstances*

I have outlined three ways of explaining cargo cults, by prophets (*a*), by followers (*b*), and by circumstances (*c*). I divided the first into expressionistic (0), intended (1) and unintended (2) theories; the second was also divided into these three categories. The third I divided into whole (0) and partial (1). This makes eight subdivisions. The possible combinations of these various factors is already 47. And these are only the simplest divisions I have made. Clearly this whole range cannot be fully surveyed in any detail so I shall have to pick and choose those combinations and recombinations of the basic theories which I shall discuss. I shall do this on the following basis. All three theories strike me as true and as unsatisfactory. Therefore to rely on any one theory, or not to rely on any one, is a mistake. Only combinations of all three theories will be considered. Next I shall rule out all irrational and expressionistic theories as having little or no explanatory power. This leaves us with prophets intended (a_1) and unintended (a_2), and followers intended (b_1) and unintended (b_2), and circumstances wholly (c_0) or partly (c_1). We can reduce still further by removing the unintended prophet and followers theories (a_1) and (b_1). (*a*) and (*b*) have a further complication:

[1] Linton (escapist); Firth ('new illusions', 1932, 'other than rational elements', 1951); Berndt (projection into fantasy world, 1952), 'trauma',1954; Burridge ('rationalisations', 1954); Hogbin ('take refuge in fantasy', p. 216; 'psychological morass', p. 220); Mair, 1959 ('fantasy', substitute for political action, p. 121).

was the cult intended as an end or as a means? Most writers assume in both cases it was a means. We shall assume it was an end. This leaves us with two combinations only: (a_1) plus (b_1) plus (c_0), (a_1) plus (b_1) plus (c_1).

We can reduce further by eliminating theories that only some of the circumstances are responsible (c_1). Any part of the circumstances is part of the whole circumstances and cannot but operate therein. Consequently the whole of the circumstances have to be taken into account. We are finally left, then, with (a_1) plus (b_1) plus (c_0). This explanation, which takes into account the aims of the prophet and the circumstances as he sees them; the aims of the followers and the circumstances as they see them; and the circumstances as they are, consisting of people, prophets, followers, white men, institutions, cosmological and moral ideas (which are institutional), is what I would call situational logic. Indeed substituting the word 'situation' for 'circumstances' all the way through should make this apparent. However, if this is situational logic, it could well be objected, haven't Belshaw, Hogbin and Burridge provided accounts of this kind? Indeed they have. I want to examine their accounts in detail to show that, good though they are, they are not quite sufficient.

6. Three Authors and their Theories

Three main logic-of-the-situation theories exist; by Belshaw, Hogbin and Burridge. Belshaw's is that the cult doctrine solves the intellectual problem of the white men. This is the crucial problem facing prophets and followers and preventing them comprehending the changed circumstances. Hogbin shows how contact with the white men breaks down the traditional social system by introducing a new set of choices the strain of which requires resort to a new religion. Burridge argues that both intellectual explanation of the white man and internal conflicts of the society are resolved by the cult; the Melanesian wants to integrate the white man into a moral community, the only circumstances which he can tolerate and manage, and his aspirations are detected and guided by prophets.

(A) *C. S. Belshaw.* For Belshaw the central problem in the native's situation is the necessity of explaining the white man. He cannot understand the white man's power, or doings. The Melanesian

has to find some explanation of European power in holding sway over multitudes; of the miraculous arrival of manufactured goods in ships and aeroplanes; of strange European behaviour which sends away piles of raw materials; of the peculiar distaste with which Europeans treat him. On the one hand, this gives him an end of activity—he must strive to attain a similar power. On the other hand, it sets him an intellectual problem and gives him an emotional experience. His emotional experience is jealousy, sometimes hatred, of the European, who neither gives him these things as a friend nor initiates him into the mysteries of the process of sale and production—indeed, tries to fob him off with Biblical education. His intellectual problem is, first, to explain European success, and, second, to achieve a method of parallel success.

The problem must be solved in terms of Melanesian experience. There is behind him the great tradition of cults such as the *Baigona*, and animism. It is natural that he should turn to find a superior cult. At first, it was Christianity in many parts, which was conceived as a superior, sometimes as a supplementary, animism. This fails, or is not understood, and is moulded on to something new. The new cult endeavours to copy significant European activities. There is the belief in shipping, that is in the origin of cargoes—for remember most Melanesians have not seen or experienced the manufacturing process. There is a mystical significance in the revolting white skin of Europeans, and in money, which circulates so strangely; in flags and flag-poles, which the European treats with peculiar reverence; in towns and houses rather than villages; in soldiers and drilling—which *must* be mystical, for what use is there in it. And in later years, of course, there is the myth of American arrival, so obviously based upon the big-handedness and freedom of American troops. These things supplied the modern elements in the cargo myth, the myth which explained European success and indicated the correct road to follow (p. 124).

Belshaw is arguing that cult doctrine is a rational attempt by the natives to explain certain things they do not understand in terms of their magical and animistic outlook. The spirit world is utilised to explain curiosities in the behaviour of white men. The reason he cannot understand the white man is because he is in contact with, *and yet excluded from*, the higher standard of life the Europeans enjoy. This disparity is appalling and puzzling to someone with a background in a co-operative social system like Melanesia, as H. Ian Hogbin explains (see below). Exclusion is not the only factor, Belshaw also lists a 'lack of intimacy' in the contact between an official or missionary and his people; low wages placing most material goods beyond their purchasing power compared with the relative affluence of the war years;

the presence of large numbers of Americans during the war which gave credence to the long-standing myth that Americans would eventually come to liberate the Melanesians and give them quantities of material goods (p. 83);

and

the deliberate stimulus given in the Solomons by the Administration to the growth of Melanesian political organisations (p. 83).

The Europeans are credited with superior knowledge (and there-fore manipulative power) *of the magical world*. Such doctrines grow out of: (*a*) ignorance; which fosters (*b*) puzzlement; and the remedy-ing of this ignorance is vitiated by (*c*) an uncritical attitude towards explanations. Belshaw does not add (*c*) which strikes me as the best way to explain continued adherence to failed cults. Or, to put it another way, Belshaw does not face the problem of why Melanesian explanation takes the form it does. Although I anticipate Chapter 5 a little I shall say something about this problem. The Melanesians, I would argue, have cargo cults because they live in a tradition of magical and religious explanations of the world.[1] This means that when they are faced with an intellectual problem the first and un-criticised assumption they make is 'this has a magico-religious explanation'. Of course, this need not be a conscious assumption; they might not even categorise things in this way; to them magic and religion are exhaustive and have no corresponding polar con-cepts[2] or contrast.[3] But once they do make such a distinction, once they become critical of the whole magico-religious framework, then they are making a break with a tradition that is an intrinsic part of their closed society.

Some anthropologists argue that this view of native 'knowledge' as magico-religious is false because primitive peoples also have some elementary technical knowledge (of gardening and fishing, etc.). That is to say, they argue that because primitive people often know how to grow crops, raise herds and fish successfully, the alleged 'backward-ness' of their knowledge is a myth. This assumes that by 'magico-religious' we mean 'backward', which is not the case. Calling them 'pre-scientific' is not the same. But the critic who objects to 'pre-scientific' with this argument assumes that 'scientific' means 'tech-nical success'. I reject this. Technical success can often be based on the most far-fetched theories and rules of thumb. So the technical success of the natives does not show that the ideology (or 'science')

---

[1] As we did at one time. One way of looking at the progress of science which I have always found helpful is in the way it has gradually extended the frontiers of what it can explain and what, therefore, is its rightful province, and has pushed back the frontiers of what magic and religion even try to explain and claim as their spheres of influence. We have gradually extended the critical tradition until all that is left outside of science now are 'fundamental ques-tions' (or 'The Big Questions' as W. W. Bartley calls them; see his 'I Call Myself a Protestant', *Harpers Magazine*, May 1959, reprinted in Hamalian and Volpe, 1960) and modern cosmology is making a bold bid for some of these. This way of looking at the progress of science has been developed by E. A. Burtt, 1928, and A. D. White, 1896, in the introductions to their volumes.

[2] Grant, 1956.

[3] Gellner, 1959, pp. 40–3; who there argues that this does not make them meaningless.

95

behind their technology is sound. Their *explanations* of why they garden and fish in such and such ways are more than likely to be in the magico-religious tradition. But even if they are not, my argument can be sustained along the following lines. Let us distinguish between theoretical knowledge and technical knowledge. Technical knowledge is useful, has a purpose; the only criterion which can be applied to it is 'how well does it work?' Theoretical knowledge claims much more; it demands to be evaluated in terms of whether it is true or false, *regardless of how well it works*. The native gardener is very uncritical of his theoretical explanation (if any) of why his rule of thumb works. A people who explain natural phenomena in in principle untestable magico-religious terms are still in a tradition which precludes the advance of theoretical knowledge. How far they have advanced can be gauged from whether, when their rule of thumb breaks down, they explain it conspiratorially, i.e. animistically, or whether they seek out a new and better rule of thumb.

These Melanesians are confronted by the problems posed by the Europeans, the problems of European wealth and power. As Belshaw says, they explain these things in Melanesian terms. Melanesians just have not the necessary knowledge, or tradition of criticising their knowledge, to enable them to explain the phenomenon of the European—although this is not to say their explanations are not very ingenious. More than this one cannot expect.

So I believe Belshaw to be right in this matter. I think the stage of a people's knowledge and the kind of problems facing them go a long way towards explaining their behaviour. These, combined with despair brought on by severely adverse material circumstances, produce a fruitful bed for the cults. The seeds of the cult are planted by the prophets who spread their doctrines and who are able to get away with merely *ad hoc* adjustments to someone else's cult because the doctrines are never held to be tested and refuted by their (falsified) predictions. And anyway an animist explanation in terms of evil forces at work, or an *ad hoc* explanation of not performing the ritual correctly, or a conspiratorial explanation of being misled by (previous) false prophets, can always be relied upon to sway uncritical believers. Cult doctrines are unlikely, if the prophets or the believers have anything to do with it, to be allowed to be put to critical test (if one can be devised; a major interest of cargo cults, with their precise predictions, is that they, unlike with most religions, *can* be devised), for the simple reason that the critical attitude does not prevail among them. Any test results which did weigh against cult doctrines would be written off as unacceptable blasphemy.

Let us touch on Belshaw on some of the other problems the

cults raise: they are highly organised, very popular, very short-lived; why?

Here Belshaw falls short of providing a satisfactory explanation in terms of the logic of the situation of people and prophet. We know from the John Frum case that not all the natives join in cargo cults. Belshaw does not tell us who does and why, and who does not and why not. He does not explain to us the popular success of cargo cults. Why, that is, quiet, easy-going Melanesians are so easily put into a mood for neglecting gardening, dissipating stocks and destroying property. We know why they do it, because the prophet tells them to, and if they are cultists they tend to do what the prophet tells them.

But how does it come about that they ever get ensnared by such an extremist crank? They are not so oppressed and poor as to be starved into dementedness. On the contrary they are normally calm and rational beings. The problem is: why do people join cargo cults instead of getting on with their work. It is a big one. The answer 'because although they are in similar social situations they are acting to realise different aims' is not sufficient. I am asking why x has this aim and y has that. In this instance, it seems, the argument leads us inexorably into psychopathology. Such a psychopathological explanation would presumably explain religion by appeal to abnormalities. But on the face of it this would appear somewhat unlikely. Are the vast majority of Melanesian cultists hysterics? Jehovah's Witnesses in Great Britain are a small sect and it would not be *in principle* impossible were someone to claim they were all hysterics. But it would hardly be convincing to assert this of the whole populations of South Sea islands.[1]

Despite the fact that he doesn't discuss the uncritical attitude, despite his failure to explain aims, I accept much of what Belshaw says. Indeed I would think that my own view is more an elaboration (and I would hope a deepening) of his sketch. But sketch it is.

(B) *H. Ian Hogbin.* H. Ian Hogbin also offers an account of the logic of the situation, but he lays the stress rather on the native society than on the contact with the new society. The stresses he pictures are internal to Melanesian society even though brought about by the white men. He presents the situational logic in such a way that it is quite apparent that certain problems exist there which

---

[1] It is my view that the sociological problems of religion cannot be psychopathologically explained. And the psychological problems of religion, how it is conceived, what its psychological function is, and so on, are the *only* problems of religion that can be tackled psychologistically. (These questions are discussed in Jarvie, 1961, sections 2.4 and 3.4.)

the cult seems to offer a solution to and for various reasons the solution is taken seriously.

. . . It is surely obvious that the native in many colonies now lives in a shifting scene and is continually faced with a series of fundamental dilemmas. Should he seek employment to earn money for the purchase of goods that are now so necessary, or stay at home to grow food for his family and care for his aging parents? Should he carry out the instructions of the agricultural officer and gather the ripening harvest in his coffee plantation, a crop his grandfather had never heard of, or fulfill his tribal responsibilities and attend the protracted funeral ceremonies of a chief in some distant village? Should he accept the judgment of his headman, who now has no power to enforce it but at least knows all the surrounding circumstances intimately, or take the charge to a European magistrate and submit to the tedious, and to him meaningless, procedure of the white man's law? Should he spend his money on a new pair of trousers, which he badly needs, or pay the traditional dues to his chief? Should he listen to the missionaries who say that he is morally entitled to choose a bride for himself, or accept the stranger selected for him according to ancient usage by his kinsmen? Should he be strictly monogamous even if his one wife is barren, or take an extra spouse to ensure the continuity of his clan? These and similar problems are cropping up all the time (pp. 38–9).

Hogbin's theory seems to be that given this is the situation the typical anonymous individual native is likely to be in after contact, if a prophet offers to resolve all or many of these dilemmas then, given what we have called a 'religion-oriented' culture, it is not particularly surprising he is taken to as a godsend; a panacea for the strain brought about by contact with civilisation.

Like other authors Hogbin believes the sense of deprivation and the real economic hardship experienced by the natives is a crucial factor in creating a favourable climate of opinion for a cult. If I understand him well he thinks that cargo cults are magical reactions to (or explanations of) these conditions; magical because of a failure to understand the chain of cause and effect in the surrounding European society. The lack of coincidence between the new wants and the known means of satisfying them, and the fact that the natives are still dominated by magical thought, causes them to 'take refuge in fantasy' (p. 216). Thus the ground is thoroughly prepared for a leader to arise who will channel these fantasies into a cult. Borrowing from Firth, Hogbin suggests that the work the cultists indulge in is an attempt to prove that their ends are morally right. This work is perhaps useless and can be compared with the building of Chartres Cathedral.

From this distance we can well argue that the citizens of Rouen were also misapplying their energies. But 800 years ago Europeans were in many respects as ignorant as the primitive natives of today. Only knowledge recently acquired enables us to say that disease is more effectively prevented by improving housing, water supply, and drainage than by holding processions and building cathedrals (p. 219).

This passage sits uneasily with his idea that the cults are an irrational 'retreat' into fantasy. To say that they are is to use hindsight and distort the sequence of events as I shall discuss below.

Hogbin further argues that the people have been plunged into a 'psychological morass' by the introduction of a second set of moral standards (p. 220). A strong, authoritarian leader offers a way out from this by revealing a ready-made answer to all problems. 'The cults may thus be regarded as a spontaneous effort to reach social integration' (p. 220).

The only other explanation Hogbin offers concerns the cause of dissatisfaction. He notes that

the majority of the settlers are strongly imbued with colour prejudice and sensitive about what they refer to as 'White prestige'. They consider that they are entitled to respect by virtue of their pale skins and argue that dignity and authority are best maintained by discourtesy and even brutality. The natives resent such treatment and project their animosity, which they are ordinarily forced to conceal, into the fantasy world of the cults (p. 221). . . . Their resentment is perhaps augmented indirectly by the work of the missionaries. Christianity, which they know to be the religion of the Europeans, proclaims the spiritual equality of man; but colonial settlers are rarely willing to practice the ethical implications of the doctrine. Such hypocrisy has repelled dependent peoples everywhere (p. 216).

While I would not claim that Hogbin's account is complete, I think its simplicity and rationality make it well worth discussion here. First he sketches the aims of the followers and the difficulties they face in the circumstances; then he mentions the aims and circumstances of the white men; and he dismisses the idea that the cults are any more irrational than the building of Chartres. In outline, at least, we have here a situational logic account.

(C) *K. O. L. Burridge*. Burridge's work is in many respects a fulfilment of the promise of the previous two authors. Burridge too gives an account of the logic of the situation facing the Melanesians, and his account is the broader and deeper of the three. But as well as this he makes explicit the final bridge between such an account and the role of the prophet which I have had to read into the previous two.

Burridge has two main works on the cults; let us deal with them in order. First, 'Cargo Cult Activity in Tangu'. Like many others, Burridge interprets cargo activity as first and foremost directed

against Europeans. He argues that Tangu (his tribe) see the relationship between black and white as a relationship 'lacking in moral
content'. This is because the Europeans have at their disposal techniques for making great wealth, yet they share neither the techniques
nor the wealth with the natives. Naturally enough these people, with
their co-operative social system, see this withholding of 'secrets' as
profoundly immoral.

Intellectually bewildered, perplexed, their social system in which their
beliefs are embedded partially disrupted by the impact of European culture, yet desirous of European wealth, Tangu attempts, within terms of
their own knowledge and modes of thought, to grasp these techniques.

Burridge felt at this time that the cargo myths were simply rationalisations of what was not understood.

On top of this the natives have a lack of strong political organisation on both community and other levels; but the system only
began to seem inadequate when it was rudely juxtaposed to European
society and subjected to the stresses and strains of culture contact.

Finally in his paper Burridge points out that different economic
activities have, corresponding to them, different alignments of social
structure. After contact, however, the principal structural alignment
became white *versus* black, and the stress tended to bear on *ties*
within the (white or black) community rather than on *cleavages*
within it.

How far does this paper, alone, go towards enabling us fully to
explain cargo cult activity? Burridge is clearly tackling a number of
problems: (*a*) what, in the circumstances, made the situation ripe for
a cult; (*b*) how do we explain the curiously anachronistic mythology
of the cults, i.e. that they are attempts to explain new things in
traditional terms; and (*c*) how is it that these primitive people come
to be capable of the amount of organisation necessary for the cult?

As to (*a*) I think Burridge has argued a good case, particularly in
his emphasis on the resentment aroused by the awareness that the
Europeans are acting immorally. In (*b*) Burridge adds nothing to
Belshaw. Inasmuch as he introduces the idea that the myths are
rationalisations I think he blunders; Belshaw's idea that they are
attempts at explanation seems to me much better and keeps us out of
the 'are the cults irrational' dispute. (*c*), which is a problem Firth
also tackled, does not seem to me to be very serious; it has its
origins in some curious primitive mentality theories which assumed
that, because the natives did not have a centralised political system,
they were incapable of any considerable degree of organisation. But
this inference was never valid. We can pose instead the very interesting but slightly different sociological problem: what factors in the

situation caused these people to organise in this new way? And here, with his structural analysis and stress on the natives being thrown together and finding themselves set over against the whites, I think Burridge is convincing.

In his book *Mambu* Burridge gives a much more elaborate treatment of cargo cults, phrased in very generalised form, although worked out in detail only with respect to his field areas of Tangu and Manam. He sees the situation like this.

Kanakas (New Guinea natives) are in a situation where they need to explain the white man. They need to explain his wealth; they need to explain his moral superiority; and they need to explain their own moral inferiority.

> The attempt by Kanakas to establish their integrity as men in relation to administrative officers and missionaries, forms a large part of the story of a Cargo cult (p. 24).

There seems to be a moral disparity between the Kanakas and the white man which does not only consist in their material differences. For example, in Tangu, to accept the gift is to accept the man and the moral responsibility for repayment. But white men accept repayment only on their own terms, they laugh at native repayments (pp. 39–40). Similarly, the Kanaka is faced with a European ambience in which one of his most important categories—kinship, which implies moral obligation—is almost useless (p. 36). Kanakas' mythology is the sole repository of truth in matters of this kind and so explanations must be sought in terms of it.

Cargo cults have as their immediate cause the white man. When

> Tangu first saw white men and their goods . . . we must record the birth of the Cargo myth-dream. White men and their goods had to be explained and accounted for (p. 125).

But they are also the latest forms an old tradition of the society has taken.

> One should not be too hasty in assuming the Cargo cults are wholly derived from the colonial situation. They may be a cultural inheritance (p. 25).

He argues that much of the Kanakas' 'knowledge' about their history and the world is embodied in their mythology and especially in the Primal Myth, a story of the origin of the people which has a mysterious and symbolic character. This myth is partly a pseudo-history and partly a moral dream. Burridge holds that they interpret much of their experience in terms of this myth and that they use it to justify their moral values. The cargo myth had to be created within Tangu terms—within the myth-dream.

They try to understand their total experience and can only do so in terms of their history—in terms of categories they know. Mere observation is neither memorable nor intelligible unless immediately related to categories of understanding. Expectations—selection of particular categories—play a major part. So Tangu make their observations, render them intelligible, and line them up with expectations. Quite a normal procedure. Only those whose categories and expectations are wider or different may perceive the end result in such a way as to call it mistaken (p. 217).

Apparently into this oral tradition of the Primal Myth has been fed the natives' experience of the white man, especially in the form of missionaries and administrators, and the dreams and expectations the white man has aroused. Until the Japanese invasion nothing much happened after the arrest of Mambu in 1938.

But the myth-dream was developing, foretelling a future and resolving certain problems on the level of myth. . . . Reappraisal was taking place—not as an intellectual activity cogitated, known to be known, but as a largely emotional or spiritual process expressing itself in myth. Tangu were, quite literally, feeling their way (p. 133).

Burridge's thesis is that this process performed a subtle transformation and that the myth of the cargo was the myth-dream made into a full explanation and a call to action. The Primal Myth gives no explanation of the European (Why are we black and poor? What went wrong? p. 40) and does not prescribe any action. While the myth-dream does solve the problems, and the cult-dream provides imperatives to action. But it is not simply goods they want.

That is, access to cargo is not simply access to European goods, but access to European goods within a particular moral relationship (p. 267).

The Kanakas strive for a 'moral renovation' out of which they can shape a new, more satisfying world.

What makes the difference between an all-too-familiar political unrest combined with the economic disability of a multi-racial society, and the occurrence of a Cargo cult, is a sudden onset of moral and emotional passion concentrated to the point of action by and in the sort of man Mambu was (p. xviii).

The Mambus and the Yalis are special in that they, steeped in the myth-dream culture, and having had some contact with the white man, add their charismatic appeal to a showing of the way—the way out of the morally invidious situation. Slowly Melanesia is beginning to grasp something of the general nature of the problem. The ideas are defined and partially articulated by such as Mambu.

It is a mistake, according to Burridge, to see the cults as anti-white. It is a misunderstanding of the moral drama of which the cults are re-enactments. They embody the fundamental desire for a return to moral equality. The Kanakas want the white men to give them equal moral status: they want to be men to the whites as well as among their own people. They do not want to be 'boys' or miscreants. Thus those prophets and those anthropologists who see the cults in terms of a total rejection of the white man and his ways (e.g. Linton) are on the wrong track. Excluding the white man will hardly assist the attempt to gain moral equality with him.

In bald and oversimplified terms the problem of Cargo is, first, how to live in an environment which is neither European nor Kanaka, but something *sui generis* compounded of both; and second, how to transcend the division and make the environment an intelligible unity. Despite the efforts of some charismatic figures . . . the objectives of Cargo cannot be achieved by excluding white men . . . the myth-dream makes it quite clear that the objectives of Cargo can only be achieved with the help of white men . . . the problem is to find ways of co-operation with white men, and to persuade white men to co-operate with them (p. 41).

All the strivings for a unified moral community are defeated by the vicious circle in which the values of the Kanakas, the administrators and the missionaries all seem to be pulling in different directions.

One other problem Burridge tackles is the employment of magical means to gain 'pragmatic' ends. His view, rejecting ideas of fantasy or irrationality, is similar to one I shall expound in Chapter 5. He argues that every constructive activity is accompanied by ritual practices, magical and/or religious. Kanakas' theory of causation is such that they think the crops will not grow, the hunt will not succeed, the wife will not be fertile, unless there is the mystical ceremony as well as the practical act. Thus mystical techniques are integral to their whole culture and survive in the cargo cult.

There are only two points on which I want to take issue with Burridge. The first is his contention that there is a 'level' of myth which is not 'an intellectual activity cogitated' but an 'emotional or spiritual process'. It seems to me, on the contrary, that myths are primitive forms of explanatory theories; they solve a problem about the world. As such they may not be critically discussed like theories but many of the modifications to them must have been attempts to make them better explanations. They are not on a special emotional level, they are thought-constructions, highly animistic explanatory theories usually in an untestable form. Tangu are not 'feeling their way' at a pre- or a-logical level, their prophets and dreamers, within their background of knowledge, are accounting, in a thoughtful way, for some of the features of the world.

The second question-mark I want to put against *Mambu* is closely connected with the first. Burridge talks of Tangu myths containing their (Tangus') 'truths'. This unfortunately leads him on to the idea that each people or culture has its truths—our's for example, are not embodied in myths. He uses this relativism to attack those who see the cults as based on intellectual mistakes or fantasies. Although I am with him in this last move I do not accept his relativism. Myths are hypothetical knowledge, not truths; they are also either false or unfalsifiable hypotheses. This is their relation to our western knowledge. Tangu myths are not intellectual mistakes, they are the best hypotheses the Kanakas can make within their magico-religious horizon of expectations.

Burridge's book is one continuous and coherent argument. The ideas are bold and excitingly expressed. I have not tried to summarise it, merely to single out one or two of his points to illustrate the quality of the thought. The single methodological criticism of him I will make is that he nowhere tries to set out systematically the closely interrelated problems of cargo cults. This is unfortunate as he gives answers to nearly all the questions I have raised elsewhere (Chapter 2, section 8). He could have done this without destroying the narrative power of his book simply by giving them in a list in the preface, and restating his answers in a parallel summary at the end.

Mambu raises one other methodological issue. It is in my view almost methodologically paradigmatic, and by far the best and most thoughtful study of cargo cults yet to be written. But in the journal *Man* it was reviewed in three column-inches by the late F. M. Keesing (1961). He treats us to a very brief summary of the book, unintelligible to anyone who has not read it, written in a slightly disapproving tone as witness the following quotations:

> The factual data are interspersed freely with patches of generalising discussion . . . the presentation tends to be involuted and repetitive. . . . The explanatory terminology [is] heavily psychological, yet adheres to no disciplined psychological system, and the writer acknowledges that his central concept of 'myth-dream' does not 'lend itself to precise definition' (p. 148).

Not only is the reader not told that this is the best, most coherent, and boldest interpretation of cargo cults yet to appear, but it is intimated that there is something wrong with interspersing facts and discussion, with repeating a complicated argument, with having bold psychological ideas which do not adhere to any 'system', and with using an explanatory concept which cannot be precisely defined. Thus Keesing, in reviewing an excellent book, not only fails to realise the fact and thus to appraise his reader of it, he also virtually commits himself to three methodological faults: he wants a separation between facts and discussion; he wants psychology disciplined and not speculative; and he wants his concepts precisely defined. All three points are faults of contemporary social anthropology and discussion of them will be found elsewhere (Jarvie, 1961, *passim*). I have argued that facts cannot sensibly be detached from the discussion which gives them relevance and even meaning; that speculation should be disciplined only by criticism; and I entirely accept Popper's critique of definitions.[1] Even, it seems, when a social anthropologist gets his method right, methodological error in others prevents its being recognised.

Burridge, then, has made a major contribution, *the* major contribution after Belshaw, to the story of cargo cults. Methodologically there is very little wrong with it. To criticise it for leaving points untouched could only be done in a full-length study which did full justice to the scope and complexity of Burridge's argument. At first when I got hold of this book I thought it made much of my meta-methodological criticism of social anthropology redundant, but when I saw how it was reviewed by a major authority in the field I realised that this methodologically paradigmatic exception tended to confirm rather than refute my methodological misgivings. I am only sorry that the present philosophical work is not the place to do the book full justice.

7. Conclusion

Credit where credit is due to the three authors we have just discussed, and their highly rational theories. Discussion of them must close this survey. It has shown, I think, that methodology can, in the form of surveys, be theoretical work in the sense that it helps us sort out and evaluate existing theories and that, by revealing gaps, allows the construction of new theories to fill them. I shall try to clinch this point in the next chapter by constructing a logic of the situation theory which fills the gaps left by Belshaw, Hogbin and Burridge.

[1] In 1946, vol. ii, chapter 11.

4

EXPLANATION AND
EXPLAINING THE CULTS

A large sea-change will undoubtedly come over theoretical anthropology as the outcome of . . . criticisms of 'structuralist' theory. In
studying the cults we simply by-pass . . . functions and structural
coexistences. . . . A complete re-analysis of the Melanesian cults
might . . . come at an interesting and appropriate time.[1]

1. *Criteria of Explanation*

I TRIED in the last section of Chapter 3 to establish that, good
though they are, the theories of Belshaw, Hogbin and Burridge do
not go far enough. Belshaw's theory is unsatisfactory because he
doesn't explain the eschatology, or the failure to abandon the cults;
moreover, while he does say that the Melanesians are trying to solve
an intellectual problem created by the arrival of the Europeans he
does not explain how they are trying to solve it, or why they are trying to solve it eschatologically. Hogbin does not say what the aims
of the prophet are, and he too neglects the recurrence of the cults.
Burridge does not say much on the prophet's aims, and does not
really deal with the recurrence of the cults. These authors are very
good, we all grant that; do I not demand too much by saying that
they are not perfect by my standards of a satisfactory explanation. Are my standards for an explanation not too high? Are they
satisfiable at all? These are the questions which prompt me to produce a theory of my own in this chapter. I do not produce it because
I am in any sense an 'expert' on the cults, or because I think I have
anything material to contribute to the literature on them. I simply
want to produce a theory and show that, simple though it is, it
satisfies my criteria for a satisfactory explanation, and that therefore
my criteria are easily satisfiable.

Most of the authors who have written on the cults, then, do not
satisfy my criteria of satisfactoriness: that the statements of fact

[1] A somewhat rearranged and cut quotation from Stanner, 1958, pp. 14–15.

which need to be explained should follow from the theory, which thus explains them; that the theory should be enlightening; and that it should be testable. Are, perhaps, these criteria too severe? What right have I to set up standards and then judge reputable authors by them? I have no *right*, of course, but I think I can show my move to be reasonable because my criteria are very weak. In the discussion in Chapter 1 I distinguished between truth and satisfactoriness and asserted that we can reasonably only demand the latter. We cannot demand truth, I said, because we can never know when we have got truth and consequently the demand for truth is too strong. To demand satisfactoriness alone is rather weak. All it amounts to is that the proposed solution to the problem should be a solution, that it should be in some sense enlightening and not too *ad hoc*. This demand is very weak. To ask that a solution to a problem should be a genuine (and interesting) solution is hardly to ask much.

As far as I can see if I abandoned or weakened my criteria any further it would be tantamount to giving up. This is why I feel justified in applying the yardstick of satisfactoriness to any theories of cargo cults, no matter who authored them. There seems to me no *hubris* in my pointing out that a number of proposed theories are not satisfactory. The best of these theories, those of Belshaw, Hogbin and Burridge, are nontrivial, noncircular and non-*ad hoc*, but they do fail in that none of them proposes a complete answer to our questions, a solution to all the main problems connected with the cults.

2. *Meeting the Criteria*

The criteria for satisfactoriness are very weak. How is it that these excellent authors have failed to meet them? One answer might be that the criteria are too strong and cannot be met. I have tried to show that not to be the case in the discussion above: the criteria are so weak that if they cannot be met social science might as well give up. On top of this I shall construct in section 5 a theory of my own precisely with the aim of showing that the criteria can be satisfied. My own answer to why the criteria have not been met is that the problems to be solved have never, even in the best works, been fully stated. Nowhere in the literature is there anything at all resembling what I did at the end of Chapter 2, namely setting out the main questions to be asked and marking them off from related questions as sharply as possible. I do not regard my attempt as anything more than a layman's notes, but I think similar notes, had they been in the hands of cargo cult authors, might have improved the situation a good deal.

Why is this business of stating your problems clearly beforehand so important? And if it is so important why is it not done? It is not done for two reasons, really: a historical reason and a methodological reason. The historical reason is that it is forbidden by Francis Bacon's philosophy of science, which is all-pervasive. Even those who are convinced that Bacon was wrong are reluctant to break the baconian tradition of evidence first and problems and theories, disguised as 'conclusions', later. The trouble with this is that 'evidence' has to be selected, whereas according to Bacon's theory it shouldn't be, so that one has to conceal the fact that it is selected. I believe this tradition should be broken. The reason it should be broken is the importance of stating your problems clearly first. This is a simple matter of intellectual discipline. If your 'evidence' will anyway be selected it is much better to articulate the principle of selection in order that it can be examined and utilised consciously and with control. Now the principle of selection will be a statement of the problem, e.g. 'why do prophets found cults?' will tell us to seek material on prophets and their aims, while 'why do cargo cults occur?' may lead us to collect evidence on many other things. Moreover, stating the problem is very often half the battle of providing a solution to it. Thus, by stating the problem clearly, one marshals the evidence consciously with one's audience following every move. If one sticks to Bacon's technique one bemuses the audience with a mass of evidence and then suddenly by sleight-of-hand produces 'conclusions'. One will pretend that the evidence is presented objectively and that therefore the conclusions are somehow 'objective'. This will not do; the principle of selection of the evidence will already have predisposed one to certain kinds of conclusions. If stating the problem in a particular way leads towards a particular solution and thus to the marshalling of the right evidence, so to speak, then this statement or principle must be brought out into the open. This is because a reformulation of the problem might lead to the selection of slightly different evidence and consequently to the overthrow of the 'conclusions' drawn from one's first presentation of the evidence.

This matter of intellectual discipline is of some importance. Bacon's theory is that the most important intellectual discipline is disciplining the intellect. He argues that the intellect is unreliable and tends to jump to conclusions. One must direct all one's efforts to taming it, to preventing these jumps. Convinced as I am that the unprejudiced, unjumping mind is impossible, I adhere to a different theory of what intellectual discipline consists in. I think the main danger is falling prey to Bacon's theory of disguising one's problems and bias and so never knowing exactly what one is doing. One then spends all one's time pursuing useless activities like observation and collection of evidence without any clear idea of what it is for or how to use it. Science is explanatory, I believe, and the most important intellectual discipline is to know what one is trying to explain and how, and then go looking for the relevant evidence. The relevant evidence is not that which fits your formulation and thus your theory, but on the contrary that which runs most against both, which seems most unmanageable. Only by first clearly formulating one's problem can one see what evidence will count against it and so begin observation. The conclusions do not, so to speak, follow from the evidence; like all conclusions, they are, and must be, built into the basis or premises from which the observations start.

Briefly: only when you know what questions are being asked can you try to answer them rationally. Precisely one of the reasons the literature on cargo cults is so large and so diffuse is this business of not stating questions and answers clearly. Indeed it is the explanation of the whole tradition of long-windedness in social anthropology. The tradition, that is, that one has to wade through great tomes of factual material before one gets to the point where the author will explain to you why it was worthwhile to read all that stuff. In some cases one is told that the material is there because that happens to be the author's fieldwork area and one may justly get angry, for anything of interest turned up is being confessed to be incidental. More often than not, though, it is painfully obvious that authors have slavishly followed Bacon and drawn their 'conclusions', i.e. decided why they wrote the book, last. Then, instead of going over it again and cutting out everything not relevant to the conclusions, they leave it in that original state. This results in many anthropological works being eminently suitable for skip reading. It also means one has to read the last chapter first—which is a minor quirk one has to tolerate with far too many books—if one is ever to get at their problems.

To conclude: because social anthropologists follow the baconian tradition they have not said explicitly what they want and so they have failed to get it. They did want satisfactory explanation but being unclear about that want and about what it is they failed to get it. Let me explain.

3. *Stating the Problems*

State the problems first, I have argued. Failure to do this has led to failure to meet the criteria of satisfactoriness. Given that this is so, what are the problems? I do not mean that question in the sense of a repetition of Chapter 2, section 8, but in the sense of 'what *kind* of problems have we here?' Clearly we have the general problem of social change and the less general one of the rise of millenarian religion. The previous statement is very vague; indeed it is so vague that many authors, who started with one problem, taking it that some equivalent of my previous statement is a sufficient specification of those problems, went on to solve different ones. But even in problems specified in more detail such waywardness is not uncommon. Mooney, for example, set out to explain the Sioux Ghost Dance, gave an elaborate explanation of why there was unrest (the Ghost Dance did occur in a time of unrest), and forgot to explain how the unrest led to the Dance. He then shoved in, quite *ad hoc*, the remark that a tribe in the vicinity of the Sioux had a messiah cult which caught on among the restless Sioux—he didn't explain that either. Again, A. C. Haddon sets out to explain five new religious cults; first he shows how messianism arises when there is religious fervour, and he says religious fervour is a frequent characteristic of periods of social unrest, but he never says why. One more example: Ralph Linton's aim was to explain nativistic cults: he distinguished four kinds and said they were attempts to revive or perpetuate traditional values, but gave no guide as to why attempts to revive or perpetuate traditional values should give rise to cults.[1] Of course there are authors, like Firth or Mair, who do state their problems and try to answer them. This indicates, I think, that I should be even more specific in my allegations.

Many authors, for example, believe their problem is how to explain social change. They find this very difficult and tend to flounder over it. I believe their problem should be how to explain social change*s*, in the plural, not in the singular. This change of formulation is significant. On the one hand an abstract and intractable problem. On the other, some people in particular circumstances whose changed actions have to be accounted for. Yet, though I think change in general is difficult, I agree that millenarianism in general is not; I think Cohn and Mair are on the right lines in their assumption that millenarianism is a general problem which has to be tackled overall and the solutions applied to particular cases of this kind of social change. Be that as it may, it seems to me that such discussions, concerning what is the problem and what kinds of solution may or may not be expected can be of considerable value *in getting solutions*. For example, to realise we want to explain this or that social change and need not bother with *the* explanation of social

[1] Robert Brown (1963) argues a related point in his chapter on functionalism. He shows how social anthropologists sometimes explain by reference to an effect something has, and how they neglect to argue the essential corollary that this effect can only be gained by this one means. The neglect means that the explanation is no explanation at all (since the conclusion does not follow from the premiss), but a mere conjunction.

change allows us to breathe more freely. I shall now discuss this matter within the framework of situational logic.

4. *How to Explain Social Changes*

Within the methodological approach of situational logic adopted here any problem of social changes presents no special methodological problems: social changes can be caused by any number of things; e.g. a vast new mineral discovery and the repercussions of its exploitation; the white man invading and conquering; the white man leaving; an influx of alien troops fighting other alien troops; the introduction of widespread education; an attempt to levy taxes; a depression in the world price of a principal export; the appearance of a new and appealing religion; and so on. Social change can consist either in changes in people's social behaviour or in changes in the society itself. But if it is changes in the society itself it will only show itself through changes in the behaviour of people. We will examine why this should be.

Less obviously, I think, situational logic can also take care of the general event of millenarian religion, as I shall show later.

If we accept the premiss of methodological individualism that all human behaviour must be explained in terms of human decisions, aims, actions, etc., then *changes* in the behaviour of people should be explained by analysing the situations of, say, the anonymous individuals who have initiated the chain-reaction of happenings that is the social change, in order to see what factors in their situation persuaded them that one course of action was more appropriate to achieving their aims than another. Social change will not be explained by accounts of natural events like earthquakes, disease or famine. That natural events have social consequences cannot just be assumed, it must be shown; famines or plagues do not automatically affect the social structure and if they do affect it then it is not necessarily in predictable ways. *Natural events only have social consequences because they affect the situations and thus the decisions of certain individuals who, on account of this, choose or are constrained to act differently from the way they acted previously.* Only thus it seems to me, do changes in social life come about from natural causes.

To put it another way. Culture contact or culture clash should not be looked on as resembling a collision between the molecules of a gas. Societies are collections or structures of individuals; 'societies' cannot collide with each other. In much the same way atoms cannot clash with each other (social institutions can and do clash, e.g. two armies, or the army and the police; but societies are not institutions). Societies are perhaps more helpfully regarded as fields of social forces, much as fundamental particles are these days seen as points in fields of force which can 'approach' one another, but never touch. To push the analogy, our social fields are made up of the aims, attitudes, circumstances and behaviour of people. Western society, for example, clashes with primitive society only through its agents; through the impact western individuals and their ideas make on the natives. This impact can take two forms which are best distinguished. It can remould their social situation and not interfere with their aims at all. An example of this would be the setting up of District Commissioners in place of chiefs. Assume that this creates a situation in which the aim 'I must not fall foul of the highest authority' would still operate. Still, actions which did not annoy the District Commissioner might be quite different from those which did not annoy the chief. In such a situation the westerners—the District Commissioner and others—and their ideas can actually change the native life-ends, their aims: it can make them materialistic, or property-conscious, and subsequently they can radically alter their behaviour to gain these ends.

We can see in this example the importance of the distinction between alteration of the situation and alteration of the aims, although both can explain changed behaviour. Because of this distinction we need to know, before explaining the cargo cult, what ends people were pursuing before the cult arrived, and we can assume, as a tentative hypothesis, that these were not changed. If their ends have not changed then their changed actions must be due to a changed situation and we should see whether that hypothesis adequately accounts for the changed behaviour. If it does not then we must reopen the possibility of the aims having been changed. We must then carefully distinguish problems concerning *how and why* their aims have changed, from problems concerning the *effects* this change has had on behaviour and society. As to the latter, the social organisation, the economic structure, the political structure, the state of knowledge and belief, etc., must all be explored to see if they show evidence of change. Almost certainly if aims *have* changed changes will be found in these areas. This will amount to a new social situation or set-up and the behaviour appropriate to realising the new aims in this new situation has to be worked out with all its consequences, intended and unintended, expected and unexpected, wanted and unwanted, in the hope that *this* will amount to an account of the social change.

Perhaps a brief comment should be added at this point on my discussion of change of aims.[1] Change of aims has not been much

---

[1] I have been greatly assisted in working out this discussion by Dr. Agassi; indeed, this, and the next paragraph, is almost a joint effort.

discussed in the literature on situational logic. Let me review briefly the development of situational logic and what has been used to explain what. The idea of situational logic comes really from economics and Max Weber. Weber said that unwanted social phenomena could be explained as the unintended consequences of the actions of the constituent individuals of the ideal type. Collingwood was the author who explicitly extended this situational explanation to actions, like Caesar's crossing the Rubicon, although the idea is perhaps implicit in Weber. Weber's position is not clear either on the matter of actions or of institutions. Change baffles Weber's theory, because it is a theory of static *types*. Therefore, in order to account for change he has to account for the rise of a new ideal type, and this is his theory of charisma. Popper's great discovery is that aims and ideal types are not enough to explain action; circumstances, material *and* institutional, are required in the explicans. Institutions are, so to speak, a third force in the society and their existence and importance is the reason sociology is autonomous with respect to psychology. Popper also agrees with Weber that aims are purely individual things, they cannot be attributed to institutions *qua* institutions (as opposed to the members of institutions). Popper handles change very easily within his theory which uses actions, aims and unintended consequences. He says social change is either: (*a*) an unintended consequence of some other changes—e.g. in circumstances or in other people; or (*b*) intended social engineering brought about by people acting deliberately; or (*c*) the development of new ideas which become a part of public opinion whether moral or scientific. Popper also shows how situational logic can explain aims as being subordinate to other aims. Popper also has explained, in lectures, how there is something like a hierarchy of aims, some more fundamental than others and therefore explicable in terms of them. For example, in a society where money determines status, anyone seeking status will first of all seek money; so the aim to get more money can be explained by the more fundamental aim of the desire for status. In the above discussion I have gone one step further and said we can explain change of aims as unintended consequences of other changes.

Already then, it has been suggested that actions can be explained by aims and circumstances, that circumstances can be explained in terms of previous circumstances, aims, actions and unintended consequences, that aims can be explained in terms of other aims. However, I have not seen sufficient discussion of the other possibility which I need to open up: the explanation of changes of aims as a result of acting to realise other aims in particular circumstances, namely as unintended consequences. Popper, so far as I can gather, tends to say that we can explain some aims by means of others, but

113

that there is a sort of limit to this process in that some aims have to be given. This is all quite true but it does not exclude the rational explanation of change of aims.

People in Melanesia, for example, may join Christianity in order to get access to the material wealth of the Christian Europeans. One unintended consequence of this move of theirs is that they become Christians; striving to use Christianity as a means it, in fact, alters their ends. It may, for example, get them to drop the idea of a material millennium. Again, the pursuit of one aim, 'do not fall foul of the highest authority', may again lead to a change of other aims. The European highest authority may demand different things and so aims may be changed by involvement with these things.

There is nothing very new or startling being said here. Indeed everything follows rather obviously from the idea of situational logic. However, I think this model for the explanation of change of aims is enlightening and needs to be clearly stated.

I now pass to the explanation of cargo cults. I shall not be trying to solve all the problems listed in Chapter 2, section 7. Rather I shall present a framework of theory and interpretation from which my answers to *some* of these problems will follow directly; answers to the others require a detailed factual treatment which I am not trying to give. But in any case, I shall try my best to make it clear to which problems each discussion pertains.

5. *An Explanation of Cargo Cults*

[In] the closed society, . . . the conscious design of institutions is a most exceptional event if it happens at all.
—K. R. Popper, 1946, vol. ii, p. 94.

In this section I first outline why I think cargo cults occur (A), then why they have the doctrines they do (B), then why they are similar (C), then why they are apocalyptic (D). My purpose, as I said, is merely to produce an example which satisfies the minimal criteria of satisfactoriness.

Cults, we have seen, centre round prophets. People listen and do what the prophet asks them—(A) Why? Because what he says is in accord with their general outlook and solves their urgent problems. (B) Why then are cargo cult doctrines what we know them to be? Because they were created as hypotheses to explain certain facts, solve certain problems raised by the presence of the white man. The explanations are within the magico-religious framework of the culture. (C) Why then are the cults similar from place to place? Because of diffusion; the diffused ideas are accepted so frequently because they suit these relatively homogeneous social situations well. (D) Why are the cults apocalyptic and millenarian? My suggestion is because of the situation which arises when a closed society is undergoing change. Before going into detail I have to say a few words to explain Popper's idea.

In a closed society the distinction between what is *natural* and what is *conventional* is not clearly made; in it what is made by Nature and what is human convention are often mixed up. But mixed-up only in one direction: the conventional is taken as natural but the natural is not taken as conventional. That is, the distinction between natural occurrences, like the annual cycle of the seasons, or the succession of night and day, are not marked off from human conventions, like the political organisation of the society, the taboos, the kinship terminology, and so on. The blurring of this natural/conventional distinction is purely asymmetrical; everything is assimilated into the natural category. The idea of humanly invented conventions is almost unknown; and it is characteristic of the closed society that those things which *we* happen to know are nothing more than human conventions are often surrounded by an aura of magic and taboo which insulate them from criticism and change.[1]

This description of the open and the closed societies may seem very obvious. The difference is between laws of nature and laws of man. There cannot, it seems, have been a closed society, because everyone knows the difference between laws of nature and laws of man. The difference is very simple, the one law you can break, the other law you cannot break. Any of us can see that difference. I, on the contrary, would like to assert that most of the societies known to man have been closed in my sense. The closed society is one where the belief is that the taboos can, of course, be broken, but that this action in itself will bring down the thunderbolt or the divine vengeance. To break the taboos is to destroy oneself, one may as well go and jump from a palm tree, for the outlook is hopeless.

[1] One of the ways of characterising the difference between natural science and social science is to note that the former deals far more with the problems of nature, while the latter's typical problems are conventional (except where there is interaction of the natural and the conventional). Most of the problems of social science are connected with social conventions. A natural scientist might be said to try to explain the known and observable in terms of the unknown and possibly unobservable—a very daring procedure. The social scientist, on the other hand, largely concerns himself with explaining the puzzling in terms of the not so puzzling. This may be why I agree with Frazer in regarding magic and religion as being very close to science—because they are both theories about the unknown which try to explain the known. It may also explain why many scholars reject Frazer's view, namely because they still hold an unmysterious (i.e. inductivist) view of science, as opposed to their view of the 'mysteries' of religion. Such prejudices should quickly break down in face of the mysterious worlds of the atomic, quantum and relativity theories.

In this sense of 'closed' surely most societies have been closed. In Christianity we have the theory that the moral laws and taboos are God's laws and that to break them will bring down the divine vengeance, sooner or later.

> In 1915 an earthquake of exceptional violence destroyed a large part of our province and killed, in thirty seconds, about fifty thousand people. I was surprised to see how much my fellow-villagers took this appalling catastrophe as a matter of course. The geologists' complicated explanations, reported in the newspapers, aroused their contempt. In a district like ours, where so many injustices remain unpunished, people regarded the recurrent earthquakes as a phenomenon requiring no further explanation. In fact, it was astonishing that earthquakes were not more frequent. An earthquake buries rich and poor, learned and illiterate, authorities and subjects alike beneath its ruined houses. Here lies, moreover, the real explanation of the Italians' well-known powers of endurance when faced with the cataclysms of nature. An earthquake achieves what the law promises but does not in practice maintain—the equality of all men.
> —Ignazio Silone, in Crossman (ed.), 1950, p. 98.

No thought is given to the fact that these rules and taboos are man-made and can be man-changed. How Christians convince themselves that man-induced changes that have happened are right (the moral prohibition on sex getting relaxed, for example) I do not know. Again, the Nuer know that to kill is to put oneself into an impure or sullied state and that only by the prescribed ritual cleansing can a man remove the stain. All this is naturalistic rather than conventional. Even in the Old Testament we find strong traces of these ideas in the cries of the prophets that the lord will take vengeance on the wicked.

(A.1) *Millenarianism in general.* If social change presents no special problems but has to be handled in detail, what about millenarianism? I believe that millenarianism presents no special difficulties but has to have an overall theory to explain it as a general phenomenon. What has to be explained is the promise of the millennium and people's interest in it. My theory is very simple. Assume that a given population suffers from some kind of stress such that they find their present condition of life insufferable. Assume further that the members of this population cannot imagine their present way of life gradually getting better but can only focus on dreams of an unreal world better in every respect than this one. A transition between the two, other than an apocalypse, they cannot imagine. Then, perhaps, they are ripe for a millenarian prophecy. Assume that what could happen is that one person, more ingenious than most, who also believes in the collective dreams of a better world, suddenly understands how the apocalypse can be brought about. He needs to draw on this common reservoir of dreams in the society if his claim to show how to realise them is to strike a chord and activate the population. Burridge has given this reservoir of dreams the excellent name 'myth-dream'. The myth-dream is, like a myth, objective and known to at least a large part of the population; it is also like a dream because it is a hope, an aspiration of the almost-unreal future. Our ingenious person, like to set himself up as a prophet-leader, must also draw, when he explains his theory of how the millennium can be realised, on the background beliefs of his fellows. They must accept his method as an understandable idea (say, a certain magical practice) and, obviously, it must be within their material resources or he will just be crying for the moon.

This theory is within the framework of situational logic. It postulates certain circumstances in which people are dissatisfied and are dreaming, but where there seems to them to be no possible rational transition from the one to the other, other than by way of an apocalypse. Their situation is intolerable; their aim is the dream. Then comes a prophet who proclaims that they can realise their aim. The aims and circumstances of the population, then, and the intrusion of the prophet are enough to explain the millenarian cult. But we want to trap a small fish in this millenarian pool: the cargo cult. Now what is special about the cult and how do we explain (trap) it? The main thing that is special is the particular form the millenarian dream takes, and the particular form of rite which, it is thought, will bring on the apolcaypse.

(A.2) *Cargo cults in particular.* The special phenomenon of cargo cults might arise in the following way. Assume a society which is small, homogeneous economically, politically, and culturally, which is suddenly pushed into a colonial situation. Either the whites come and take over, or they call occasionally at the islands and behave in an authoritative manner, or word that they do these things precedes their arrival. These white men are a surprise. Belshaw vividly describes the figure they cut: they are wealthy, successful and powerful, and they do not act towards the natives as men are expected to act. Their strange behaviour and appearance runs counter to native expectations of other men. This behaviour, especially in connection with their possessions, which seem to have power, is envied and copied in an attempt to get the possessions, to get the power, to become equal. The attempt fails; the problem remains: how to get them? Into this situation there suddenly comes a man who solves their problem, who says that he knows why the whites are so successful and how the copying can be made successful.

The significance of the white men is that they are external agents. Why should the social change not be spontaneous? Obviously because we are dealing, in Melanesian cargo cults, with the problem of social change in a closed society; that is to say, with an upset in the social system of a society that is old, stable, and has deeply-rooted ways and traditions.[1] Since *ex definitione* social change can occur only in the field of what we know as the conventional (which is not to say that its causes need be conventional) it becomes obvious why very little spontaneous social change ever occurs in the closed society; those things that people might want changed are so hedged about with tabooistic magic that some external agent almost *has* to be introduced if change is to succeed in coming about. Given that society has a certain on-going impetus (institutions are modified, people succeed each other in roles) then only some powerful natural cause like famine or flood can bring about social change. No individual deliberately brings about and moulds the direction of change (in normal conditions) because the society is so organised that individuals can hardly think in such terms. There is one possible exception to this, namely, the exceptional; the man with a liberating genius. We know that it is perfectly possible, human capacities being what they are, for someone to transcend the limitations of his education and upbringing. This sort of person, if he is not suppressed, can be the initiator of vast movements and social changes. All the founders of the world religions are examples and so, surely, are the prophets of some of our cargo cults. It is possible that in this way some sort of spontaneous social change, i.e. change independent of outside influence, is brought about. But on the whole with cargo cults, the doctrine and techniques of the prophets smack very much of the West and its religions and so we are perhaps justified in pooh-poohing this possibility of spontaneity. Moreover, to use this explanation you have, as I do, to believe in the unfashionable doctrine of the power and influence of ideas, especially new, or liberating ideas.

Perhaps the presence of the white man, and his very individualistic way of behaving, impresses the native, who now wishes to emulate this acquisitive individualist. When this happens we seem to be witnessing the breakdown of the closed society, and the attitudes it engenders, under the pressures created by constant failures to explain things within its *intellectual* framework of religion, magic and taboo. White men have to be explained. All the closed society can produce is new magico-religious doctrines. As explanations these do not produce the goods—they fail. Faced with this situation the men of the

[1] It is not 'closed' in the ordinary sense of that word, like China or Japan were, since white men have irrupted into it.

118

closed society are critical—*of the man, not the theory*.[1] They argue that it was the charlatan *x* who tricked us, who deceived us, with a false doctrine. The general theory of magico-religious explanation underlying the particular doctrine is not challenged.[2] But over and over again this approach fails. The very desperation apparent in the way some areas have an accelerating series of cults, each lasting less time than before, can easily be pictured as the death throes of the closed society. The upshot is that people lose faith, or that their resources are exhausted, or the authorities are repressive, or the cults become mystical, or some or all of these. Perhaps eventually someone hits on the idea of overtly political action which manages to get results before all enthusiasm has been drained away. For a time he still has to cloak it as a cult. Sooner or later, though, it turns out that straight political demands, and actions (pressures, strikes, theft),[3] are far more effective than doctrine and ritual.

Whatever else may be said, it is generally agreed that basically cargo cults are, in one form or another, a reaction to, or form of, social change in the closed societies of Melanesia; social change brought about, somehow, by the impact of western civilisation. It is my view that cargo cults are among the first social institutions in the societies where they arise to be consciously designed, created and manipulated by man. They are the first stirrings of a (quasi-) conventionalist attitude to things social. The reasons why such a tacit recognition of conventionalism takes the form of a religious innovation is that explanations of the world are sought in religious terms there; and so it is religious offices which are sought when changes come about. Social change is prior and creates a problem: then comes a religious explanation of it: and a religious solution to it. Here we have a clear-cut case of a social institution being set up in order to realise certain ends—in this case the obtaining of cargo. It is not the case that the people setting up the cult know that their

[1] Here again they show their precritical attitude; to attribute the failure of a theory to its evil or conspiring inventor is naïve. This is not to say that it has been anything like superseded even today. Cf. my various remarks and references *re* inductivism.

[2] To quote Attenborough (see p. 123, n. 3): 'It's nineteen years now since John Frum first promised that he would bring the cargo,' I said. 'He hasn't brought it yet. Aren't you getting a little worried?' Sam looked at me for several seconds before replying. 'If you can wait two thousand years for Jesus Christ to come,' he said, 'I can wait more than nineteen years for John Frum.'

[3] Cp. Burridge, 1960, pp. 30–1: 'Others . . . have seen that if mystical techniques cannot obtain the cargo then other means may have to be used.' He relates how in Bogia prudent cult organisers stole goods and cash and laid them up in a secret *cache* for use when the time came. This time the cargo *was* to materialise.

means are inadequate or inappropriate to the realisation of their ends; on the contrary, they are fully convinced that they are.

To put it differently: we can see, in cargo cults, the seeds of the first step towards 'the open society' in that the merging of nature and convention has been broken down by this creation of a social institution. Furthermore, when the cults, which constitute a solution to a problem, *fail* (or are refuted), and fail over and over again, *criticism* of them is likely to get under way. Admittedly not, as yet, criticism of their whole magico-religious basic hypothesis.[1] Still, there is no need to assume that the criticism will continue to overlook this common assumption or the large areas of common ground between the doctrines of successive cults which have arisen (in the same area).

Where the cults have come under strong or even militaristic leaders the whites have found them provocative and have often violently suppressed them. Most of the societies concerned are acephalous, i.e. not politically centralised, and it was easy for a powerful cult to forge a new hierarchical system of its own which completely cut across the old ties and boundaries between people, and thus channelled their loyalty in a new direction. In this way the movements become, in white eyes, political. Some form of central organisation is attempted which can channel the natives' demands.

But this is not to say that the cargo cult is essentially the attempt to centralise acephalous societies. In other parts of the world acephalous societies coexist alongside centralised societies without either copying its organisation from the other; there is thus some doubt that the Kanakas are attempting to organise what the white men would recognise as a centralised form of political resistance to them. In other words, the theory that Melanesian society is becoming politically more central simply because it is adjacent to a centralised society is unsatisfactory. The following hypothesis may help to fill this gap.

White society understands and responds to the language of political demands better than it responds to the language of magic and religion. I think this is clearly so; the disputes and problems of western society are very largely politicised where the native would resolve them by appeal to magic or taboo. It is this that the cultists, after a succession of failed cults, may come across more or less by trial and error. They learn that a cult which overtly goes after what it wants, and stages it in political terms *vis à vis* white society, will get more results (if not always perhaps the results desired, but how can

---

[1] In the face of refutations there is always a tendency to tinker with details rather than to question the whole background knowledge or basic interpretation of the world—in this case the magico-religious world view.

they know that)[1] than will a purely religious cult which the whites don't understand and therefore tend to write off. For example, if a cult's predicted aeroplane just does not come then the prophet may be hounded out of the society. But if he organises his cult and directs its activities in such a way that the whites will react,[2] then he has both a good excuse for failure and, in effect, a greater chance of success in that the whites might take notice of the problem and yield up some of their secrets. And if they put the prophet in gaol no one will ever be able to say *his* cult failed. Politicisation is not, then, I would say, a natural outcome of the cults, but something some cultists learn.

It is not the only thing they learn from the white man, they also, I would argue, pick up some of the individualistic ideology of the white men who have so suddenly irrupted into their society.

This is another way of putting the 'movement towards the open society' thesis. In the West religion acts as a mechanism whereby within the open society certain closed subsocieties are defined and maintained. Here, in Melanesia, we have a closed society. Query: is the cult movement something like a collective reaction to the impact of the individualistic open society brought by the European? The European breaks down the cohesion of the old society by undermining its organising principles of kinship, loyalty to parents, respect for elders and so on—which are collectivist; he introduces money, acquisitiveness, wage labour and Christianity (a new in-group)—which are individualistic. Are cargo cults the first desperate attempt to sustain or re-establish the collectivism of the closed society in the face of this new force? Are they nativistic—i.e. in so far as the closed society is nativistic? It might seem that in face of the undermining pressures of white behaviour and ideology cults grow up which hope to resist or overcome them by a sort of total yielding. Only, they reason, when the practices and goods of the Europeans are delivered over to us will the European himself be delivered over to us, and only when the European is delivered over to us will his pernicious influence be stayed. The cult is the answer because religion is as yet their only answer to anything; it is their intellectual panacea.

Earlier (in section 4) I suggested that the cults might be explained as caused by changes in the objective situation or in the aims of the people involved, or both. One way in which aims could be changed would be if, with Christianity, the peculiarly western neurotic concern about the future was imported. Preoccupation with the future

---

[1] After all, present-day African nationalists know that provoking the Europeans is better than letting things slide—when a fuss is caused attention is paid to their case.
[2] E.g. Marching Rule, which is well described in Inglis, 1957.

is a characteristic of western society; people plan for it, save for it, and are always looking forward to it. This outlook, which has us in such strong grip, could well have stemmed from Christianity: a religion that constantly stresses present sacrifice for future rewards. Other roots may be found for it, no doubt; what is sure is that it is not the only possible view of life. Another and equally powerful one takes life as essentially cyclical and looks no further than the next harvest or the next winter. Such an outlook is characteristic of many primitive people, and judging from the literature, of much of Melanesia. What I am suggesting is that cargo cults are in part a result of attempts to assimilate the western philosophy of the future; the Melanesians catch the white man's futurity neurosis.[1] The result of this neurosis is that people come to evaluate much of the present in terms of its future worth.

This is a new and quite fetching idea to the Melanesians, I conjecture, but in its pure Christian form a little sophisticated. However, when it is made concrete—when the offer is not of spiritual joy in a mysterious life after death, but of material wealth in six weeks' time—it is both more intelligible and more attractive. The impact of this new way of looking at things and its sudden crystallisation in a very attractive form go some way, I suggest, to explain the rapid and enthusiastic reception of the cargo cult.

We can then see how different the Melanesian cargo cults are, for example, from the potlatch. The potlatch is a curious kind of feast held among N.W. Coast American Indian tribes. The lavishness of the feast is a measure of status. Those who have been to a feast are obliged to repay their hosts with something larger. There is thus a competition in feasts. This competition also consists in conspicuous consumption or wastage of valuable items, like the copper objects of the potlatch. To throw away and destroy things during the feast is a way of gaining prestige.

On the surface there is much that resembles the potlatch in cargo cults. There is the consumption of food stocks, the throwing away of money, and even the burning of houses (also sometimes an event in a particularly spectacular potlatch). But the reasons behind these two sets of similar actions are completely different. The cargo cultists gain no prestige by their actions: they do it as a gesture of their faith in the Coming. They sacrifice the present in an effort to control the future. In the potlatch the attitude seems to be more like, to hell with the future, what counts is my prestige now! This shows, I think, that ritual cannot properly be studied and understood, let alone be explained, without bringing in belief.

[1] I owe the idea of the 'futurity neurosis' to Professor Popper.

(B) *Cult doctrine.* Cargo cult myths are theories, hypotheses, conjectures, guesses—I use these words interchangeably.[1] All theories are the result of trying to solve a problem. Cargo cult doctrines are hypotheses to explain the problem, 'what is white society and how does it get the wonderful material things it has?' The theories explain where these things came from and how. The theories lead to viewing certain actions as being appropriate to call forth the required goods for black society as well. These actions, when performed, or rather these consequences, constitute *tests* of the theories on the basis of which they are performed.[2]

On the whole the cultists are very poor people. And on the whole colonial whites are far from being poor. The native sees the white man in his comfortable house talking into a box. Later a ship appears loaded with all sorts of desirable goods. The native perceives that the white man associates the two events. He says 'ship' into the box and expects a ship to appear; and sure enough a ship appears. He specifies his cargo requirements into the box confidently expecting them; and lo, the ship is carrying just these. Obviously this is very powerful magic. (Indeed, science was advocated by people like Porta, author of *Natural Magick*, and Bacon, as magic which, because it works, is more powerful.) Note that I conjecture that the native thinks of it entirely in terms of magical causation, because such is the state of his theoretical knowledge. Therefore, there seems to me to be no particular difficulty in explaining why he goes off into the jungle, gathers all the people around, declares he has at last fathomed the white man's magic, makes a crude model of the box, gabbles into it and then tells everyone to come to the seashore to build a jetty at which the expected ship can unload its cargo.[3] The assumption of his ignorance and naïveté explains it all.

[1] I use them interchangeably only when I am speaking about their logic, which is identical. There are, of course, differences. Belief in myths, as Dr. Hogbin has pointed out to me, is obligatory if one is to retain membership of some religious groups. This can hardly be said of most hypotheses and theories, although it has happened.

[2] Strictly speaking statements about action (or about anything else) cannot be deduced from, and therefore be explained by, theories alone; they can only be deduced from theories plus initial conditions; but we need not worry about this here.

[3] In *The Sunday Times* of April 24, 1960, David Attenborough (Attenborough, 1960) quotes a missionary as follows:

'They are started by things like this,' the missionary said, picking up the shiny paraffin lamp that stood on the camp table. 'A New Guinea native, who has lived all his life in the Stone Age [an unfortunate parenthesis in an otherwise unexceptionable statement], sees this lamp—or a refrigerator, a can of beer, a motor-car, or a radio-set—and he is totally bewildered.

'When he examines it in detail it is quite clear to him that such a thing is not of human origin—how could you possibly chip or weave a chromium-plated

The prophet exhorts them before performing his magic to have faith in him, to do what he tells them and to give him certain commodities. This they do. I think we can assume that they obey him because what he promises, the problems he claims to have solved, are so close to their hearts, something they want so much, that they are prepared to do almost anything to get it (including, as we have seen, large-scale building, giving the prophet women and produce, and destroying money, produce and animals).

That such a cult, once begun, should develop, be elaborated, rigidified or transformed, is not at all surprising in view of our knowledge of the typical way the world religions have developed.

A slightly more cynical interpretation of this utilisation of European magic to obtain European goods can be given when the additional factor of Christian missionary activity is introduced. It is possible to assume that native peoples associate European power and prosperity with European religion (especially when they hold a general theory of causation which is magico-religious). They join the European's religion in the hope that they will thereby obtain similar benefits. When, however, these benefits fail to materialise, it is not unreasonable to assume, they think some trick is being put over on them by the missionary (we have already argued that they do not consistently apply a critical attitude to their theories but prefer to criticise individuals for seeming-refutations); the more especially if,

---

lamp like this? If it isn't man-made, he says to himself, then it must have come from the gods.

'But why should it only come to the white man? The white man does no work. Instead he does stupid, useless things: he sits in front of a metal box with dials on it and listens to it making odd noises; he dresses people up in identical clothes and marches them up and down.

'And then the New Guinea man devises an explanation. These activities are a peculiar ritual which the white man performs to make sure that the gods send to him all these strange new goods—or, to use the pidgin word, the cargo. That is the secret.

'Therefore, if the native wants the cargo, he must do the same things. So he dresses himself up in pathetic improvised uniforms; he talks into tin cans in the same way as a European talks into a microphone. He believes that an ancestor or a god—a sort of messiah—will bring all the cargo and give it to the tribe.

'As everybody will have everything they want when the cargo comes, there is no need to work any more. No one goes to the mission school. When the apocalypse comes, the whites will be thrown out or be the servants of the natives, so the authority of the District Officer is ignored. The people spend their time building dummy airstrips and great warehouses to receive the cargo when it comes.'

Attenborough criticises this explanation for being too simple and logical; what other qualities an explanation should have in addition or instead he does not say.

124

as is common, although they are allowed access to Christianity, the colour bar prevents them from worshipping in the white men's churches. This looks to them as though they are being excluded from initiation into the true mysteries of the white man. By a trick, it is conjectured, the True Christianity—which delivers the cargo—is being concealed from us—so as to prevent us from having the cargo. Consequently, attempts are made to find the True Christianity without the help of the white man; all sorts of hypotheses about what is being concealed are formulated; some of these hypotheses are of a baffling mixture of naïveté and ignorance with cleverness and ingenuity. The idea that the first page of the Bible has been deliberately torn out of all the natives' Bibles and suppressed is particularly common. An explanation of it may be as follows. Great stress is laid by the missionaries on the importance and truth of what the Bible says on everything—yet there is, curiously, no mention of the native peoples in it. This puzzles the natives. God, the creator of all, would surely have mentioned the natives (cf. the motto of Chapter 2); *ergo*, some of God's word has been suppressed. And it is this suppression of essential injunctions or spells which prevents the natives getting the cargo and which enables the white man to stay on top. As a result of such reasoning, breakaway, but still recognisably Christian sects start up, which claim to have discovered the contents of the suppressed passages.

Again, the natives' lack of knowledge of white ways, the white indifference to this and to them, the natives' old beliefs in ancestors and spirits, have had to be grafted on to hypotheses of a simplicity marred only by the tragic consequences of their falsity.

We can also tackle the problem of the content of the cult doctrine (the promises of goods and of power) with the following further psychological explanation. We could present a theory which states that the Melanesians are in some sense projecting their political aspirations, their political demands for the end of colonial rule and/or the 'benefits' of colonial rule, into a religious form, the only explanation-form they know. The theory would further state that, given sufficiently astute leaders, the people can be organised behind such a cause in a way that is already politico-religious. This theory would complement, while remaining independent of, the theory that they are learning the efficacy of the language of political demands.

(C) *Similarities of the cults.* Within this framework, what can we say about why the cults follow similar patterns and preach similar things? Earlier we have seen that these could be explained either by evolution, or by diffusion. I now want to argue for a combination of both. There is no reason, it seems to me, for jettisoning 'directional' evolution. If we recall the discussion (in Chapter 1) of our short kinship memories in this country, and that we explained this by reference to disuse, the reason for preserving evolution in our explanations will become clear. Here was what looked like the macrophenomenon of a society dropping a useless institution; what we had was the microphenomenon of people in a situation such that there were no reasons for them to go on doing something—something which took time and effort. Some institutions, perhaps because they take up no time and effort, or because they take more time and effort to get rid of, or replace, than to go on with them, have a sort of inertia; they continue to exist after they are redundant even in a competitive system, or a system with the survival of the fittest. Fitness need not be simply a matter of eliminating the useless, it may also be a matter of not bothering to do anything about what doesn't get in the way. It is a mistake, I believe, to imagine societies as like racing cars in which every non-essential part is a burden: there are survivals even in the healthiest of surviving societies. In this way, it seems to me, some aspects of the present state of society can be explained as outcomes of a limited sort of evolution which is to be understood as a macro-effect or magnification of what goes on at the more fundamental level of situational logic. If so, then there is no reason why the cultural and linguistic homogeneity of Melanesia might not have a lot to do with the fact that the originally similar peoples who populated the area, having faced similar sorts of situations, evolved in very similar ways. But, as I have said, the application of evolutionism within situational logic is limited because the pure darwinian account of the elimination of everything inessential does not apply. The human beings who make up the society are not efficient mechanisms for carrying out adjustments because they do not always make that their overriding aim.

Secondly, the *prima facie* implausibility of diffusion can also be disposed of. Here in Melanesia we have similar peoples in similar locations and situations, and, in particular, speaking the same language: pidgin. They are nearly all exposed to a diffused culture: the culture of the white traders, priests, and administrators. These latter, too, especially to the Melanesians, are extraordinarily homogeneous, quite apart from the fact that in contrast with the natives all Europeans are almost identical. Moreover the priests, traders and administrators, with their radios, planes, boats and loud voices *were themselves the agents of diffusion* (along with the few natives who moved around with them). But there is a limit to the applicability of diffusionism within situational logic too: what diffuses are elements and what they do is alter the situation—but not always.

The similarities of both doctrine and pattern, then, can be in principle explained by means of situational logic supplemented by evolutionism and diffusionism. Basically the situation of culture and myth is similar and the intrusion is similar and both the intrusion and the myths they cause are diffused and have a similar outcome.

(D) *The apocalyptic aspect.* Whether the cause be natural occurrence or liberating genius, when a change does occur in the closed society, be it externally or internally caused, it usually takes the form of a sudden, apocalyptic upheaval which is likely to result in the introduction of new taboos, or in religious conversions or repulsions. Why so? Here is a society of such long-standing stability that no one can remember it any differently, and suddenly some form of change occurs. Clearly in such face-to-face groups, the effect must be electric. The humdrum is suddenly interrupted by a new and exciting turn of events which is, at the same time, a frightening sort of threat to stability, to the system of magical and religious belief. Thus there can either result a tightening up on this system or a complete breakdown in it. Cargo cults are *such* violent intrusions into the established society which is so unprepared for the intrusion that breakdown is usually what happens. Such violations of tabooistic constraint are naturally followed by a sudden release of emotional energy. Frazer, in this passage, perhaps explains why:

. . . in primitive society the rules of ceremonial purity observed by divine kings, chiefs, and priests agree in many respects with the rules observed by homicides, mourners, women in childbed, girls at puberty, hunters and fishermen, and so on. To us these various classes of persons appear to differ totally in character and condition; some of them we should call holy, others we might pronounce unclean and polluted. But the savage makes no such moral distinction between them; the conceptions of holiness and pollution are not yet differentiated in his mind. To him the common feature of all these persons is that they are dangerous and in danger, and the danger in which they stand and to which they expose others is what we should call spiritual or ghostly, and therefore imaginary. The danger, however, is not less real because it is imaginary; imagination acts upon a man as really as does gravitation, and may kill him as certainly as a dose of prussic acid. To seclude these persons from the rest of the world so that the dreaded spiritual danger shall neither reach them nor spread from them, is the object of the taboos which they have to observe. These taboos act, so to say, as electrical insulators to preserve the spiritual force with which these persons are charged from suffering or inflicting harm by contact with the outer world.—Frazer, 1909, vol. i, pp. 294–5.

The religious hysteria built up by particular prophets and the violent breaking of the old taboos has resulted often enough in fits of dancing and other involuntary motor behaviour. Let us try to explain this. White rule, white repression, the vagaries of world commodity prices and therefore the payment the natives get for their copra—all these were more or less unintelligible to these simple people. Zinsser explains reaction to such situations as: 'mass hysterias, brought on by terror and despair, in populations oppressed, famished, and wretched to a degree almost unimaginable . . .' While Sargent (1957) adds these words

> It should be more widely known that electrical recordings of the human brain show that it is particularly sensitive to rhythmic stimulation by percussion and bright light among other things and certain rates of rhythm can build up recordable abnormalities of brain function and explosive states of tension sufficient even to produce convulsive fits in predisposed subjects. Some people can be persuaded to dance in time with such rhythms until they collapse in exhaustion. Furthermore, it is easier to disorganise the normal function of the brain by attacking it simultaneously with several strong rhythms played in different tempos [*sic*] (p. 92).

This is a beginning.

6. Conclusion

I feel I should point out that my attempt to explain cargo cults essentially turns on what Stanner calls a 'belief in belief'; a belief, that is, that people's theories and beliefs influence their actions and can, to a certain extent, explain their actions. I shall discuss this topic more fully in the next chapter, but I should like to add a brief postscript on the theme here. The chief criticism of 'belief in belief' is the anthropological platitude that rituals are not (not always, at least) derived from beliefs since, if anything, rituals precede beliefs in the order of historical succession. I want to make only two points in reply to this criticism. The first is that in the special case of the cargo cult the claim is false; in cargo cults we know it to be the case that beliefs did precede ritual. Of course there were religious rituals in Melanesia before there were cargo cults. But these previous rituals bore little resemblance to cargo rituals which were, in my view, invented to implement cargo beliefs. Secondly, I do not understand why rituals, which admittedly cannot be explained merely by reference to the beliefs which justify them, cannot be explained by reference to these beliefs plus other factors; and demanding that beliefs should not be part of explanations of rituals amounts to the demand that rituals are not to be explained at all. For unless we can state the aims and means of the actors, in this case the performers of the ritual, unless we state their beliefs, how can we explain their actions? Of course, statements of rituals cannot be derived from statements of beliefs alone: there are far more factors involved in the justifications of a ritual than one. But an explanation of ritual would certainly need some statements about beliefs, as well as some other statements of the situation, such as those about previous rituals which have either been modified or sustained in the light of the (perhaps new) beliefs. (I have argued, then, that belief is *logically* prior to the ritual it justifies: this is all I need here.)

An example may be useful. It is certainly not traditional ritual in Melanesia to build air-strips and jetties. However, it is fairly traditional to build ceremonial houses. In order to explain the new ritual, we can assume that there was a shift in ritual, and in order to explain this shift one has, I think, to mention the beliefs modifying the actions. And perhaps the potlatch comparison will be useful here too. The potlatch and cargo cults are two very similar rituals, with quite different religious and social meanings. We can only know about, and explain, these differences of meaning, if we accept that different beliefs can, under some circumstances, lead to similar actions, even though it is also quite true that similar beliefs can also lead to different actions (e.g. the varieties of Christianity). Yet without different beliefs, to begin with, there is no possibility of different meanings in the first place.

Having said all this I think I can permit myself one reflection on cargo cults, unconnected with the main purpose of this book, but nevertheless arising from my own views in a significant way, a reflection which I have not seen strongly enough made elsewhere. My own feeling is that the most important problem the cults raise is the practical administrative one of how to stop the burning of goods, the dissipation of resources, and noncooperation which is often their sad and wasteful outcome. This is a serious human problem to which the governments of the area must turn their attention. It is also an extremely difficult problem the solution to which will no doubt require much trial and error. While I don't for a moment wish to suggest that I have a solution, I have a suggestion as to where the solution may be found; it would be, moreover, a testable solution, and would not involve vicious social experiment. For according to my theory the most significant roles are played in cargo cults by ignorance, prejudice, discrimination and mixed-up goodwill. There is nothing to stop attempts being made to improve the situation in these matters on both sides of the contact situation. Education for native ignorance, a campaign against settler prejudice and discrimination, tolerance and understanding towards native attempts to gain community and understanding might well do it. We must really convince ourselves and our agents in Melanesia that the Kanakas are people and deserve to be treated as such. To do this will be a long-term and initially disheartening process, but if we are to be true to our values, we really should try. To try it would do no harm—for even partial education is of value.

129

We have had occasion to mention the faith of the social anthropologists in the brotherhood of man; we have to acknowledge that this belief has done much to ease the situation in some colonies, but not by any means enough. Since the belief in the brotherhood of man has turned in the hands of modern anthropologists into a disbelief in belief, into a kind of relativism of rituals, the hope of solving *specific* social problems by education has never seriously taken root, although we are all in favour of education.

5

METHODOLOGICAL DISCUSSION
OF THE THEORIES

IN my survey chapter I presented theories and criticism of theories in the broadest of outlines only. I want in this chapter to discuss in a little more detail several criticisms of cargo cult theories, criticisms which can also be used to allege the unsatisfactoriness of the situational logic solution. These criticisms say situational logic is no good: (*a*) because it explains these religious movements rationally and these movements in particular and even religion in general are not rational; (*b*) because it tries to explain all these cults together whereas each one is a unique phenomenon; (*c*) because it does this by assuming that the people in this situation are acting rationally, but they are not; (*d*) because it does this by assuming that what people believe or say they believe will explain what they do, but this is false.

1. *Religion is not Rational*

My theory of millenarian religion in general and therefore of cargo cult religion in particular is a rational one. I attribute reasonable aims to the actors in the situation and try to show that, within their frame of reference, their actions, if interpreted as trying to realise those aims, are perfectly rational. Against this way of approaching religion two attacks can be discovered in the literature: one that the religious reaction in this case is not a rational one, and the other that religion in general is not rational. The first is a theory put forward by Raymond Firth, the second a generalisation of it by Dr. Lucy Mair.

In anticipation of some difficulties up ahead I want at the inception of this discussion to make some preliminary distinctions connected with the idea of rationality. There seem to me to be at least three questions which the concept of rationality can be used to answer. (1) Is a given doctrine rational? (2) Is *belief in* a given doctrine rational? (3) Is a given action rational?

Our first question, (1), is a question about the rational status of some particular doctrine or belief, like the existence of God, or the succession of cause and effect. Normally rationality is attributed to those views which can be shown to be based on facts; or on science: which can, in other words, be justified. (It seems to me that this is a mistake and no doctrine can of itself be designated rational. I accept the view, so well argued by Popper and, following him, Bartley (1962, *passim*), that no doctrine can be justified. I therefore do not think there is much sense in trying to talk of rational doctrines at all.)

The second question, (2), concerns belief *in* a doctrine: is belief in God rational belief? There are a number of ideas all tangled up here. By a rationally held belief is very often simply meant something widely held, something which is, in fact, reasonable, or based on common sense, or on facts, or on modern science, or what not. This can be summed up in the term 'justification': belief in a doctrine is rational if that doctrine can be justified. (Since I have already stated that I do not believe any doctrine can be justified it follows I do not believe in rational belief. On the other hand, belief in any doctrine at all is not equally rational in every case. Bernard Shaw in his preface to *Androcles and the Lion* shows how belief in the Bible is not rational. He suggests asking a number of people whom one considers rational to say what parts of the Bible they believe in; he suggests the answers will vary in a random manner, i.e. be arbitrary, and therefore not rational. There is a strong school of modern philosophy, justly and severely criticised by Bartley, which believes that in fact the situation with all doctrines must be like this Bible case, because all positions are in the end irrational commitments, equally arbitrary and irrationally chosen. I would follow Popper's suggestion here that no doctrine can be justified or rationally believed in, but that we can adopt a more or less rational attitude to a position the more or less account we are prepared to take of the criticism of that doctrine.)

Finally, what about (3), rational action? Clearly the most common criterion for calling an action 'rational' is when the action is based upon rational belief. (Since I don't believe in rational belief I reject this criterion too.) Other criteria have been suggested, utilising the idea of the goal-directedness of an action, explicability of an action and of psychological reasonability of an action (i.e. action that is non-neurotic, or non-fanatic). (For my part I accept the idea of goal-directedness as the criterion of rationality.)

With the end of this short interpolation I return to my topic and discuss Firth's and Mair's idea of the irrationality of cargo cults.

Firth's reasons for believing the cargo cult religion to involve essentially 'other than rational elements' (see below) are two. First that the cults involve ethical demands, and second that they are, by native standards so to speak, nonrational. Both of Firth's arguments are to be found in his book *Elements of Social Organisation*. On p. 111, after some discussion of cargo cults, he suddenly says 'Such is the line of argument at the rational level. But other than rational elements enter into the situation.' I find some difficulty in understanding Firth's division of the discussion of the cults into that dealing with the rational elements and that dealing with the other than rational elements. There are two strands to his thinking from that place onwards, two kinds of things are discussed under this category of the 'other than rational elements'. The first of these things, the fact that ethical beliefs and demands are involved with the cult—as Firth puts it, ' "What we want is right" '—I shall deal with now.

We can have no reason for doubting Firth's contention that these demands are an inextricable part of the cults. What I do not accept is the idea that there is anything nonrational about these demands. It strikes me as being residual positivism to talk of ethics as 'other than rational'. We can accept some of the implications of Firth's distinction, even if we do not accept them all. We usually take ethical demands as a given part of the situation within which the actors act, rather than attempt to give a rational explanation of them. But because we do not (or cannot) give a rational explanation of ethical demands does not make them, say, psychologically nonrational, or incapable of being held open to criticism and thus not rational in those senses. By holding our ethical demands open to criticism and improvement we are being rational to some extent in ethics. Under this interpretation there is no essential rationality possessed *ipso facto* by certain doctrines like those of religion and ethics; what rationality there is consists mainly in the attitude towards rational discussion of the view in question.

I now want to examine how the beliefs are irrational within the native frame of reference. First of all Firth points out that there is an 'incompatibility between wants and their means of satisfaction' (p. 113). Basically the natives simply lack the knowledge necessary in order to get what they want (European goods) and this *impasse* has 'turned [them] to fantasy' (p. 113). Why fantasy? Fantasy in *their* terms because here they are resorting to magic without scientific accompaniment. When the natives want crops they don't just chant: they chant *and they plant seeds*; they chant and they cast their fishing-nets; they pray and go out and hunt. That they indulge in magic does not mean they have no science; they fully realise that the two must go together. Perhaps this has been best put by Malinowski:

If by science be understood a body of rules and conceptions, based on experience and derived from it by logical inference, embodied in material achievements and in a fixed form of tradition, . . . then there is no doubt that even the lowest savage communities have the beginnings of science, however rudimentary. (1948, p. 17, quoted in Barber, 1952, p. 56.)

Earlier, on pages 95*ff*, I mentioned that against my kind of view that cargo cult action is rational because based on a genuine doctrine, it is sometimes argued that cargo cult mythology is 'fantasy' even in native terms. The argument is that the natives have a store of knowledge of farming, fishing, what is good to eat, how to construct boats and houses and so on, and that this matter-of-fact knowledge somehow shows they are not the naïve magicians I make them out to be. Doubtless this argument is correct: they have a store of solid, technical knowledge. Further, Guiart has pointed out that some native magic is very recent. But he is not denying that some is also antediluvian. All this supports the case of those who would have us believe that it is not lack of technical knowledge but lack of means, techniques, and natural resources which make the natives so nonrational, so prone to 'fantasy'.

Against this I would argue that it is by no means clear that the Kanakas think in these categories—magic *versus* technique. According to my opponents the natives themselves consider their religion and magic as one—as we would say, irrational or fantastic—way of thinking about things; whereas they consider their practical, technical knowledge as another—as we would say, rational or sensible—way of thinking about things. I should imagine, on the face of it, that such a picture is highly unlikely. In reply it could be said that it is indeed highly unlikely and that it is not what was meant at all. The distinction being made is between the traditional religion and its beliefs and the new and fantastic doctrines of the cargo. Now these are new and fantastic within native terms; within native terms they are arbitrary and other-than-rational. Were he so inclined, then, such a person could well argue that it is the arbitrariness of the cargo myths, within the traditional world-view, that makes him suspect their rationality.

I think this would amount to a good case for attributing a degree of nonrationality to the cults. Still I think the position can be criticised. The first criticism would be that unless the theory were carefully applied it would make all innovation and change rationally suspect. A high price to pay for so viewing the cults. The decisive point would be whether the new myths embodied a coherent horizon of expectations. If they did I think the cults would be rational; if not perhaps my opponent would be right. My second criticism is factual. Some authors do claim that similar cult-activity is part of the Melanesian cultural inheritance. This, if true, and if flexible enough to see the cargo cults as simply another variation on the tradition, would clinch the rationality of the cults on the criterion of arbitrariness.

I have asked two tricky questions: are all social changes nonrational, and, is the cult integrated into the previous background of myths and rituals of the people? One possible answer could be: only those social changes which are integrated into the background are rational. The question is a simple empirical one: check whether they are integrated or not. This label of 'nonrational' is, then, more or less a confession that functionalism cannot handle social change; this we have known all along, the only new move is to disguise the failure under the label 'nonrational'. But why should anyone say that only integrated changes are rational? Answer: functionalists would say so because they are only interested in what is observable, in the ritual, not the belief; therefore social change to them is the changes that have taken place in what people do, and its rationality is the extent to which these changes are integrated.

Let us leave this digression which interprets the cults as nonrational because arbitrary and return to the problem of whether or not a person adopting the 'inadequate means' view provides us with a clear distinction between previous myths and their related technical knowledge, and the new fantastic myths. The question, in fact, of the integratedness of the cult. We would need more detail on the explanation-patterns of the natives.

Just how do the natives explain their practical information, rules, and rules-of-thumb for gardening, fishing, building houses, and so on? Just how different are these accounts from their magical and religious doctrines? My guess is that, if pressed, they would give a 'fantasy' explanation of their technical knowledge. And even if they give recognisably scientific explanations of their techniques we still have to be shown that they see any rational/nonrational discontinuity between this and their magico-religious beliefs. One need not go to the South Seas or to Central Africa to find evidence against the view that people separate technology and magic. Our own society, in the Middle Ages and in isolated villages and suburbs now, manifests high technology with magical justifications for it, not to mention the mumbo-jumbo of the modern advertising industry.

The reason I suspect the natives will produce fantasy explanations of their technology is the theory I have developed out of Belshaw, that what is lacking is not technical knowledge (we admit they have a lot of that), but theoretical knowledge, *which explains the technical knowledge*. That is to say, native explanations of Europeans and of cargo are either fanciful and untestable, or concrete and already falsified. Certainly, had the native the production techniques explained to him, and had he the necessary natural resources available, he could make the cargo goods without benefit of a western scientific and philosophical background. But wouldn't he then be like the Indian Ph.D. in physics who still believes in astrology? Is it not the whole animistic world-view, in which I include the natives' theoretical knowledge of the physical world and of the society of the white men, which marks them off from us? The cargo cult prophet Yali of the Garia (Lawrence, 1954), remember, who had seen the manufacturing process at work in Australia, could still have an obscure connection with a cargo cult. Although I have said this before, I think here it must be again stressed that technical knowledge, i.e. predictions for practical use, are deduced from explanatory theories. It is quite possible to get the right results from the wrong theories, as readers of Mr. Koestler on Kepler will know.[1] Native ignorance of the rationale of the white man's *mores* and of his cargoes is theoretical; they explain us animistically, which, when it says that cargo is made by the spirits, or that we are misappropriating cargoes intended for them, is false, but they have no way of finding this out independently. The difference between the native and the westerner is that faced with such evidence we would revise our theories radically (or we ought to) while the native tends to invent *ad hoc* corrections to his explanations, as would bad scientists.

The foregoing is intended to combat the doctrine that the incompatibility of wants and their means of satisfaction turned the natives to irrational fantasy. My view is that the fantasies were entirely rational attempts, within the native framework, to explain the incompatibility. Now how is it that Firth, and many another anthropologist, advanced such a theory? I have a tentative theory which might answer this question: how anthropologists came to muddle up the rationality of the natives with their nonpossession of science. The theory is philosophical, so I apologise for it. First of all what the natives have is technology not science. This is not a verbal quibble but a vital distinction between rules-of-thumb and scientific theories; between 'knacks' which work and theories which are articulated and lay claim to truth. The natives' technique does not give them a claim to comparison with us, only their explanatory (magical, animistic) theories can be so compared. Secondly, social anthropologists have confused technique and science precisely on account of their slogan 'study the ritual, not the belief'. This slogan leads them to ignore the fact that the natives do not have on the one hand scientific theories of their technique and on the other hand magical ones of their magic, but that both the technology and the magic are explained

[1] Koestler, 1959, e.g., pp. 326–8, where false hypothesis and mathematical mistake yield the right result.

magico-religiously. Thus Malinowski, speaking about this primitive science, and saying,

detached from the craft, that is certainly true, it is only a means to an end, it is crude, rudimentary and inchoate, but with all that it is the matrix from which the higher developments have sprung. . . . (1948, *ibid.*)

utterly misses the point and the vital distinction between the two. Having agreed that the fantasies were rational, let me turn to whether the resort to fantasy was also rational. Firth in 1932 suggested that the native creates new illusions to counter disillusion and strain. He is more or less suggesting that the cult fantasies are a form of escapism from the reality of disillusionment. Now is this flight into fantasy nonrational or rational (psychological) behaviour? Are there good reasons for it or not? Let us take it for a moment that he means escapism is nonrational, there are no good reasons for it. To this it might be replied that it could equally well be a psychologically rational move. After all, if we interpret 'nonrational' as 'neurotic' then we can say that Freud provided rational accounts of the formation of neuroses. That is, he tried to show how people's resort to neuroses was, from their point of view, reasonable. But this attribution of neuroses to the cultists is not very plausible. First of all it is not clear what is being escaped from: is it the problem which has brought on the disillusionment, or is it perhaps the anxiety and strain brought on by the unsolved problem? Secondly, who is escaping from what? Can we even talk sensibly of the whole society experiencing disillusion and anxiety? I am not altogether convinced that we can. The question is whether we can explain the escapism rationally and, if we can, can we criticise Firth for not providing such an explanation? Such a rational explanation is provided, I think, by Cyril Belshaw on lines Firth employs elsewhere. Belshaw argues that within the native frame of reference cargo myths are not illusions but attempts to solve certain problems in native terms. The fact that their myth-explanations are in native terms does not warrant them the label nonrational; rather, the very fact that the natives use their belief to try to explain facts shows the natives to be rational about their beliefs. Rational activity is goal-directed. What is the goal of the myth-making activity? Its goal is, one may assume, to explain the Europeans, their wealth, native poverty, and so on, as Belshaw has shown. If this explanation is true the activity of resorting to fantasy is rational.

It is surprising from my viewpoint that Firth, who in another place stresses the resort to native means to achieve new ends, should have neglected the possibility of arguing in parallel that cargo myths are explanations, in native terms, of new problems. Why this oversight?

Precisely because Firth, it seems to me, is assuming that we can judge the whole native magical frame of reference to be non-rational. My evidence is his very use of the word 'fantasy'. He is judging their *theories* to be fantastic. What Firth is judging nonrational is magico-religious explanation; the reason he is judging it nonrational is because it is magico-religious. But, I would say, the fact that we, with our western scientific knowledge, can see that the actions prescribed by these explanations will not bring about the promised ends tells no more about these natives than that their knowledge is inadequate—although that is a very tendentious way of putting it. What is it inadequate for? How do we know that it is inadequate? Only because it clashes with the 'rational' beliefs of modern science. But not only does the native not know of modern science, he might not believe it if he did. Would that be *ipso facto* nonrational if the native had never heard the arguments in favour of the scientific explanation? It would not; it would only be nonrational if, faced with all the arguments, *and able to appreciate their force*, the native still refused to accept that a western scientific explanation was any improvement on his own.

More specifically, I think that once the word 'fantasy' has been introduced we have to be very careful. What justification is there for thinking that native ideas are, by their form, fantastic, while Europeans' are sensible and down-to-earth? Firth says that the natives 'turned to fantasy' (p. 113); might one not construct an equally plausible case to the effect that the natives were discovered in fantasy (i.e. animistic magico-religious world-view) by the Europeans, but were never brought out of it by education and missionary teaching? It has been said of many scientific theories that they are fantastic; many scientists have boldly claimed that scientific theories, including the ones they have produced, were products of the imagination. Did Firth wish to imply that these or their adherents were nonrational? I suspect not.

As far as I understand it Firth has tried to show that this magico-religious fantasy belief present in the cargo cults is 'other than rational'. I do not know whether he would say religion in general is other-than-rational, or fantasy. Many social anthropologists would. This is because there is a long tradition on the topic in social anthropology. Social anthropology has for a long time been intimately connected with the Rationalist movement. I mean the movement grouped around The Rationalist Association whose efforts perhaps culminated in Frazer's monumental *Golden Bough*—which explicitly sets out to discredit present-day religion as primitive and irrational. Believing as Rationalists do, that all religion is superstitious mumbo-jumbo, it is not surprising that when they come to study religion they

138

prefer to concentrate on ritual rather than belief. At least ritual is an understandable, tangible thing, which is more than you can say for the superstitions behind rituals. This is one explanation, anyway, for anthropologists' persistent talk of 'ritual activity'. I can think of at least one other explanation of this oddity. By and large social anthropologists seem to have found religious beliefs terribly difficult and problematic to deal with, and for that reason they have sheered off them. Perhaps their position is defensible, for certainly the difficulties of the matter are immense. A casual glance at the volume *African Worlds* or at *Nuer Religion*, which are exceptional cases of attempts to study religious beliefs, will soon convince anyone of that. Nevertheless, I think the attitude some anthropologists adopt is highly arguable. Their attitude is not merely to avoid talk about religion if they can avoid it, but rather an over-readiness to talk only about its observable aspects, namely ritual. This is not leaving religion alone but giving an empiricist or even behaviourist twist to religious studies. The move is justified on intellectual grounds by a theory of Radcliffe-Brown's that religion does not explain ritual. By this he means that if you ask why a man goes through the motions of prayer it is no answer to say he is worshipping God (since different people worship the same God in different ways). According to Radcliffe-Brown the motions of praying may have developed before the notion of worshipping God. It might either have been originally justified differently or it might be the case that the ritual action in itself is valued and the religious justification was *post hoc* or perhaps parallel and *ad hoc*. (Remember the transfer of pagan ritual to Christianity.) Thus anthropologists feel free to describe and discuss the actually existing, observable, ritual without having to bother much about the religious 'explanations' that are given of it. Indeed these, being origin explanations, are unacceptable to most social anthropologists. They accept a durkheimian theory that ritual foregatherings are to be explained by their social or collective function of the reaffirmation of ties and community.

Before I go on, let me stress that this discussion of Rationalism extrapolates from Firth's arguments. It is not intended to attribute any beliefs to him. My extrapolation helps me to understand his position, by seeing it as a direct descendant of what might be called 'the frazerian tradition' (of interpreting religion).

Consonant with this whole tradition comes the explicit argument of Dr. Lucy Mair that religion as such is not rational.

Her thesis is most interesting and is based on a number of intriguing arguments. She believes religion to be nonrational in the sense that: (*a*) religious performances are recognisably different from other, nonmystical activities which are rational; (*b*) that religion prescribes means which the actors know cannot possibly achieve their ostensible ends. There is, I would say, still a third, somewhat more subtle, argument behind her position. We are trying to explain the actions of people more or less rationally. We all accept that rational action is action directed to an end. Objectively speaking, however, we can say that some actions are more likely to realise their end than are others. Thus we might say that, given the knowledge and belief of the actor, he acts the more rationally the better suited, from an objective point of view, are his means to the realisation of his aims. Clearly praying for rain is objectively much less likely to produce rain than is dropping dry ice into the clouds. Therefore, objectively, (c) science is more rational than religion.

Dr. Mair states her view of religion in a review-article of Worsley (1957) called 'The Pursuit of the Millennium in Melanesia' in *The British Journal of Sociology* for June 1958. Although primarily an Africanist, Dr. Mair's book on Melanesia, *Australia in New Guinea*, gives her words extra interest:

His [Worsley's] line of argument is indicated . . . by the terms in which he criticises the description of the cargo cults as 'irrational'. In so far as his strictures are aimed at people who regard them as an expression of mental confusion or even derangement, all modern students will join with him. But in the sense in which religious beliefs are recognised, by those who hold them as well as those who do not, to be at anyrate non-rational, the cults surely deserve the term; and also in the sense in which the word is applied to means which cannot possibly achieve their ostensible end. Indeed, it usefully distinguishes them from the recognisably political, non-mystical movements which have superseded them in some places.

I shall now counter-attack Dr. Mair on this point that religion is non-rational or irrational. I shall proceed point by point and consider each of her arguments as comebacks to mine. My main point against her is the same as against Firth. But the issue is broader and merits being treated a second time.

In arguing that religion is rational, whatever its protagonists or opponents may say, I am saying that the cults are rational too. The fact that some religious people agree that religious beliefs are irrational is a red herring. In the sense that religious beliefs are theoretical explanations of things and events in the world, they are as rational, I would say, as any other (say scientific) explanation, in one sense of 'rational'; in another sense science is more rational than magic, of course.[1] Dr. Mair then brings up the argument that calling

[1] Namely in that the theories of empirical science are testable, tested and have survived tests. These *theories* are no more rational than magical ones, but some philosophers (Popper, Watkins, Bartley) have argued that they are more rationally held. If something like this is what Firth and Mair had in mind they have not made this clear, for they seem to go much further. In such case, my arguments can be read as directed against those further parts of their views only.

the cults irrational serves usefully to distinguish them from later 'non-mystical' movements. The force of this argument is difficult to see. These other movements are nonreligious, while cargo cults are religious; this seems an adequate distinction. It is surely better than introducing the heavily value-loaded term 'irrational', with its overtones of 'unreasonable' and even 'bad'. Perhaps a better use of 'rational' is to apply it to purposeful behaviour. The religious elements of cargo cults, in so far as they have the *purpose* of explaining something—of solving the problems created by contact—seem to me to be rational.

Against this Dr. Mair brings a final argument that the cults and, perhaps, religion, are irrational in the sense that they propose means which cannot possibly achieve their ostensible ends. This, I happen to believe, is true. But how can the *natives* or religious people know that the means are inappropriate to the achievement of the ends? The answer is they cannot; not, at least, without the kind of prior knowledge which Jarvie, Dr. Mair, and the reader of *The British Journal of Sociology* have. I suggest that the only criterion by which we could find out if there was any relation between cult means and cult ends would be the success or failure of the cults. If successful (like modern science) then there is a relation, if not, not. How can we argue like this? The aim of Dr. Mair's review is to show Worsley is in error. Were we to show (by Gallup poll) that her review had failed to do this would we then be allowed to call the review irrational? Of course not. Moreover, how do we know that all religion is unsuccessful, 'cannot possibly' achieve its ends? If some religious performance suddenly brought it off what would we do? Call it 'science' and rational? It would hardly be fair to use our (scientific) knowledge of the relations of means and ends as criteria for judging theirs irrational. Another argument, that the natives (and religious people) *do* know that the means cannot achieve the ends because they have technical knowledge of means-ends relationships in, e.g. fishing and farming, has been discussed earlier. In line with Firth, Dr. Mair wants to see the cults and religion as 'irrational'; I resist this move because I find the inference that is often drawn from it, namely, that religion and the cults are retreats into fantasy and escapism, has no explanatory power. I find it difficult not to believe that anthropologists' keenness to introduce the word 'irrational' is partly an attempt to label the cults 'unreasonable'; this, the contrary of my own view, is *ad hoc* psychologism.

Before I conclude this section there are a few more things I want to say. First, I have sometimes interpreted and expanded the arguments of Firth and Mair. This is to facilitate exploration of a direction of discussion they have opened up but not pressed to its conclusion. In trying to press the points home I have added to my opponents' arguments and I hope I have said clearly where I have done this.

Secondly I think a tribute is due to Firth and Mair for reopening discussion of one of the basic metaphysical issues of the study of man: the rationality of man: the rationality of man and of primitive man. This is a deep and intriguing problem which they have tackled despite the heat it is likely to generate. Their solution to it seems to be that to some extent we are all a bit nonrational; namely to the extent that we are religious men. While I disagree with their solution to this problem because I believe we can be rational as well as irrational in religion and in ethics, my entire discussion owes its existence to the work of these two authors. Were it not for their rediscovery of this fundamental problem, and their challenging solution to it, I would not even have noticed it, never mind have been able to work out a position of my own or be in a position to criticise them.

2. *The Rationality of Ignorance*

I think the position of Mair and the Rationalists on the rationality of magic and religion is so singular that it deserves a separate discussion. As far as I can see this whole tradition in social anthropology takes the line that pure belief in magic and religion is either irrational or nonrational, even within the framework of the believer himself. After all, those who believe in God's vengeance do not abandon the vengeance of the law; similarly the rational savage does not just chant the spells he also plants the seeds. Therefore, those who simply pray or chant are behaving irrationally within their own terms, they are neglecting a previously essential aspect of the ritual. This argument is not quite correct. For it would also follow, on this idea of rationality, that the man who planted the seed without chanting the spell was also behaving irrationally. Thus it follows that, on this account of rationality, the modern scientist, including the social scientist book reviewer, is acting irrationally if he mixes the chemicals or publishes the review without chanting the requisite spells or prayers. So, were Mair and Firth to adopt the native frame of reference, that only the whole ritual taken together is rational, this somewhat bizarre conclusion would follow.

However, my own position may seem equally curious. What is really under discussion here is savage ignorance *versus* civilised knowledge. My position has been that savage ignorance is just as rational as civilised knowledge. Now this is a very curious position to be in. Can I be sincere? If I mean it then what possible grounds can I have for believing in western civilised knowledge and not ignorance and magic?

If this is the worry at the back of the minds of the Rationalist anthropologists it must be admitted they have discovered a somewhat difficult point. Nevertheless, I still think my solution to this difficulty is more satisfactory than theirs. My solution is this. Magic and religion, to many people, are a part of common sense. As a part of common sense it is reasonable for them to hold it. If another part of their common sense is an uncritical attitude towards belief, an acceptance of the received or traditional ideas, then their belief in common sense is reinforced and doubly rational. In our society superstition and elementary popular science are all mixed up. But part of common sense in our society is the attitude of being critical towards traditional or received ideas. Once one becomes critical, and establishes standards of being critical, then I personally believe it is no longer reasonable to hold on to the more simple-minded magico-religious beliefs in prayers and spells. So I can provide a reason why I accept western science and not magic in, say, the matter of farming. At the same time I can insist that, within his common sense, or frame of reference, the savage is also being reasonable.

This sounds a trifle like relativism again. Having chastised relativism so much I must hastily disavow any tint of relativism. Within both savage and civilised frames of reference it is possible to appraise the system of belief of the other, but I think it can easily be shown that a critical attitude towards beliefs and ideas is better than an uncritical one. No relativism here then. Both we westerners and the savages have a degree of rationality in believing what we do. But our reasons for believing what we do are somewhat better than their reasons, at least by our standards of critical discussion. And our standards of critical discussion are better than no standards of critical discussion, and that latter is the situation of the savage.

On this one place, then, where the Rationalist functionalists briefly allow themselves a twinge of absolutism towards primitives, I think they make a blunder. The question is, how did this blunder come about? My answer is, through an inability to conceive that ignorance may be rationally held, and even have a functional significance. Functionalists, believing that societies, like darwinian species, strive towards an adjustment to the environment by means of internal adjustment and harmony, cannot quite bring themselves to believe that something as gross as ignorance could survive. Surely, if savages believe the moon is made of green cheese that is no matter. But if they believe tigers are wonderful and kind, then, provided they inhabit a tiger area, that society will not long survive to propagate such gross ignorance. Similarly, if a society believing in rigid exogamy moves to a remote desert island it too will not last long.

These, however, are simply extreme cases which prove nothing at all. Disharmony-promoting doctrines need not destroy societies, and sheer ignorance within a society can even promote its harmony. As an example of disharmony-promoting false-doctrines let us take the belief of many white men in the Southern United States in myths of negro racial inferiority. These may have been of no importance at one time. But for the last hundred years or more they have been the source of severe conflict within the United States. Certainly all efforts are being made to ease this conflict, but the conflict is not destroying the society, though it may be hindering its progress somewhat. As an example of pure ignorance creating harmony let us take the recent case of soldiers, anxious to get out of the British army, beginning to run in Parliamentary by-elections. Before this method of getting out of the army was discovered, ignorance of it served to conceal the conflict in British society between the law which said soldiers couldn't get out of the army for less than £250, and the law which said that soldiers standing for elections must be discharged. Now this conflict between our desire to keep soldiers and our desire not to let politics get militarised has been shown up by the discovery of this route to get out of the army cheaply. Ignorance of the conflict of laws promoted social harmony; now the ignorance has been dispelled, the harmony is lost. Consequently action will now have to be taken to remove the conflict of laws.

Functionalists, believing in the rational adjustment of societies, seem to have sought to pretend sheer ignorance didn't exist, that there is no pure magic. But they could not account for the case where the empirical rules-of-thumb were discarded and only the spells relied upon. Here, where they shouldn't have, they became absolutists.

3. *All Historical Events are Unique*

This criticism of the situational logic theory amounts to saying that any theory, such as my own, which is a general account of social change, millenarianism and cargo cults, is mistaken. Mistaken because there is reason for believing that the events so lumped together require particular explanations in every case. This argument has been put forward by Judy Inglis.[1]

She begins by taking umbrage with those who constantly stave off giving explanations of the cults by pleading that there is not yet enough factual information to go on. Her thesis is that there is already enough factual information available for us to be sure that no general explanation of the cults can be given. She concludes that each is a unique and unpredictable historical occurrence.[2]

[1] Inglis, 1957; see also Stanner, 1958, and her reply, Inglis, 1959.
[2] 'The search for a general explanation in terms of a common historical factor, leads to formulations too general to be useful' (p. 249).

(Positively, she argues that a fundamental underlying cause of cargo cults is a 'cultural disposition' to react to certain situations (perhaps of culture contact or culture clash) in this messianic way. Quite what particular form and content this disposition would take in any particular case would be unique and unpredictable.)

Inglis' criticism of other authors because their explanations are vague and do not account for every feature of the cults, does not seem to me an argument for the position that no general explanation *can be* given. It would be very difficult to show the impossibility of general explanations and lack of methodological sophistication may have prevented Miss Inglis from fulfilling this part of her programme.

For a start she begins with a necessitarian idea of the general explanations of science. By 'necessitarianism' I mean the view that science aims to predict, and that only that explanation is satisfactory which enables us to predict with certainty or necessity, say, the next occurrence of a cargo cult given a particular situation; namely enables us to assert without qualification that in a given situation a cargo cult must necessarily arise. Necessitarianism is a common mistake which pervades some of the cargo cult literature and therefore demands a little discussion. Two muddles are involved: one that science aims to specify the necessary and sufficient conditions of an event, and the other that this knowledge allows science to predict the event. Both muddles are serious. Take the statement that all swans are white. It says that anything that is a swan will be white, in other words, swanness is a sufficient condition for whiteness. It certainly does not say that swanness is a necessary condition for whiteness, this would mean that everything that was white was a swan! Science, then, aims at sufficient condition explanations. The second muddle fails to appreciate the logical role of prediction within science. The aim of science is to explain, not to predict; prediction is a subordinate aim to be used to test explanatory theories. It is subordinate because retrodiction can function in the same way as a test.

Having said this, let me come back to Miss Inglis' principal thesis: that cargo cults are unique historical occurrences and necessary and sufficient conditions for them cannot be found. Of course it is true that each cult is a unique occurrence and cannot be predicted, no doubt. So what? Well science, for example, deals only with repeatable, or generalisable, events. Social events are not repeatable. For this reason we can never, on Inglis' account, have general explanations of cargo cults. But is the difference between natural and social science so very great? Does anyone believe that any two events in a cloud-chamber are the same? Does anyone believe that rolling a ball down an inclined plane can be done in identical conditions? In a metaphysical sense of 'identical' there is no identity here and no scientist would claim that there was. They would claim that from the point of view of this experiment or test the two events were sufficiently similar for their purposes. They would operate in fact, with a less, strict test of identity: identical for the purpose in hand. And they are being fairly precise in this; they always leave open the possibility that their purposes are not well enough specified and that minute differences of conditions may change the way they look at the event completely. It is obvious to me that social science is in no worse a position here than natural science. We have our theoretical interests or point of view, and our beliefs as to what influences are relevant and what not. We can therefore say that cargo cults are repeatable events, sufficiently similar for our purposes. After all, it is the relevant similarities we want to explain first. When we have done that we can go on to account for individual variations from cult to cult.

4. *People aren't Rational*

This criticism of theories of cargo cults—although it doesn't insist that religion need be irrational, does accept the view that there is a common explanation of cargo cults—is not necessitarian, but says simply that the actors in the cargo situation were not rational, but confused. I think I can turn this argument back on itself and to my advantage. Its proponent is F. E. Williams.

Williams' problem was simply to explain the odd behaviour attendant on the cults. His fundamental thesis is that the madness was a result of

certain effects of contact with and subjection by a superior people.

He mentions among other factors which, he thinks, had something to do with causing the cults,

The effort to assimilate a body of new and difficult ideas, and a resultant mental confusion.

The new and difficult ideas would, one supposes, be Christian teaching and the mysterious ways of the white man, e.g. the way he obtains goods. This mental confusion is the factor

largely responsible for the emergence of the leading ideas of the movement.

I find myself differing considerably from those anthropologists who cannot resist pouring scorn on Williams' theories and making him look a little foolish. Theirs is the wisdom of hindsight. It is always easier to caricature someone's views than it is to make a real effort to understand what he is getting at. Williams seems to me

146

perfectly correct in saying that the natives have not been able to assimilate many of the new ideas to which they have been exposed. Of
course it is easy to make fun of this theory of 'mental indigestion', as
it has been called—slightingly in intention but, to my mind, quite
correctly in description. If we put it a little differently, I think
Williams' theory stands revealed as a very sound idea. The whole
explanatory scheme of the world brought by the whites and their
missionaries is so utterly alien to the traditional knowledge of the
natives that they are unable to grasp it fully. Put it the other way: the
whole explanatory scheme of the world held by the natives is shaken
by the mysterious appearance of the whites. For example, the natives
regard the fact that the white men cropped up from nowhere, and yet
seem very prosperous, as something in need of an explanation, just
as we might see the need for an explanation if numbers of people
with wings and harps and happy expressions suddenly descended and
colonised us. In both cases physical explanations and magico-
religious explanations are possible; and the more uncritical your
tradition is the more inclined you are towards the latter type.

The point might perhaps be put a little more sharply. Popper has
argued[1] that our background knowledge of unrefuted theories and
(perhaps unarticulated) anticipations adds up to something he calls
a 'horizon of expectations'. This is the set of the expectations we
have of the world; how we expect the world to behave. Most of it is
taken for granted most of the time. When a new fact comes along
which is not expected, not accounted for within the present horizon,
it, so to speak, makes a breach in this horizon; it knocks out a theory
or belief and has itself to be taken into account when the breach is
repaired, or when a new horizon is built. This inclusion of the new
fact into the reconstructed horizon causes the horizon constantly to
expand.

There are two possible ways in which the possessors of the horizon
can attack the problem of breaches in that horizon. Either they can
make an *ad hoc* adjustment which serves simply to take care of the
breaching fact, or they can look thoroughly into the reasons the
breaching fact breached and try to revise as much of the horizon as
they can in the light of it. These approaches can be termed *ad hoc* and
radical. In a way they correspond to the uncritical *versus* the critical
approach to beliefs. The person with a magico-religious belief who
simply makes an adjustment to deal with a difficulty (like that a particular spell didn't work, say, because the rites weren't properly
carried out) is acting in a very uncritical and *ad hoc* way. While the
same believer who subjects his whole theory of spells to scrutiny

---

[1] Popper, 1963, chapter 1, section 5. See also Wisdom, 1952, pp. 7 and 50–1;
and Gombich, 1960, p. 60.

because of that failure and, perhaps, revises or abandons it, is adopting a radical or critical approach. Neither of these approaches quite approximates to what I have in mind as a theory of what happens with cargo cults. My theory would be in some ways a compromise between the two. There is certainly the *ad hoc* or uncritical tendency in the Melanesians: they would like to patch over cracks with minor repairs. Unfortunately circumstances will not allow them to do this because the impact of the European on their thinking and values is such that it would be more accurate to say he smashes, not just breaches, their horizon. In these circumstances I would say that the turning to eschatology is a desperate attempt to do an *ad hoc* repair that is as radical as possible: it is still a magico-religious repair, but it is the most radical one.

The arrival of the white man on isolated South Pacific islands in some way smashes, not just breaches, the inhabitants' horizon of expectations. The white man's arrival is disruptive and not easily explained away. Thus it both undermines and overthrows the native horizon or world-view; the native, faced with the collapse of many expectations and a multitude of new facts to be accounted for, naturally tends to move in the direction of least resistance: towards the vague, *ad hoc* and irrefutable magico-religious explanation. The great virtue of such magico-religious accounts being that the new horizon built with their help is very nearly unbreachable. A new world-view can be erected which incorporates both the disruptive and the 'metaphysical' aspects of the white man, i.e. those respects in which his arrival is mysterious and therefore not amenable to tests.

In support of the view outlined above we might do well to remember that the whites did very little in the way of enlightening the natives in any systematic manner on the subject of their ways of life and thinking. The missionaries, perhaps the obvious people to perform such tasks, were on the whole much too preoccupied imbuing the natives with the sexual morality of puritanical Christianity to pay any attention to such work. Not that they would have had any success. The problem of communication between world-views so vastly distant as the Melanesian and the modern European is daunting.[1] Even when some of those involved in cults had been to Australia and been shown cities and factories there, the white men remained a mystery for them: either their subsequent cult was based on doctrines they did not believe and hence they were charlatans, or as I would suggest, their *ad hoc* attitude towards their horizon, or mental set, prevented them from taking the cities and factories as refutations of their world-views. You can only observe what you are looking

[1] See chapter 1 of the witty and thoughtful book by Becker, 1932.

148

for, and these chaps were not able to look at what they were shown the way the white men wanted them to look at it.

All in all, then, that the natives have a pretty garbled picture both of Christianity and of what we know to be the truth of the white man's world, is not really surprising. And Williams' hypothesis that this picture is the source of the very strange mish-mash which constitute cult ideas, seems to me a good, if as yet vague, one. But to say that it is confused and mad and therefore irrational is much different and much worse.

5. *Belief does not Explain Action*

This very simple and rather startling thesis was introduced by Stanner, in an exchange of papers he had with Judy Inglis. It will be recalled that she was a devotee of situational logic. She argued that all cargo cults are unique historical phenomena which grow out of particular combinations of people and circumstances. No general theory of them is possible because the logic of every situation must be slightly different. Stanner took her to task for the whole idea of a situational logic account:

It is as though we were being told: 'here are the Melanesians, with this kind of culture, and living this kind of life; here are certain historical circumstances; here is the cult of cargo; and, since the Melanesians believe this-and-that about the source and provenance of valuable goods, it is hard to see how anything but cult could result' (p. 5).

Stanner further says that

A large number of facts are being brought together without a truly persuasive link other than the axiom that belief leads necessarily to action (p. 5).

But how, he asks, can belief explain the *form* of the cult? He points out that the idea that belief necessarily influences action has been under attack by anthropologists for the last half-century. Their principal argument against it has been that, obviously, conduct can influence belief, that new rituals can be incorporated and only justified later; Stanner cites Radcliffe-Brown's alternative theory: 'what really happens is that the rites and the justifying or rationalising beliefs develop together as parts of a coherent whole' (p. 8).

Stanner attacks Inglis' assertion that

from the best accounts of particular cults in which there are references to the history of a certain area, to the beliefs of its inhabitants, to the attitudes of its administrators, and so on, we can understand why one community has reacted as it has (p. 263).

He says:

Short of assuming precisely what anthropology exists to demonstrate, it seems to me that none of the desiderata mentioned by Miss Inglis reveals the logic which prompts the impassioned Melanesians, acting jointly, to neglect their gardens, forsake their villages, waste their pigs, dissipate their valuables, whore their women, dance themselves to ecstasy, and go out to wait for wealth to come by means which never were on land or sea (p. 19).

Indeed

Our insight into the cults will grow in the measure in which we abandon the effort to base interpretations on the primacy and efficacy of belief.... We have no sure means of knowing if a man believes what he may say he believes. Belief can be simulated from any number of motives which themselves are beyond our sure knowledge, but the external activity need not differ from that of a true believer.... In the Melanesian cults, the natives do not seek cargo because of anything they believe about the provenance or source of cargo. I would prefer to say that they do so because cargo has value or meaning for them, and that they enhance their belief in consonance with that value or meaning. The fantastic nature of the one is a function of the inordinateness of the other. I am thus not denying that Melanesians have and may hold beliefs; nor am I saying that we should not record and analyse what they may purport to be their beliefs; I am contending only that a structure of theory built upon a belief in belief assumes what is neither warrantable nor necessary (p. 25).

This passage needs some comment. First, 'We have no sure means of knowing if a man believes what he may say he believes', says Stanner. Quite true, we have no access to other people's minds. Does it follow that because we can't be sure we are right we shouldn't bother to answer the questions? Yes, on the false view that hypotheses are Bad. Second, he says that belief can be simulated and yet the external activity remain the same. Again true, but does anything follow from it except that our answers about belief will be conjectural? 'Study ritual not belief', all over again, so that our discussion (of the activity) will not be conjectural. Finally, Stanner contends that the seeking of the cargo is attributable not to the seeker's beliefs about where it comes from, but to the high value they place upon it; our knowledge that they do value it highly may perhaps explain the fantastic stories they give of its source and is certainly enough to explain the cult; we need not assume their beliefs to be their beliefs in order to explain their activity.

I find some difficulty in following all of this. I especially don't see why Stanner's theory that the natives value the cargo goods is significantly less conjectural, less sure, than Belshaw's and Attenborough's contentions about the natives' 'beliefs'. What kind of argument is it to say that we can discount their beliefs because these involve 'means which never were on land or sea'? Who knows these means never were on land or sea? Who dares say that he knows the natives know they never were on land or sea? Or is this a permissible conjecture while a statement about 'beliefs' is an impermissible one? I would suggest we have here a recurrence of Firth and Mair's attempts to discount the significance of religious beliefs; the assumption that one's own beliefs are obvious and true, whereas opposing ones are merely conjectural, nonexistent or dismissible as irrational.

It is perhaps necessitarianism which makes Stanner regard situational logic as unsatisfactory. He is right in contending that situational logic seems to say it is hard to see how anything but a cult could result; explanations of human behaviour in terms of the logic of the situation, however, always fall short of a complete account because they cannot eliminate the human factor; they can only go so far, they cannot do more than leave the human element open: if we reconstruct the situational logic of an event we still do not account for it happening: in an emergency quick thinking might or might not save the day; whether it will or not is a prediction beyond our reach. Two people, identically situated, may act differently because: one is a Christian, the other not; one thinks quickly, the other slowly; one always does the obvious, the other never does the obvious, and so on. Any theory which eliminated this human element would be explaining human thought and will, and any explanation of human thought would be an explanation of itself, i.e. it would explain too much.

However, despite the limitations on it, situational logic is the best explanation of human behaviour we have; indeed it is virtually the only one we have. But it must be combined with a theory which allows belief and aims to influence action.[1] True, the two may interact, and it may be difficult in any particular case to say which has primacy. But that in the ultimate analysis belief must have primacy seems an inescapable conclusion. In fact, I would contend that this *is* the uneliminable human element.

If we remain adamant that belief does not affect action then I do not see how we can explain anything social or human. Of course the cultists want the cargo because they value it. But why do they have a cult and not something else? Can there be any other answer than that they genuinely believe that the cult will bring them the cargo? Yes. If they do not believe in the efficacy of the cult then the cult is perhaps performed for some other end or is enjoyed for its own sake: we may say that the cult is futile, or a deception, and has no connection with the desire to get the cargo, yet unless we say it is for

[1] Talk of belief 'necessarily' influencing action is something of a red herring; few would hold to anything as strong.

some end, we have no explanation at all. The theory that it is performed although known to be futile is saying the cult is somewhat irrational, but it is not an explanation of it; the theory that the cult is enjoyed for its own sake and is known to be otherwise futile runs so counter to all common sense, attributes such a degree of deviousness to the cultists—that they ruin themselves for the sake of ruining themselves and disguise their behaviour as rational—that it reduces to the theory that it is a deception to conceal some secret pleasure enjoyed by all, and this is a kind of conspiracy theory. I have discussed conspiracy theories in Chapter 3. Thus I think these theories which rule out a belief in belief will not do. Although Stanner utilises the theory of Radcliffe-Brown's that we needn't believe that belief and action are related in the way we normally believe they are, he does not, as we saw in the motto to Chapter 4, believe that structural-functionalism *à la* Radcliffe-Brown will do to explain the cults either. To discuss this second point we shall have to turn away from Stanner.

6. *The Lack of a Structural-Functional Explanation*

The final criticism of my theory which I want to deal with would be simply: my theory is not a structural-functional theory. My reply would be that the charge is quite true. Moreover, and even more interesting, as far as the literature I have looked at is concerned, no structural-functional explanation of cargo cults has so much as been seriously attempted. I shall discuss this last fact in sections 6, 7, 8 and 9.

While there are indeed no strictly structural-functional theories of cargo cults in the literature, there are some functional or proto-functional ones. Haddon, of course, argued that religion sanctions social aspirations and, as the aspirations were changing because of contact the religion had to change too so as to sanction the new social aspirations, Firth in 1951 explained how the cults sanction the moral striving of the cultists; by working on warehouses and jetties, the participants showed their faith that what they demanded was right and would be forthcoming. His ideas were further developed by Burridge. Stanner presents a slightly different thesis. He believes that the things the cultists want have social values (their value to the society as a whole); that the natives misvalue, or more precisely overvalue, the cargo by founding a cult; and that this overvaluation explains why the cult must die; were such overvaluation to become established it would lead to social chaos (1958, p. 4). He also believes that contact with western society has shown up certain functional inadequacies in the native society and that the cult is an attempt to get the native society to adjust, and this attempt it magically (and *post hoc*) sanctions (p. 24). Worsley holds that cults function as means of uniting diversified societies. Mair holds that religion validates the social structure and is only changed when it disappoints expectations, i.e. cannot handle a new situation (p. 119), so that the cult is a result of the failure of the old religion in the new situation.

All these explanations obviously smack of structural-functionalism because they talk of institutions 'sanctioning' others, of social values, and of functional adjustment. Yet they are not strictly structural-functionalist theories *of the cults* because they give no explanation of the shifts in the structure. Thus, Haddon doesn't explain structural-functionally why the social aspirations changed; Firth and Burridge do not give structural-functional accounts of why the new moral strivings; Stanner gives no structural-functional account of the overvaluation; Mair gives no structural-functional account of why the religion disappoints expectations. Worsley's remark, to complete the list, is not an explanation of the cults at all, but of their consequences. But I wish to stress, that these are my own comments not the comments of the authors themselves; according to the authors' own view they are all, except Worsley (who is a marxist), like most British social anthropologists, orthodox and practising structural-functionalists.

As explained earlier, most British social anthropologists are structural-functionalists. This doctrine of theirs is both a heuristic and a metaphysical theory. My dissatisfaction with the theories of cargo cults can be explained by the fact that their authors have by and large followed the kind of inductive heuristic embodied in structural-functionalism, but they have not followed it as a theory. That is, they have plunged straight into ethnographic fact about the society in which the cults arose and about the cults themselves, *before* saying what problems the cults raise, i.e. why we should take an interest in all these facts about them. That is not to criticise structural-functionalism as a body of theory. Yet none of the writers we have discussed has attempted to construct a structural-functional explanation of cargo cults. Even Firth, a very distinguished member of the British structural-functionalist school, does not do so. Also, none of the writers *mentions* the fact that structural-functional method—the method of analysis usually used in social anthropology—is not being, or has not been, applied to cargo cults. This silence in itself is interesting. Either the fact was not noticed,[1] or these strange emanations of religious mania were felt to be nontypical of the problems of social anthropology and therefore were not to be treated in the usual way.

[1] D. F. Pocock is the first writer I have come across who mentions this point. See Pocock, 1961, pp. 110–11.

7. *Structural-Functionalism's Difficulties with Social Change*

In this section and the next two I present my account of why there has been no structural-functional *theory* of why cargo cults occur and proceed in the (very similar) way they do.

It seems to be generally agreed that cargo cults are phenomena of social change. Firth deals with them in his chapter 'Social Change in Peasant Communities' in *Elements of Social Organisation*; Stanner covers them in his book *The South Seas in Transition*; Hogbin tackles them in his aptly titled *Social Change*; Guiart, Bodrogi and Worsley all think that somehow or other they represent the first stirrings of nationalism in a society previously without it. To be more precise, all authors agree that the cults are at the same time parts of the reaction of societies to new and changing situations, and a *sign* that the societies in question are undergoing some sort of change (besides being, in a way, agents of change too).

So in seeking a causal explanation of cargo cults we are seeking a causal explanation of one kind or manifestation of social change. We recall that structural-functionalism is anti-history.[1] I have already mentioned the difficulty that structural-functionalism has with time. Inasmuch as the functionalist tries to take a snapshot of society, to explain everything at a frozen instant of the here-and-now by describing its relations with everything else in the here-and-now, the doctrine cannot but exclude time. The doctrine does not exclude the idea of change as such, but since every change leads to quick adjustment or to destruction, according to this theory (see my remark on Malinowski's evolutionism, Chapter 1, section 6), the theory demands that we view society as a series of snapshots, not as a moving picture. How can a doctrine which explains an event or an institution by indicating its place in the fixed social structure and specifying its interdependencies with other parts of the structure account for changes in the structure? Some anthropologists argue that a change in the structure can be shown to be a consequence of other changes in other parts of it and that there is no special difficulty in explaining social change. I contend that structural-functionalism can indeed provide good accounts of this sort but that it needs to be supplemented if social change is to be explained properly. Indeed, the functionalist and the structural-functionalist tacitly admits this when saying that he only needs study stills because any change will lead to a quick adaptation or annihilation. Even if this justification

[1] See chapter 1, section 6, and chapter 6, section 5. Undoubtedly the case of the antihistorists was helped by the fact that the primitive societies in question were all without written history. This may seem no reason for ruling out *a priori* possibly fruitful (and possibly testable in due course—who knows what evidence may yet be unearthed?) historical interpretations of social institutions.

were true, we may still wish to inquire into the mechanism of the quick adaptation. Suppose we want to explain change in the place where married couples settle—from, say, virilocal (living in the settlement of the groom's family) to uxorilocal (living near the bride's family). Suppose also we are able to show in a structural-functionalist fashion how this change is a consequence of certain changes in religious beliefs brought on by the activities of missionaries and that in turn the changed marriage pattern will cause changes in the political structure. Nonetheless, to explain the change of residence pattern we still have to account for the decisions of certain leaders of opinion to accept the new religion. And this cannot be done structurally. For, this kind of change is essentially an individual matter, the best approximation to an explanation of which we can so far hope for is one stated within situational logic. We might show how people were using the new religion as a means to something else (say, to strengthen ties with the white men), or how the new religion had changed people's aims and they had decided that, as the traditional residence pattern was irksome, couples should choose freely and that this free choice led to the changed pattern we wanted to explain. The anthropologist could point out that the social structure is part of a person's situation. True enough, but it is just this idea of a situation which must be added to structural-functionalism. I think this argument shows us that although structural-functionalism is needed when we are dealing with social change, it must be combined with situational logic. (I take up the argument again in section 8.)

An exclusive concentration on structural-functionalism then, has proved in the large and important field of social change to be inadequate. However, this methodological inadequacy cannot take all the blame for the difficulties experienced with social change. The leading anthropologists whose influence is strongest today tended to study, and so be preoccupied with, small-scale, face-to-face societies. These societies fit the idea of social structure as a coherent whole very well. Thus a holistic idea of social structure was somewhat uncritically accepted and later anthropologists considered it their job to give a picture of the society they were studying as a coherent, on-going, whole system (see Chapter 6, section 3). Thus their first concern was to identify and describe the principal social institutions which constituted the social structure of the society. They even resorted to aged informants in order to get a picture of the social system as it was prior to modification by contact and change. Thus the preoccupations of the holistically-trained anthropologist left him time and interest only for the unchanging, underlying structure; he did not bother with or bother to notice social change. The limitations of the method thus went uncorrected.

If the functionalist were to adopt situational logic as a theory of adjustment from still picture to still picture, then the next step would be to reject the stills as based on the false idea of either annihilation due to no adaptation or quick and complete adaptation, and as thus both redundant and false. Redundant because situational logic can explain the events without 'freezing' the situation, and false because adaptation is neither quick, nor uniform nor necessarily towards equilibrium.

8. *The Failure to Find a Structural-Functional Explanation of Cargo Cults*

We are now in a position to explain why there has been, as yet, no structural-functional explanation of social change and thus of cargo cults.

There has been no attempt at a structural-functional explanation of social change as exemplified in cargo cults for two principal reasons:

(*a*) Briefly: functionalism explains institutions by their consequences; it seems not to have been noticed, though, that this does not causally explain them at all. We would expect change to be explained causally in a science of society. But to narrate the unintended consequences of some happening is not to explain it causally. It would have been absurd if any author had said 'cargo cults ease the adaptation to western society, therefore they occurred'. Quite possibly they do ease adaptation. Possibly, even that the prophet saw this to be the case. But then they happened *because* that prophet did such and such and those people responded to him, and perhaps the prophet so acted *because* he wanted adaptation. But this is very different from saying that the prophet's and people's actions took place because these actions promote adaptation. Sometimes anthropologists slip from the latter into the former sort of explanation without noticing it; in the case of cargo cults, perhaps, such confusion would be too obviously noticeable.[1]

(*b*) The second reason for the lack of a structural-functional

---

[1] Professor Gellner has suggested that the teleological-type criticisms of functional explanations can be evaded if they are read as causal explanations written backwards: 'The "explanation" of institution X is not really the proper, causal explanation of *it*, but of the manner in which it contributes to the society as a whole. The "real" explanation of X is provided when the functional accounts of the *other* institutions are given . . .' (Gellner, 1963, p. 162). Applying this to cargo cults we can ask: how did it come about that this society adapted itself to western society and that society failed to do so? Answer: because this society had a cargo cult, and cargo cults promote adaptation, and that society did not. This is all true and very illuminating, but why ever did anthropologists start writing their explanations backwards and why do they not now stop?

account of cargo cults is this. Authors have been unwilling or unable to give a situational account of the people involved. This has to be added on to a structuralist account. Let us examine a structural explanation of something. Assume that the event *e* to be explained is a fall in the *Financial Times* (*FT*) share index of five points. The explanation runs: the index fell means prices fell; prices fell because people wanted to sell, not buy, securities. On a free market the price tends towards the point where the amount offered by those who want to sell will be equal to the amount demanded by those who want to buy. Therefore a sudden increase in selling was followed by a drop in price to tempt more buying. Query: who are these people? Answer: typical buyers of securities. Why did the typical anonymous individual buyers of securities want to sell rather than buy? Answer: a balance of payments crisis shook the investor's confidence and his liquidity preference increased so he decided, for the time being, to increase his cash ratio.

This use of an example from economics is deliberate in that it gives a clear model of the *kind* of explanation a structural explanation is, and it enables us to see clearly the role of structural relationships in the explanation. The explanation *presupposes* an economic *structure* of such and such a kind with such and such links between its institutions so that if something happens in one area (the balance of payments) you get a (predictable) reaction in another. Two parts of the structure—the *FT* index and the balance of payments situation—are functionally related.

Note that the explanation *presupposes* the structure; it is necessary to add a situational account of the rationale behind the investors' decisions to sell, not buy, if the explanation is to be satisfactory.

9. *Can there be a Structural-Functional Explanation of Social Change?*

Given that for the various reasons discussed there *has been* no structural-functional explanation of cargo cults offered, the question we must now attend to is whether it is possible that there *can be* such an explanation of these phenomena. At this stage, the question amounts to whether I can see how to evade my own arguments and sketch lines along which such an explanation might be effected, at least in principle.

Obviously if situational logic is ruled out the answer is no, for the reason that situational logic is an explanation of adaptation to change. As I shall argue in Chapter 6, section 6 (ii), situational logic is, one way or another, employed by structural-functionalists; indeed it explains the success of structural-functionalism. The question now is, allowing a situational interpretation of structural-functionalism, how much can we explain with its help? What kind of questions can be answered along its lines? My own view is that more or less can be done structural-functionally, depending upon whether the cults are assumed to be internally or externally caused change.

On the assumption that cargo cults are internally caused, structural-functional explanation of many factual details will be possible. Internally caused change is change not due to the impingement of external factors (either social or natural) but to spontaneous changes within the society. In Britain the development of a high level capitalist economy was internal; it was not entirely positive, and thus led to certain attempts to adjust the economy in 1926 (e.g. keeping wage rates low) so as to overcome the deficiency resulting from these changes; the attempts, in their turn, resulted in the upheaval of the General Strike. Thus, one may say the series of events was the process of structural adjustment. Similarly, one can imagine a situation in a primitive society where a collective decision militating against a substantial number of its members might result in a great change, and even a religious upheaval, as attempts at readjustment. (A case is known of the overpopulation problem being solved by one section of the population driving the other into the sea.)[1] Once the balance of present living was upset in this way we could use structural-functionalist models to explain their consequences. And a situational analysis, presupposing the structure, may be sufficient in turn, to explain why the disruptive decision was taken in the first place.

Where the change is the result of some external agency (be it natural like an earthquake, a crop failure or disease; or social like colonisation) then no explanation in terms of the structure and function of the society affected will do. One would either have to resort to some overall theory like the geological theory of earthquakes, or Marx's account of the reasons for colonisation, to handle all cases; alternatively, one would have to produce an individual historical (geological or social) explanation of each particular case.

An argument an anthropologist could at once raise against me here would be that I have discussed the question of the causes of the external events whereas the question anthropology has to answer is, why the society in question reacted *that* way and not *this*, to these external events.

My answer would be that the anthropologist is right, of course. Knowing the structural set-up of the society helps us trace the *effects*, the repercussions of the initial changing agency throughout the society. But if we explain the reaction of the society to the intrusion (be it the cult or colonisation) we do not explain the intrusion

---

[1] Reported by Firth in 1936.

of the change-bringing agency in the first place. It is the earthquake, the disease, the colonisation, which we cannot explain structural-functionally; whether it is the job of the anthropologists to explain earthquakes, disease and colonisation is quite a different matter. I would agree that the anthropologist need not try to explain these things but he cannot leave them out of his account. And when he does refer to them their importance is largely in altering the situation of one part of the society which then has to get functionally adjusted to the other parts. This is one reason why situational logic is pre-supposed by functionalism.

Internally caused change, then, is explained by the structural-functional anthropologist more easily than externally caused change. Practically every author we have looked at has assumed that the cults are a reaction to culture contact or colonisation, i.e. that they are externally caused. Because cargo cults are *externally caused change*, no structural-functional explanation of them (as opposed to their effects or receptions) *can* be given. This, in my view, is the most powerful reason why none has been given or, so far as I am aware, attempted; we need no longer find this lack surprising.

10. *Other Faults of the Theories and of their Presentation*

One fault common to the cargo cult writers we have already re-viewed: the discrepancy between their lip-service to structural-functionalism and their understandable failure to use it. Now I want to present some further methodological criticism of their work and to suggest that the literature reveals open problems.

The various theories of cargo cults were surveyed (in Chapter 3) more or less in a logical order rather than a chronological order. In the normal course of the publication of learned journals one would have expected articles proposing theories, other articles confuting them and proposing alternatives to have appeared as the quarterly issues succeeded one another. This is the usual way in which progress in deepening and extending knowledge is achieved in academic sub-jects. Nothing much like this has happened in the case of cargo cults. With the exception of Worsley's book where he criticises Ralph Linton's theory and the weberian theory of charisma, there is very little overt intellectual cut-and-thrust.[1] To some extent it is going on below the surface; assertions are being made with the purpose of contradicting another piece of work and, if one is well up in the literature, it is possible to detect this. It seems as though a tacit anti-polemical convention discourages explicitness about who and what

---

[1] Inglis and Stanner have criticised each other, Mair has criticised Worsley, and almost everyone has criticised Williams; that is about all.

is under attack. This is unfortunate simply because it can retard the growth of knowledge. It is esoteric; esotericism excludes the vulgar; but the vulgar can often contribute. Muted controversy prevents their contributing.

On a first impression the published material looks as though it is the work of writers each of whom has come to cargo cults afresh, his mind unsullied by the views of other people (except insofar as the opinions of someone like Williams are paraded so that their absurdity can be pointed out). At least, this would appear to be the impression the authors want to give. Each just launches out into his analysis with little or no attempt to state the problems, and discuss the solutions so far put forward. This procedure of posing problems and criticising earlier solutions to them is the heart of the critical tradition. Although vigorous in natural science and, perhaps, in philosophy, the critical tradition is still weak in social anthropology;[1] anthropologists are reluctant to stick their necks out. It might be worth offering an anthropological conjecture about why this is so.

It is a product, I believe, of the inductivist myth that the 'scientific' character of social anthropology (which I fully accept) consists in its 'scientific' fieldwork. In my opinion the 'scientific' character of the excellent fieldwork done by British social anthropologists is a scientistic myth.[2] A myth bolstered by the further myth that science proceeds by induction from the facts. These myths encourage the belief in scientific expertise and thus perfect agreement between scientists.[3] Since their mythology makes agreement the proper state of affairs it is not surprising that anthropologists are reluctant to take to pieces the conclusions of their colleagues. I have already explained how Popper's view of the scientific character of a discipline, which I accept, is different from this (see Chapter 1, section 9). His view

[1] The main disputes which I recall are those over: the explanation of kinship terminology, the nature of social structure, evolutionism *versus* diffusionism, the interpretation of bride-wealth, and over social *versus* cultural studies. Unfortunately this latter debate between anthropologists on different sides of the Atlantic (see Murdock, 1951, and Firth, 1951*b*) does not seem to have been particularly fruitful. (Professor Firth has kindly reminded me of Leach *versus* Gluckman (on father-right) and Needham *versus* Homans and Schneider (on cross-cousin marriage).)

[2] It has to be emphasised that fieldwork, like laboratory work, is scientific only in so far as it is publicly checkable. Mostly we trust our scientists, of course, but the public nature of their results is an essential check on their objectivity.

[3] Perhaps this is a by-product of the inductivist tradition that science seeks only verified truths, and that the true scientist speaks only the truth. This involves: (*a*) never making bold assertions because they might be wrong; and (*b*) when something inductively arrived at does turn out to be wrong the victim must have been misled by a conspiracy or have been a charlatan (conspirator) himself—depending upon his status. See chapter 1, section 4.

amounts to saying that a discipline is scientific to the extent that its theories are testable. *There is nothing particularly 'scientific' about the procedures of the laboratory, or the field, except insofar as they are means of testing particular theories.*

It is difficult to understand, to return to cargo cults, why in all cases the writers have left to the reader the task of sorting out what problem is being tackled at any one time. Too frequently authors have tackled more than one problem simultaneously without stressing, or even noticing, that they were distinct, especially when they were closely interrelated. At the end of Chapter 2 I made a somewhat unsystematic attempt to list the principal problems the cults raise for a social anthropologist. On the whole other writers have preferred to 'analyse' cargo cults without, apparently, meaning by that the distinguishing and discussing of problems.

Not only are problems not strictly separated off from one another (even in the longer tracts of Worsley and Burridge), but an astonishing, almost bewildering, variety of different sorts of explanations is paraded, often mixed up together. There are economic explanations, sociological explanations (i.e. explanations within situational logic and especially explaining facts as unintended consequences), socio-cultural explanations,[1] historical explanations, psychological explanations, diffusionist explanations and evolutionist (often enough historicist) explanations.

Yet with no exceptions these explanations stand outside the official explanatory framework of British social anthropology. Since these authors were often structural-functionalists tackling a problem which, according to their own claims at least, should have been accessible to their doctrines, and since their explanation by-passed it, they are in a definite sense unsatisfactory.

There is no objection to any of these explanations *per se* (with the possible exception of historicism). No more is it being argued here that these are all separate and separable disciplines which ought not to be mixed up. But I do want to insist that problem and explanation be of the same order. Psychological problems, for example, *cannot* be explained in terms of historicist sociology unless there exists 'bridging laws'[2] leading us from the one to the other. Economics and history, to take another example, can be brought to bear upon sociological problems insofar as there are links between these three disciplines. If in a problem-situation economics, social history, psychology and theory of culture are all mixed up then our explanations may utilise theories from all four; but more often than not we

[1] I have spared the reader most of these by passing over German, Dutch and most American work.
[2] For the idea of bridging laws see Wisdom, 1952*b*.

find that an analysis by means of the general method of situational logic suffices to explain it.

Why, then, are the writers on cargo cults so methodologically dubious; why is their often high-calibre work presented so poorly? My conjecture is that they are insufficiently critical. The writers would all doubtless affirm their adherence to the rational approach, but they fail to carry it out fully in practice. Too few seem to have sat down with a problem, analysed it, then combed the literature for other people's solutions; or to have started by criticising the solutions of someone else, proceeding to tackle the problem *via* criticism of those views. One of the exceptions to these strictures is Firth's 1955 paper where he seems to pose himself the problem: 'all right, you have tried to give an explanation of cargo cults; but what about your special field, Tikopia, is not it, *prima facie*, a counter-example to your theory—for most of the conditions seem to exist there but no cult has occurred?' Here Firth is taking a critical attitude *to his own work*. This is *the* most difficult part of criticism: even some of the most critically-minded scientists find it hard to be sufficiently critical of their own ideas, yet Firth has done it. But Firth is very unusual in this: lack of criticism is the rule. A consequence of this normal lack of criticism has been the ever-increasing muddling up of the various problems (mentioned earlier). Authors started out to say what *causes* cargo cults and ended up holding forth on the necessary *preconditions* of cults; or they began with the problem of explaining them sociologically and ended up talking confusedly of the cultists' mental confusion; and so on.

11. *How far have the Theories Solved the Problems they were Intended to Solve?*

Having gone into the theories proposed by the various anthropologists in some detail it is now time to conclude this discussion of the literature by trying to answer the above question.

At the end of Chapter 2 I listed some of the problems of cargo cults. Now let us find out which of them, on the basis of our literature survey, may still be considered open.

(*a*) The straight empirical problem of who joins the cults. There is a cluster of questions to be answered: is it only the deprived who join (if so, what are they deprived of—wealth, status)? or is it those who have been abroad? or those who have never left their village? or those who have accepted Christianity (themselves, or their neighbourhoods)? or those who have later been neglected (by the missionaries, white administrators)? or disappointed by Christianity (did not receive expected wealth, status)? or those who have never accepted Christianity? and so on. Despite the quite extensive descriptive literature which exists on the cults,[1] some of which has been reviewed in Chapter 3, at least for myself I can say I do not know the various authors' answers to these questions. It is useful, I think, to seek out such genuine gaps in the literature, since this may lead someone to filling them, perhaps authors of previous works who think they did but who did not so far answer them. Admittedly, no anthropologist who has written on the cults has had the luck to be on the spot from the very inception of a cult (with the exception of those who—like Williams—were administrative officials; yet this was hardly an ideal role from which to attempt a dispassionate sociological analysis). Indeed, many of the anthropologists who have written on the cults have never been to Melanesia at all (Linton, Bodrogi, Cohn, Inglis, Worsley); some have been there but done no fieldwork on the cults (Haddon, Firth, Stanner, Mair); and of the rest Hogbin never researched in a cargo area, while Williams and Belshaw were administrators. This leaves Lawrence, Guiart and Burridge the degree of whose actual experience of cult activity first-hand, under their noses, is not public knowledge. But certainly many of these anthropologists arrived not long after cult activity had ceased and would have been in a position to get, by questioning, answers to most of our questions.

The general problem underlying the questions asked above is 'what are the special conditions in their circumstances which have caused these individuals to act in this and this way?' Each of the questions is designed to test a particular hypothesis, like 'people acted this way because they were poor'. We do not have to bother with the plausibility of the hypothesis if we can show empirically that it is either unsatisfactory or not true; namely, either that there are cultists who have never been poor or that there are poor people who did not join the cults.

The literature mentioned in Chapter 3 yields some fragmentary information about the structural and economic set-ups of particular societies and thus about the *situation* of the typical individual. It is not so forthcoming about the *aims* of individuals. Various isolated attempts have been made to give a picture of the structural and economic set-up as the native sees it; but a really thoroughgoing attempt to do this is still wanting. Right up to the appearance of Burridge's book in 1960 we have nowhere a thorough and detailed rational reconstruction of the native's actions in terms of the ends he would like to achieve given the situation he faces, *as he sees it*. With the appearance of that book most of the literature has been superseded. So much for the problem (*a*), who joins the cult?

[1] Listed in Ida Leeson's bibliography: Leeson, 1956.

(b) Very much the same as what was said under (a) goes for the problem, who does not join the cult? We want to know where non-participants stand socially and economically in relation to the people who did join the cult. We also want to find out why they *say* they did not join. No adequate explanation of a cult can be given unless we have the answers in (b) to the parallel set of questions asked in (a) and for the following reason. The existence of noncultists refutes every theory using one of their characteristics. If there are nonpoor cultists then the theory that all cultists are poor is false. All those negative categories must be listed so that we can write off as many hypotheses as possible. While there is a paucity of problems and theories there are a great many popular ideas floating about and these need to be confuted as systematically as possible.

(c) Questions concerning the prophet. Whatever Worsley may say against charisma, the problems connected with the prophet are close to the heart of the matter. A great lack of information about the prophets confronts us, which is especially hard to understand as most of them are still alive and there to be interviewed. Margaret Mead's *New Lives for Old* does concentrate on a prophet—Paliau—but it is so laudatory of Paliau and his achievements that one has to treat it as an excessively biassed case-history.

Our questions about the prophet should be designed to test very similar hypotheses as in (a). Was the prophet relatively rich, or poor, or neither? was he a deprived person (if so, in what ways), or did he have all the advantages? was he a Christian, a disillusioned Christian, a pagan, an atheist, or what? what kind of education had he had? what was his previous career? what were his aims—what precisely did he think he was trying to do? was he sincere? This list is long and obvious so I need not try to make it complete. Another thing which might be mentioned, though, is how far the cult turned out just as the prophet expected; how far, even in this limited sense, the prophet succeeded in realising his aims, and how far the unintended consequences (which there surely were) interfered with both the prophet and his plans. To take an example from our own experience: many western politicians have as a main aim the achievement of power. Their aims when they have got this power interact in a complex way with their desire to get and maintain power. A man may be swept to power on a wave of reformist sentiment. His attempts at reform may then be so disastrous that he has the choice of abandoning his programme or losing his power. On one interpretation, Macmillan became Prime Minister to repair the damage created by Suez, in which he was thought to be a devout believer. He did the job, but it is an open problem whether he intended, or was simply forced, to do it by playing down and then quietly burying the whole affair. There is little doubt that the vacillations in Russia between priority for heavy industry and then priority for consumer goods are examples of leaders trying to be flexible in an effort to stay on top.

All this is very obvious but occasionally more complicated events occur. Occasionally some slogan—'Liberté, égalité, fraternité', or 'Freedom of the press'—endowed with an almost magical force, carries its believers into power. It not infrequently happens that its believers try to implement it—the French Revolution, the Constitution of the U.S.S.R.—and what in fact happens is that the magical force is retained with the slogan, which has not in fact been realised for obvious reasons of power politics, but it is fervently asserted as an official myth. It was an official myth that 'all animals are equal' long before 'but some are more equal than others' was added. Official myths depend on doublethink, the sloganeers must believe the Ministry of War is in fact a Ministry of Peace, that the news in the rewritten *Times* is true. So not only do leaders manoeuvre to stay on top, they also create official myths and by doublethink believe in them and thus continue to uphold their cause.

(*d*) The next problem is connected with detailing the myths and doctrines of the cults. Regarding this fascinating aspect of the cults little or no fault can be found with the literature. The descriptive material available detailing the different legends and ideas underlying most cargo cult movements is, as may have been gathered from the three examples cited in Chapter 2, both extensive and thorough. Reservations, however, are in order regarding the interpretation and explanation of this material.

(*e*) Now we come to the problem of why the cults are so similar in pattern and belief. The following two competing hypotheses more or less crystallise the great conflict which raged in the first quarter of the century between the diffusionist and evolutionist schools of thought (see Chapter 1, sections 2 and 3). The diffusionist explanation of similarity is the theory that cultural borrowing goes on across the vast distances of the Pacific. The evolutionist alternative is: similar conditions have led to a similar outcome. It would be difficult to test either theory and more difficult to get a crucial test. For, in order to refute the diffusionist explanation, every possible way in which diffusion could have taken place should be checked, which is barely possible and makes diffusionism: 'there exists a process of diffusion', metaphysical. At the same time, since the evolutionist theory turns on the phrase 'similar conditions' it would be testable only in conjunction with a theory which gave us some manageable criteria for interpreting some existing conditions as similar. It is a pity that Worsley discussed neither theory seriously along these lines, especially as he is trying to defend a theory along evolutionist lines, according to which cargo cults are similar because they were brought about by certain specifiable states of affairs in the socio-economic set-up such as price fluctuations. Marxist theory does give him criteria for interpreting states of affairs as similar; fortunately, though, the testable variant of marxism has been refuted. Thus, although as they stand the two theories are not testable, by further specification in different ways we can attain a variety of testable hypotheses.

(*f*) The problem of why the cults flare up so very rapidly is very different. One explanation I can imagine is that the cults irrupted into some sort of vacuum; they filled such a yawning gap in the lives of people living in a small face-to-face society where news travels fast that they could not but spread rapidly. I have already aired this view (in Chapter 3 and I develop it in Chapter 4), when stating that in my opinion this gap was the strong need for some sort of solution to the intellectual problems raised by the white man. People were deeply troubled by the unanswered questions connected with this phenomenon and the cargo cult myth answered them all in intelligible terms; it has the additional attraction besides of not only explaining the white man's position but also of showing how to obtain the more attractive of his advantages.

Admittedly this explanation is sketchy but I hope I have said enough to show that an explanation in terms of a purely intellectual *craving* of this kind makes unnecessary any explanations using abnormal psychology. Indeed the desire to solve an objective intellectual problem amounts to a sociologically objective *aim*; thus our explanation sketch is sociological and not psychological. Whether my explanation is worth testing or can be tested are questions for the fieldworkers. It may at least be possible that the explanation is less *ad hoc* than one using abnormal psychology; that is, it is conceivable that independent evidence for the existence of the aim of explaining the white man may be found, whereas the cult is the only evidence for psychological abnormality.

But there can be still other sociological solutions to the problem, even other intellectual sociological solutions. We know that certain movements have in other places developed rapidly without the enabling condition of an intellectual vacuum, e.g. when two highly alluring and rather popular doctrines are united by some minor prophet. Examples would be Christian Science, or Christian Socialism, or National Socialism, or Freud-Marxism. These may take place where there is intellectual confusion between competing doctrines and their unification resolves the problem; or they may take place simply because the doubled allure is too strong to resist. There is a sense in which cargo cults could be interpreted as based on the

166

intellectual unification or supplementation of the previous world-views (magic plus religion) and Christianity. The lure of the priest and witch-doctor suddenly has added to it the allure of the wonderful things the white preacher preaches, giving the new unified doctrines a glamour that sweeps everything before them.

(*g*) What information we have relevant to the question why the cults collapse is interesting but rather scrappy. Many possibilities have to be followed up: the failure of the millennium to materialise; violent repression; loss of faith for other reasons such as fatigue, or distraction, or inability to sustain the excessively heavy demands the prophet made; etc. Each of these possible causes needs investigation which they have not had.

To succeed in solving this problem only brings one up against a rather more intractable puzzle. We have discussed explaining the speed of the cult's development, the emotional vigour which they engender in their participants. Now, assuming the cults are not violently repressed, what has happened to all that energy? Why does the cult dissipate so rapidly? Assume, as I do, the following theses. (1) The initial enthusiasm was purely intellectual—a craving for a solution to a problem. (2) Intellectually, the acid test of the solution to the problem was whether the cult fulfilled its promises. (3) Intellectually, admitting that the cult failed should amount to the admission that the result of the test was negative, to the admission that the cult's solution to the problem was *refuted*. On these three suppositions it is possible to explain the rapid dissipation of the cult as a disappointment of a purely intellectual kind (as a result of critical *post mortems*, of thinking the whole matter out again in the light of new facts).

(*h*) Despite the desire, *qua* sociologists, to avoid psychology, we should consider the question of the importance of abnormal psychological factors in the cults, for most anthropologists seem to think that they are there. In general we demand of any satisfactory explanation that it should not be *ad hoc* but testable independently of the evidence to be explained. The cargo cult must not be the only evidence of neurosis. But even granted the presence of neurotic elements, what do they explain? Either the neurosis is a sort of causal force which *makes* people act; we would then have to assume it to be typical and construct an account of it in ideal-typical terms (see the discussion of 'futurity neuroses' above). Or the neurosis could be regarded as part of the knowledge-situation of the individual to be taken into account when making a rational decision. Such as if one thought: 'were I to do so then my guilt feelings would torment me'. This explanation assumes a degree of self-knowledge in the typical individual which just may not be there.

Neurosis seems to be both a causal drive which one cannot control and a factor in one's situation of which one may or may not take account.

12. *Conclusion*

My purpose in this chapter was simply to sift the literature and seek out lacunae. My reasons for doing this were primarily two only. First I wanted to show that questions concerning cargo cults have not been seriously enough gone into in a search for lacunae, and secondly I wanted to show that searching for lacunae from an armchair on the verandah (no doubt an uncomfortable position in which to type, but that's the image we have to abide by) can be successful and fruitful.

It behoves me now, before passing into the rather long recapitulation and coda of this book, to answer some possible misunderstandings of this chapter. I can imagine someone thinking that the concealed purpose of the chapter, if not of the book, is subtly to discredit social anthropologists by making a lot of seemingly obvious but in fact rather complicated points against them. I can but assure them that this is no intention of mine and that I have done all I can to remove anything which suggested that. I have again and again said how much I admired social anthropology and social anthropologists, how much their results excited me, and such things. My criticisms of them are far from attempts to discredit. On the one hand I think I can show the way to deal with problems over which they are at the moment stuck. On the other hand I firmly believe that they can improve and advance their study a great deal by adopting a new tradition of presentation and methodology, one more closely resembling that in natural science. Indeed my belief is that they are closer to natural science than the most enthusiastic of them realise. This is hardly to their discredit.

A second, somewhat more specific complaint, might be about this 'discovery' of lacunae. Someone could with justice say that we all know there are lacunae, and we don't need your analysis to point them out. In fact we are so aware of lacunae that we certainly don't need to bother 'discovering' them. What do we do about them? What do you think fieldwork is? We spend all the time we have on fieldwork because societies are dying out which may fill lacunae we need filled. There isn't time for systematising the lacunae, we must rush to the field.

My answer to this is first that it is a gross exaggeration. It doesn't take that long to sort out the lacunae, indeed there's no reason at all why it shouldn't be done while the social anthropologists are in the field. Second, I have to remark that this programme of fieldwork seems to be endless. All the societies we know of are undergoing change, so no sooner have they all been done by one anthropologist than there will be a legitimate clamour that they should have a follow-up study by another, and so *ad infinitum*. When, I might ask, is this endless fieldwork going to have a stop?

This final question brings me on to a last justification of the foregoing chapter which I haven't stressed very much. I wanted to settle once and for all the quarrel between social anthropologists as to whether we already have enough field material to explain cargo cults or whether the work of several more generations is required before we can start synthesising the material. I have listed a set of fairly straightforward questions, the answers to which simply do not exist in the literature. This shows, in my opinion, *pace* Judy Inglis (1957), that the field material is hardly adequate as yet. Yet I am not for a moment suggesting that all thinking should stop and that we should rush to the field in search of answers to these questions. These questions are those of an amateur. Any social anthropologist could easily improve upon them. My suggestion is that more fieldwork is needed, but that it must be preceded by discussion and formulation of as many specific questions as possible. Fieldwork will then be much more short, sharp and easier to organise and write up when the fieldworker returns. He will go to Melanesia armed with his questions, seek out the answers, and come back.

Something of this sort used to exist in that out-of-date volume *Notes and Queries in Anthropology* which, even in its most recent edition, is hardly a good enough guide for the modern fieldworker. But I believe that every fieldworker should have a problem, not a society to study, and then his list of questions will be pertinent, not endless. Fieldwork should in fact be shorter, thus enabling the same worker to study the same problem in several societies.

Any social anthropologist would have an answer to this at once. Contextualism tells us, they could say, that you cannot study a specific problem in a society and ignore the rest of the social organisation without distorting the facts and failing to understand the society properly. However they would make this remark within the framework of contextual functionalism and at that, and the reasons why it should be abandoned in such a strong form, I have already glanced, and will now in the last chapter deal with more thoroughly.

6

THE AIMS AND METHODS OF SOCIAL ANTHROPOLOGY

> But reflection and enquiry should satisfy us that to our predecessors we are indebted for much of what we thought was most our own, and that their errors were not wilful extravagances or the ravings of insanity, but simply hypotheses, justifiable as such at the time when they were propounded, but which a fuller experience has proved inadequate. It is only by the successive testing of hypotheses and rejection of the false that truth is at last elicited. . . . Therefore in reviewing the opinions and practices of ruder ages and races we shall do well to look with leniency on their errors as inevitable slips made in the search for truth, and to give them the benefit of that indulgence which we ourselves may one day stand in need of: *cum excusatione itaque veteres audiendi sunt.*
> —J. G. Frazer, *The Golden Bough,* p. 341

1. *Back to Frazer*

M Y main contention in this book on the revolution in anthropology has been that the revolution, however many benefits it brought, went wrong. This wasn't noticed at once but began to be only when the initial post-revolutionary enthusiasm and high hopes turned stale and flat. Social anthropology only came into professional academic life with Frazer's Liverpool chair in 1908, and that was honorary. It was established in the universities on a wave of enthusiasm created by Malinowski. But although popular in the 'twenties and 'thirties in the *avant-garde* way that Freud was popular, as an academic subject for undergraduates, it did not boom until the 'fifties. In the 'twenties and 'thirties, though, the few pioneers and their students had a precious thing: a messianic intellectual enthusiasm. Like marxists and freudians they felt a great truth had been revealed to them, and their job was to carry it forth. Today, there is boundless enthusiasm for departments and journals and teachers and fieldworkers, but there is little or no intellectual progress and so little or no intellectual enthusiasm. Perhaps the messianism had to be given up to get consolidation under way. The consolidating process has been marked, however, by the most tortuous disputes as to what the aims and methods of social anthropology are. Now it is surely a very curious position that in a period of consolidation, of training students, sending them to the field, building up a substantial literature, there should be widespread doubts and calls for rethinking the subject. Curious from one point of view but not perhaps from another. The revolution in anthropology was in many ways a typical political revolution. First there came the prophet and his messianic call to salvation. Then he was joined by the first followers whose enthusiasm was so great partly because they were an *avant-garde*, perhaps even a slightly persecuted *avant-garde*, or at least an *avant-garde* not sufficiently appreciated in the academic world. Then came the success of the revolution and the accession to power and the excitement and confusion which always follows. Out of the confusion emerged a drive for consolidation; and here the trouble always begins. Messianic activity leaves little time for going into the detail and the consequences of the doctrine. But consolidation amounts precisely to going over the doctrine in detail and working out the consequences. What if, then, the detail should turn out to be shaky and the consequences unpalatable? One answer would be: rethink. Another would be: pretend to rethink while actually trying not to.

My theory is that the second answer is at present tacitly accepted by social anthropologists. It would be easy to challenge my theory and to point to attempts to rethink seriously. The best example probably being a book by Leach called *Rethinking Anthropology*. But J. D. Freeman, incidentally an anthropologist whose work I greatly admire, has already given, in his review of that volume in *Man*, the reply I would make. Freeman argues that Leach's rethinking has been within the structural-functional framework. But in concentrating its energies on this level of analysis social anthropology

has ceased to be 'the science of man' and has become little more than the science of man's customary social behaviour. This, in my view, is a retreat from the historic task of anthropology. The time has come, I would suggest, when we ought to turn to the rethinking of even more basic issues; and, for my part, I would hope that during the decades that lie ahead there will emerge a unified science of man. . . . (1962, p. 126).

In other words, Freeman wants to see anthropologists go over from rethinking inside the framework to rethinking the framework. This is what I mean when I say the anthropologists have adopted the policy of pretending to rethink while not doing so. What they are trying to do is rectify with a minimum of rethinking. Dr. Marjorie Topley has expressed this in conversation by saying that attitudes to

The Aims and Methods of Social Anthropology

fieldwork among some social anthropologists have come to be rather like attitudes to the belief in the existence of God among some religious people. The belief in both cases has become so integrated into the lives of these people, that the tendency is to immerse themselves deeper and deeper into the activity of worshipping God, of fieldwork, simply in order to avoid the disturbing and perhaps catastrophic question 'does God exist?', 'is fieldwork worthwhile?' It is preferred not to ask such questions precisely because so much turns upon them. A very understandable reaction.

But if social anthropologists are afraid of it, why do they constantly play with the fire of pseudo-rethinking or even semi-rethinking? Mightn't they accidentally do some and mightn't it be catastrophic? Why don't they leave well alone and not go near any kind of rethinking? My answer to this is that honest intellectual curiosity drives them towards the question; that is to say, they try to rethink but have not carefully distinguished rethinking within the framework from rethinking the framework. But what is their intellectual curiosity about? About, I would say, the much-lauded revolution in anthropology. In a semi-intuitive way, perhaps, they know the revolution perverted the subject so that it is no longer the true science of man. And perhaps they fully know it. Why, then, should they bother with post-revolutionary social anthropology? Why not just get on with building a new and proper science of man? I suppose they have two good reasons for not giving up post-revolutionary social anthropology entirely, even if they fully know that it has been perverted. First, it is a good rule of method not to debunk a school or a tradition because it is in error. One is only justified in debunking if one considers the error silly. Certainly I, for one, would never think of calling the revolution in anthropology silly. What, then, does this same rule prescribe for traditions in error? It is very explicit. It says: criticise the error and rescue from the doctrines everything you can. Second, because social anthropology is the only candidate for the job of the science of man, and it is nearer than it seems at first glance to being the genuine science of man. That it is nearer than it seems is my explanation for the tortuous internecine disputes on the aims and methods of social anthropology. Fearful that they have betrayed their interest in man some anthropologists repeat the malinowskian catechism of function and fieldwork, to comfort themselves. Others, bolder spirits, know that their subject is on the right lines, play with the fire of rethinking, and constantly berate the others for standing pat. (E. R. Leach's function in this respect has almost become institutionalised: he stands for the peace in the feud, as Professor Gluckman might say. His stimulus keeps everyone awake but its more positive function is unclear.) Yet almost no one dares to face

172

the prospect of a complete revaluation of the post-revolutionary aims and methods of the subject as compared and contrasted with what it is conjectured the aims and methods of the science of man ought to be. They dare not face it because if the inquiry turns out badly their life's careers are at stake.

Such an attitude is very understandable and easy to sympathise with. My view is that it is quite unnecessary because social anthropology is *so* successful, despite its recent stagnation, that any criticism, however severe, is likely in the end to strengthen and invigorate the subject, rather than debilitate and undermine it. The whole drift of my argument in this book is that a purge of some methodological error (and, e.g. the consequences of such a purge like adopting selective fieldwork, but this is optional) will enable a new leap forward to take place. All along I have maintained that social anthropology is the Science of Man and that it is its present *impasse* which is of concern. I believe that what I have argued here is a revaluation of its aims and methods that will reaffirm the status of social anthropology as the science of man *and will change almost nothing in the organisation and teaching of the subject*; all changes will be presentational. They will be nonetheless vital for all that, because they may get social anthropology out of the structural-functional rut.

I am able to propose this 'reinterpret but change almost nothing' line because it is my view that all that needs to be gone back on is the history of the subject; and in particular the history of the revolution is too much an official myth. What is needed is a new appreciation of what it is that happened in the revolution that has caused the subsequent stagnation and soul-searching confusion over aims and methods. I hope and believe I can provide that account but because it is a confused and difficult question I shall do so in two ways. First I shall present my interpretation straight, with no argument or documentation, then I shall proceed to detail it. My account will thus, I hope, be seen to be coherent, a necessary but by no means a sufficient condition of its being true. After giving my hypothetical historical reconstruction of the revolution in anthropology I shall sketch the subsequent developments we will deal with, also as coherently as I can. Where the story is more straightforward I think one should get down to cases right away; yet this is not such a case; when first I wrote this without preliminaries it was unintelligible. Therefore I unblushingly request indulgence for doing it twice.

Bronislaw Malinoswki plotted and directed the revolution in social anthropology. It was a genuine revolution, aiming to overthrow the establishment of Frazer and Tylor and their ideas; but mainly it was against Frazer. Frazer committed a number of crimes and thought-crimes, the post-revolutionary literature has sensationally

revealed. He had a thesis, of an evolutionary and historical character, of the development of magic (most primitive), religion (next most
primitive), and science (least primitive but also liable to be superseded). This seemed to offend against the beliefs of those who
believed in the unity of mankind. It was reinforced by his refusal to
live among, or even to go to see, savages, and by his affection for his
armchair. Frazer also enjoyed a great *avant-garde* extra-academic
success—when Freud and T. S. Eliot thought about anthropology
they thought about Frazer. Moreover Frazer was a classically-
trained amateur scholar, refreshingly unpreoccupied with the
methodological status of his studies. He was unsystematic and unscientific and relied on dubious material.

For having the burden of all these crimes, Malinowski declared
Frazer's regime had to be overthrown.

One should not be misled by the curiously affectionate personal
relations between Malinowski and Frazer. Admittedly Frazer wrote
a nice foreword to *Argonauts* and Malinowski wrote a magnanimous
tribute to Frazer after the latter's death; but this should not disguise
the fact that Malinowski started a war for control and won it.

Frazer, no doubt, believed he was doing the science of man, but
he was not given to going on about 'science'. Malinowski's revolution took terribly seriously the claim to scientific status and made it
the basis of his revolution. No doubt what Malinowski intended was
to preserve the science of man and make it really a science. This was
why he had to overthrow Frazer and his influence. Frazer, while full
of ideas, was like a man who pretended to be a scientist but who had
never been inside a laboratory and who had never personally checked
the results that were communicated to him. What was needed then
was a methodological revolution; new ways and new standards for
building the science of man.

Malinowski's new ways were fieldwork ('come down off the
verandah'), and functionalism ('study the ritual, not the belief').
They were both very powerful methods; they made mincemeat of
some bothersome problems and they made the intellectual theories
of the evolutionists look silly. In all these ways Malinowski had
provided what was called for. Unfortunately, however, action is only
one category in sociology, there are also the unintended consequences of our actions. It seems as if Malinowski had pioneered a
method that was too powerful, it got out of hand. I mean this quite
specifically. To begin with, Malinowski intended a revolution in
method, the better to achieve the aim of discussing the unity of mankind, and instituted what turned out to be a revolution of aims. But
this result was more than was expected. The difference between
Frazer's work and Malinowski's is not merely in methodology, as it

should have been. In Malinowski's hands the science of man was twisted into an inductivist and relativist science, with no clear connections with the basic metaphysical problem of the unity of mankind at all. In all this I think the role of Radcliffe-Brown was that of a consolidator. His contribution was to strengthen the doctrine of functionalism by bringing in the element of structure; in almost all else connected with the revolution he went along with Malinowski. Although they disagreed, over basic needs, for example, he did not come to dominate the scene until Malinowski left for the States just before the war.

So much for my historical reconstruction of the revolution.

My thesis is that social anthropologists come to the subject full of interest in people and society. They are entranced by the idea that these interests can be given scientific authority. But in learning how to 'scientise' their interest they actually lose or forget what their primary interests are. Something like an unconscious confidence trick is played on them. But they are left suspicious that something is missing from the science they have been taught. What about Man, they ask? 'Fieldwork', is the answer they get. Yet Lévi-Strauss is the only post-radcliffe-brownian social anthropologist I know of who has written a really magnificent and humane book (his *World on the Wane*) on Man as he is seen by an anthropologist and a fieldworker.[1] All the rest is cold, dehumanised, structuralist sociology. The early monographs of Malinowski, Firth and Schapera are full of 'human interest' but their later works are less so. My plea, then, is for a 'Back to Frazer' movement, or for an 'Over to Lévi-Strauss' one.

As I have said, my attack on the revolution is not the only attempt there has been. Self-doubt has possessed the post-revolutionaries for some time. From various sources, including the centre, some criticisms of the revolution have been put forward. (i) That the methods it advocates are not those of science; (ii) its methods prevent the explanation of social change; (iii) that functionalism as a theory is obviously false because it assumes harmony; (iv) that functionalism is relativistic; (v) that functionalism is inhumane and positivistic; (vi) that Frazer's problems have been abandoned or neglected.

The task I have set myself in this chapter is the revaluation of the revolution precisely in order to evaluate these criticisms. I want to know which of the criticisms can be avoided and which demand deletions of part of the revolutionary innovations from the science of man. And I want to ask the question whether the criticisms are so severe that the whole of the revolution has to be abandoned. I shall

---

[1] Perhaps I should also mention W. R. Geddes' *Nine Dyak Nights*. But virtually nowhere in social anthropology today does one find works with the human interest content of, say, Van der Post's *Lost World of the Kalahari*.

argue that it cannot be, that there is much of value in it. Then I shall look at the only alternative I know of, the most radical of the counter-revolutionaries, those who want to reintroduce history into the subject. I shall criticise this programme too and rescue what I can from it. I shall then be in a position to rescue all I can of functionalism, especially those good ideas which led to its success. After evaluating the criticisms in this way I want to suggest what positive steps should be taken in order to build the science of man. (I shall even attack the idea that 'building' is the right image.) This will be making explicit what I have tried to argue towards throughout this book: that social anthropology can and ought to be the Science of Man. Indeed more: if social anthropology is not the science of man it is nothing worthwhile. But if it is to be a true science of man it must: (1) never forget its basic problems—(*a*) the problem of the unity of man, on the metaphysical level; (*b*) the explanation of *prima facie* differences or similarities (depending on your answer to (*a*)) on the scientific level; and (*c*) the problem of what can be done to improve man's lot, on the practical level—and (2) overthrow the scientistic myth that science is sober, and the myth that it consists in (sober) generalisation from observed compared facts. From my first encounter with social anthropology, in the works of Frazer and Robertson Smith, I found it exciting and enlightening. The deeper one goes the more enlightening it gets. This success must be trumpeted from the rooftops: here is a social science with genuine results. Social anthropology is interesting and exciting and: that which is interesting and exciting in it is already the embryo science of man waiting to be hailed and boosted, not guiltily concealed like a secret vice.

2. *Remarks on the History of the Revolution in Social Anthropology*

No adequate critical history of social anthropology has yet been written.[1] A critical history is an attempt to trace the development of a subject from the emergence of its basic problems, through the various attempts to solve them, the refutation of these attempts, their modification or replacement, the appearance of new problems and so on. The attempts to provide something like this on the revolution in anthropology that I know of are Malinowski's brief essay 'Social Anthropology' (1929*a*), Evans-Pritchard's little book *Social Anthropology*, the passage in H. I. Hogbin's *Social Change* quoted in Chapter 1, and D. F. Pocock's *Social Anthropology*. With all of these works I disagree, but they are in their way excellent,

---

[1] But then there are few, as yet, of natural science: see J. Agassi, 1963*a*.

particularly Evans-Pritchard's, which is a model of clarity and simplicity. As I shall discuss Evans-Pritchard later in this chapter (section 5), have discussed Hogbin in Chapter 1, and have reviewed Pocock elsewhere (1963), I will now confine myself to Malinowski. Suffice it to say that the stories of all four do not diverge in essentials. All the other writings I have seen on the history of the subject are either inductivist over-simplifications, whose authors are forced to regard people who held previous (now refuted) theories as somehow deranged;[1] or polemical works like Lowie's *History of Ethnological Theory* (1937); or else introductory books trying to expound the 'subject' as though it were a system of thought, devoid of history, problems or conflicts. These simply foster an uncritical attitude which looks on the revolution, if it is mentioned at all, as an inevitable victory of reason over error and not at all problematic.

Malinowski's effort to say what the revolution in anthropology was is not as satisfactory as one might wish. He systematically violates the following methodological rule (which I accept): first present an opposing position in its most plausible and sensible formulation and only then criticise that opposing position—which is now in its strongest form. His whole account is coloured, besides, by his contentiousness, by his debating-point techniques, and by his conviction that virtue and right are on his side (so that his opponents and predecessors can hardly be anything but fools and knaves); but at least he makes some attempt to present the history of anthropology in terms of problems and solutions. Like many of his writings his history of the revolution suffers from an exaggerated estimate of the importance and value of his own theory—functionalism. In Chapter 1 I presented Hogbin's synoptic sketch of the development of social anthropology out of anthropology. We might now usefully discuss Malinowski's somewhat more elaborate treatment to see if he throws a little more light on the development of social anthropology, and especially on the problem of whether there is anything to my thesis that the problems of study, as well as the methods, underwent change during the revolution.

When, in the last century, people began to do social anthropology (it was not yet so named), 'the religion of inductivism'[2] was still

---

[1] (See the second sentence of the next paragraph in the text.) I have learned from Professor Popper that historians of science have been led into exactly the same mistake by their inductivism. Consequently they write entirely in terms of 'discoveries' without ever being able to say why a particular discovery is important.

[2] Dr. J. Agassi's apt phrase (see Agassi, 1956). Prof. Gellner argues that inductivism is mostly an unquestioned assumption. This may be true although I think it cannot explain the aggressive empiricism of not only the bulk of

flourishing. On account of this nearly all methodological criticism consisted then, and still consists, of accusations and counter-accusations of a faulty application of the inductive method.[1] Another reason for the present short rehearsal of the history of the revolution in the science of social anthropology is to show that it can be made perfectly intelligible without using the idea of induction.

Malinowski begins with this:

> Social anthropology really begins with a pre-scientific [sic] interest in the strange customs and beliefs of distant peoples, and in this form it is as old, at least, as the Father of History (p. 862).

Malinowski is admitting that the diversity and unity of mankind is the problem behind interest in social anthropology, that such curiosity started science; yet he dismisses it as 'pre-scientific'. I need hardly say that I strongly disagree; and I even claim that curiosity is the basic impulse behind much of science, pseudo-science, and pre-science; the desire to know is the continuing motive-force behind them all. It is understandable that Malinowski is suspicious of curiosity since it is indeed behind pre-science and pseudo-science also, yet one might expect him to admit that curiosity may be, in some cases at least, healthy and fruitful. Apparently, as far as Malinowski was concerned, this is not so. For,

> we have not yet succeeded in eliminating this cruder curiosity in 'Ye Beastly Devices of Ye Heathen' from modern anthropology, where the thirst for the romantic, the sensational and the thrilling still plays some havoc with the sober scientific attitude (p. 862).

Understandable as is this attempt to eliminate 'cruder curiosity'—what one might call the journalistic elements from anthropology—Malinowski exaggerates this case. Already he seems to have forgotten the problem of the unity of mankind and is off on an inductivist temperance campaign which has nothing to do with that problem at all. Even were we to accept the inductivist idea of disinterestedness as characteristic of good, sober, science, still, woe betide the

[1] The first anthropologist I have heard explicitly attack the inductive method of factual comparison and generalisation was Dr. Edmund Leach of Cambridge in his Malinowski Memorial Lecture delivered at the London School of Economics on 3 December 1959 (now in Leach, 1961). But even his criticism was phrased as a typical recriminating attack by one inductivist on other (bad) inductivists. He recommended that anthropologists define their problems and then be not afraid to propose bold and speculative solutions to them. This he labelled 'induction'. In the published version of the lecture this idea regrettably is not as clearly expressed as in the spoken version.

philosophy but even of many a social anthropologist. I accept Agassi's view that the religion of science was an inductivist religion—a sort of empiricist anti-established-religion religion.

science which cannot accommodate a certain amount of romance and excitement.

Despite its largely sober and scientific attitude, Malinowski admits, modern social anthropology still consists of a large diversity of schools with differing views on the same problems. The primary problem on the solution of which they are divided is the problem of similarities in custom, institution and belief in separate societies. ('Pre-scientific . . . crude curiosity' is at last admitted at the back door.) The fundamental division of opinion is between (*a*) the evolutionist school and (*b*) the diffusionist school. Malinowski proceeds to discuss both.

(*a*) The evolutionist theory states that it is a characteristic of human nature that it 'produces at the same level of development identical or similar [social] forms' (p. 863). Initially the model of evolution envisaged was unilinear: *all* human societies go through the same stages during their development. Later this model became unworkable; it just did not fit the facts. Instead a multilinear model was substituted, which postulated that different societies go through different lines of development, but that at least all societies go through *some* development.

(*b*) Diffusionism, according to Malinowski, turns on the theory that 'similarities in implements and weapons, in beliefs and legends, in social organisation and decorative art are explained by spread from one or several original centres' (p. 863). Cultural borrowing (or 'the rubbish-heap view of culture', as it was derisively nick-named) was scorned when expressed in its more extreme form, i.e. *all* culture derives from *one* area by diffusion.

This point may merit a comment. In its most extreme form diffusionism is, I suppose, either self-contradictory or question-begging. The question is, how do cultures develop? The extreme answer would read: *all* culture is borrowed. But if so, then there can be no culture to begin with. We see at once why the theory assumes that culture derives from postulated 'centres'. This raises a new problem: how did culture get to these centres in the first place? Either it evolved there or it was borrowed from elsewhere. Were it borrowed then it could not be a 'centre' and we would be in an infinite regress; while to admit that it evolved would be to concede a vital point to the evolutionist 'enemy'. We thus easily see why *in their weaker* forms the diffusionist and evolutionist theories do not conflict with each other; the evolutionist's weak version of multi-lineal progress leaves ample room for diffusion and diffusionism must allow for some evolution. This may be one reason why the post-malinowskian anthropologists of today have resolved the dispute by tacitly combining modified versions of both theories.

To return to Malinowski's history. The evolutionist/diffusionist dispute was superseded by the development of social anthropology into an empirical science (this, according to Malinowski) over the period 1875–1900. The way was led by Pitt-Rivers, Tylor, Mac-lennan and Lubbock. As far as I can see—Malinowski is not too explicit here—the problems of study underwent some change too. Instead of tackling the problem of similarities of society and custom —which had divided the evolutionists and diffusionists—anthropologists embarked on the explanation of the working of social or cultural wholes. Interest crystallised around the problem of the nature of cultural processes and the complexities of social organisation. Here Malinowski cites the names of Robertson Smith, Frazer, Westermark, Granley and Hallind, Durkheim and Wundt. More specifically, the great advance in Malinowski's eyes to *direct observation* began under Haddon, Rivers, Seligman, Spencer and Gillen (Mooney is nowhere mentioned and Morgan, curiously, is not in this list). Out of this development there grew up two further schools whose divisions cut across those of the evolutionists and diffusionists. These new schools are called by Malinowski the psychologistic school and the sociological school.

The psychologistic school again divided into two: the primitive mentality theorists; and the psychological process theorists. The former group, which was led by Lévy-Bruhl, held that savages had odd quirks in their social organisation because they had odd minds; they had a primitive mentality, structurally different from ours, sometimes called 'pre-' or 'a-logical'. This theory was not popular for very long; perhaps it lent itself too easily to prejudiced distortions.

The psychological process group—Frazer, Van Gennep, Sumner, Gromby and Westermark—had respectable origins in Comte and Mill. They argued that culture is to be explained in terms of human psychological processes. This is a bold and powerful theory which is still influential down to our own day. It is more usually known as 'psychological reductionism' or 'psychologism'.

Malinowski makes no secret of the fact that his sympathies, though, are squarely with the sociological school; indeed, he saw himself as its chief advocate. Curiously, he is concerned to differentiate this sociological approach from the school advocating the method of conjectural history, not from the psychologistic school.[1]

---

[1] It never seems to have struck Malinowski that the critics of functionalism were not asking (for historical accounts of) how social institutions have or could have become the way they are; but that all they were asking was, given the social structure, how do we explain typical (as distinct from historical) social events? Questions about social events—'Why did typical individual *x*

Unlike sociological theories

historical hypotheses . . . suffer from a lifeless and inorganic view of culture and treat it as a thing which can be preserved in cold storage for centuries, transported across oceans and continents, mechanically taken to pieces and recompounded (p. 863).

Whereas genuine history is

based on definite records or on archaeological evidence, [and] gives results which can be empirically verified, and therefore are of scientific value (p. 863).

Malinowski seems to merge, not to say confuse, history and diffusionism; he seems to assume that historical records ('evidence') can be informative even if we do not have hypotheses; to assume, further, that 'hypotheses' are unscientific (he makes it rather clear that all conjecture, preconceived assumption, and hypothetical schemes, have to be banned from this new science of social anthropology). The great fault of 'conjectural history', then, is that it is unscientific because it is conjectural, rather than that it is history; that it makes the grave mistake of explaining the actual, observable, by means of an hypothetical prior state of affairs. The objection might be raised that all natural science seems to explain the known in terms of the unknown; i.e. natural objects and phenomena are explained by means of a mysterious world of fields of force, fundamental particles, atoms, etc., all unobservable and some definitionally invisible. But a stronger objection would be that Malinowski assumes all historical explanations of society to be conjectural and all nonconjectural explanations of society to be sociological. This, for one thing, leaves no room for social history on the lines of Trevelyan. One would have thought that historical explanation of the state of our society would be as well supported by evidence as any sociological explanation and therefore as little conjectural too. Moreover Malinowski's formulation leaves no room for hypothetical or conjectural sociological explanation like that, for example, of Van Gennep, to who he himself refers.

So there is a rather interesting mistake or slip of the pen in Malinowski's formulation of his view of the revolution in anthropology. He wanted to distinguish between conjectural and nonconjectural explanations and he muddled this with his attack on history and

---

do *y*?'—are precisely the sort of sociological questions which are all-important in the study of social change. When faced with such a question Malinowski's injunction to be concerned not with 'history dead and buried, but with tradition alive and at work' (Malinowski, 1929*a*) is no help at all. It is no help, for it is because *y* is a deviation from tradition alive and at work that we want an explanation of it.

support for sociology. This latter attack was in turn explained in Chapter 1 as a reaction against his intellectual forbears plus an inflated idea of his own innovation. Clearly history is marked off from sociology mainly because history means Frazer and sociology means Malinowski. Father-Killing again (see Chapter 1, section 7).

3. *Functionalism*

What, then, is this sociology which Malinowski stands for and which constitutes the heart of his revolution? It is largely to consist in the functional analysis of culture. By culture, if I understand him, Malinowski simply meant a distinct way of life of a people; a something which is comprised in that unique combination of social organisation, religion, language, economy, polity, art, and so on, that exists in only one space-time area. This whole complex of beliefs, customs and behaviour was, for him, *the* culture—the only tangible 'thing' the anthropologist could be said to study. The functionalist analysis of culture sets out to find the functional relationships between the parts of a whole culture and thence to explain it as a coherent system. It seems to have assumed that the whole always did form a coherent system and that therefore the object of a functional analysis could be to find out what each part contributed to that system, and in what manner the parts were related to each other, and to the ecological surroundings. It is assumed that every custom, object, idea, and belief fulfils some vital function (with the stress on 'vital'), some task which is responsible for its continuance as a part of the working whole that is culture, some task without the performance of which the working whole that is culture would not be able to survive. The theory portrays a culture as a whole which is greater than the sum of its component parts; it is to the life or survival of this extra something that it is the *function* of these parts to contribute. Hence we may title this 'sociology' of Malinowski's the 'functionalist theory of social institutions'.

At this point I want to offer a conjecture as to how Malinowski arrived at his notion of total culture. Like Radcliffe-Brown before him, Malinowski gained his principal and formative fieldwork experience in a small-scale island society: he spent four years off and on studying the Trobriand Islands of Melanesia. It is this fact, I think, which tended to make his idea of 'culture'—the thing he said he was studying—a thing which could be grasped as a whole. An accident of geography, then, led Malinowski to develop the essentially vague notion of a social or cultural whole as though it were something precise and demarcatable. The same accident permitted the theory that every part of such a whole culture had a function in that culture, to go unchallenged by him. It was precisely because he was *not* thinking in terms of a huge-scale, diversified, abstract[1] society that he was able to conceive of studying any interrelations between any two given parts of a culture. Such societies as he had opportunity to analyse sociologically were peculiarly prone to encourage the mistaken idea that societies, like organisms, consist of interlocked, interdependent and mutually adjusted parts.

This functionalist theory is incompatible with the evolutionary anthropology of the nineteenth century, for implicit in it is the methodological prescription: 'never mind history—let us concentrate on illuminating the way any one institution is related to or influences other parts of the system of institutions. What relationships does it help to maintain? What does it contribute to the on-going of the whole?' This plainly rules out all sorts of questions the evolutionist might have wanted to ask: 'What stage in the development towards civilisation are those people in? How primitive is this particular institution?' There is in these latter questions no interest in the working of the system now; everything that possibly could be was to be explained historically in the light of certain general theories concerning the evolution of society. This incompatibility of the two theories was not enough for Malinowski, he went one step further and introduced the quasi-darwinian conjecture that dysfunctional or even nonfunctional cultural elements (i.e. elements which are impediments or even just useless) would have been eliminated in the struggle for survival. Societies (or cultures) in striving for an efficient adjustment to their social and ecological surroundings would have disencumbered themselves of disturbing or even of useless institutions. Nothing now extant in any society, therefore, could be a functionless survival from a previous age; no historical explanation would suffice to explain any cultural component; no historical statement would be necessary in the explanation since no anachronistic institution was possible.

If functionalism was *generated* (as I have argued in Chapter 1, section 6) by the peculiarities of the Trobriand *kula*, as Malinowski saw it, the doctrine *fed and grew* on a fundamental suspicion of, and urge to attack, nineteenth-century evolutionary anthropology. As Nadel describes it, nineteenth-century anthropology was an attempt to use accounts of primitive people as chapters of universal history on the assumption that once we were very much like the present-day

---

[1] For the idea of the abstract society, see Popper, 1945, vol. i, pp. 174 ff. This, and its contrast, the concrete or face-to-face society, seem to me to be extremely useful sociological ideas—especially when we are comparing primitive and advanced societies—which have been strangely neglected. See also my discussion in section 4 of Chapter 1.

primitive. The problem to them was why hadn't the present-day primitive moved on to where we were? One suggestion was that the primitives were inferior; another was that they got side-tracked from the main stream of evolution. But the most widespread explanation was that the social customs and institutions of present-day primitives which needed explanation *were* bizarre, irrational phenomena. For example, their curious use of kinship terms was a hang-over from a previous, curious, marriage custom. The malinowskian functionalists flatly denied this; they held, on the contrary, that customs or institutions were viewed as bizarre only because of the ethnocentric prejudice of the anthropologist. To get rid of this he must get off the verandah. To a functionalist every social system constitutes a reasonable and ordered way of life and nothing need be explained as 'irrational'; in particular if a survival occurred it would be irrational; hence survivals are impossible.

To be sure, there is much truth in the functionalist case. It is too easy to write off any problematic custom as a 'peculiar' survival. Especially as a heuristic which challenges us to try to go beyond such an easy assumption, to at least see if an institution has a function, the functional theory has great value. But functional theory was not presented as a conjecture to be discussed and criticised, or even as an heuristic; instead dogmatic acceptance of it became almost an article of faith of what Malinowski called (only half self-mockingly I should say) 'the Functional School of Social Anthropology'.[1] That this school was imbued with the quasi-religious fervour[2] which often gathers round an exciting and fruitful new idea may explain why the reaction against history was so violent. Evolutionism was attacked with such force that for a time all historical study of societies was discredited in its wake (cp. Chapter 5).

Although Malinowski rejected conjectural history because it was uncritical of the implausible assumption that primitive people are in some sense retarded and stuck in a stage analogous to that of an earlier period of our own social development, he did not go on to develop the opposite view that present-day primitive societies are as different from their own historical antecedents, and ours, as our present-day society is different from them. Instead he put all such speculation aside and concentrated on fostering the idea that the task of the social anthropologist is to record a cross-section or snapshot of the society as it is when he is there. This is the practical

[1] See Firth, ed., 1957, p. 11.
[2] Malinowski was, in a sense, the founder of a cargo cult in academic social anthropology (the cargo was a Science of Society, the faith functionalism, and the ritual fieldwork and functional explanation). But his was a cargo cult with a difference: an abundance of goods *was* forthcoming. Not, admittedly, a full-scale Science of Society; but some magnificent achievements nevertheless.

formulation of the theory that all social institutions have functional interrelations with all others. To carry out this programme demanded prolonged and intensive fieldwork and thus explains the importance Malinowski attached to the latter as being the result of his insistence that if you only see enough of an institution you cannot escape seeing its integration with other institutions.

It may seem surprising that Malinowski managed to reconcile in functionalism the conflicting strains of an empiricism (stressing observation) with an apriorist metaphysical idea of societies as wholes. *A priori* his positivism should have allowed that only the actual, observable *behaviour* of human individuals was 'real' and to be discussed; an acute methodological individualism might have been expected. All talk of unobservable, occult 'social wholes', 'social relations', and so on, would have been ruled out (as it is ruled out by some positivists, e.g. Hempel). Malinowski appears not to have noticed this problem of reconciling conflicting philosophies. Yet he did reconcile them, either because he did recognise this problem or because of other reasons, thus not noticing it. His demand that everything be described and functional relationships between the described phenomena be sought combines both induction and positivism with a metaphysical holism. I suggest that he achieved this synthesis by combining the view that science proceeds by induction from the evidence, with the machian idea that there is no distinction between explanation and description because 'explanation is nothing but complete description'. Mach's idea was that causality is metaphysical and hence to be excluded from science; by *a* causes *b* we only relate a mere function—*a* appears before *b*—an observable function, that is. It follows from these two assumptions that complete explanation will involve complete description of the whole of society.[1] Now Malinowski took over, it seems, Mach's empiricist functionalism and loaded it with a new metaphysical meaning—he added the idea of integration instead of the idea of causality which Mach had just expurgated. Moreover, he explained integration causally on evolutionist lines!

The above discussion has been a bit abstract.so before making any further objections against Malinowski I want to give a single illustration of functional analysis, of the way a malinowskian deals with

[1] The Mach passage is quoted from Nadel, 1951, p. 202. I criticise it in my paper 1961 (section 3.2). I try to show that it is misleading to reduce explanation to description in the inductivist way. (Cp. my discussion of the same issue in chapter 1, sections 3 and 5.) There is, however, a sense in which explanation *is* description, but not necessarily of observed facts. A statement is explained by another we call a theory, and it is our aim to seek true theories, i.e. theories that should be descriptions of the structure of the world. But this way of putting it is a long way from the phenomenalism of Mach.

185

a social institution. Let us take magic. Traditionally, evolutionists and particularly Frazer, held that magic is a primitive form of science—it embodies causal theories and empirical apparatus. Malinowski (in 1929*a*) denies this similarity between magic and science, claiming that magic is not primitive science, but rather a system whose function is to strengthen belief, to substantiate morals and to enhance tradition. His argument here is ambiguous; does he mean to say that these two views are incompatible? How does his functional view contradict the view that magical myths are primitive science? Cannot primitive science strengthen belief, substantiate morals, and enhance tradition? Such effects may, after all, be part of the social functions (or rather, I would prefer to say, unintended consequences) of science. I think Malinowski in places virtually asserts that this is impossible, but also virtually admits that this may be so—when he points out that magic explains what the native cannot control. If so, in view of the fact that science too sometimes explains what we cannot control or understand, one has almost no escape from admitting that at least in some respects magic *is* primitive science. Not only is the intellectual role of magical and scientific theories similar but their social function is similar too (see Barber, 1952, p. 67).

Here we see an example of (functional) discoveries of the unintended consequences of actions—magical operations—in a social system; they fill the anthropologist with such excess enthusiasm for the method that he is blinded to the fact that he is not actually contradicting the views of his predecessor; that his predecessor, namely Frazer, also has something relevant to say. The urge to kill the father gets out of hand, and it is not noticed that the doctrine of studying the ritual not the belief covers up important resemblances between magic and science. True, magic and technology are both present in primitive society and are viewed as two different rituals. Because the ritual of technology superficially resembles the rituals of western science the two are confounded. Thus a completely untenable distinction is drawn between the rituals of magic and of science because the similar intellectual and functional meaning of the two has been neglected on the basis of the dogma, 'study the ritual, not the belief'.

I want to make two further criticisms of Malinowski, both concerning his use of the organic metaphor for the social or cultural whole.

There is much sense in Malinowski's attack on the 'lifeless' view of culture; it is certainly absurd to think of culture as a preservable and transportable 'thing'. But does this general point apply to any particular component or institution? True, combinations of institutions cannot easily be moved around; but surely single institutions or cultural elements quite easily *can*. It is true that gardens cannot easily be moved, but quite a few plants can be transplanted—not all, of course. What, then, is behind Malinowski's view? Contextualism, I would suggest, is what he is stressing. Just as in a language a certain word will have different uses and thus different meanings, so in social life a custom, like shaking hands, or taking off hats, will have a different social significance in one society than it will have in another. One cannot just see New Guineans shaking hands and immediately suppose they are greeting each other in a friendly way. In their social context the gesture of shaking hands might have a completely different meaning. (Indeed, already in our society it can be a gesture of greeting or the clinching of a business deal.) Similarly, similar meanings can be conveyed in any number of ways: think of the number of ways there are to salute an officer in an army, everything from the Nazi raised-arm to the American hand-to-forehead. Clearly Malinowski has a good point here when he points out that both evolutionists and diffusionists tend to ignore this kind of contextual significance. He wants to say that to understand the gesture or custom you must understand the whole social context in which it is embedded.

Here, I think, he goes too far. While the significance of a gesture may differ from society to society we cannot assume that it *must* differ. We should begin with our preconceptions from our own society and improve on them by refuting them. A handshake *may* mean the same thing, so why not assume it does and then test? Were we to accept Malinowski's view that every context makes a difference we should have to accept the so-called paradox of democracy that says: democracy cannot work without the base of a strong democratic tradition; but you cannot have a strong democratic tradition unless you have had democracy for some time. Confirmed as this is by many events since world war II it is, nevertheless, happily false. There are countries in the world into which Parliamentary democracy has been successfully transplanted. This refutes the paradox and Malinowski's view that institutions are alive in the sense that they cannot be transplanted *and stay the same*. This shows that understanding of the relevant parts of the context rather than of the total context is all that is required.

My second criticism simply takes the metaphor of society as a functioning organism one step further. Man, who stands at the highest point yet known of the evolutionary scale, has in his body, we are told, nonfunctional survivals (e.g. the appendix). There is thus every reason to suppose that society (which is only metaphorically 'living') also may contain uneliminated redundant parts which remain on account of a sort of social inertia (and perhaps on account of their being rather harmless). This raises the problem, how did Malinowski come to believe there were no survivals? My Trobriand *kula* explanation (see Chapter 1, section 5) says that he generalised his account of the *kula* and then realised this ruled out survivals. I now present an alternative explanation. I do not know how to decide between the two. Malinowski's situation was this. He was out to do fieldwork in Melanesia. As an Austrian subject he was technically an enemy alien, but although an eye was kept on him, he was allowed to continue his studies. His movements seem to have been only somewhat restricted. It is not altogether clear whether he would have stayed quite so long among the Trobrianders if he had been quite free to come back to Britain. Anyway, there he was, in the middle of nowhere. There were a few white men on his island but he deliberately pitched his tent among the native huts so that he would be forced to seek out native companionship. He really put himself in a situation such that he had to find his way around Trobriand society in much the same way he had had to find his way around English society when he had arrived from Poland. A man in such a situation who manages to succeed in finding his way around in that society, and to enjoy living there and experiencing the special flavour of its social life, is going to be disinclined towards theories which view as bizarre survivals many institutions of that society. Malinowski, in short, trying to find his way around in Trobriand society, was forced to look for the significance of every act. To his surprise, even with the most complicated and bizarre things, he was successful; he found that *everything* he had noticed could be given some social significance. My thesis is: he was so impressed by this discovery that he generalised it into the functionalist theory: every element of a culture had a function; there are no functionless survivals. He may even, in the early stages, have come across what looked like survivals, but he found that, with hard work, they could be functionally understood. The trouble is, he didn't see that what he was doing was applying a methodological rule—'look for the function'. Since the rule always gave results he mistook it for the theory 'everything has a function'. I am not here criticising Malinowski's taking the Trobrianders as archetypal primitives. Leach (1961) censures Malinowski on this count that he generalised from the Trobriands; for my part I think generalising from single cases an excellent method. My criticism would be merely that Malinowski's 'Trobriandcentricity' prevented him from refuting this obviously false no-survival theory. This, however, is criticism, not censure; though quite possibly his followers' blind adherence to his error was vicious.

We may now leave functionalism and turn to its replacement, structural-functionalism.

4. *Structural-Functionalism*

Radcliffe-Brown, the creator of structural-functionalism, was older than Malinowski. He was doing fieldwork in 1906–8 (in the Andaman Islands of the Bay of Bengal) when Malinowski was still doing physics and mathematics at Cracow. Yet his first book in social anthropology, *The Andaman Islanders*, was completed in 1914 but published only in 1922, the same year as Malinoswki's *Argonauts of the Western Pacific*. It went quickly out of print for many years. Despite this publication lag and lack of initial success, Radcliffe-Brown shares equal responsibility with Malinowski for moulding, through his academic work, British social anthropology into the shape it takes today. In the 'twenties and early 'thirties Malinowski's influence was the stronger, among both anthropological professionals and the public at large. Unfortunately, perhaps, Radcliffe-Brown never achieved the kind of public esteem which Malinowski enjoyed. However, from the mid 'thirties the influence of Radcliffe-Brown's thinking on social anthropology became increasingly marked. If in fieldwork Malinowski is still the peerless master, then in theoretical social anthropology Radcliffe-Brown still reigns almost unchallenged.

Radcliffe-Brown's contribution to the revolution in anthropology might be summed up by saying that he changed 'functionalism' into 'structural-functionalism' (although the latter neologism is, I believe, due to Talcott Parsons). I would say that in a way this was another historical accident. Radcliffe-Brown's life was an itinerant one: he seems to have moved every few years from one university to another. In the 'twenties he was in Australia encouraging students to go out into the interior to study the aborigines. It just so happens that one of the most complex problems social anthropologists have ever come across is the kinship system of these very primitive peoples. Details are unnecessary here; suffice it to say that their system of naming kin and of who was allowed to marry whom was very complicated to a westerner. Both the organising principles of the system and how it could possibly work seemed ununderstandable. It was Radcliffe-Brown's great achievement (*a*) to demolish, on the general grounds we have gone over above, all the 'survival' explanations of such systems; (*b*) to criticise severely the 'psychologistic' explanation of them given by some American scholars; and (*c*) to take a big step towards providing a rational account of how the system works which, at the same time, represented a considerable advance in the theory of kinship. Briefly his theory is: that marriage rules follow the lines along which kinship terms are extended and thus from an examination of the kinship terms we can understand the marriage rules. My conjecture is that this success—for whether true or false[1] this theory is a breakthrough from the attitude that the whole system was a bizarre and complicated oddity—with a particularly abstract and intractable problem, strongly coloured Radcliffe-Brown's subsequent view of social institutions. The social relations of kinship constituted a system or 'structure' which could be mapped; Radcliffe-Brown came to regard all other institutions likewise as (perhaps mappable) structures. He interpreted people's social relations in such a way that there was, besides the kinship structure, an economic structure, a religious structure, a political structure, a legal structure, an educational structure, and so on. Each of these structures was part, or an aspect of, a total structure made up of all the social relations between people and called the *social structure*. This notion, in various disguises, and somewhat elaborately worked out, is the base on which much of present social anthropology rests.

The first difference to be remarked between functionalism and structuralism is a slight shift of the metaphor from the organic to the mechanical. Functionalism conceives society as like a human body and the function of the parts is to contribute to the sustenance of the whole, the function of which in turn is to satisfy the needs of the members. In a way, the structural theory is also organic, but with a slightly mechanical twist. The basic structure of the body, for example, is the skeleton. Now the skeleton aids the sustenance of the whole in a specific way: it holds it together or integrates it. In the words of Sol Tax, Radcliffe-Brown 'believes that the necessity for social integration is the fundamental cause of all social institutions—that they have the function of keeping the society integrated.'[2] This is not quite coherent, since integration needs a basic prop and this must, I think, be the social structure. One might characterise structural-functionalism roughly as the method of exhibiting the way any social institution under discussion interlocks with and contributes to this structure of structures the social structure. Its contribution can be either to the maintenance or continuity of the total structure, i.e. to the steady on-going of the whole system; or to the cohesion, integration, or hanging-together of the whole thing, i.e. its amelioration of conflict with the rest of the structure and with its social and natural surroundings. Social anthropologists vacillate between these two meanings the second of which I do not understand. The purposes, or ends, in terms of which Radcliffe-Brown explained social institutions, were those of the integration, stability, and maintenance of the system. Institutions were (almost) explained by their survival-value

---

[1] It has come under heavy and, I think, convincing attack from G. P. Murdock, 1949, pp. 50 ff.

[2] Quoted in Murdock, 1949, p. 121.

to the society. Malinowski also operated with survival values. But his were those of human beings, not of societies.[1] He argued that the function of a society was to satisfy the basic biological needs of people and that to the extent they did this social institutions had a function and would continue as part of the system. Another difference between functionalism and structural-functionalism which this brings out is that biological needs can either be satisfied or not satisfied, they can neither be 'negatively satisfied', nor made more acute. Social structures on the other hand can have elements making for disintegration, instability and destruction of the system. Thus Radcliffe-Brown and his pupils were able to sophisticate their ideas by inventing the idea of dysfunction, a negative value or end with which to explain some institutions.

A word might be said here about the relationship of the functional and structural theories to the philosophies of Malinowski and Radcliffe-Brown. Both were positivists. Both believed in inducing theories from the facts; both rejected conjectural history because it was conjectural, i.e. hypothetical, i.e. not based on induction from facts. Malinowski was more under the influence, I think,[2] of the Mach-Kirchhoff school of phenomenalism; Radcliffe-Brown was under the influence of Durkheim who was in the tradition of Comte. This positivism explains Malinowski's aggressive empiricism and also, I suspect, Radcliffe-Brown's scorn of psychologism. It is not surprising to find a positivist being against the 'unseens' of psychologism mainly because they are unobservable. To the positivist observation is god: thus both the armchair conjectural historian and the unobservable postulates of psychologistic theory are anathema. Malinowski did not come to hold this latter position until he got over his freudian period of the early 'twenties. Yet Radcliffe-Brown, to his credit, had the courage to interest himself in social ties and social structures which were patently 'invisible'.[3] He salved his positivist conscience by insisting that social structure was a real observable thing. I do not know of any arguments he used to back this view. Leach, for example, has argued pretty conclusively that if social

---

[1] I mean, of course, that this is the theory he held at one point. That he held others at times is amply illustrated by the essayists in *Man and Culture* (Firth, 1957).

[2] I cannot agree with Leach's view (1957) that Malinowski was a jamesian pragmatist. Leach's argument that that was the intellectual climate of Malinowski's time is not sufficient to establish such a thesis. Anyway, I think Malinowski retained an absolutist view of truth. His background in physics was almost certainly machian and his philosophical background probably hegelian. See section 3 above.

[3] Following in the footsteps of his mentor Durkheim. See Agassi, 1960, footnote 14.

structure is anything it is a model we make and if models exist anywhere they exist in our heads (1954, Introduction). Positivistic talk about social structure being observable is hard to defend. As often seems to happen to positivists, the theory they adopted, that there is a tendency towards the functional integration of society, turned into metaphysics and even teleology in their hands (Jarvie, 1961, section 3.7). Perhaps without his knowing it, it was Radcliffe-Brown who liberated social anthropology from positivism when he followed up Durkheim's interest in social relationships, in the abstract. In so doing he cleared the way for those who did not believe that all social phenomena were directly observable.

As to what social structure *is*, a great deal too much ink has already been expended on this. Suggestions have been: the relations of persons to persons; the relations of persons to institutions; the relations of institutions to institutions; or various combinations of these. Detail of the tortuous arguments which have taken place need not concern us here. I prefer to say simply that 'social structure' is a metaphor to describe the mechanical relations between entities in the social order. Its 'reality' is of importance only to the positivist. Instead I want to turn back to my narration of the revolution in anthropology. Certainly all this talk of functional integration and structure has a very remote bearing, if any, on the metaphysical problem of the unity of Man, and the practical problem of what we can do to aid men. My thesis is, in short, that Malinowski, aided and abetted by Radcliffe-Brown, changed the problems their subject set out to study by concentrating on the method of study. As anthropologists they wanted to study Man. As academics they wanted their study to be scientific, i.e. systematic and sound. But the price of doing that was forgetting (for the time being, at least) about Man and worrying about method. Although I do not endorse this 'scientific' motive, I do not oppose methodological rethinking: as I said at the beginning of the book, I think methodological discussion has a rightful and fruitful place in scientific discussion. But the danger is that wrong-headed methodological discussion, in the absence of a strong tradition in the science, can lead it haywire. I suggest this is what has happened in social anthropology. Earnest young students who want to do the subject because they are interested in people are gradually shown how the ideals of science and scholarship demand fieldwork and structural-functionalism.

Worse, though, is yet to come. Next to economics, social anthropology is far and away the most vigorous and interesting of the social sciences. I have already listed a sample of the problems so far solved. Social anthropology is therefore in a strong position to make a take-over bid for its neighbour, sociology. Now this is precisely what has happened. More and more anthropologists believe that sociology is a branch of their subject, and an increasing number of sociologists are flirting with social anthropology. This would be all to the good were it not that social anthropology means, not situational logic, but structural-functionalism. So that soon structural-functionalism may take over completely.

The strongest formulation of this theme is a recent paper by Prof. Kingsley Davis of Berkeley (1959). Davis argues that structural-functional explanation *is* sociological explanation; that the characteristic problems and explanations of functionalism are those of sociology itself. Thus we have come the complete circle; Malinowski's revolutionary view that social anthropology is functional has come again *via* the view that social anthropology and sociology are identical, and the position that (structural-) functionalism is the method of social science.

On the surface Davis' paper may seem like nothing more than a proposal to legislate away the use of the word 'functionalism' (where this is a contraction of structural-functionalism). Instead we should just say 'sociology' or 'sociological explanation'. He argues first that the meaning of the word 'functionalism' has been stretched so far—that it now encompasses so much—as to be virtually the equivalent of 'sociological explanation' or 'sociological method'. So why not, he goes on, stop talking of 'functionalism' as though it were some sort of special method and instead speak simply of 'sociological explanation (or analysis)'?

. . . the definitions most commonly agreed upon make functionalism synonymous with either reductionist theories or pure description . . . the issues raised with respect to functionalism, except insofar as they spring from the ambiguities of words like 'function', are really the basic issues or questions of sociological theory . . . historically the rise of functionalism represented a revolt against reductionist theories, anti-theoretical empiricism, and moralistic or ideological views under the name of sociology or social anthropology. Although functionalism may have been salutary at the time it arose, the ambiguities of its special terminology make the myth that it is a special method a liability now. It seems wise to abandon the myth for the sake of increased clarity and efficiency.[1]

The only argument Davis adduces in support of his thesis which is not mentioned in the above summary is that he tries to show (moderately successfully) that those things which have been said to be the

[1] If functionalism is either reductionism or pure description it is difficult to see how it can have arisen as a reaction against *both* reductionism and anti-theoretical empiricism. 'The definitions most commonly agreed upon' seem to make functionalism identical with what it rose against. Davis could, with advantage, have made this point explicit.

unique distinguishing marks of functionalism are simply the common-or-garden characteristics of 'scientific analysis in general' (p. 760).

In fact I prefer to think that Davis is saying that functionalism in practice is the same as sociological analysis, and is not trying to equate them by a mere verbal device. If this is Davis' thesis then, I would say, it is false because functionalism cannot explain social change, while sociology in general is not similarly impotent. Davis deals with this point in his paper. His argument is two-pronged: on the one hand he holds the accusation to be trivially true if functionalists take their static model of society literally; otherwise it is false because 'some of the best analyses of social change have come from people labelled as functionalists' (pp. 766-7).

Both of these replies are weak. It is not a question of whether or not functionalists take their static model literally. It is difficult to see how they can do otherwise. Take, e.g., economics: a simplified model of a market is there used to help understand the concomitant variation of supply and demand. But every economist well knows the impossible complexity you quickly get into if you add and vary parameters to make the model more 'realistic'. Now functionalists are trying to understand the whole of society, not just a partially quantifiable aspect of it like economics. All they can do is try to construct highly simplified hypothetical models about the relationships obtaining between social institutions; models which cannot but be on a *static* principle. They cannot avoid taking this model literally; it is all they have to take. *Ipso facto* they must consign the explanation of change to some other model.

The second reply of Davis is purely *ad hominem*. I would answer that the fact that Levy, Merton, Schapera, etc., have been responsible for 'some of the best analyses of social change' proves nothing at all about functionalism, while revealing a great deal about those authors; in particular—since they do not use functional analyses in their studies of social change—that they intuitively recognise the limitations of functionalism which I have already outlined and break the injunction to seek the integrative purpose of every institution.

Two things emerge from this criticism of Davis. First: were Davis' thesis true, and were it the case (as I think I have shown) that functional explanation was not always satisfactory explanation, then the whole of present-day sociology would be toppling. (This is not so shocking a conclusion: nobody really thinks that sociology is coterminus with functionalism.) Second: I have already tried to establish that there is at least one set of sociological problems—those of social change—which has to be tackled in other ways. As a matter of fact I think there are many such sets, but to establish that there is one is sufficient for my purposes. Thus either sociology is toppling or Davis' argument is mistaken. I opt for the latter alternative.

Elsewhere (1961) I have tried to dissect the various structural-functional theories with which social anthropologists operate. I want now, with a quotation from Timasheff, to present the doctrine of the revolution in its most acceptable form. I shall then summarise my criticisms of it.

> In the first place (and this starting-point is often obscured in the writing of functionalists), the maintenance and the possible extension of a group and its social system, as well as the persistence and possible improvement of the group's culture, are defined, at least implicitly, as the group's objectives or goals. Empirical study should reveal a given system's *functional requisites*, that is, the conditions under which these objectives can be achieved. It can then be shown that specific parts of the group's social structure and culture operate as mechanisms that satisfy (or do not satisfy) the functional requisites. Further propositions follow as broad theoretical guides. First, universal functional needs can be met in different ways, illustrated by social and cultural variation; and individual societies, so to speak, have 'selected' their particular procedures from a wide range of cultural possibilities. But, second, the number of such choices is always limited, limited by the biological characteristics of man and by his social and psychic needs; hence the prevalence of independent and parallel inventions in different societies (a phenomenon which served the evolutionists as one of their strongest arguments). Third, the range of 'choices' for a specific society is further limited by the interrelationship and, in some measure, the interdependence of the choices themselves; thus, the adoption of one type of kinship system, for example, restricts the number of possibilities in other institutional areas. (More concretely, as it has often been noted, modern industrial growth in traditionally agrarian societies no doubt limits, but does not determine, the number and type of possible political and other institutional developments.) A major task of functional analysis is to discover the number and type of cultural possibilities under diverse social conditions. . . .
>
> . . . The function of a partial structure, that is, a culture trait, custom, institution or subsystem (A), more exactly, of its *operation*, is not identical for system N with the consequences of the operation of A, but with the *meaning* of these consequences or of the specific contribution of these consequences for N. Let us designate them by M. Then we can say that the specific contribution which A makes for the persistence of N is M. Or, expressed in another way: a contributive cause of the persistence of N (say, the family) is A (e.g. the incest taboo) because of M (prevention of confusion in family roles). It would not be functional, but teleological reasoning, however, if one claimed that the prevention of confusion of roles in the family is the cause of the incest taboo. . . .
>
> —Timasheff, 1957, pp. 228–9.

So: a group has the objectives of maintenance and extension of itself and its culture and there are certain requisites if these objectives are to be achieved. The requisites are selective but the selection is limited in various ways. The function of an institution is its consequences for the persistence of system N. The question is: does it explain an institution to specify the manner in which it satisfies the functional requisites of this society?

My answer is: a functional theory would explain an institution causally only if it contained the assumption that societies indeed have aims *which have means of realising themselves*; i.e. to say that societies have requisites is not enough; they must also have ways and means of obtaining these requisites. To this it is often answered that these are requisites of survival, so if the society has survived that shows it has managed to obtain these requisites. I would answer that this is circular reasoning: why do societies survive: because they have obtained all their requisites: how do we know they have obtained their requisites: because they have survived. Some little more independent argument is required to show there are requisites which are obtained, as there happen to be alternative accounts of why societies survive and of how institutions should be explained which do not operate with requisites at all. Besides, powerful attacks have been launched on the idea of functional requisites or societies' needs as such.[1] If the theory is to be taken seriously, these demand an answer.

Sometimes it is replied to such an argument that, of course, structural-functionalism is not causal explanation, but something else (Davis calls it 'pure description' but that takes us back to machian phenomenalism). The only suggestion I can make here is that perhaps teleological explanation is meant. I would regard that admission as already a criticism, but if functionalists are happy in teleology I do not wish to argue but simply to point out this puts them beyond the pale of science. Science is usually understood to give causal explanations and I see no reason why that should not apply to the Science of Man. Now to go on with the causal claims of functionalism.

I will commence with an example. Problem: why did the price of gilt-edged securities plunge on such and such a date? Answer: because the price of gilt-edged is an inverse function of Bank Rate and Bank Rate went up $\frac{1}{2}$ per cent on that day. This is a satisfactory explanation if and only if it postulates a causal connection (not just correlation) between the price of gilt-edged and the Bank Rate, i.e. if we can construct a theory or model which shows *how* the one affects the other.

Explanations in natural science generally explain the known in terms of the unknown. For various reasons, including the rationality

[1] For both see Gellner, 1958, and Agassi, 1960.

196

principle and the sort of 'privileged access' (see section 6 (ii) below) we have into behaviour, in social science we tend to explain the mysterious known in terms of the unmysterious known. Whether the explanation of the price-shift of gilt-edged is satisfactory depends to a large extent on whether the explanation in terms of a rise in Bank Rate is problematic or not to the person posing the problem. If it is, it is perfectly easy to give a situational explanation of why the Governors of the Bank of England raised their discount rate to the money market at this time. Having gone this one step further it will also be necessary to go on to explain the structure of the Bank and how it is controlled by Governors who are subject to Treasury directives, and so on.

Generally speaking, then, functional explanation is satisfactory when it succeeds in tracing the cause of a social happening to an unproblematic event or institution. For example, Radcliffe-Brown explained extended kinship terminologies in terms of the extended social relationships to which the terms referred. He explained the problematic kinship terminology by specifying its reference to the 'given' social-structural set-up. Were the social-structural set-up in its turn to be queried he could explain it only as a unique configuration, historically developed.

Where, then, does functionalism go wrong, if at all? To put it in general terms first: it goes wrong when it tries to smuggle in, under the guise of producing a causal explanation, the unintended consequences of an event as a cause of that event.[1] An example is the explanation cited above (section 3) where Malinowski argues that magic serves as an organising force in society. If this means that it so happens we can see that magical practices result in a certain reinforcing of the social structure—well and good. But if it is being insinuated that the reason there is magic there is that it serves as an organising force for society—then the explanation is dubious. He has muddled antecedent and consequent. If we say 'if magic then enhanced organisation in the society' we have a statement of the form 'if a then b'. Now in this b is being explained by a, it is simply a logical mistake to think a (magic) is explained by b (its tendency to strengthen organisation); b (organisation) only is partly conditioned by a (magic) not a by b. The reinforcing is an *effect* of magic and cannot, for that reason, be said to explain it *causally*. That magic has the *disposition*[2] to integrate a society is not a causal explanation

[1] A good account of this, the teleological fallacy, may be found in Levy, 1951, and in Agassi, 1960, footnote 5.

[2] Hempel in Gross, 1959. This noted methodologist turns his heavy guns to the task of criticising the types of functionalist theory I have not dealt with in detail. He tries many formulations of the theories to see if there are any ways of

of the presence of magic. The fact that this disposition has such an effect *might* be the reason why it is maintained in existence. If, that is, we can talk of parts of society needing 'reasons' for their existence. If the consequent cannot causally explain the antecedent it can be said *teleologically* to explain it. However, in science the status of such explanation is dubious even with regard to living organisms. Teleological explanation can be usefully compared to the following. Why did the stone fall? Because it wanted to hit the ground. The point being that the stone fell *because* its support was withdrawn and gravity dragged it down. It was the (unintended?) consequence of this that it fell and hit the ground.

Few would defend the idea that the stone *intended* to get to the ground, that magic *intended* to be an organising force in society. But it might be argued that these explanations are quasi-intended. That is to say, that the evolution of society *can look as though* it had a definite direction, was being intentionally guided. There can be the appearance of a Hidden Hand operating, but it is no more than an appearance for it can be explained as the disposition of the stone and the magic. Far from disregarding this, I regard it as a crucial reformulation which avoids the teleological criticism and leaves functionalism free from this difficulty. I have therefore tried, in section 6 (ii) and Chapter 4, section 5, to sketch a possible account of such 'directed' evolution which utilises only situational logic. Thus functionalism can be rescued from both teleology and anti-history, and can be rehabilitated with the help of evolutionism. It thus allows those historical explanations it was designed to exclude. This has led some anthropologists to insist that social anthropology is thus shown to be an historical study.

5. *Anthropology is History: Evans-Pritchard and Worsley*

Malinowski's revolution, then, was a revolution in method: he proposed the abandonment of historical conjecture and its replacement by functionalist sociology. Radcliffe-Brown followed up by rectifying the functional theory to include the social structure and substituted what we might call the needs of the structure, or its essential interdependencies, for Malinowski's biological needs.

---

putting them that will make them satisfactory. He always ends up with vacuousness or covert tautologies. Finally, all he can say in favour of functionalism is that, despite its illuminating, suggestive and fruitful past, it must now be largely regarded as a useful heuristic or simply as 'working hypotheses'. This last point is not altogether fair because if we look into it, we find that all the illumination, suggestion and fruitfulness that has stemmed from functionalism derived from this single form of it as heuristic.

But this revolution of method had also become a revolution of aims, or problems. The science of man, conceived of structural-functionally, explains neither the problem of man's unity nor that of his practical problems. In fact its relativism makes the first no problem: man is assumed to be equal everywhere and differences are assumed to be contingent, the problem is simply to catalogue these contingent differences. Moreover the practical problems are disposed of too because its relativism is conservative and omnitolerant: societies which have survived are harmonious and do not need reform. Even on the level of cataloguing the differences of soceties there is no attempt causally to explain these differences. The aims and methods of the science of man, then, are hardly prescribed adequately in structural-functional terms. One consequence of this inadequacy, or perhaps its central part, the rejection of the past as having any relevance, has stirred up the most prolonged and intensive controversy between anthropologists. Evans-Pritchard has said that this throwing out of history is a mistake and he comments that the revolution is scientistic and inhumane. Worsley follows him in this to a very considerable extent. However, he counter-rejects Evans-Pritchard's anti-scientism and argues simply that Malinowski's non-historical scientism was an error. I shall now discuss this deviation.

I have not finished with functionalism, though, for after this digression I shall return to it with a new theme: since it was so successful there must have been something in it. Question: what worth preserving is there in structural-functionalism? My answer will be: those parts of it which overlap with situational logic and explanations using the unintended consequences of actions. The digression will, I think, be worthwhile because it will enable us to review certain arguments against functionalism and against anthropology as the science of man, and thus further our quest for the worthwhile elements in functionalism that can be used in the science of man.

The third view of the aims and methods of social anthropology which I am going to discuss, then, is the view that anthropology is a branch of history. According to Evans-Pritchard this makes it a humanity: according to Worsley it makes it a science.

Evans-Pritchard has outlined his case in three places; his Marrett lecture 'Social Anthropology: Past and Present' of 1950; his magnificent little book of Third Programme talks, *Social Anthropology* (1951); and his lecture at Manchester, 'Anthropology and History' (1961). The first two seem to have been written at the same time and they even have parallel passages, so we shall consider them together. As always with Evans-Pritchard these items are written in an admirably clear and lucid style; one always knows what he is saying.

Both Worsley and Evans-Pritchard, it seems to me, view social anthropology as the Study of Man. Evans-Pritchard, finding the views of those who see that Study as a Science repellent, decides that while the aim is to study *Man*, the only decent way this can be done is by coming off the verandah and seeking to understand *men*. He feels that a scientific approach involves the cold detachment of the verandah. The reason why Evans-Pritchard turns aside from science to history and not something else, is explanation. It is scientific explanation which Evans-Pritchard is specifically repelled by. As an alternative he looks to that humane study of the lives of men, history. History, for him, is attempting to understand men, not to predict and dehumanise them. Worsley on the other hand says this is precisely what the science of history does do. Evans-Pritchard was right, according to Worsley to campaign for more history in social anthropology, but we only do this because by examining the past we can detect the historical laws of society and so predict the future.

In the hands of Evans-Pritchard and Worsley, then, the central methodological conflict has shifted from sociology *versus* history to history (humane) *versus* history (science). Malinowski argued that historical or origin explanations were not satisfactory and must be replaced with sociological, that is functional explanations. Malinowski and Radcliffe-Brown in fact opted for slightly different kinds of functional explanation which, because of certain resemblances to biological explanations, were thought to warrant the claim to scientific status. Evans-Pritchard objects that functional explanation has to be supplemented by the more humane approach of the historian or else a positivistic science will result. Worsley concurs with Evans-Pritchard but adds that the approach of the historian is to build a science too. Round and round goes the dispute. Now for a little detail.

Evans-Pritchard begins, in his chapter 'Later Theoretical Developments', by sketching in the rise of evolutionism and mentioning the psychologistic, diffusionist and functionalist criticisms of the doctrine. He lodges strong reservations about functionalism framed largely as criticisms of the pronouncements of his teacher and predecessor in the chair at Oxford, Radcliffe-Brown. The latter's fundamental position is outlined in this passage:

The function of culture as a whole is to unite individual human beings into more or less stable social structures, i.e., stable systems of groups determining and regulating the relation of those individuals to one another, and providing such external adaptation to the physical environment, and such internal adaptation between the component individuals or groups, as to make possible an ordered social life. That assumption I believe to be a sort of primary postulate of any objective and scientific study of culture or of human society.[1]

Evans-Pritchard becomes critical when the view is given a scientistic twist with the argument that:

> social systems are natural systems which can be reduced to sociological laws, with the corollary that the history of them has no scientific relevance (1951, p. 57).

His argument against this scientism is simply that nothing resembling such laws has ever been produced:

> Up to the present nothing even remotely resembling what are called laws in the natural sciences has been adduced—only rather naive deterministic, teleological, and pragmatic assertions. The generalisations which have so far been attempted have, moreover, been so vague and general as to be, even if true, of little use, and they have rather easily tended to become mere tautologies and platitudes on the level of common sense deduction (1951, p. 57).

He adds that he is not obliged to prove that there can be no such laws because 'it is for those who say that there are, to tell us what they are' (p. 58).

My comment would be that to say that no sociological laws have been found is not to show that none will be found. To *assert* their nonexistence will not shake their proponents one iota; to do that it is necessary to *show* the impossibility of such laws. But already Evans-Pritchard seems to have gone a step further, for he adds that the examples which actually have been produced (so some do exist, then) are 'even if true', common-sense tautologies and platitudes. Again, to say that the laws are commonsensical, or platitudinous, is not to say that they have no explanatory power, much less that they do not exist. The law that all men die when their heads are cut off is undoubtedly trivial, yet it helps to explain a great many events in political history. The law that people buy more when the price is low is also a platitude, but economists have done a lot with it.

To this Evans-Pritchard has another reply. His objection is now to the whole approach, to the whole philosophy which sees man as part of an explicable law-obeying machine:

> Social anthropologists, dominated consciously or unconsciously, from the beginnings of their subject, by positivist philosophy have aimed, explicitly or implicitly, and for the most part still aim—for this is what it comes to—at proving that man is an automaton and at discovering the sociological laws in terms of which his actions, ideas and beliefs can be explained and in the light of which they can be planned and controlled.

[1] Radcliffe-Brown, 1931, quoted by Evans-Pritchard, 1951, p. 55.

This approach implies that human societies are natural systems which can be reduced to variables. Anthropologists have therefore taken one or other of the natural sciences as their model and have turned their backs on history, which sees men in a different way and eschews, in the light of experience, rigid formulations of any kind (1950, p. 123).

This is a not altogether fair mode of argument; positivism does not imply the desire to plan and control people's actions, ideas and beliefs. On the other hand the motive of the passage is clearly that positivism forgets that Man means men, not parts of machines. Having said that he rejects the whole notion of conceiving human beings as machines, i.e. predictable natural systems, Evans-Pritchard goes on to outline his own view in the same passage (1950, pp. 123–4):

There is, however, an older tradition than that of the Enlightenment with a different approach to the study of human societies, in which they are seen as systems only because social life must have a pattern of some kind, inasmuch as man, being a reasonable creature, has to live in a world in which his relations with those around him are ordered and intelligible. Naturally I think that those who see things in this way have a clearer understanding of social reality than the others. . . .

Evans-Pritchard then advances the strongest metaphysical objections to the sociology of extreme functionalism, that they forget man; I share his dislike: we should never forget that the social sciences are about people. Metaphysically, Evans-Pritchard's heart is in the right place. Moreover it leads him to give an appreciative account of the work of his colleagues. He explains anthropological work and the intriguing results gained superbly. Unlike Firth, who calls cargo cults partly other than rational, Evans-Pritchard shows, in one of his most important works (1937, *passim*) that magic is rational. All this even though in his radio talks he never for one sentence explicitly says that social anthropology is about the rational unity of mankind—although he constantly operates with the idea at the back of his mind.

On the other hand, his strictures about 'reducing' social systems to laws and the rest, are less palatable. They give his views a slightly irrationalist twist, very much the opposite of the view advocated here. Yet I find Evans-Pritchard's idea that social life has patterns (i.e. regularities) because of a need for order fits in with my own view.

I would, then, endorse the consequences of Evans-Pritchard's favour of history, e.g. that the history of cargo cults must be taken into account if they are to be understood fully. My only contention here is that both science and history try to explain things and that both use—must use—universal sociological laws. The difference is simply that in science it is new laws we are trying to discover whilst in history it is new facts (or initial conditions) which, in combination with old or trivial laws will yield explanations of other facts. If Evans-Pritchard is saying that social anthropology does not explain but only describes then he himself is accepting the crude positivism he so reviles; if he admits social anthropology explains, that is enough. If he does admit this, then I do not understand how he is using 'understanding of social reality'; to me it would essentially involve explanation.

Evans-Pritchard rejects explanation because it involves sociological laws which are somehow connected in his mind with deterministic explanations of society.[1] He thinks causal explanation an unattainable and repugnant aim because it would involve predictions. He shows that explanation of social phenomena must involve history (a point made here earlier). But since primitive peoples by and large have no history, 'how' (explanatory) questions are ruled out. We must ask 'why?' not 'how?'; seek to understand, not explain. However, as I have said above, I believe the difference between the two to be illusory (see my 1961*a*).

There is little point in discussing whether every explanatory discipline is scientific (if the explanation is independently testable I happen to believe this to be the case). The question only worries those who object to being labelled 'scientific'.

In his latest lecture (1961) Evans-Pritchard argues that sociological explanation involves historical explanation and thus that social anthropology is a form of history and history is a form of social anthropology.[2] He does not say that this is so because they both employ situational logic. (We shall come to this point in section 6.)

While on the whole I find Evans-Pritchard's views a valuable corrective I think he understresses the rational kernel in the functionalists' anti-historism—namely the desire to avoid the fallacy of origins: the recalcitrant fact that the past cannot provide a complete explanation of the present. That is, the present is only in part a product of the past; it is also, in part, independent of the past.

Dr. Peter Worsley takes what Evans-Pritchard says and gives it a scientistic twist. His book on cargo cults contains an appendix (1957, pp. 257–76), where he explains the method he employs in his book, and discusses the relationship between social anthropology and history. His views derive from Marx, as he points out, although

[1] Necessitarianism again; see Chapter 5, section 3.
[2] In his Presidential Address of 1962 Professor Schapera criticises Evans-Pritchard by demonstrating the very considerable extent to which social anthropologists always have utilised historical materials. He thus does not resolve the dispute as this could easily be a case of practice conflicting with theory.

he follows Evans-Pritchard in saying that social anthropology is a branch of history. The view of history he expounds, however, is far from that of Evans-Pritchard; for I think Worsley is clearly a historicist of the most blatant kind, a fact which would surely cause Evans-Pritchard to reject his view, because it is scientistic.

To my mind, the fact that Evans-Pritchard can never for a moment bring himself to say of the life and society of the Nuer that it is, at least, poor, nasty and brutish, suggests he is relativising. While Evans-Pritchard would probably be horrified to be accused of relativism, I have little doubt that, in a way, he is. As a person I am sure he is nothing of the sort, no more than is Worsley, but by a sort of 'guilt by association' argument I think I can show that he is. Evans-Pritchard does not state clearly his views on the 'primitive'/'civilised' issue, and his acceptance of the idea that fieldwork, however unpleasant, is a chastening experience is similarly significant. Worsley seems to object to this relativism: he argues that there is an evolution from 'primitive' to 'advanced' although in a strictly limited sense:

> There is no suggestion that the individuals who compose any one society are in any way inferior to any others, either actually or potentially, but merely, to state the matter broadly, that development has been mono-directional from stateless to State societies. And objectively, some societies have achieved a more complex and richer technological, artistic and scientific development than others (p. 259).

He then adds some animadversions on those social anthropologists who say that they are studying primitive peoples. He prefers to mark off as 'primitive' only those peoples living in stateless societies. *Qua* marxist Worsley is a sort of relativist too. Marx's 'moral futurism'—the morality of bloody revolution is justified because the end it is directed to, the future society, is right—relativises morals to the hypothetical future (when of course, revolution would not be justified). Worsley, then, like Evans-Pritchard, is decidedly opposed to the anti-evolutionism, anti-historism of positivists like Durkheim and his British followers. His specific argument is that following its first flush of success with other problems, the appropriateness of functionalism for treating problems of social change came into question. This criticism threw severe doubt on its *general* efficacy as a method.

Having recorded doubt about functionalism in general Worsley turns to the argument that history should be rejected because it is not science. Here he deviates completely from Evans-Pritchard, who gladly admits that history is not a science.

Professor Nadel considers that anthropology is a science, and *therefore cannot be history*, while Professor Evans-Pritchard considers that social anthropology is not a science, *because it is a branch of history*. Yet there is a common term in both these sets of propositions; history is not science (p. 264).

This last sentence is the crux of the matter; for Worsley thinks that history *is* a science. And since it is a science it can find a legitimate place in the Science of Man. Therefore anti-historism must be overthrown.

Worsley is prepared to use Evans-Pritchard's attack on anti-historism despite their deviation on the history/science question:

The claim that one can understand the functioning of institutions at a certain point in time without knowing how they have come to be what they are, or what they were later to become, as well as a person who, in addition to having studied their constitution at a particular point of time, has also studied their past and future, seems to me an absurdity (1950, p. 121).

I don't find this argument of Evans-Pritchard's too convincing. It is one thing to call something 'an absurdity'; it is quite another thing to give us arguments that show it is absurd. I do not see anything at all absurd in the anti-history attitude as outlined in this quote; history would be irrelevant here. Do I need any knowledge of the 'past and future' (*sic*) of the Bank of England to understand the effect of the Bank Rate on the price of gilt-edged? Did I need it then understanding would be impossible because *ex definitione* we cannot have 'knowledge' of the future. Everything here turns on the ambiguous word 'understand'. If 'understand' involves full knowledge of the past, present and future of an institution, then history is required and Evans-Pritchard's advocacy of it is trivially true (although it remains logically impossible for anyone ever to have such 'full' knowledge). But if all that is meant is 'can give a satisfactory explanation of the effect of this institution on some other', then to drag in history is a red herring.

Let us, then, come now to the obtaining of the science. Again Worsley uses the arguments of Evans-Pritchard: we carry out successive studies of a phenomenon and we find that:

each study reaches, as our knowledge increases and new problems emerge, a deeper level of investigation and [teaches] us the essential characteristics of the thing we are inquiring into, so that particular studies are given a new meaning and perspective. This will always happen if one necessary condition is observed: that the conclusions of each study are clearly formulated in such a way that they not only test the conclusions reached by earlier studies but advance new hypotheses which can be broken down into fieldwork problems (p. 123).

This is excellent and bold: we will reach the essential characteristics of a thing if we test old hypotheses and advance new ones. Presumably Evans-Pritchard thinks that historical understanding is sought by means of coming to know what the essential characteristics of a thing are; while science seeks whatever it does seek by means of laws. Worsley, on the other hand, clearly believes the 'essential characteristics' will lead to the laws of historical development: really aristotelian. It is curious that, in Evans-Pritchard's sense, 'nonscientific' history should seek 'essential characteristics' by means of a scientific method, i.e. formulating hypotheses, testing them (and presumably refuting some) and going on to invent new ones.

I would accept Evans-Pritchard's point that social anthropology is required by some of its problems to take account of history; and I would accept Worsley's point that history is scientific (or empirical) even though he advocates it for the wrong reasons, not that it tries to explain by rational means. Worsley wants to argue that history uses 'scientific methods', like concomitant variation, to build up laws, and therefore, *on account of those laws*, is science. Here Worsley has fallen into two traps at one and the same time: induction and historicism.

Notice how he wants to treat the specific problem of the cargo cults; he seems to follow Evans-Pritchard when he describes the method of his study of cargo cults thus:

An attempt to define the conditions under which one particular social phenomenon, the millenarian cult, occurs. Such a study must be comparative and historical in approach (p. 257).

In other words he wants to solve the problem of cargo cults by discovering the (essential?) social and historical factors which bring them about and which, presumably—he is rather vague on this point—will provide us with sufficient conditions to explain their occurrence and thus allow us to *predict* them. So, unless I read too much into him, the 'accumulated mass of field material' (p. 258) of social anthropology is to be comparatively studied in harness with an extension of the marxist theory of historical evolution to primitive (i.e. in his usage, stateless) societies.

If Worsley meant by laws of history, laws used in historical explanation like 'all men die when their heads are cut off' I would agree that history uses laws and therefore is scientific. But clearly this is not what he means. He means first of all that we should inductively seek out correlations between phenomena—these we shall try to reify into laws. Now this is not the procedure of science as I understand it; moreover this inductive procedure is logically invalid. So these generalised laws are not scientific laws; and as to the logical invalidity we can refer to the arguments of Hume.[1] and Popper.[2]

On top of this it is obvious that these nonscientific 'laws' are to be historicist laws of the 'mono-directional' evolution of society. Seeing the anti-historicist objections coming Worsley comforts himself with a piece of wish-fulfilment by asserting that 'the high-tide of anti-historicism has now passed' (p. 266).[3] My own impression was somewhat different; namely that historicism had been refuted, and that it was *its* high-tide that had now passed. So, if I am right in interpreting Worsley's scientific history as seeking out induced historicist laws of the development of society then he is already demolished (by Popper, 1957).

6. *Social Anthropology as the Science of Man*

In this book I have criticised the aims and methods at present adopted in social anthropology because I believe they can be shown to thwart the aim of building the Science of Man—the aim, I would argue, with which most would-be social anthropologists start out. My argument so far in this the last chapter has been that the doctrines of Malinowski, Radcliffe-Brown, Evans-Pritchard and Worsley will none of them do as specifications of the aims and methods of social anthropology, the science of man. I have already conceded that Evans-Pritchard is right in demanding that history be reintroduced into social anthropology; I have also conceded that Worsley is right in arguing that this first concession does not make the subject nonscientific (he is right for the wrong reasons, no doubt). But apart from a few scattered remarks in the text, and the hackneyed point[4] that structural-functionalism is a useful heuristic, or methodological rule, I have made no serious attempt to concede what is acceptable in structural-functionalism, to rescue structural-functionalism, or at least some of it. Now this is a bad situation to be in. It would be *hubris* to be caught saying that all these intelligent anthropologists were simply accepting in functionalism a gross error. Were I to say this I should still have to explain why it was such a successful method and thus gained wide acceptance; why, in fact, it is a good heuristic. Of course I suppose it is possible that structural-functionalism was a side-tracking error like phlogistonism. But I

---

[1] Hume, *Enquiries*, quoted by Popper in the item cited in the next note.
[2] Popper, 1959, new appendix *10, and 1963, Chapter 2.
[3] There is a curious piece of what looks like verbal borrowing here: the second volume of Popper's *Open Society* is entitled 'The High Tide of Prophecy: Hegel and Marx'.
[4] Cf. Gellner, 1958, and Agassi, 1960.

don't for a moment think that structural-functionalism, either as a method or as metaphysics, at all resembles phlogistonism. I believe on the contrary that, stripped of its positivism and inductivism, structural-functionalism is a powerful doctrine with considerable truth in it, and that this truth explains its success.

This, the last section of the book, will be devoted to the question of the true core of structural-functionalism, and the reconciliation of that doctrine with my own views about method. I want to show that structural-functionalism relies heavily on, and can be explained in terms of, situational logic, and that therefore there is a hard rational core even in the doctrine according to which the harmony, or the tendency towards equilibrium, between various institutions is a characteristic of every society.

To carry forward this argument for social anthropology as the science of man, then, I shall describe present-day social anthropology to bring to the fore the question (in (i)) where it conforms to, and where it deviates from, its truly scientific character. I shall then go on to characterise (in (ii)) the relation between those parts of contemporary social anthropology which are scientific and my own views, for I believe they are closer than at first sight they seem and can easily be reconciled.

(i) *Contemporary Social Anthropology as Science.* The principal topic of this subsection is the claim that social anthropology is a science because its methods are scientific. This is an attractive claim. Radcliffe-Brown's penultimate and posthumous book, to give an example of how far the claim is taken, is called *A Natural Science of Society*.

This claim to scientific status is justified in various ways depending on the view of science held by the proponent of the scientific status. As a first approximation let us take the following account.

We have built up, in social anthropology, a systematic method of classifying societies—a scientific system of classification; we have a method of detailed and intensive observation of our raw material— a scientific method of observation; and we build by means of these methods interesting and illuminating hypotheses about the nature of social organisation which we can verify on a comparative basis—we have scientific hypotheses; these hypotheses could only be achieved by comparing similar aspects of different peoples, by inducing generalisations from the scientifically observed material—they are achieved by the proper scientific method. Thus our work is not limited to single societies, much less *ad hoc*; our method consists in comparative sociology which gives our hypotheses a broad-based, universal and scientific character.

Let me now detail a little this account of the system of classification, the observation of facts, and the building of theories from these facts. British social anthropology today largely conforms to Radcliffe-Brown's ideals: it concerns itself mainly with the varieties and structural principles of social structure. Over the years since the revolution in the subject anthropologists have developed a classification system for social structures, dividing them by means of it into different types. The classification is based on various key factors like: kinship, i.e. modes of descent, succession and inheritance (matrilineal, patrilineal, bilineal, nonunilineal; patriarchy, matriarchy, gerontocracy, etc.; primogeniture, ultimogeniture, etc.); religion (animistic, magical, monotheistic, polytheistic, etc.); economy (subsistence agriculture, pastoral, mercantile, industrial, etc.); similarly with politics, law and ethics. There can be, for example, a type of society which is patrilineal, acephalous, and monotheistic; a society, that is, in which descent, succession and inheritance pass through males; which has no centralised political system; which worships one spirit. (The Nuer, subject of the classic treatise by Evans-Pritchard, are of this type.) Most of the technical words of social anthropology derive from this useful shorthand developed for characterising the key features of a social organisation and its customs.

Written in terms of the above classifications, there is a mass of descriptive material on particular groups, tribes and peoples. This is descriptive ethnography. The collection of these collected facts of descriptive ethnography has proceeded for years with a gradually heightening standard (progress resulting, I conjecture, from key centres of problem-interest becoming clearer). The standard has improved particularly in the continual reduction of the amount of misunderstanding and ethnocentric bias involved in the description of a society; in the past these factors were responsible for a good deal of the 'curiosity value' of anthropological materials.

We see the way this system of classification is used mainly in the training of social anthropologists. Most professional social anthropologists, for example, have a thorough knowledge of the available ethnography on the peoples of the area (or areas) where they carried out their fieldwork. These 'areas' of specialisation are very large: e.g. North America, Oceania, South, East, West, or North Africa, and so on. The luckier anthropologists may be familiar with two or more such areas, but as the literature is vast it is very difficult to keep track of much of it. Scientific observation and building of theories is seen at work partly in the training and partly in the practice of the subject. A large part of the training for social anthropology consists of the student working through a mass of the ethnographic material to become familiar with the great range and diversity of human society. He is then able to go out to observe with a true scientific detachment.

We see this in practice in that he goes and lives among the people he studies; he breaks his stay in order to think out the implications of what he has so far observed and then can go back refreshed to fill in gaps. He then carefully and slowly builds his hypotheses (called 'writing-up'). This has all been beautifully described by Evans-Pritchard (1951, p. 76):

if his work has been sufficient merit, and if he is lucky, [he] obtains a grant for field research and prepares himself for it by a careful study of the literature on the peoples of the region in which he is to conduct it, including their languages.

He then usually spends at least two years in a first field study of a primitive society, this period covering at least two expeditions and a break between them for collating the material collected in the first expedition. Experience has shown that a few months' break, preferably spent in a university department, is essential for sound fieldwork. It will take him at least another five years to publish the results of his research to the standards of modern scholarship, and much longer should he have other calls on his time; so that it can be reckoned that an intensive study of a single primitive society and the publication of its results take about ten years.

So much, then, for a first approximation to the claim that social anthropology is a science. The claim that social anthropology has a scientific classification system, a method of scientific observation, and a method, the comparative method, of building universal sociological generalisations. These resemblances to the natural sciences warrant the claim that social anthropology is a science.

By saying that this is a first approximation I mean that although I have heard and seen this account of the scientific claims of social anthropology, I think the most methodologically aware anthropologists have gone far beyond it. This means that I need not criticise the account in detail but can refer to these criticisms by other anthropologists.

Basically the account is inductivist: by observing and classifying we build science. We must begin with clear minds (or else the science we build will be all mixed up with prescientific prejudices), and we must try to observe as much and as systematically as possible for only then will we be able to build up a full picture of society to compare with others.

Malinowski and Radcliffe-Brown, followed by Nadel and Leach, have all severely criticised this account. They have all said thinking must begin with problems, and observations must begin from theories A horizon of expectations, to use other language, is required before anything can be observed. Fortes (1949*a*, p. vii) in his preface to the Radcliffe-Brown *Festschrift*, has put this well. He describes Radcliffe-Brown's differences from the approach of the inductivist first as rejecting unbiassed observation, second as stressing comparative study and third

> that comparative sociology must use the standard scientific technique of starting from an hypothesis, testing it by intensive fieldwork, modifying the original hypothesis in the light of the field results, and continuing thus to build up a systematic body of knowledge (p. vii).

Leach (see note 1 to page 178 above) has stressed that anthropologists must start with a problem; this was also a basic element in Malinowski's teaching.

The reader will appreciate how much a methodologist like myself welcomes this methodological sophistication. Before, however, discussing our common agreement on *problemstellung* I have to catalogue our differences. Reluctant though I am to do it, I must point out that the appearance of methodological agreement is merely an appearance. Whether they know it or not, and most do not, Malinowski, Radcliffe-Brown, Nadel and Leach are inductivists, and inductivism is the error I want to persuade anthropologists out of. The ways in which these scholars are inductivists are: (1) their retention of classification as an aim of science (Leach excepted); (2) their belief in science as something systematic and cumulative and therefore authoritative; (3) their belief that you test hypotheses and modify, not refute; (4) the belief that there are a certain number of possible hypotheses only one of which can emerge from the testing.

I am forced to expand this a little to explain myself. I am not on the attack because these anthropologists who are trying to get on the right lines haven't quite got it straight. No, my concern is this. Were there such a perfect agreement between my view and that widely accepted by the leading anthropologists there would be no call for me to criticise them. Yet I have argued throughout this book that something went wrong with the revolution. One of the things that went wrong is method, and the methodological faults of social anthropology can only be explained on the hypothesis that attempts were made to be critical and non-inductivist but that they ended up merely as sophisticated inductivist. Let me illustrate.

(1) That Radcliffe-Brown was all for classification is well known. (See Leach, 1961, pp. 2–3.) That classificationism is a form of inductivism is also well known. The aim is to classify social structures in order to compare them and build generalisations out of the *classified facts*.

(2) Almost any thinker who talks of 'building science' is speaking

inductively. The assumption is of facts or theories being accumulated, rather than of theories *and of facts* being overthrown. This inductivist view is stated clearly in the passage from Fortes quoted above. That this is also closely connected with the idea that science, as a systematic body of knowledge, has authority, is revealed in another passage from Fortes (1949*a*),

> Radcliffe-Brown . . . held unwaveringly to the belief that the only road to the solution of the ills of human society is the long and arduous one of first building up the scientific knowledge upon which effective remedies can be based with some hope of success (p. x).

In other words, science provides the authority for success. But scientific success cannot even tell us if the sun will rise tomorrow, never mind if social reforms will have some hope of success. If science is conceived of as a conglomeration of guesses with no authority, such statements would not be made.

(3) Again, the idea in the first Fortes quotation is of theories being modified in the light of tests. But what if the theory is just false and has to be given up in its entirety? What about the anthropologist just being left with no answers at all? This I believe is never seriously considered because of (4).

(4) Here the idea is that there will only be a few hypotheses possible and that tests eliminate and modify until there is only one left, which is thus verified. Leach:

> Generalization . . . consists in perceiving possible general laws in the circumstances (p. 5).

And what if some of the possibilities, which are after all infinite, are not perceived, and all those perceived are false? Answer: fieldwork doesn't refute, it modifies and verifies. Fortes again:

> his [Radcliffe-Brown's] emphasis on the critical importance of the test of fieldwork in the verification of sociological theories (p. viii).

Tests verify, then? But if so, are they tests?

I hope this shows that even in the best writers inductivism remains.[1] But perhaps all this could be swept aside if we could agree just to discuss problems and speculate. We would all know what we were talking about, ideas would flow and we could leave it to others to refute them. All my teachers and friends assure me that they are all preoccupied with problems and begin discussions by saying 'what is your problem?'

Very good, I say. I can imagine, however, a critic saying 'but to demand all this specification of problems is to impose our dogmas. What is a problem', he could say, 'depends upon your framework

[1] For references to Nadel, see Jarvie, 1961; to Malinowski, see Chapter 1.

and this framework is thus imposed upon the person questioned. If he frames a problem within a different framework to yours there is no communication, so in order to discuss with him in terms of problems you or he must impose his framework.' My answer to this is that all discussion should begin by discovering if the participants hold different frameworks, and if so which. Then they should choose which to use. There is no dogma here. The choice can be rational because rationally discussed, because frameworks and their relative merits can be rationally discussed. To illustrate let me take the problem of ancestor-worship. First we begin with 'what is the problem?' My opponent says 'why does society x have ancestor worship?' I say, 'very good, now what would constitute an answer?' He says, 'some specification of its structural necessity.' I answer, 'I refuse to accept your framework because I think I can show that your answer within that framework is not satisfactory because it answers a different question.' Here we must discuss our frameworks. By posing a problem and specifying the kind of answer we would accept, our frameworks are at once revealed.

Although social anthropologists say they are problem-oriented, since all problems are within a framework, they and I still do not communicate because our frameworks differ. In advocating stress on what is the problem my main aim is to start discussion as to what a solution will look like. My view is that the problems posed by our social anthropologists today are similar in verbal form to those of Frazer, *et al.*, but there the resemblance ends because they are interpreted differently; patently unsatisfactory answers are expected and the obvious answers (this society worships ancestors because they believe ancestors have power over their future) are dismissed as superficial.

Not only then do I argue that Malinowski changed the problems of social anthropology, but he confused everyone by retaining the same form of words for very different problems.

Anthropology lost its continuity because not only the theories and methods, but even the problems of the older generation were summarily scrapped. Of these steps the latter is the most serious. To seek new problems is all very well: but to condemn others as being concerned with pseudoproblems you have to be very sure of your ground. Here, I think, social anthropology swerved in slightly the wrong direction; this is only beginning to be realised and, perhaps, rectified as the task of having field reports on every major society gradually nears completion and anthropologists' minds can come back to theoretical and methodological questions. I should guess the time is now ripe for a reconsideration of the classics of nineteenth-century anthropology to see how far their problems were pseudo; to see how far they have been replaced by real problems in their functional formulations; and to see how far they remain open problems into which research might be conducted.

My suggestion is that social anthropologists have an underlying sense of all this and it has finally caught up with them and they have got stuck. There is a widespread feeling that social anthropology is not making theoretical progress nowadays.[1] I have blamed this on misconceived attempts to copy what are thought to be the methods of science. These sentiments have also been expressed by Leach (1961), who explains how the reaction has been to plunge, ostrich-fashion, ever deeper into fieldwork and ethnography (p. 1). I conjecture that this is because here is one clear case where their scientific pretensions cannot be challenged: the sober recording of hard facts. Here is Evans-Pritchard speaking with modest pride of the Ph.D. theses of his students:

> You will note in the first place that *there is nothing very exciting about the subject of these theses*, no searching after the strange or colourful, no appeal to antiquarian or romantic interests. All are *matter-of-fact enquiries* into one or other type of social institution (1951, p. 13, italics mine).

Here, at least, we are soberly getting on with solid work.

The origin of these temperance sentiments is clearly the inductive belief in the sober and scientific collection of facts. (It should be noticed, in this context, that functionalism is inductivist in the sense that it offers a way of turning a set of facts into a theory; in this case a self-explaining system. This means: (*a*) that no problems can arise involving two systems because each is completely self-explanatory on its own unique terms and therefore there can be no problems which need to be solved by comparison, so the comparative method of explaining social events is in conflict with universal functionalism; (*b*) heavy stress is placed on the idea of the 'system'. What you define as the system also defines the limits of what you can functionally explain at one time. The problem here is whether systems are natural or conventional. If they are natural then well and good; they explain themselves and each needs an explanation to

[1] 'Since 1930 British Social Anthropology has embodied a well defined set of ideas and objectives which derive directly from the teachings of Malinowski and Radcliffe-Brown. . . . But during the last year or so it has begun to look as if this particular aim had worked itself out. Most of my colleagues are giving up the attempt to make comparative generalisations; instead they have begun to write impeccably detailed historical ethnographies of particular peoples.

'I regret this new tendency for I still believe that the findings of anthropologists have general as well as particular implications, but why has the functionalist doctrine ceased to carry conviction? To understand what is happening in social anthropology I believe we need to go right back to the beginning and *rethink* basic issues. . . .' (Leach, 1961, p. 1).

itself, the only problem is detecting the systems. If they are conventional then there is nothing to prevent the whole of social life
being defined as one huge interacting system, which whole thing
explains itself (thus avoiding what may appear to be problems
involving several societies and which may prove awkward), and parts
of which cannot be explained independently of the rest. It is worth
recalling here that Radcliffe-Brown became a conventionalist late in
life with his theory that 'society' was simply the convenient area of
study.)

Taking refuge in fieldwork has however its problems. By his own
admission, the social anthropologist requires a theory before he can
observe. We all accept that the human mind is such that it cannot
make observations unless it has an expectation, a problem or a
point of view in the light of which it can 'read' the world.[1] A problem is usually the attempt to explain some disappointed expectation
or theory. The above argument recommends that theoretical and
methodological thinking should be very much prior to fieldwork and
observation: you must know what you are going to test before you
start testing. Obviously, if this is true, 'undirected' fieldwork—just
going in and observing and absorbing—is impossible. They *must*
have a point of view, a basis of selection and interest, which they are
employing. All I would say is that it would be better were this out
in the open where it could be scrutinised and discussed. For then it
might be made sharper and clearer, so that observation could be
more economical and directed.

To this it could easily be answered that detailed discussion of the
problems beforehand can only be vague, because problems may only
be discovered in the field by someone who tries to keep his mind
open. Let me explain. Basically, this answer could proceed, we are
interested in getting to know and understand the richness and
diversity of human society. Our problems before fieldwork are a bit
vague; but perhaps it is better this way. What we do in fieldwork is
to go among totally alien peoples and learn to live as a member of
their society. Only in this process do we discover problems. With most
of the alien culture it might be easy to get along; but more often than
not there will be peculiar institutions and usages which it will take
a long time to grasp. Only a prolonged stay will *discover* these; only
longer will suffice to gain an *understanding* of them. These will be
the principal centres of problem-interest in fieldwork reports because
they need some explanations. The rest will just be background information, a context into which to fit these problems. Jarvie may be

---

[1] (See Chapter 1, section 1.) Or, to deepen the metaphor, unless the mind
has a searchlight beam with which to explore the world. See Popper, 1946,
vol. ii, pp. 260–1; and 1963, chapter 1, sections 4 and 5.

right in saying that what we find it difficult to get used to or to grasp will depend on expectations engendered by our society and by the study of other societies we have made. The fact remains, however, that our problems prior to fieldwork *have to be* vague.

There is a lot of truth in this. But the problem which is really at the heart of such fieldwork is 'can all human societies be rationally reconstructed in terms of orderly conjectures?' This is not at all vague; it is merely very broad. (I take it that the argument is not just trying to show that getting the 'feel' of the field is an excellent and humbling liberal education. It is; but it is also a long and expensive one.) Also, it is limited to one society at a time and fieldwork was supposed to be the sole remaining, basic claim to scientific status of social anthropology. But investigation into particular theoretical problems which are larger than any one society cannot really be advanced by this 'undirected' fieldwork at all. None, for example, of the theories of cargo cults discussed in Chapter 3 and my 1964 paper is taken from fieldwork, but rather from general sociological and philosophical thought. I suggest that were this thought prior to field research then very much more useful library material would exist on cargo cults. Social anthropology has a strong claim to be a science because its hypotheses are empirical and it has a field method and a large literature to facilitate their testing. But knowing what to look for with this method and in this material can only come about as the result of reflection and speculation on particular problems.

(ii) *The Logic of the Situation and the Unintended Consequences of our Actions.* 'Undirected' fieldwork, then, is mainly reconstructing the logic of the situation of the typical individual in the society under study. It is learning to live in that society. Some of these reconstructions are more difficult than others, and it is here that the fieldworker 'discovers' problems. I want now to discuss these problems and then their solutions, a little further.

First it might be of some help to contrast problems of social anthropology with those of natural science. There are always two problems: what are the problems (this is the framework); and how do we solve them? As to the first, namely, what the problems are. There is some difference here between natural and social science. The choice of a framework in physics can be done purely on intellectual grounds. The choice of a framework in social anthropology may involve moral considerations (for example, behaviourism). There is thus a moral constraint on our freedom to choose a framework in social anthropology; this means there is a constraint on the permissible revolutions of frameworks. Another difference is that since the subject of social anthropology is man, namely us, we have an immediate possibility of checking any proposed framework. We can check it against ourselves. We cannot immediately check field theory or atomic theory in physics. So much for what the problems or framework or subject-matter is.

As to the second, how do we solve the problems? First of all we settle on a framework, one way or another. From then on there is, in my view, an exact parallel between natural and social science. They both try to solve these problems by means of theories and the critical discussion of these theories. I will now discuss explanation within the framework of situational logic.

We begin by dividing actions into those to be explained intentionally and those to be explained as unintentional. For intentional explanations we use a model of so-called 'rational action' relative to a given situation. Other behaviour—that which is decidedly irrational relative to the situation—is beyond the purview of social science. Action is explained by means of assumptions about the actor's knowledge and beliefs (including those about his situation) as well as his aims, from which that action can be shown to be directed towards the realisation of that aim. If, for example, a person wants to get more power over others (which Dr. Leach assumes is a universal human attribute[1]) then, in normal circumstances, it would be irrational for him to go off into a desert, alone; but it might be rational for him to ingratiate himself with the powers that be. To elucidate why this 'might be' so in any particular society is an important task of social science, involving as it does, elucidating the social context within which the decision was taken and including the background knowledge of the institutional means available to achieve an actor's ends. One might characterise social anthropology as the attempt to make the behaviour of alien peoples intelligible by discovering the situational logic underlying it.[2]

The situation of the anthropological fieldworkers is rather like that of the well-trained spy dropped into enemy territory he has never visited before. However well the spy has been trained and briefed, however well the anthropologist has studied the literature, both still have a lot to learn when they land. They have to find their way around in that society, getting to know the unspoken as well as the spoken rules, the nuances of behaviour in given situations. All this must be acquired before the intruder can properly become a member of that society—which is the explicit aim of both spy and fieldworker. The only assumption both spy and fieldworker rely on as

[1] See Leach, 1954, p. 10: 'I consider it necessary and justified to assume a conscious or unconscious wish to gain power is a very general motive in human affairs.'
[2] A point also made by Hayek, 1949, ch. 3.

they do their reconstruction is that the behaviour of the people they are among can be rationally explained; that it is intelligible; they adopt the rationality principle. Situational logic, then, is based in the rationality principle.

(I would just comment here that there is also something like an irrationality principle: people may be acting irrationally and inexplicably but we go on trying to explain them. All explanations are necessarily oversimplifications; in reality things are probably not like that. But situational logic is the only way we have of explaining these things. We can't explain everything—but then we don't want to; rational, oversimplified explanations may be quite adequate to our *problem*. We don't know of any other way to go about explaining things which doesn't lead to arbitrariness and lack of testability.)[1]

To illustrate, assuming that in times of drought rational farmers will want rain, our martian in Chapter 1 found the behaviour of the people on the Bible Belt unintelligible. This was only because he knew nothing of the state of knowledge of these people. It had to be explained that certain theories they held about God made their actions in such a situation highly intelligible. It would have been pure sophistry had the martian argued, for example, that the 'real' explanation of their behaviour was that during a time of drought there is a tendency for the social group to break up, or to be torn by dissension, but that this ritual foregathering—ostensibly for a religious ceremony—was in fact a way of demonstrating as well as reinforcing the solidarity of the group.

The reader could not be blamed were he to find such an 'explanation' by the martian pretty far-fetched. Yet precisely this sort of 'explanation' is paradigmatic in the classical texts of British social anthropology. (It derives from Durkheim.) The obvious explanation is by-passed for the recondite one. And it is apparently not noticed that this results in an attempt to solve one problem ending up solving a different one. For example: 'why do people worship their ancestors?' is the problem. Answer: 'because they have a theory that their ancestors have some influence on the course of events in this world, or that the ancestors can help them in the next, or both; and that the ancestors' temperament is such that they require to be worshipped if one is to get anything out of them.' If we are told: 'no, rather is the explanation that they worship their ancestors "because their social structure demands it"',[2] then we must reply that this misconstrues the problem, is an answer to some other, totally different,

---

[1] This paragraph is a condensed report of a discussion I had with Professor Popper.
[2] This odd explanation from Fortes was pointed out by Scheinfeld; see Chapter 1, p. 41, n. 1.

problem (perhaps: 'who do some societies have a religion structured in this and this way?'). Again, the problem: 'why do people worship this rather than that ancestor?' asks about the origin and development of the ancestor theory; no relevant answer can be given purely in situational or in functional terms. Instead of following up functionalist by-paths we should ask whether the straightforward theory about the belief that ancestors influence this world provides a satisfactory explanation; and, later, whether it is false. Of course, when I say that structural-functional explanations are recondite I am not registering some objection to difficult or complex explanation *per se*. Indeed, where such an explanation goes deeper, i.e. explains more, we may prefer it. But it is still a good rule of scientific method to prefer the least complicated, the simplest explanation of all the facts. We prefer the theory that people worship their ancestors because of a theory they hold about ancestors to the theory that their social structure demands ancestor worship, because the first theory is simpler and more satisfactory. Moreover, we believe the theory about the influence of ancestors to be false; but then the second theory amounts to the idea that the social structure 'demands' a false theory. It thus seems to be heading straight for the relativist muddle that the ancestor theory is true-for-them in their social structure, although false-for-us in ours.

The way out of the muddle is not to apply different methods to an alien society from those we apply to our own society. The answer to 'why do some Englishmen worship God?' is, 'because they believe there is a supreme and all-powerful being called "God" who demands to be worshipped.' It is no answer to that question to talk about the social structure of England. Of course some people go to church for social rather than religious reasons. But this only illustrates yet again the futility of studying the ritual not the belief. The belief of a man in God is part of his situation, as is his belief that the way to express that belief in his society is to go to church. The problem of 'why do people go to church?' which may be answered by social reasons, is not the same as 'why do people worship God?' unless one operates on the principle 'study the ritual not the belief'. Again, someone may say, 'but that man is worshipping God in order to curry favour with those people'. All right, but that is an answer to the question 'why does that man pretend to worship God?' Beliefs are an essential part of the logic of a person's situation. One of the great strengths of situational logic is that it seems to be an account of what most of us do all the time as we move around in and learn about our own society. In a sense we are all spies parachuted into our own society. As soon as we begin to explore society, as children, we are trying to understand how to behave in particular situations. Sometimes we copy others unquestioningly. Far more than we realise, though, we consciously adopt modes of behaviour thought appropriate in different situations by the other members of the society. This is because, to a very large extent, we accept the ends of others, even to the extent of being 'reasonable', not rebellious. Even the most radical of us wants to preserve quite a lot. This is because situational logic is the sole rational method we know of finding our way around in social life. But even the most reformist-minded of us requires some stability and order in our social lives and if we were to reject all the aims and mores of our fellows we should feel we were being sucked into a chaos. Few of us can tolerate this.

So much for our society in detail. To explain large-scale events like the course of cargo cults and of wars situational logic has to be combined with descriptions of how actions chain-react and rever- berate through the complex of social institutions, sometimes having consequences neither their initiator(s), nor social scientists en- visaged. Doubtless Christ never dreamt that one day his mission would result in the Inquisition. And it is doubtful if the Bible Belt farmers realise that their religious rituals promote social cohesion. But an economist because of his knowledge of our institutions would expect that a higher Bank Rate would tend to promote unemploy- ment. Knowledge of the institutions and of the interconnections between the institutions helps us trace *the intended and unintended consequences of our actions*. Unintended consequences are, of course, not necessarily unexpected. To Christ the Inquisition might have been both unintended and unexpected. The Kansan farmers would probably be baffled and astonished at the news that they are ritually reaffirming the ties of the group. But a 7 per cent Bank Rate would result in unintended (in the sense of unwanted) unemploy- ment which was nevertheless expected and deemed unavoidable in those circumstances given those aims. So we must further dis- tinguish unintended and unwanted. We can have: (i) unwanted and unintended, e.g. the Inquisition from a humane Christian point of view; (ii) unintended but wanted, e.g. social cohesion—we might say it was a good thing without being able to plan for it;[1] (iii) in- tended but unwanted, e.g. a necessary evil such as unemployment as

---

[1] Much of the revelatory character of Adam Smith's economics stems from his working out of this idea. He was one of the first thinkers to show clearly how—without any conscious intention on our part—there can be something like a tendency, in his model of the economic system, for selfish actions to have highly desirable and desired consequences. He, however, does not make the functionalists' mistake of using these consequences as explanations of the events of which they are consequences. He does not elevate the Hidden Hand to an explanatory theory; rather, he explains the Hidden Hand institutionally and situationally. (See below.)

the cost of suppressing inflation; and (iv) intended and wanted: the rare (possibly even impossible) case where we set out to get something and we get it, *and nothing more*.

This analysis applies *en bloc* to social anthropology: I have yet to come across a problem there which was solved other than by elucidating the situational logic, or else by starting from commonplace (or unproblematic) actions and tracing repercussions through the complex of institutions until the problematic event is explained; except for those which were historical questions in disguise (although very often situational explanations played a large part here too). To take some examples. Kinship classifications which differ from those in our society can be explained by showing how they mirror differences in social groupings (see Chapter 1, section 8). Mother-in-law avoidance and ancestor worship can be shown to be due to certain theories about mothers-in-law and ancestors. Some have given structural accounts of how these theories were formed; this only goes to show how easy it is to slip over from the problem of why people act the way they do into the different problem of how the theories upon which they base their action were formed. The Chinese worship the immediate agnatic senior because they have a theory about the influence this ancestor exerts over their present fortunes. The question 'how did this theory arise?' is merged with the original problem of 'why do the Chinese worship their ancestors?' which has already been solved. The new problem is tackled as follows. A Chinese father has great power during his lifetime so far as family life is concerned. Therefore, it is argued, it is reasonable that there should be a theory which gives him parallel powers after death. Yet, so far as I at least know, there does not yet exist a psychological theory which allows us to infer from importance before death to the formation of a theory about importance after death. A second line of attack is to say that the structural set-up explains why the theory is held, why it fits into that world-view. But this is another question again.

Anthropologists do not carefully enough distinguish explanations in terms of situational logic from pseudo-explanations consisting of descriptions of the socially desirable or beneficial unintended consequences of some action. This is easily illustrated. Nadel (1951, p. 214) describes a first fruits ceremony which is a straightforward implementation of certain fertility beliefs. He then goes on to show that a first fruits ceremony also prevents the eating of unripe crops and the premature dissipation of food resources. But he does not say that these are unintended consequences of the first fruits ceremony. What he does do is to ask us, without evidence, to accept that this has all been thought out and then brought about by someone or something; that it is 'quasi-intended'. And he further asks us to believe that this 'explains' the first fruits ceremony. Now either he has to attribute this quasi-intention to a durkheimian 'society' or to say that it arose in the evolutionary struggle; or he has to postulate some far-seeing individual(s) who brought it about.

The last explanation rather over-rates individual possibilities and a very strong and detailed historical case for every such explanation would have to be given. The quasi-intentional explanation is vague: either the 'intentions' are attributed to society, or they are explained as the unintended consequences of other events which make them appear intentional (an outcome of the evolutionary process perhaps; see below). If the intentions are attributed to society we will find either a group-psychological explanation or an evolutionary explanation. Group psychology might seem a bit *ad hoc* to be useful;[1] so we come to evolution, the second of our possible explanations.

Clearly this is the one which deserves to be taken really seriously. It has the advantage of being able to explain explanations of the first kind. The only trouble with it is that it is, and it remains, a possibility of an explanation. Either evolution is directed to an end (by whom), or it has an implicit end (it is a struggle to *survive*). No one has yet been able to give a really convincing account of social evolution because societies cannot be said to have natural goals like survival and reproduction, or to have environments with which they *must* come to terms. To speak in this way, transposing human and animal characteristics wholesale to social wholes, is highly misleading. So misleading that 'holism', as it has been called, has been specifically attacked.[2] The point is that in some respects social wholes are like individuals and in others they are unlike individuals. Failure to take this carefully into account has dogged most discussions of the evolution of societies. With this in mind we may perhaps be able to make some headway.

Clearly structural-functionalism is unsatisfactory in so far as it abandons historical explanation and solves historical problems with holistic or quasi-intentional theories. Also clearly, its conspicuous success with a lot of problems reflects the fact that it is a really valuable approach. How can we reconcile these two? By, I would suggest, a broader view which *explains* the success of structural-functionalism and avoids its defects. This broader view I believe has been outlined by Popper. Nothing is less mysterious than a structural-functional explanation; it is simply a combination of situational logic and tracing the unintended consequences of some action. We solved the problem of extended kinship terms by conjecturing the

---

[1] See Agassi, 1960, pp. 269–70, note 18, and text.
[2] Especially by Popper, 1957, sections, 23–4; Hayek, 1952; and J. W. N. Watkins, 1953, 1955, 1957*b* and 1958*a*.

reasons for their extension. Once this initial extension had taken place the gradual blurring of the distinction between sociological kinship and physical kinship could be seen to be an unintended consequence of it. We have thus accounted for the novelty-explaining character of structural-functionalism.

We can also see why structural-functionalism cannot explain history: it is a narrower idea than that of situational logic, and situational logic explanation *is* historical explanation. It is narrower in the sense that, because it *presupposes* the social system, it can only explain things which happen within that social system. It cannot explain the external event, although it can explain its effects, if they do not break down the social system (as they do with cargo cults). Then, with no social structural background against which to explain, they are helpless. Situational logic has no trouble at all with social change.

One other advantage of situational logic which we have not explained is its ability to explain the equilibrium-restoring character of society. The persistence of societies as well as their changes have to be explained, for neither is explained by functionalism. This is done with situational logic by presupposing the system's parts to be mutually interdependent in a way that disturbances are compensated for and eventually smoothed out (except in cases like cargo cults). But again we have no difficulty if we remember that Adam Smith invented a model of our economic institutions which restored its own equilibrium and yet the Hidden Hand can be explained entirely situationally as the unintended consequence of people acting in what they conceive to be their best selfish interests.

To return for a moment to cargo cults. 'How did the social situations in these societies become so similar' may require an evolutionary explanation. This too can be explained in situational logic terms: a society jettisons unwanted or unnecessary institutions simply because they are institutions which have lost their function, *that is*, people no longer see them as a part of the set-up which their situation requires that they maintain. The lack of kinship records in the U.K. is an unintended macro-effect of the situationally explicable decisions of the people of that society not to bother to remember their kin. Our preservation of certain antiquated traditions is a similar macro-effect of a decision to retain certain actions, which is again situationally explicable.

Does this then mean that the theoretical social anthropology we sought in the beginning of this work is situational logic plus unintended analyses? Answer: 'no'. Theoretical sociology can look to laws (often trivial, but when counter-intuitive not so) like those of economics; Parkinson's law; 'every social change creates vested interests which resist further changes';[1] and so on, with which behaviour can be explained. But these will not be generalisations. They will be universal[2] laws made intelligible because why they hold *can be explained with situational logic and unintended consequences analyses*. Just as 'all planets move in ellipses' can be explained in terms of masses, velocities, forces, etc., so 'all social changes create vested interests which resist further change' can be explained as the consequences of people's actions.

(iii) *The Value of a Method*. I want now to emphasise that, although I have followed the method I have advocated in this book, that method does not stand or fall with my particular solution to the problem of cargo cults. I did not 'derive' the solution from the method; the method has not led me to the solution although it did help me to see what sort of a solution was required. The method is no substitute for simple inventiveness and imagination. My explanation is probably false—most theories are—but should it actually get falsified then this would tend to vindicate rather than vitiate my method, in as much as a falsification is explicitly to be sought after and welcomed, according to my method. To have proposed a theory and then to have had it falsified is to have learnt a great deal—and not of an entirely negative character.

Moreover sceptics should not seek the comfort of regarding the failure of my solution (i.e. its falsification, which is a failure only in a certain sense) as showing that there is no foolproof method. No one says there is. The method I advocate is a procedural convention, a proposal to adopt a way of doing things, not a *formula* for getting the truth. If this convention encourages people to present bold and speculative theories, to expose them to criticism to which they succumb, then that is enough. We cannot reasonably ask for more, *from a method*.

[1] For other examples see Popper, 1957, p. 62.
[2] J. W. N. Watkins, in an interesting unpublished broadcast talk, has suggested that this universality is a purely numerical one.

APPENDIX I

EISLER: CHRISTIANITY AS MILLENARIAN CULT

ABOUT this time there appeared a man—if it is possible to call this royal beggar, glowing with faith in his God and filled with Divine inspiration, this poor and crippled wandering workman, whose words have now for almost two millennia resounded through the world, by the same miserable name which designates also the fearful sheep of the human herd, as well as the rapacious beasts eager for power, against whose obtuseness and hardness of heart this incomparably precious and fragile vessel of the spirit was to be shattered.

Descended from the progeny of that ill-fated Zerubabel, sunk into oblivion and misery for centuries, or at least believing himself to be thus descended, and brought up with the faith and in the tradition of such fateful lineage, he grew into the consciousness of having been chosen for a liberator-king, of having been destined to unheard-of grandeur and unheard-of suffering, to be the martyred 'servant of God' and at the same time the future world-ruler. The mysterious healing power emanating from the glance of his kindly dark eye, from his consoling word, and from the light touch of his skilful hand, convinced the crowds of the sick and the afflicted, the possessed and the burdened all over the land, of the saving nearness of the secret king. He himself is carried, by the confidence of the cured and the steadily increasing number of the believers, far above himself and his everyday consciousness. Filled with admiration for the great herald of the final days who had initiated the struggle for the kingdom of God and prophesied the coming of the messiah for the nearest future, he had formerly followed the 'Hidden One', whose sect was akin to his own, either by birth or by marriage, in order to fulfil all the law and to be taken into the new community of the regenerated Israel. Yet what he himself announces goes far beyond the strict demands of the old hermit. If the latter had required the fulfilment of all righteousness as the condition of the coming of the Anointed, Jesus taught the 'better righteousness' of 'non-resistance', the hard and quiet heroism of the weak. Not to do wrong to anyone, *shimsa*, as again in our time a great spirit, a *mahan atma*, a religious genius, is trying to teach in India; not to resist even the oppressors, but to conquer their hardness by a victorious kindness; not to judge a brother nor to seek justice against him; not to strive for gain, but to help everyone by giving kindness; not to rule over anyone, but to serve all, nay, even to love one's enemies.

225

Along with this superhuman demand of disinterested pacifism he prom-ises the poor, the oppressed, and the heavy-laden an easier yoke, a new law of God, a new constitution, a redemption from the pressure of the hierocratic state become unbearable, redemption also from the pressure of the superimposed hostile world-empire and the incarnate arch-enemy of God ruling over it until the end of this aeon. The people who listened to his preaching were attracted not so much by the narrow path he pointed out to them, as by *the alluring hope of a golden age in which the first would be last and the last would be first, when those who hunger and thirst would be fed, whilst those who are satisfied now would then be hungry; and still more by the dark rumour that the despised sinners would partake of that kingdom before the righteous.* . . .

Having collected a small band, he started on the laying down of a constitution . . . of his kingdom: twelve are to go out to call the twelve tribes of Israel; seventy-two ambassadors are to go to the seventy-two nations of the Gentiles to demand their submission to the kingdom of God, after the manner of the Persian great king asking for earth and water. The notion of pacifying the world by a mere message and an announce-ment of the peace and goodwill of the only true God had long before Jesus driven the Pharasaic missionaries over land and sea, to convert all people; it is taught here, with a childlike trust in God which has never again been attained, in these speeches addressed to the Royal messengers.

After the return of those 'of little faith', who only in the nearness of the mysterious powers of their master were capable of sustained enthusiasm there followed the first falling-away of this pious confidence in the kind-ness of an all-loving Father in heaven.

The terrible God of the fathers, who according to the teaching of the prophets rejects the animal offering of this priestly code, demands an infinitely harder sacrifice: nothing will satisfy Him but the decisive deed—to renounce everything dear to man: fathers, mothers, children, if they refuse to follow the call, to give up all possessions, horses, fields, the beloved land of promise itself, to assume the mark of the cross distinguish-ing the homeless, wandering tribes, to follow after the liberation into the desert, the land of freedom, to emigrate from the inhabited world which is subject to the Romans. As the fathers had left Egypt, the house of bondage, to go into the desert, following the call of God from Harmel under their leader, so the select are again to follow their prophetic guide on a new exodus. This is no revolt, but merely a 'breaking out', an escape from unbearable oppression, which seems to him the true path of salvation. After the example of the achievements of the Macabee Mattathia, of the Baptist and of Judah of Galilee, he will make the solemn announcement to Israel on the great pilgrims' assembly at Jerusalem on the Passover, and thence will lead his elect . . . of the new and true Israel, into the desert.

The Zealots and *Barjonim* among his followers are not afraid of this enterprise; but they know better than . . . their 'prince of peace' who intends to enter Jerusalem mounted on an ass, that even this road into the desert must lead through the prophesied war of the last days. 'Armed for war' like their fathers in Egypt they expect to leave Palestine. When their leader, with a heavy heart, has realised this stern necessity and not only permits but even commands them to buy swords, each one for himself, they have anticipated him, and each pulls two daggers, the weapons of the sicarii, from his bosom.

From the heights of Mt. Homen, in the north of Galilee, where Simon Barjona in wise forethought would have pitched the camp and would have liked to call the elect for an exodus into the desert, the expedition marches to Jerusalem instead, for the last decisive manifestation, headed by their leader, who for some time past has been expecting captivity, suffering, and death, but who is still secretly hoping for a miracle of God, a shortening of the predestined time and a passing of the cup. To the most faithful of his inner circle he confides that he is going to his death, as the 'servant of Yahweh', to take upon himself the guilt of his people, according to the words of the prophet. No other peoples are to be the scapegoat for Israel's sins; Israel's own King and chosen high priest must fall as a piacular sacrifice to force from heaven at last the longed-for redemption.

Thanks to the joining of other pilgrims marching to Jerusalem, and of scattered adherents here and there in the country, the little band grows to a size of several hundred men, encamps in front of the city, on the Mount of Olives, among the tents of the other pilgrims, still increasing through the reputation of the wonder-worker which mysteriously clings to Jesus. About a thousand men enter the city, preceding or following the prophet, who rides into the city sitting on his *Slebi*'s donkey, and proclaim him Davidic king of Israel. A passionate cry of the multitude, 'Osanna', 'Deliver us', accompanies the solemn entry. The prophet is carried forward by the ever-increasing pressure of the crowd into the temple, suddenly occupied by surprise by men carrying hidden arms. The levitic guard offers no resistance—nay, the priestly youth, the 'buds' on the staff of Aaron, which, though dry, blooms once again before its definite end, greet the son of David with cries of joy. The temple, with its castle the Antonia, then without a Roman garrison, is in the hands of the Galileans, whilst the *Barjonim* of Jerusalem have at the same time seized the tower standing above the *Shilosh*, the aqueduct through which according to an old saga, David himself had once entered the old fortress of the Jebusites.

The Roman cohort in the castle of Herod is far too weak to win back these two strong points, the keys of the fortifications in the extreme north and the extreme south. The movement might even then, like the one of a later day started by the *segan* 'Ele'asar b Hananiah (A.D. 66), have carried with it the leading families of the priestly nobility, had not the attack on the temple banks and the expulsion of the dealers in sacrificial animals, as well as the decisive utterances of the newly proclaimed king against the temple itself, shown to the high priests with unmistakable clearness what the present masters would have to expect in the event of the people remaining the victors.

Thus the messengers sent by the military tribunes of Herod's castle vie with those of the high priest in warning the governor in far-off Caesarea of what had taken place, and in clamouring for the speedy dispatch of his legion. Pilate approached in forced marches, and on the preparation day of the Passover the rebellion was well repressed, the temple reconquered in the same manner in which it had been taken—that is, by a band of apparently peaceful pilgrims. The altar and precincts were flooded with the blood of the Galileans cut down in vast numbers; the tower of *Shilosh*, laid low by the Roman machines, was covering the corpses of eighteen of the rebellious Jerusalemites. In the night, a few hours after the sounds of the Hallel announcing the end of the Passover meal had vanished, in the stillness a Roman cohort, increased by a guard of loyalists hurriedly armed by the high priests with clubs and daggers, surrounded the Mount of Olives. After a weak attempt at resistance, given up almost immediately by the express command of Jesus, the leader of the revolt, in Roman eyes only the one-day king of a belated and bloody *Saturnalia*, was captured, promptly condemned that same night according to martial law, and crucified along with two other 'robbers', leaders of the revolt. (1931, pp. 567–571, italics mine.)

APPENDIX II

MILLENNIAL DREAMS IN ACTION

ELSEWHERE in this volume I have said that one of the special problems connected with cargo cults is that until recently there were no major works devoted entirely to them. At that time, when I wrote, there was only Worsley's book. Now already we have Burridge's masterly work and a *Beiheft* of the journal *Comparative Studies in Society and History*, called *Millennial Dreams in Action*. This, which appeared in mid-1962, is a collection of papers read at a symposium in 1960, before Burridge's work appeared. I want, in this brief appendix, to discuss this volume, or at least the relevant parts of it, as an illustration of the state discussion of the topic is in.

Millennial Dreams in Action, edited by Sylvia Thrupp, who also edits *Comparative Studies in Society and History*, is subtitled 'Essays in Comparative Study' and contains eleven papers, five appendices and an editorial introduction. Its scope is the general anthropological and sociological study of millenarianism. The papers cover Africa, Melanesia, China, Borneo, Jamaica, the Middle Ages in Europe, and Brazil. Of interest to us are four of the papers (by Cohn, Shepperson, Guiart and Eliade), two of the appendices (by Aberle and Kaminsky), and Dr. Thrupp's editorial introduction. I shall discuss these in the order in which they are printed.

1. *Thrupp's report on the Conference*

In her editorial report on the conference Dr. Thrupp first of all notes that there was a general rejection of 'reductionism'. As examples of reductionism she mentions the following theories: (1) that millennial movements are 'cultural devices for relieving the painfulness of social changes that degrade or seriously jeopardize the status of a group'; (2) that 'through ritual and the stimulus of new leadership the movement may "revitalize" the tribal culture'; (3) 'it will rally those who have been uprooted and dispersed into what is for them at first a social vacuum, giving them something to live for until the wider society may offer more satisfactory alternatives'; (4) 'it enables people to work themselves up into states of excitement in which they can either assure themselves of a speedy solution to their problems or ignore them'; and (5) the cultists' emotional state of mind reflects a social situation, more or less directly.

The conference rejected reductionist interpretations on logical grounds, and because if one attempts comparison of a broader scale the development of ideas has to be taken into account as well as states of emotion. In any culture the thinking in which a millennial dream is embedded has a logic of its own that is not an automatic reflection of social situations. The variety and the development of ideas are a part of our problem (p. 12).

I cannot follow everything here but I think I grasp that the aged philosophy of 'study the ritual not the belief' which I have berated so hard in the text of this book is being explicitly given up. Ideas, it is being said, cannot just be superstructures of social situations; they have life and meaning of their own. We are told that the Conference's alternative was historical and comparative study, especially of the 'negative instances', situations similar to those where millenarianism occurred but which did not have it.

Dr. Thrupp ends her summary (I skip entirely her discussion of individual areas) by putting forward tentatively four kinds of explanation which were taken seriously at the Conference. (1) That the cults are a reaction to deprivation. (2) That they are a form of (endogenous) distress and anxiety. (3) That they are the result of an aesthetic liking for cultism. (4) That they are the result of tension between traditional leadership and an upstart rival. Dr. Thrupp points out that explanations (1) and (2) are refuted because these difficulties have alternative responses. She does not comment much on (3) and (4).

2. *Cohn on the Middle Ages*

As might be expected, the paper by Professor Norman Cohn on millenarianism in the Middle Ages is very interesting. He begins by defining millenarianism as the belief in collective, terrestrial, imminent (soon and sudden), total, supernatural, salvation. He then writes an enthralling study of medieval millenarianism which confutes the idea shared by marxists and right-wingers that they were mass or poverty-stricken uprisings. There are several circumstances which separately or together enabled the cults to occur in medieval Europe: (1) catastrophe or fear of catastrophe; (2) the defection of the power which normally controls relations with the Power behind the Cosmos; (3) emotional frustration in leisured yet statusless and functionless women; and (4) the non-availability of secular means to groups who are aware that power can change hands. Again in four points Cohn then puts forward his own theory: (i) there is the religious promise of an age of bliss; (ii) there is a prophet who adopts this promise and has a suitable personality; (iii) there is a latent human yearning for salvation from suffering; (iv) there is a discharge of emotional tension which gives energy to the movement.

3. *Shepperson on the Comparative Study of the Movements*

The concept of a millennium, says Shepperson, is conceived of as transitional. On the one hand there are some movements which think the deliverer will appear in a cataclysm because human agency can do nothing and only an upheaval will change things—this is the theory that the deliverer will be premillennial; on the other hand there are those who think the millennium comes as the fruit of human agency and the second coming or deliverer will arrive only afterwards—this is the postmillennial or reformist attitude. He compares millennialism to secular utopianism: the latter is a search for perfect space, while the millennium is a search for perfect time. There is no smooth progression in millennialism. He asks the following questions: How far is the messiah-mechanism external? What is the role of women as leaders? And he says that research is needed on millennialism in G.B. and the U.S.

4. *Guiart on the Cargo Cults*

Guiart poses the problem: Why do cargo cults occur here and not there?

He begins with the idea that Christianity is not just an intrusion but a new factor in the situation, a new religion significantly altering the situation. He says that more research is needed into this topic. Guiart suggests that in an intuitive way the natives applied structural-functionalism to the white man. They wanted to be like the white man so, operating on the principle that if they acquire one institution the others, which are indissolubly linked to it, will follow, they decided to accept one institution of the white man. The institution they decided to start with was Christian religion; after all, this institution was being offered, even thrust upon them by white men (missionaries). But wealth, the institution they coveted most in the ensemble, didn't follow on their acceptance of the religion. The native prophets denounced the missionaries for this. Guiart gives instances. On Tanna early converts to Christianity wanted to be paid, early missionaries indulged in trade, lived in great luxury, and did reward natives (e.g. for building). Early converts are known to have been well-dressed. But this rewarding of converts could last only as long as they were a minority. There was a lot of stress in missionary teaching on hellfire; therefore catastrophes were blamed on God (since his priests talked so much about his wrath . . .) On New Caledonia, missionaries were at first looked upon as gods and asked to bring rain. Then there was a reaction. Natural disasters were again interpreted as God's wrath. The mass conversions were made in the hope of gaining life, that is a better deal, better treatment, a hope of resistance to the 'death' of colonial rule. The missions by educating the natives helped them the better to resist the settlers. On Espiritu Santo attempts were made to avoid white incursions by re-organising the society around the mission.

On Tanna most people were Christians in the early years of the century: this was the 'Tanna law' period of native courts trying people for immorality. The strictness was thought to be a defence against the traders and recruiters. There was a sudden return to paganism in 1941 in the form of the John Frum cult (see Chapter 2) who was a reincarnation of a traditional god known as karapenmun.

Guiart points out that the native society was more flexible than it is usually credited with being. They were able to divest themselves of institutions like exogamy and bride-price. This is a refutation of structural-functionalism, of course.

Guiart ends by saying that conversion was a form of protection (a sort of 'if you can't beat them, join them' philosophy) from European cheating, abusing, kidnapping, disease and weapon-bearing.

5. *Eliade on Cosmic Regeneration*

In his paper Dr. Mircea Eliade argues that to some extent millenarian cults are a cultural inheritance: these cultures have the annual return of the dead and cosmic regeneration as parts of their normal cycles. Cargo cults take over and amplify this.

> If so many 'cargo cults' have assimilated Christian millenarist ideas, it is because the natives have rediscovered in Christianity their old traditional eschatological myth. The resurrection of the dead . . . was to them a familiar idea. If the natives came to feel disappointed in the missionaries . . . it was . . . because the missionaries and their converts did not seem to conduct themselves as true Christians. . . . The millenarist movements became savagely anti-Christian when their leaders realised that the missionaries . . . did not really believe in the arrival of ships of the dead bearing gifts, that in effect they did not believe in the imminence of the Kingdom, the resurrection of the dead, and the establishment of Paradise (p. 143).

6. *Aberle on Relative Deprivation*

Aberle begins by saying that deprivation, so often used as a partial explanation of the cults, can be important when it is relative as well as when it is absolute (the so-called 'subsistence line' might approximate to what Aberle means by absolute deprivation). Relative deprivation he says is deprivation relative to reasonable expectations. These can be of three kinds: comparing the present with the past; comparing the present with the future; and comparing self with someone else. All three comparisons are possible only when there has been change. When empirical means of rectifying the deprivation are blocked, the author argues, remedial action may be taken in any one of four spheres: the attempt to possess what there is a relative deprivation of; or there may be simply attempts to regain the status lost by the deprivation; or there may be an attempt to restore behaviour that has been stopped by the deprivation; or there can finally be simply an attempt to raise the worth (in the eyes of other groups) of the group, as a group. Any of these deprivations is a basis for remedial action but none is sufficient. The doctrines of any resulting cult will be related to the kind of deprivation they suffered.

Finally Aberle discusses four theories. The first is the theory that the cults are caused by boredom; this he does not criticise but says is not the case with most cults. The second is what he calls utility theories (not elaborated on by him) which he dismisses because they use constants (utility values) to explain variables (different cults). The third is the theory

that the cults are caused by deprivation, but he says that doesn't point
to a particular type of deprivation. Finally, out of pure prejudice, as he
confesses, Aberle is unwilling to explain the cults on purely spiritual
grounds. He ends by suggesting the theory that there is in the cults a
desire for the renewal of the social order.

7. *Kaminsky on Explanation*

Kaminsky argues that we can infer from the cults that the participants
have lost their powers of self-criticism and their sense of reality—they
empty their present social order of all value. He therefore suggests that a
psychological theory of the cults 'based solidly on the positive evidence'
(p. 216) would be an advantage.

8. *Conclusion*

Even in a symposium devoted entirely to the topic we still, I think, find
the methodological faults of which I have complained. There is a lack of
specification of the problems. There is almost no give-and-take in argument and discussion between the papers: they might almost have been
published just as they were read. Those discussions, which obviously
were of interest, on the rejection of reductionist theories and on Kaminsky's psychological ideas, are not reported at all, only alluded to. Consequently we have a mass of unrelated and unrefined ideas on a variety of
the subproblems of the cults. Only Guiart writes a really straightforward,
simple, and understandable paper on the general problem of a theory of
the cults. Cohn, of course, provides excellent comparative material on the
Middle Ages. In short, this symposium, despite the participation (see p. 5)
of Cyril Belshaw and Reinhart Bendix, was badly lacking some methodological guidance.

APPENDIX III

LAWRENCE ON THE EXPLANATION OF
CARGO CULTS[1]

I

LAWRENCE (1964) begins by asserting flatly that cargo cults must be understood both in their socio-political and epistemological dimensions and that these are not the same. He announces his intention of studying their systems of ideas as extensively and intensively as he will study their sociology. This is at once a very bold breakaway from the Radcliffe-Brown/Durkheim dogma that people's ideas are either to be ignored or sociologically explained away.[2] Lawrence then goes on to outline the social structure and religious systems of several Southern Madang societies as a prelude to his history of western contact in the area. He attempts to sort out the traditional value patterns and epistemological assumptions against which the intrusions of the white man can be silhouetted. An outline history of European incursions and settlement in Madang is then given. This story runs from 1884[3] to date. The history of the area is to a certain extent documented and not conjectural, but there are many lacunae at which Dr. Lawrence has speculatively to reconstruct events. The anthropological prejudice against using historical data thus is simply pushed aside. Of course, in the matter of the logical inability of the past to explain the present,[4] Lawrence does not intervene. He uses history as an essential background; it does not explain everything, it is part of the initial conditions.

This history of Madang is the story of five successive phases of cargo cult activity over more than some seventy years. In the course of it Lawrence pays a great deal of attention to the individual lives and doctrines of several important and influential native prophets, especially the famous Yali. The action of Chapters V–VIII centres entirely on the fascinating career and personality of Yali. Thus Dr. Lawrence allies himself firmly with those thinkers who claim that individuals and their ideas, their unique

[1] I am grateful to J. Agassi, H. I. Hogbin and P. Lawrence for critical discussion of the first draft of this appendix, which is part of a paper to appear in the *European Journal of Sociology* entitled 'On the Explanation of Cargo Cults'.
[2] See above pp. 149*ff.*
[3] Contact began in 1643, but intensive contact and administration began only in 1884 under the Germans.
[4] Gellner 1965, pp. 15–20.

personal compounds of influences and novelties, can decisively affect society. Indeed Dr. Lawrence goes further and explains how both the actions of individual government officials and those of Yali were a complicated mixture of the intended and unintended; that is, intentional acts with intended consequences and intentional acts which were dictated more by the events of the situation than by any general aim, and both acts and consequences which were not intended at all.

Thus for the reader there is built up a very striking picture in depth of Southern Madang society, the character of native-European contact there, and the interpretation of that contact by the natives. To accomplish this task Dr. Lawrence has expended close on thirteen years, including several field trips. The result in my opinion is a classic of social anthropology, showing how its unique 'feeling' and 'depth' when combined with conventional historical, biographical and sociological techniques can produce a work that hangs together as a coherent story.

From this general discussion we come to Lawrence's actual explanation of the cults. He breaks down the problems posed by cargo cults into only three. They are: why did the natives want cargo; why did they believe ritual alone would get it; and what is the political significance of their attempts to do so? This simple division into *motives, means* and *effects* is very convenient. However, for purposes of discussion I want to break down the problems still further, along the lines adopted in chapter 2 section 8. This will I believe enable us to evaluate Lawrence's book in detail.

II

The problems begin with (A) who joins the cults and (B) who does not? Lawrence's answer on these points cannot easily be summarised. He says that definitely more than fifty per cent of the Southern Madang population were involved in the third of the cargo cults he distinguishes (less in the other four), and from his material it seems that in certain small areas entire villages would be caught up while others would be entirely left out. Lawrence says that two categories of people definitely did not join: those with a prolonged and thus better grounding in true Christianity (although not all the cults had a Christian basis), and those who had had insufficient contact with Europeans and their culture to be caught up in talk of cargo.

It is difficult to bring his evidence to bear on the deprivation theory, the theory that traces the cults back to a sense of injustice aroused in the Melanesians by their being deprived of certain things. While there was some exploitation, and some expropriation of land, the cults spread far beyond the pockets where these things happened. If one cares to say the Melanesians were deprived simply in not participating in the European standard of living then deprivation explains nothing since both cultists and non-cultists were deprived. But if one restricts the description 'deprivation' to those who seem to have suffered some specific injustice, the difficulty arises that this does not explain the attraction and presence of the cult among these who did not so suffer.

The next problem (C) is, 'to what extent are charismatic leaders involved?' Lawrence argues that they are sometimes involved but that they are a precipitating rather than an enabling cause. The ideological background has to be well prepared before the prophecies of an individual can take root. All cults seem to have begun with a prophet, but sometimes they seem to have gone on to develop their own impetus and to dispense with organised leadership; sometimes, again, they have been organised and run by one man (e.g. Kaum); and sometimes, yet again, they have centred on a charismatic figure, but much organisation and attention to detail has been handled by men behind the scenes (Yali's secretaries, etc.).

Worsley (1957, pp. 266–72) argues that the elements of organisation and direction in the cults cannot be explained as rational on Weber's characterisation of charismatic authority. This is a sound point, but it is difficult to see why the aura of charisma should not be used to explain 'pull' or following,while something else is used to explain organisation. BillyGraham's 'follow-up organisation' is merely his recognition of the non-permanent effect of his charismatic appeal. On the other hand, Worsley is justly severe when he suggests the cults explode Weber's characterisation of traditional and charismatic authority as irrational. In fact, of course, all these impulses to action can be shown to fall under the rational category of goal-directed action. A respect for tradition or a proneness to yield to charisma are factors in a person's situation, *limitations* within which he pursues ends, or even determinants of his ends. Thus Worsley's attack on Weber's charisma as 'subjectivist' perhaps creates more problems than it solves.

Problem (*D*) deserves the most extensive treatment since it is, 'how did the myth of the cargo arise?' Lawrence argues that social relations in traditional Madang society centred on exchange and cooperation; moreover knowledge and wealth were thought to have a religious origin. Native society became increasingly heavily dependent on European goods —steel tools and cotton especially—after the turn of the century. The first cults which can properly be 'dated' are those involving Christian services from the 1920s onwards. But Lawrence traces cargo beliefs back to the 1870s. The traditional religion was not so much a spiritual theology, it was more like a technique for obtaining material well-being. Thus, faced with Europeans who neither entered into relations of cooperation and exchange with the natives, nor accepted their religion, yet who seemed to possess material well-being of a particularly glamorous kind (cargo), the natives constructed a series of hypotheses to explain these successful intruders. (I here compress Lawrence's five beliefs into four.) The first hypothesis was that the Europeans were gods and received cargo from their home. The second hypothesis was that the Europeans were another island tribe; superior manipulators of religious forces, they were able to conjure up immense supplies of goods. The third hypothesis was that the whites were another tribe and that they were piratically intercepting goods destined for the Melanesians, and that the missionaries were white renegades offering the Melanesians the secret of their techniques in the form of Christianity. The fourth hypothesis was a kind of final disillusionment in which even the missionaries were thought to be involved in the conspiracy to misappropriate cargo, by deliberately withholding the vital secrets of the manipulatory technique. The reaction was then to formulate hypotheses about the content of what was thought to be being withheld. Around any of these hypotheses, cults could be formed. These hypotheses incorporated a great many fragmentary pieces of knowledge about Europeans. Their gadgets, their rituals, the interesting fact that they had huge collections of native gods in Brisbane in 'museums', that Europeans kept large numbers of totemic animals as 'pets' or in 'zoos', etc.

Of course this presentation of a series of hypotheses is an excessively neat rational reconstruction; the progress from one hypothesis to another was by no means smooth or general. A look at the comparative table of the five cults Dr. Lawrence provides (p. 240) shows that the hypothesis of the Europeans as hostile misappropriators took hold only gradually. Had communications been better, had techniques of ordering and systematically discussing ideas been available, we might have seen a swifter and more uniform progress from one hypothesis to another. Yet it still seems that each successive hypothesis must have been refuted. If the Europeans were gods then if they were treated like gods cargo should be forthcoming. It was not. Conclusion, they are not gods. If the Europeans were another tribe of human beings then making friends with them or spying on them should reveal the secret of their manipulations. Again, disappointment. If the Europeans were intercepting native goods their missionary renegades should produce the answer. No luck. The final move is just to guess at their technique of manipulation and interception. It is a depressing story and yet one which, unless the colonisers were equipped with the kind of deep understanding of the native world that it took Dr. Lawrence almost thirteen years to put together, could not, it seems, have been avoided. So much of what the Europeans were doing could not have been rendered intelligible to the natives. Native beliefs were, according to Lawrence, homogeneous; it was inconceivable to them that there could exist man-produced knowledge. All knowledge was timeless and revealed. They could not see how people could live together when some believed in Adam and Eve and others believed man came from a monkey. They concluded there must be at least two tribes, one believing in Adam, one believing in monkeys. How else would an orderly social organisation be possible? The distinction between secular learning and religious learning was unknown; the former having no counterpart in the traditional system was useless to them, whereas western religion had a very definite counterpart and could be absorbed (albeit in a garbled form). Even native conceptions of time were different. Their cyclic mythological system was hardly adaptable to explaining why European societies were rich, etc.

So in the end the natives were striving for a syncretic formula which would give them the vital trade goods and wealth which seemed to be the barrier to their being acknowledged in their true dignity as men by the Europeans. They accepted a purely ritual solution, rather than a ritual plus a secular solution, because they had never seen Europeans work, they had no conception of the production process. Cargo must be the work of the gods; gods were manipulated by rituals; as the Europeans do, so must we.

Problem (*E*) is how to explain the cults' swiftness of spread. This is partly explained in Lawrence by the relative homogeneity of the native society and the consequent prevalence of the enabling conditions. These were mainly cosmological and religious. The problem of the Europeans—their not entering into cooperative relations or exchange relations with the natives—was a widespread problem. As was the aspiration to achieve a proper relationship with these prosperous newcomers. Failure to achieve this threatened their whole view of the world. Fitting the new phenomena in involved attaining a new cosmic vision, a new horizon of expectations as a defence against the terrors of the truly unknown, the chaos and darkness, the sheer not knowing what will happen next and the consequent paralysing of action which the European presence had brought about.

In addition Lawrence picks out three aids to the spread of the cults; the widespread dependence upon European goods, leading to the ready acceptance of any plausible way of getting them; secondly the reliability of communications along paths and trade routes; and thirdly the deliberate propagation of the cults by some native mission helpers. Lawrence of course does not touch on the problems of inter-island communication in Melanesia as a whole.

Problem (F) is why similar cults keep on appearing after each successive failure. Lawrence thinks this is involved with the natives' mythic conception of the world and of time. Lacking a linear chronology, they did not see a history of failed attempts stretching behind them.

The most perceptive knew, of course, that within the span of the previous three or four generations there had been five major attempts to explain and get control of the new situation, and that as each attempt failed it was succeeded by another. Beyond this, however, they regarded each attempt at explanation—each cargo belief or myth—as in itself a separate and complete 'history' of the world. It bore no relation to earlier attempts at explanation, which were all in error and had been, as it were, erased. (p. 241).

This striking passage illustrates the immense difficulties in the way of any true communication between the Melanesians and the Europeans. Happily Lawrence draws no relativist conclusions from this; he is properly convinced that however viable their cosmology and chronology, it is mistaken; the main problem as he sees it is that of finding means to educate the New Guineans out of their cosmology and chronology.[1]

Problem (G), the similarity of the cults, is relatively easy to solve for Southern Madang. There are sufficient similarities in the societies and ideas and in the character of the experiences of contact, and there are sufficiently efficient communications, to make similarity no more difficult to explain than dissimilarity. Again, the situation on scattered islands beyond New Guinea is harder to explain. For myself I would guess that diffusion of the cargo cult idea must take place somehow. Despite the homogeneity of the region it is asking a lot to have us believe the cargo cult was invented and reinvented hundreds of times.

[1] Some philosophical difficulties with this sort of argument have been raised by P. Winch, 1964. But see the trenchant criticisms of Gellner 1967 and my own in 1966.

Lawrence on the Explanation of Cargo Cults

The final problem is what Lawrence calls effects—meaning, one supposes, unintended effects (*H*). Lawrence strongly denies that the cults were 'nativistic', that is, that they tried to emphasise or reassert selected aspects of the traditional culture. Rather is it that insofar as they used old ideas and values to approach the changed situations this was because they knew of no others. There were both conservative and rebellious tendencies in cargo cults, and Lawrence would classify them rather as rebellious than either revolutionist or reformist. In a rebellion the main object is to alter the relative statuses within the given framework.[1]

Fighting and feuding were outlawed in New Guinea, but there were still hostilities. In addition there were sectional cleavages between language groups. In a word, then, the Southern Madang District lacked any sense of local or national identity. Lawrence argues that the cults to a certain extent helped weave these diverse societies into a whole with some sense of identity. Cargo cults cut across sectional cleavages and engendered a form of embryonic nationalism, an embryonic sense of identity as 'we' the natives, *versus* 'them' the whites. And this identity was one of self-interest. Such nationalism as there was, was to be found in this tendency to see the situation in which 'we' must militantly oppose 'them'.

Worsley forecast (1957, p. 255) that the religious stage of the nationalism would be shaken off and the cults would become purely political. Lawrence doubts this, especially in the short run 'which may be all we are allowed to' forecast (p. 265).

If it is allowed that the culture I have described is fairly typical of coastal Melanesia, it would be naïve to expect people, for whom the religious and secular are so inextricably interwoven in the same order of existence that it is impossible to classify any important event as exclusively either one or the other, to switch from a non-rationalist to a rationalist outlook in the matter of a few years. (p. 265).

As it is the cults form an obstacle to progress, a rallying point preventing desirable changes being understood in the terms the Europeans want them to be understood. The main problem they thus pose is how to break out of them, how to break out of the circle of mutually reinforcing beliefs.[2]

Lawrence's answer to this problem is two-fold: economic and linguistic. Writing about the situation as he found it fifteen years ago, he stresses that any new institutions needed not to be put in at random as isolated customs, but according to a careful plan which might give them some chance to take root. First of all the New Guinea economy must be built up so that more natives can buy European goods and more of them can go abroad and learn about the manufacturing process. But if this is not to founder on the preconceptions built into the natives' present ideology, they must be given a powerful alternative set of concepts and categories. The practical answer would seem to be education in proper English. At the moment

---

[1] Reform is tinkering with the framework, revolution completely changing it, see Lawrence, p. 256, *n.* 2.

[2] On this point see the forthcoming paper by myself and J. Agassi, 1967.

most communication in New Guinea is carried out by means of Pidgin English: this is the language of cargo. Only by teaching the New Guineans real English will it be possible to give them access to a way of understanding the world remotely resembling that of the European. There is no barrier *in principle* of course to the New Guineans breaking out of the cargo system of ideas while still using their own languages. The objections in practice are that those who would disabuse them can hardly be expected to master dozens of very complex tongues, and tongues moreover with no written literature. Thus the critical approach must come through English. A sad conclusion but, it seems, an inescapable one. Giving them a language is of course not enough. Practical education of various sorts, including participation in the manufacturing process, will be a minimum requirement. English will give them the conceptual apparatus; active use of it will enable them to organise their experience in terms of it. A good part of the road has already been travelled in the years since Lawrence's research began.

III

I want now to set down a few reflections stimulated by Lawrence's most exciting and illuminating book. The story of the academic discussion of cargo cults is in some ways a classic case of how a problem is discovered, refined, and redefined. When the cults were first noticed they were felt to be very special and peculiar, unlike anything seen before. Then, piece by piece, parallels were discovered or dug up in all sorts of places, from Haiti to the middle ages. And slowly they came to be assimilated to the general phenomenon of millenarianism. Perhaps the culmination of this tendency is to be found in the symposium edited by Thrupp (1962), and the recently translated volume by Lanternari (1963), where they are treated in the course of studies of millenarianism in general. But, moving in a completely different direction, we now find their peculiarity being dispelled in the works of Lawrence and Burridge by the discovery of more and more similarities between the cult doctrines and traditional native views of the world. They now seem like a typical kind of millenarianism *and* a typical Melanesian religion. It seems that as parallels to the cults are found there is less and less that is peculiar about them, less and less to explain. Is this always the pattern with new phenomena? Is it the case that we consider it necessary to explain a phenomenon only while it is peculiar, out of the ordinary? And indeed does the assimilation of the cults to millenarianism in general make any difference? Do we not try to explain religion despite its universality as a phenomenon of human society?

This is all very puzzling. Perhaps some such conclusion as this is possible. Both the familiar and the unfamiliar require explanation. Sometimes in terms of the familiar, sometimes in terms of the unfamiliar. In general the social sciences explain by reference to the familiar, the natural sciences by reference to the unfamiliar. But of course all explanations are revisable and familiarity and unfamiliarity are purely relative terms.

Having raised this general issue I want now to discuss just how typically millenarian cargo cults are. In the first place some millenarian religions are revolutionary rather than rebellious, whereas cargo cults are not revolutionary. Cargo cults do not necessarily involve the belief in an apocalypse, or in a total rejection of the past, or in a totally new future. Thus a good many of the points made by Yonina Talmon (1962, pp. 136–8) in her general characterisation of millenarianism do not apply to cargo cults although she includes cargo cults in her remarks. My view would be that the above factors usefully distinguish cargo cults from millenarianism in general. Cargo cults do not involve an apocalypse, a golden age, etc., and there is no question of a 'merger of the spiritual with the terrestrial'; these are already merged in the original culture. Perhaps the most interesting place where Dr. Talmon's generalisations break down, however, is over time. She says millenarianisms view time as a linear process leading to a decisive consummation. And on p. 139 we find the hypothesis:

Clearly, religions in which history has no meaning whatsoever and religions which have a cyclic repetitive conception of time are not conducive to millenarism.

Now either cargo cults are not millenarianisms or, since Dr. Talmon thinks they are, Lawrence has refuted her hypothesis. It seems that New Guinea time conceptions are *especially* susceptible to successive millenarian religions *because* time is not conceived as linear, as an arrow.

Of course this question of classification—millenarian/non-millenarian—could easily degenerate into a discussion of words. The question in its concrete form becomes, 'can we provide a general explanation of millenarianism which embraces cargo cults?' The answer seems to be: only to a certain extent; indeed we can provide a general explanation of millenarianism only to a certain extent. This shows clearly from reading Lanternari. There are many points of contact between millenarianisms, and some general explanations can be given. But these are only in general terms. If a full explanation of any one millenarianism is to be given, general sociological background must be combined with historical material on the situation as it grew up, and on the main personalities involved.

The final point to be taken up is that of the rationality of native acceptance of the cults. It seems to me that this very easily becomes a verbal issue. Mair (1958) says that all religions are at least non-rational. Worsley says that the cults are 'objectively' not rational, but otherwise rational. Mair means religion is not like science. Worsley means that science is objectively true while millenarian doctrines are objectively false. But the real problem of the rationality of the cults is: given native knowledge, aims and circumstances were their actions in joining the cults rational? The answer is, of course, yes; Lawrence shows that cargo cults involved no change in aims, only in the content of aims (i.e. what constituted well-being). Lawrence also shows that there was little improvement of native knowledge, despite the new circumstances. In fact the natives' fundamental tragedy is that they tried to give traditional explanations of the Europeans *because they knew no other*. There is no whiff of Whorff-Sapir in Lawrence. The natives were not *imprisoned* by their cosmology; they were, however, unable to transcend it without help. And nobody really tried to help them.

IV

The ready accessibility of material on the cults, the considerable publicity they have received, partly accounts for the widespread interest in them. But the chaos of psychological, cultural, marxist, structural, and mixed explanations of them reflects a lot of confusion. It is fascinating that Lawrence uses sociology, epistemology and history, and that he weaves from them a satisfactory account. He is not the first to study cosmology; he is the first to get at just how it is a barrier to culture contact and to be clear that not all cosmologies are equal in their truth-values. He is by no means the first to reintroduce history. But he is the first to use it in an *essential* way in a full explanation of what is going on in a society now. We can perhaps hope that his ideas and methods will be taken up and successfully applied to other cargo areas and that a great anthropological problem will prove to have been solved.

BIBLIOGRAPHY

WORKS CITED

AGASSI, J., 1956, *The Function of Interpretations in Physics*, Ph.D. thesis, University of London, typescript.

1959, 'Epistemology as an aid to Science', *Brit. J. Phil. of Sci.*, **10**, 139–46.

1960, 'Methodological Individualism', *British Journal of Sociology*, **11**, 244–70.

1963, 'Towards an Historiography of Science', *History and Theory*, Beiheft 2.

1966, 'Sensationalism', *Mind*, **75**, 1–24

ALLAN, C. H., 1951, 'Marching Rule', *Corona*, **3**, 93–100.

ATTENBOROUGH, D., 1960, 'The Cargo Cult and the Great God Frum', *The Sunday Times*, April, 24, p. 5.

BARBER, B., 1941, 'Acculturation and Messianic Movements', *American Sociological Review*, **6**, 663–9.

1952, *Science and the Social Order*, Glencoe, Ill.

BARROW, G. L., 1951, 'The Story of "Jonfrum"', *Corona*, **3**, 379–82.

BARTLEY, W. W. III, 1959, 'I Call Myself a Protestant', *Harpers*, May, 49–56; reprinted in Hamalian and Volpe, 1960.

1962a, 'Achilles, the Tortoise, and Explanation in Science and History', *Brit. J. Phil. of Sci.*, **13**, 15–33.

1962b, *The Retreat to Commitment*, New York.

BEATTIE, J. H. M., 1959, 'Understanding and Explanation in Social Anthropology', *British Journal of Sociology*, **10**, 45–60.

BECKER, C. L., 1932, *The Heavenly City of the Eighteenth Century Philosophers*, Yale.

BELSHAW, C. S., 1950, 'The Significance of Modern Cults in Melanesian Development', *Australian Outlook*, **4**, 116–25.

1954, *Changing Melanesia*, Melbourne.

BERNDT, R. M., 1952, 'A Cargo Movement in the Eastern Central Highlands of New Guinea', *Oceania*, **23**, 40–65, 137–58 and 202–34.

1954, 'Reaction to Conquest in the Eastern Highlands of New Guinea', *Oceania*, **24**, 190–228.

BODROǴI, T., 1951, 'Colonization and Religious Movements in Melanesia', *Academiae Scientiarum Hungaricae-Acta Ethnographica*, **51**, Fasc. 1–4, 259–90.

243

Bibliography

BOTT, E., 1957, *Family and Social Network*, London.

BROWN, R., 1963, *Explanation in Social Science*, London.

BUCHDAHL, G., 1959, 'Sources of Scepticism in Atomic Theory', *Brit. J. Phil. of Sci.*, **10**, 120–34.

BURRIDGE, K. O. L., 1954, 'Cargo Cult Activity in Tangu', *Oceania*, **24**, 241–53.
1960, *Mambu*, London.
1962, 'The Cargo Cult', *Discovery*, February, 22–7.

BURTT, E. A., 1928, *The Metaphysical Foundations of Modern Physical Science*, London.

COHEN, P. S., 1963, 'The Aims and Interests of Sociology', *Brit. J. Phil. of Sci.*, **14**, 246–61.

COHN, N., 1957, *The Pursuit of the Millennium*, London.
1962. See Thrupp, 1962.

CROCOMBE, R., 1961, 'A Modern Polynesian Cargo Cult', *Man*, **61**, 40–1.

CROSSMAN, R. H. (Ed.), 1950, *The God that Failed*, London.

DAVIS, K., 1959, 'The Myth of Functional Analysis as a Special Method in Sociology and Social Anthropology', *American Sociological Review*, **24**, 757–72 (The Presidential Address to the American Sociological Association).

EISLER, R., 1931, *The Messiah Jesus and John the Baptist*, London.

EMMET, D., 1958, *Function, Purpose and Powers*, London.

EVANS-PRITCHARD, E. E., 1937, *Witchcraft, Oracles and Magic among the Azande*, Oxford.
1940, *The Nuer*, Oxford.
1950, 'Social Anthropology: Past and Present', *Man*, **50**, 118–24.
1951, *Social Anthropology*, London.
1956, *Nuer Religion*, Oxford.
1961, *Anthropology and History*, Manchester.

FIRTH, R. W., 1931, 'Totemism in Polynesia', *Oceania*, **1**, 291–321 and 377–98.
1932, 'Anthropology in Australia 1920–1932 and After', *Oceania*, **3**, 1–12.
1936, *We, the Tikopia*, London.
1951a, *Elements of Social Organisation*, London.
1951b, 'Contemporary British Social Anthropology', *American Anthropologist*, **53**, 474–89.
1955, 'The Theory of Cargo Cults: A Note on Tikopia', *Man*, **55**, 130–2.
1956, *Human Types*, 2nd ed., London.
1957 (ed)., *Man and Culture*, London.

FORDE, D., 1954, *African Worlds*, ed., London.

FORTES, M., 1945, *The Dynamics of Clanship among the Tallensi*, Oxford.
1949, *The Web of Kinship among the Tallensi*, Oxford.
1949a, *Social Structure*, ed., Oxford.
1959, *Oedipus and Job*, Oxford.

FORTUNE, R., 1932, *Sorcerers of Dobu*, London.

FRAZER, SIR J. G., 1909, *The Golden Bough* (abridged ed.), London.

FREEMAN, J. D., 1962, Review of Leach, 1961, *Man*, **62**, 125–6.

FREUD, S., 1919, *Totem and Taboo*, London.

GEDDES, W. R., 1958, *Nine Dyak Nights*, Oxford.

GELLNER, E. A., 1956, 'Explanation in History', *Arist. Soc. Supp.*, **30**, *Dreams and Self-Knowledge*, 157–76.
1958, 'Time and Theory in Social Anthropology', *Mind*, **67**, 182–202.
1958a, 'How to Live in Anarchy', *The Listener*, **59**, 580 and 582–3.
1959, *Words and Things*, London
1960, 'The Concept of Kinship', *Philosophy of Science*, **27**, 187–204.
1963, 'Concepts and Society', *Proceedings of the 5th World Congress of Sociology (Washington)*, 161–89.
1965, *Thought and Change*, London.
1967, 'The New Idealism', to appear in *Problems in The Philosophy of Science, Proceedings of The International Colloquium, London 1965*, ed. I. Lakatos and A. Musgrave.

GLUCKMAN, H. M., 1949, *An Analysis of the Sociological Theories of Bronislaw Malinowski*, Oxford.
1955, *Custom and Conflict in Africa*, Oxford.

GODIN, W. and BECK, F., 1951, *Russian Purge*, London.

GOMBRICH, E. H., 1960, *Art and Illusion*, London.

GORDIMER, N., 1952, *The Soft Voice of the Serpent*, London.

GRANT, C. K., 1956, 'Polar Concepts and Metaphysical Arguments', *Proc. Arist. Soc.*, **56**, 1955–56.

GRAVES, R. and PODRO, J., 1953, *The Nazarene Gospel Restored*, London.

GROSS, L., 1959 (ed.), *Symposium on Sociological Theory*, Evanston (Ill.).

GUIART, J., 1951, 'Forerunners of Melanesian Nationalism', *Oceania*, **22**, 81–90.
1952, 'John Frum Movement in Tanna', *Oceania*, **22**, 165–77.
1956, 'Culture Contact and the "John Frum" Movement of Tanna, New Hebrides', *Southwestern Journal of Anthropology*, **12**, 105–16.
1962. See Thrupp, 1962.

HADDON, A. C., 1917, 'Five New Religious Cults in British New Guinea', *The Hibbert Journal*, **15**, 455–63.

HAMALIAN, L. and VOLPE, E. L., 1960, *Essays of our Time*, New York.

HAYEK, F. A., 1949, *Individualism and Economic Order*, London.
1952, *The Counter-Revolution of Science*, Glencoe.

HECKER, J. F. C., 1833, *The Black Death in the Fourteenth Century*, London.

Bibliography

HEMPEL, C. G., 1959, 'The Logic of Functional Explanation', in Gross, 1959, pp. 271–307.

HOGBIN, H. I., 1958, *Social Change*, London.

HOMANS, G. C., and SCHNEIDER, D. M., 1955, *Marriage, Authority and Final Causes*, Glencoe.

INGLIS, J., 1957, 'Cargo Cults. The Problem of Explanation', *Oceania*, 27, 249–63.

1959, 'Interpretation of Cargo Cults—Comments', *Oceania*, 30, 155–8.

JARVIE, I. C., 1961, 'Nadel on the Aims and Methods of Social Anthropology', *Brit. J. Phil. of Sc.*, 12, 1–24.

1961a, Review of P. Winch, *The Idea of a Social Science, Brit. J. Phil. of Sci.*, 12, 73–7.

1963, Review of D. F. Pocock, 1961, in *Brit. J. Phil. of Sci.*, 13, 327–9.

1963a, 'Between Adult and Child', unpublished.

1964, 'Theories of Cargo Cults: A Critical Analysis', *Oceania*, 34, 1–31, 108–136.

1964a, 'The Idea of Social Class', unpublished.

1966, 'On the Theory of Fieldwork and the Scientific Character of Social Anthropology', unpublished.

1967 (with J. Agassi), 'The Problem of the Rationality of Magic', forthcoming in *Brit. J. Social.*

KANT, I., 1885, *Kant's Introduction to Logic*, trs. T. K. Abbott, London.

KEESING, F. M., 1942, *The South Seas in the Modern World*, London.

1961, Review of Burridge, 1960, *Man*, 61, 148.

KOESTLER, A., 1959, *The Sleepwalkers*, London.

KROEBER, A. L., 1909, 'Classificatory Systems of Relationship', *J. Royal Anthro. Inst.*, 39, 77–84.

1917, 'California Kinship Systems', *Arch. and Ethn. Publ. Univ. Calif.*, 12.

LANCASTER, L., 1958, 'Kinship in Anglo-Saxon Society I and II', *Brit.. J Sociol.*, 9, 230–50 and 359–77.

LANTERNARI, V., 1963, *The Religions of the Oppressed*, London.

LAWRENCE, P., 1954, 'Cargo Cult and Religious Belief Among The Garia', *International Archives of Ethnography*, 47, 1–20.

1964, *Road Belong Cargo*, Manchester.

LEACH, E. R., 1954, *Political Systems of Highland Burma*, London.

1957, 'The Epistemological Background to Malinowski's Empiricism', in Firth, ed., 1957.

1961, *Re-thinking Anthropology*, London.

LEESON, I., 1952, 'Bibliography of Cargo Cults and Other Nativistic Movements in the South Pacific', *South Pacific Technical Commission*, Paper, No. 30.

LÉVI-STRAUSS, C., 1961, *A World on the Wane*, London.

LEVY, M. T., 1952, *The Structure of Society*, Princeton.

Bibliography

LINTON, R., 1943, 'Nativistic Movements', *American Anthropologist*, **45**, 230–40.

LOWIE, R. H., 1937, *History of Ethnological Theory*, New York.

MACRAE, D. G., 1961, *Ideology and Society*, London.

MCLENNAN, J. F., 1876, *Primitive Marriage*, London.

MACBEATH, A., 1952, *Experiments in Living*, London.

MAIR, L. P., 1948, *Australia in New Guinea*, London.
   1953, 'African Marriage and Social Change', in A. Phillips (ed.), *Survey of African Marriage and Family Life*, London.
   1958, 'The Pursuit of the Millennium in Melanesia', *British Journal of Sociology*, **9**, 175–82.
   1959, 'Independent Religious Movements in Three Continents', *Comparative Studies in Society and History*, **1**, 113–36.

MALINOWSKI, B., 1922, *Argonauts of the Western Pacific*, London.
   1926, *Myth in Primitive Psychology*, London.
   1929a, 'Social Anthropology', *Encyclopaedia Britannica*, **20**, 862–70.
   1929b, *The Sexual Life of Savages in North-western Melanesia*, London.
   1948, *Magic, Science and Religion*, Glencoe.

MAYER, P., 1954, *Witches*, Grahamstown.

MEAD, M., 1956, *New Lives for Old*, London.

MOONEY, J., 1892, 'The Ghost Dance Religion and the Sioux Outbreak of 1890', *14th Annual Report of Bureau of Ethnology to the Secretary of the Smithsonian Institution*, 1892–3, ed. J. W. Powell, Washington, D.C.

MORGAN, L. H., 1877, *Ancient Society*, London.

MURDOCK, G. P., 1949, *Social Structure*, New York.
   1951, 'British Social Anthropology', *American Anthropologist*, **53**, 465–73.

NADEL, S. F., 1951, *Foundations of Social Anthropology*, London.

PERRY, W. J., 1923, *The Children of the Sun*, London.

POCOCK, D. F., 1961, *Social Anthropology*, London.

POPPER, K. R., 1945, *The Open Society and Its Enemies*, London (fourth edition, 1962).
   1957, *The Poverty of Historicism*, London.
   1959, *The Logic of Scientific Discovery*, London.
   1961, 'On the Sources of Knowledge and of Ignorance', *Proceedings of the British Academy*, 1960, **46**, 39–71. (Reprinted in 1963.)
   1962, 'Julius Kraft, 1898–1960', *Ratio*, **3**, 2–12.
   1963, *Conjectures and Refutations*, London.

PORTA, G. B. DELLA, 1957, *Natural Magick*, New York.

POST, L. VAN DER, 1958, *The Lost World of the Kalahari*, London.

RADCLIFFE-BROWN, A. R., 1922, *The Andaman Islanders*, London.
   1931, 'The Present Position of Anthropological Studies', Presidential Address, *British Assoc. for Advancement of Science*, Section H, p. 13, quoted by Evans-Pritchard, 1951, p. 55.

Bibliography

1950, *African Systems of Kinship and Marriage* (ed. with Darryl Forde), London.

1952, *Structure and Function in Primitive Society*, London.

1957, *A Natural Science of Society*, Glencoe.

RIVERS, W. R., 1914, *Kinship and Social Organisation*, London.

SARGENT, W., 1957, *Battle for the Mind*, London.

SCHAPERA, I., 1930, *The Khoisan Peoples of South Africa: Bushmen and Hottentots*, London.

1953, 'Some Comments on Comparative Method in Social Anthropology', *American Anthropologists*, **55**, 353–61.

1955, 'The Sin of Cain', *J. Royal Anth. Inst.*, **85**, 33–43.

1962, 'Should Anthropologists Be Historians?', *J. Royal Anthro. Inst.*, **92**, 143–56.

SCHEINFELD, D. R., 1960, *A Comparative Study of Ancestor Worship*, M.A. thesis, University of London, typescript, unpublished.

SHAW, G. B., 1931, *Preface to Androcles and the Lion*, London.

SMITH, M. W., 1959, 'Towards a Classification of Cult Movements', *Man*, **59**, 8–12.

STANNER, W. E. H., 1953, *The South Seas in Transition*, Sydney.
1958, 'On The Interpretation of Cargo Cults', *Oceania*, **29**, 1–25.

STEINER, F., 1956, *Taboo*, London.

SUNDKLER, B., 1948, *Bantu Prophets in South Africa*, London.

TALMON, Y., 1962, 'The Pursuit of the Millennium', *European Journal of Sociology*, **3**, 125–48.

THRUPP, S. (ed.), 1962, *Millennial Dreams in Action*, The Hague.

TIMASHEFF, N. S., 1957, *Sociological Theory, Its Nature and Growth* (Rev. ed.), New York.

TYLOR, E. B., 1871, *Primitive Culture*, London.

WALLACE, A. C., 1956, 'Revitalization Movements', *American Anthropologist*, **58**, 264–81.

WATKINS, J. W. N., 1953, 'Ideal Types and Historical Explanation', in Feigl and Brodbeck, eds., *Readings in the Philosophy of Science*, New York.

1955, 'Methodological Individualism: A Reply', *Philosophy of Science*, **22**, 58–62.

1957a, 'Between Analytic and Empirical', *Philosophy*, **32**, 1–20.

1957b, 'Historical Explanation in the Social Sciences', *Brit. J. Phil. Sci.*, **8**, 104–17.

1957c, 'The Haunted Universe', *The Listener*, **57**, 837–8 and 883, 886.

1958a, 'The Alleged Inadequacy of Methodological Individualism', *J. of Phil.*, **55**.

1958b, 'Confirmable and Influential Metaphysics', *Mind*, **67**, 344–65.

1960, 'When are Statements Empirical?' *Brit. J. Phil. Sci.*, **10**, 287–308.

Bibliography

WHEATLEY, JON, 1962, Review of F. A. Hayek, *The Constitution of Liberty*, in *Mind*, N.S. **71**, 435–6.

WHITE, A. D., 1896, *A History of the Warfare of Science with Theology*, New York.

WHITE, M. G., 1956, *Towards Reunion in Philosophy*, Cambridge, Mass.

WILLIAMS, F. E., 1923, *Papua: Anthropology Reports No. 4, The Vailala Madness*, etc., Port Moresby.
1934, 'The Vailala Madness in Retrospect', in *Essays Presented to C.G. Seligman*, ed. E. E. Evans-Pritchard, R. W. Firth, B. Malinowski and I. Schapera, 369–79, London.

WINCH, P., 1964, 'Understanding a Primitive Society', *American Philosophical Quarterly*, **1**, 307–24.

WISDOM, J. O., 1951, Review of *The Concept of Mind*, by G. Ryle, *Inter. J. Psycho-Anal.*, **32**, 62–5.
1952a, *The Foundations of Inference in Natural Science*, London.
1952b, 'A New Model of the Mind-Body Relationship', *Brit. J. Phil. of Sci.*, **2**, 205–301.

WORSLEY, P., 1956, 'The Kinship System of the Tallensi: A Revaluation' (Curl Bequest Prize Essay, 1955), *J.R.A.I.*, **86**, 37–75.
1957, *The Trumpet Shall Sound*, London.

ZINSSER, R., 1937, *Rats, Lice and History*, London.

INDEX OF NAMES

Aberle, D. F., 229, 232–3
Agassi, J., xvi, xxi, 10n, 26n, 75, 112n, 176n, 177n–178, 191n, 196n, 197n, 207n, 222n, 234, 239
Aristotle, 7–9
Attenborough, D., 119n, 123n–124n, 150

Bacon, F., xiii, xvi, 5–6, 108–9, 123
Barber, B., 82, 89n, 134, 186
Bartley, W. W. III, 79n, 95n, 132, 140n
Batari, 60
Beattie, J. M., 26n
Becker, C. L., 148
Belshaw, C. S., 82, 85, 88 and n, 89n, 90n, 91, 93–7, 100, 105, 106–107, 117, 135, 137, 150, 163, 233
Bendix, R., 233
Berndt, R. M., 82, 89n, 92n
Bodrogi, T., 82, 84n, 87n, 88n, 89n, 91, 154, 163
Bott, E., 47n
Brown, R., 110n
Buchdahl, G., xvi
Burridge, K. O. L., 58n, 82, 83n, 84 and n, 86n, 87n, 88 and n, 89n, 91–3, 99–105, 106–7, 119n, 152, 161, 163, 229, 240
Burtt, E. A., 95n

Caesar, J., 113
Carlyle, T., 87
Christ, J., 9, 63, 119n, 225–8
Cohen, P., 78 and n
Cohn, N., 51, 83, 88 and n, 89n, 91, 110, 163, 229, 230, 233
Collingwood, R. G., 113
Comte, A., xiii, xx, 191

Crocombe, R., 56
Crossman, R. H. S., 116
Cuvier, G. L. C. F. D., 41

Darwin, C., 10, 40
Davis, K., 193–6
Dennis, N., 234
Durkheim, E., 1, 180, 191 and n, 192, 204, 218, 234

Eisler, R., xxi, 52, 62n, 225ff
Eliade, M., 229, 232
Eliot, T. S., 174
Emmett, D., 4
Evans-Pritchard, E. E., 4, 6, 21–2, 30, 31n, 42, 46n, 47n, 176–7, 198–210

Faraday, M., 76
Firth, R., xxi, 6–7, 20, 31, 33n, 82, 86n, 87n, 88n, 89n, 91, 92n, 100, 110, 131–42, 151–4, 158n, 160n, 162–3, 175, 184n, 191n, 202
Fortes, M., 31, 33n, 34, 46n, 211–12, 218
Fortune, R., 47n
Frazer, Sir J. G., 2, 32–3, 38, 43, 67, 115, 127, 138, 170, 173–6, 180, 182, 186, 213
Freedman, M., xxi
Freeman, J. D., 171
Freud, S., 1, 25n, 78–9, 137, 170, 174

Galileo, G., xiii
Geddes, W. R., 175n
Gellner, E. A., xix, xxi, 4, 27, 29n, 46n, 95n, 156n, 177n, 196n, 234, 238

251

van Gennep, A., 1, 180–1
Gluckman, H. M., 33*n*, 47*n*, 160*n*, 172
Gombrich, E. H., 147
Graham, Billy, 236
Granley and Hallind, 180
Grant, C. K., 95*n*
Graves, R., 52
Gromby, 180
Gross, L., 197*n*
Guiart, J., 61, 82, 88, 89*n*, 90*n*, 91, 134, 154, 163, 229, 231–2

Haddon, A. C., 2, 82, 88*n*, 89*n*, 91, 110, 152–3, 163, 180
Hartland, S., 38
Hayek, F. A., xiv, 78*n*, 80, 217*n*, 222*n*
Hegel, G. W. F., 207*n*
Hempel, C. G., 185, 197*n*
Hogbin, H. I., xxi, 37, 40, 42, 59–60, 83, 87*n*, 88 and *n*, 89*n*, 90*n*, 92*n*, 93–4, 97–9, 105, 106–7, 123, 154, 163, 176–7, 234
Homans, G. C., 21, 33*n*, 160*n*
Hume, D., 26*n*, 207 *and n*

Inglis, J., 83, 89*n*, 90–1, 121*n*, 144 *and n*–145, 149–50, 159*n*, 163, 169

James, W., 2

Kaum, 236
Kaminsky, H., 229, 233
Kant, I., xx
Keesing, F. M., 104
Kepler, J., 136
Koestler, A., 80, 136 *and n*
Kroeber, A. L., 45

Lancaster, L., 24
Lanternari, V. 240
Lawrence, P., 55, 61, 63, 82, 88*n*, 89*n*, 136, 163, 234 and *n*., 235–42
Leach, E. R., 31, 160*n*, 171–2, 178*n*, 188, 191 *and n*, 210–14, 217 *and n*
Leeson, I., 163*n*
Levi-Strauss, C., 175

Levy, M. J., 194, 197*n*
Levy-Bruhl, L., 180
Linton, R., 82, 86*n*, 88*n*, 89*n*, 92*n*, 103, 110, 159, 163
Lowie, R. H., 177
Lubbock, Sir J., 180

Macbeath, A., 4
Mach, E., 185
McLennan, J. F., 1, 38, 180
Macmillan, H., 164
Macrae, D. G., 29*n*
Maine, Sir H. S., 1, 37–8
Mair, L. P., xix, 47*n*, 58–60, 68*n*, 83, 87*n*, 88*n*, 89*n*, 91, 92*n*, 110, 131–2, 139–42, 151, 153, 159*n*, 163, 241
Malinowski, B., ix–x, xv, xix, 2–4, 6, 11–14, 16–19, 21–2, 28, 30–2, 35*n*, 39–44, 133, 137, 154, 170, 173–89, 191 *and n*, 192–3, 197–9, 207, 210–14
Mambu, 102
Mancheri, 62
Mann, T., x
Marett, R. R., 38
Marx, K., 53, 78–9, 91, 158, 203, 204, 207*n*
Mayer, P., 47*n*
Mead, M., 84, 164
Merton, R., 194
Mooney, J., 82, 89*n*, 90–1, 110, 180
Morgan, L., 1–2, 10, 37–8, 180
Murdock, G. P., 160*n*, 190*n*

Nadel, S. F., xv, xviii, 185, 204, 210–12*n*, 221
Nasser, G. A., 85
Needham, R., 160*n*
Neguib, M., 85
Neloaig, 63
Newton, Sir I., xiii, 80

Paliau, 84, 164
Parsons, T., 189
Perry, W. J., 38
Pitt-Rivers, G. H. L.-F., 1, 180
Plato, 7–9*n*, 78–9
Pocock, D. F., 153*n*, 176–7

Podro, J., 52
Popper, K. R., ix–xi, xiv, xviii–xix, xxi, 8*n*, 19, 25*n*, 26*n*, 40, 45, 48–9, 53*n*, 56, 67 *and n*, 68, 72, 75, 77, 78*n*, 79–80, 105, 113–15, 122*n*, 132, 140*n*, 147 *and n*, 160, 177*n*, 183*n*, 207 *and n*, 215*n*, 218*n*, 222 *and n*
Porta, G. B. Della, 123
van der Post, L., 175*n*

Radcliffe-Brown, A. R., ix, 2, 13, 35*n*, 46 *and n*, 47*n*, 139, 149, 152, 175, 182, 189–92, 197–8, 200, 201*n*, 207–15
Rivers, W. R., 2, 38, 45, 180
Robertson Smith, W., 1, 176, 180

Sargent, W., 128
Schapera, I., 14, 27*n*, 31, 33*n*, 46*n*, 47*n*, 175, 194, 203
Scheinfeld, D., 41, 218*n*
Schneider, E. D., 21, 33*n*, 160*n*
Seligman, C. G., 2, 180
Shaw, G. B., 132
Shepperson, G., 229, 230–1
Silone, I., 116
Smith, A., 220*n*, 223
Sollas, W. J., 38
Spencer, Sir B. and Gillen, F., 2, 180
Sprott, W. J. H., xxi
Stanner, W. E. H., 64, 82, 84*n*, 85*n*, 86*n*, 87*n*, 88*n*, 89*n*, 91, 106 *and n*, 144*n*, 149–54, 159*n*, 163
Steiner, F., 21, 25*n*, 33*n*

Sumner, W. G., 180

Talmon, Y., 240
Tax, S., 190
Thrupp, S., 229, 230, 240
Timasheff, N., xxi, 195
Topley, M., 32*n*, 171
Toynbee, A., 53, 91
Trevelyan, G. M., 181
Tylor, Sir E. B., 1, 37–8, 173, 180

Vinogradoff, P., 38

Watkins, J. W. N., xxi, 57*n*, 67*n*, 75, 140*n*, 222*n*, 224*n*
Weber, M., 113, 236
Westermark, E., 180
Wheatley, J., 6
White, A. D., 95*n*
White, M. G., xxii
Williams, F. E., 59, 61, 82, 87 *and n*, 88*n*, 89*n*, 146–9, 159*n*, 160, 163
Winch, P., 238
Wisdom, J. O., 147, 161*n*
Worsley, P., xv, xvii–xix, 33*n*, 34–5, 52, 60–1, 65 *and n*, 70, 72, 83, 86, 87*n*, 89*n*, 91, 140, 153–4, 159 *and n*, 161, 163–5, 198–200, 203–7, 236, 239, 241
Wundt, W., 180

Yahweh, 51
Yali, 64, 102, 136, 234–6

Zinsser, H., 53, 91, 128

INDEX OF SUBJECTS

't' indicates that the term is discussed; *'n'* that the reference is to be found in a footnote.

abstract society, 23*t*, 183*n*
acephalous societies, 68*t*
'armchair' approach, xv

Bacon, F., *see* method
'belief in belief', 128*f*, 149*ff*, 234
bridging laws, 161*t and n*

cargo cults—Melanesia, ch. 1, §9, §11, ch. 2 *passim, esp.* §2*t, and* §6, appendices I–III—Malinowski's, xiii–xiv, xix—theories of, ch. 2, §7
chosen people, doctrine of, 51–2
Christianity, 8–9, 235
classificatory kinship terminology, 20
closed society, 114, 116, 118*f*, appendix III
'come down off the verandah', 44*ff*, 168
comparative sociology, xvi*t*, xvii, 14, 20*ff*, 33, 44*f*
conventional *versus* natural, 115*t*, 118*f*, 215
culture contact, 86, 111, 235

description, *versus* explanation, 185 —the problem of preliminary description, ch. 2, §1
diffusionism, 11, 13, 19*ff*, 90, 126*f*, 165, 179*ff*, 187, 238
doublethink, 165

enlightenment, the 3, 8
equalitarianism, 12, 43, 76
ethnography, xvi*t*, xvii, 26*f*, 209

evolutionism, 11, 16*ff*, 37*ff*, 43, 127, 154, 165, 174, 179*ff*, 184, 187, 200, 207
explanation, true *versus* satisfactory, ch. 1, §3, 75, ch. 4, §1–2, 162*ff*, 200, 213—circular, 17—*ad hoc*, 17—metaphysical and methodological frameworks of, 34, 44, 75, 171*ff*, 216—of the known in terms of the unknown, 77, 80, 115*n*, 196, 240—teleological, 156 *and n*, 197–8

face-to-face society, 23*t*, 183*n*
fantasy, the resort to, 133*ff*, 138
fieldwork, 5, 11–13, 20, 33, 172, 175, 212—advantages of, 28*ff*—disadvantages of, 31*ff*—selective, 169*t*, 173, 216
frameworks, *see* metaphysics
function, 11, 21, 35*t*, 40*f*, 47, 174, ch. 6, §§3–4—of institutions, xiv—functionalist criticisms of Frazer, 32*f*— antihistorism of functionalist anthropology 42*f*—contextualism, 169, 187
futurity neurosis, 122*t*

horizon of expectations, 147*t, and f*, 238
human differences, ch. 1, §2 *passim*

induction, 5–6, 14, ch. 1, §4, 28–9, 33, 42, 47, 160 *and n*, 175, 177*f*, 206, 208, 210–12—inductive style, xix *n*

254

inertia of social institutions, 126

'kill the chief priest', 43*ff*, 182, 186
kinship, 189—social and physical, 46—extended kinship terms, problem of, 45, 197
kula, 18, 39, 183

leopard-skin chief (Nuer), 21–2
local problems, 21*ff*, 35*ff*, 44*ff*
logic of the situation, (situational logic), xvii, 19, ch. 1, §6, 45, 86, 99, 111, 113, 117, 151, 218–19, 223–4—development of, 113*ff*, 126, 163*ff*, 236*ff*,

magic,—as primitive science, 67–68, 174, 186—magico-religious outlook, 94–95, 118, 138—*versus* primitive technique, 95, 134*ff*
meta-language, xviii*t*
metaphysics, xix, ch. 1, *passim*, 76, 81, 175, 202—and the interest in human society, ch. 1, §2 *passim*
method, xiv, xvi, 25, 48*ff*—rules of, 18, 188—methodology, uses of, ch. 1, §4—too much of, xiii–xvi—Bacon's xiii, xvi, 5–6, 108*ff*, 123
methodological individualism, 185
mother-in-law-avoidance, 23, 46, 221
myth-dream, 101*ff*

necessitarianism, 145*t*, 151 *and n*, 203*n*
needs, biological, 12, 22, 191—social 190–1, 196
Nuer, leopard-skin chief, significance of, 21–2

object language, xviii*t*
open society, 121
origin explanations, of institutions, xiv

philosophical anthropology, xix

positivism, 16, 19, 28, 185, 192, 202, 208
potlatch, 122*f*
pragmatism, Malinowski's, 191*n*
preferential cousin marriage, 23, 26, 37
primitive/civilised issue, 6–7, 142*ff*, 180, 204
primitive promiscuity, theory of, 45
psychologism, 46, 97*t*, 166, 180, 189, 191

rationalist association, the 138*ff*
rationality, of actions, 36, 77, 81, 92, 94, 134, 217—of beliefs, 6, ch. 5, §§1–5—of explanations, 78–9, 202, 213—principle, 79, 218
relativism, 12, 14, 16, 104, 143, 175, 199, 204, 238
religion oriented culture, 88*t*
rethinking, 170*ff*
revolution in anthropology, the xv, ch. 6 *passim*

scientism, xiv
sobriety in science, ch. 1, §1, *passim*, 30, 214
social anthropology, history of, 1, ch. 6, §§1–4—revolution in, 42, 48 —and sociology, 1, ch. 6— stagnation in, 1, 5, 214*n*—problem of the scientific character of, 3
social change, xix, 5, 19, 44*f*, 56, 86, 110*ff*, 118*f*, 135, 154—internally caused 158*t*, *and ff*—externally caused 158*t*, *and ff*
social structure, 190*t*, 192, 209
structural-functionalism, xv–xvii, xix, 28, ch. 1, §6, 35*t*, 45, 47–8, 56, 72, 152*ff*, ch. 5, §§6–9, 190*t*, 231
study of man, xx
'study the ritual not the belief', 44*ff*, 150, 186, 219, 230
survivals, 46, 188

taboos, 25
testability, 17
theoretical terms, 26*f*

unintended consequences of actions, xvii, 24, 235
unity of mankind, 3, 10–11, 15, 174–5*f*, 178, 237

The International Library of
Sociology
and Social Reconstruction

Edited by W. J. H. SPROTT
Founded by KARL MANNHEIM

ROUTLEDGE & KEGAN PAUL
BROADWAY HOUSE, CARTER LANE, LONDON, E.C.4

CONTENTS

General Sociology	3	Sociology of Religion	10
Foreign Classics of Sociology	3	Sociology of Art and Literature	10
Social Structure	4	Sociology of Knowledge	10
Sociology and Politics	4	Urban Sociology	11
Foreign Affairs: Their Social, Political and Economic Foundations	5	Rural Sociology	11
		Sociology of Migration	12
Criminology	5	Sociology of Industry and Distribution	12
Social Psychology	6		
Sociology of the Family	7	Anthropology	12
The Social Services	8	Documentary	13
Sociology of Education	8	*Reports of the Institute of Community Studies*	14
Sociology of Culture	10		

PRINTED IN GREAT BRITAIN BY HEADLEY BROTHERS LTD
109 KINGSWAY LONDON WC2 AND ASHFORD KENT

GENERAL SOCIOLOGY

Brown, Robert. Explanation in Social Science. *208 pp. 1963. (2nd Impression 1964.) 25s.*

Gibson, Quentin. The Logic of Social Enquiry. *240 pp. 1960. (3rd Impression 1968.) 24s.*

Homans, George C. Sentiments and Activities: Essays in Social Science. *336 pp. 1962. 32s.*

Isajiw, Wsevelod W. Causation and Functionalism in Sociology. *165 pp. 1968. 25s.*

Johnson, Harry M. Sociology: a Systematic Introduction. *Foreword by Robert K. Merton. 710 pp. 1961. (5th Impression 1968.) 42s.*

Mannheim, Karl. Essays on Sociology and Social Psychology. *Edited by Paul Keckskemeti. With Editorial Note by Adolph Lowe. 344 pp. 1953. (2nd Impression 1966.) 32s.*

Systematic Sociology: An Introduction to the Study of Society. *Edited by J. S. Erös and Professor W. A. C. Stewart. 220 pp. 1957. (3rd Impression 1967.) 24s.*

Martindale, Don. The Nature and Types of Sociological Theory. *292 pp. 1961. (3rd Impression 1967.) 35s.*

Maus, Heinz. A Short History of Sociology. *234 pp. 1962. (2nd Impression 1965.) 28s.*

Myrdal, Gunnar. Value in Social Theory: A Collection of Essays on Methodology. *Edited by Paul Streeten. 332 pp. 1958. (3rd Impression 1968.) 35s.*

Ogburn, William F., and Nimkoff, Meyer F. A Handbook of Sociology. *Preface by Karl Mannheim. 656 pp. 46 figures. 35 tables. 5th edition (revised) 1964. 45s.*

Parsons, Talcott, and Smelser, Neil J. Economy and Society: A Study in the Integration of Economic and Social Theory. *362 pp. 1956. (4th Impression 1967.) 35s.*

Rex, John. Key Problems of Sociological Theory. *220 pp. 1961. (4th Impression 1968.) 25s.*

Stark, Werner. The Fundamental Forms of Social Thought. *280 pp. 1962. 32s.*

FOREIGN CLASSICS OF SOCIOLOGY

Durkheim, Emile. Suicide. A Study in Sociology. *Edited and with an Introduction by George Simpson. 404 pp. 1952. (4th Impression 1968.) 35s.*

Professional Ethics and Civic Morals. *Translated by Cornelia Brookfield. 288 pp. 1957. 30s.*

Gerth, H. H., and Mills, C. Wright. From Max Weber: Essays in Sociology. *502 pp. 1948. (6th Impression 1967.) 35s.*

Tönnies, Ferdinand. Community and Association. *(Gemeinschaft und Gesellschaft.) Translated and Supplemented by Charles P. Loomis. Foreword by Pitirim A. Sorokin. 334 pp. 1955. 28s.*

SOCIAL STRUCTURE

Andreski, Stanislav. Military Organization and Society. *Foreword by Professor A. R. Radcliffe-Brown. 226 pp. 1 folder. 1954. Revised Edition 1968. 35s.*

Cole, G. D. H. Studies in Class Structure. *220 pp. 1955. (3rd Impression 1964.) 21s. Paper 10s. 6d.*

Coontz, Sydney H. Population Theories and the Economic Interpretation. *202 pp. 1957. (3rd Impression 1968.) 28s.*

Coser, Lewis. The Functions of Social Conflict. *204 pp. 1956. (3rd Impression 1968.) 25s.*

Dickie-Clark, H. F. Marginal Situation: A Sociological Study of a Coloured Group. *240 pp. 11 tables. 1966. 40s.*

Glass, D. V. (Ed.). Social Mobility in Britain. *Contributions by J. Berent, T. Bottomore, R. C. Chambers, J. Floud, D. V. Glass, J. R. Hall, H. T. Himmelweit, R. K. Kelsall, F. M. Martin, C. A. Moser, R. Mukherjee, and W. Ziegel. 420 pp. 1954. (4th Impression 1967.) 45s.*

Jones, Garth N. Planned Organizational Change: An Exploratory Study Using an Empirical Approach. *About 268 pp. 1969. 40s.*

Kelsall, R. K. Higher Civil Servants in Britain: From 1870 to the Present Day. *268 pp. 31 tables. 1955. (2nd Impression 1966.) 25s.*

König, René. The Community. *232 pp. Illustrated. 1968. 35s.*

Lawton, Denis. Social Class, Language and Education. *192 pp. 1968. (2nd Impression 1968.) 25s.*

McLeish, John. The Theory of Social Change: Four Views Considered. *About 128 pp. 1969. 21s.*

Marsh, David C. The Changing Social Structure in England and Wales, 1871-1961. *1958. 272 pp. 2nd edition (revised) 1966. (2nd Impression 1967.) 35s.*

Mouzelis, Nicos. Organization and Bureaucracy. An Analysis of Modern Theories. *240 pp. 1967. (2nd Impression 1968.) 28s.*

Ossowski, Stanislaw. Class Structure in the Social Consciousness. *210 pp. 1963. (2nd Impression 1967.) 25s.*

SOCIOLOGY AND POLITICS

Barbu, Zevedei. Democracy and Dictatorship: Their Psychology and Patterns of Life. *300 pp. 1956. 28s.*

Crick, Bernard. The American Science of Politics: Its Origins and Conditions. *284 pp. 1959. 32s.*

Hertz, Frederick. Nationality in History and Politics: A Psychology and Sociology of National Sentiment and Nationalism. *432 pp. 1944. (5th Impression 1966.) 42s.*

Kornhauser, William. The Politics of Mass Society. *272 pp. 20 tables. 1960. (3rd Impression 1968.) 28s.*

Laidler, Harry W. History of Socialism. Social-Economic Movements: An Historical and Comparative Survey of Socialism, Communism, Co-operation, Utopianism; and other Systems of Reform and Reconstruction. *New edition. 992 pp. 1968. 90s.*

Lasswell, Harold D. Analysis of Political Behaviour. An Empirical Approach. *324 pp. 1947. (4th Impression 1966.) 35s.*

Mannheim, Karl. Freedom, Power and Democratic Planning. *Edited by Hans Gerth and Ernest K. Bramstedt. 424 pp. 1951. (3rd Impression 1968.) 42s.*

Mansur, Fatma. Process of Independence. *Foreword by A. H. Hanson. 208 pp. 1962. 25s.*

Martin, David A. Pacificism: an Historical and Sociological Study. *262 pp. 1965. 30s.*

Myrdal, Gunnar. The Political Element in the Development of Economic Theory. *Translated from the German by Paul Streeten. 282 pp. 1953. (4th Impression 1965.) 25s.*

Polanyi, Michael. F.R.S. The Logic of Liberty: Reflections and Rejoinders. *228 pp. 1951. 18s.*

Verney, Douglas V. The Analysis of Political Systems. *264 pp. 1959. (3rd Impression 1966.) 28s.*

Wootton, Graham. The Politics of Influence: British Ex-Servicemen, Cabinet Decisions and Cultural Changes, 1917 to 1957. *316 pp. 1963. 30s.*
Workers, Unions and the State. *188 pp. 1966. (2nd Impression 1967.) 25s.*

FOREIGN AFFAIRS: THEIR SOCIAL, POLITICAL AND ECONOMIC FOUNDATIONS

Baer, Gabriel. Population and Society in the Arab East. *Translated by Hanna Szöke. 288 pp. 10 maps. 1964. 40s.*

Bonné, Alfred. State and Economics in the Middle East: A Society in Transition. *482 pp. 2nd (revised) edition 1955. (2nd Impression 1960.) 40s.*
Studies in Economic Development: with special reference to Conditions in the Under-developed Areas of Western Asia and India. *322 pp. 84 tables. 2nd edition 1960. 32s.*

Mayer, J. P. Political Thought in France from the Revolution to the Fifth Republic. *164 pp. 3rd edition (revised) 1961. 16s.*

CRIMINOLOGY

Ancel, Marc. Social Defence: A Modern Approach to Criminal Problems. *Foreword by Leon Radzinowicz. 240 pp. 1965. 32s.*

Cloward, Richard A., and **Ohlin, Lloyd E.** Delinquency and Opportunity: A Theory of Delinquent Gangs. *248 pp. 1961. 25s.*

Downes, David M. The Delinquent Solution. A Study in Subcultural Theory. *296 pp. 1966. 42s.*

Dunlop, A. B., and McCabe, S. Young Men in Detention Centres. *192 pp. 1965. 28s.*

Friedländer, Kate. The Psycho-Analytical Approach to Juvenile Delinquency: Theory, Case Studies, Treatment. *320 pp. 1947. (6th Impression 1967). 40s.*

Glueck, Sheldon and **Eleanor.** Family Environment and Delinquency. *With the statistical assistance of Rose W. Kneznek. 340 pp. 1962. (2nd Impression 1966.) 40s.*

Mannheim, Hermann. Comparative Criminology: a Text Book. *Two volumes. 442 pp. and 380 pp. 1965. (2nd Impression with corrections 1966.) 42s. a volume.*

Morris, Terence. The Criminal Area: A Study in Social Ecology. *Foreword by Hermann Mannheim. 232 pp. 25 tables. 4 maps. 1957. (2nd Impression 1966.) 28s.*

Morris, Terence and **Pauline,** assisted by **Barbara Barer.** Pentonville: A Sociological Study of an English Prison. *416 pp. 16 plates. 1963. 50s.*

Spencer, John C. Crime and the Services. *Foreword by Hermann Mannheim. 336 pp. 1954. 28s.*

Trasler, Gordon. The Explanation of Criminality. *144 pp. 1962. (2nd Impression 1967.) 20s.*

SOCIAL PSYCHOLOGY

Barbu, Zevedei. Problems of Historical Psychology. *248 pp. 1960. 25s.*

Blackburn, Julian. Psychology and the Social Pattern. *184 pp. 1945. (7th Impression 1964.) 16s.*

Fleming, C. M. Adolescence: Its Social Psychology: With an Introduction to recent findings from the fields of Anthropology, Physiology, Medicine, Psychometrics and Sociometry. *288 pp. 2nd edition (revised) 1963. (3rd Impression 1967.) 25s. Paper 12s. 6d.*

The Social Psychology of Education: An Introduction and Guide to Its Study. *136 pp. 2nd edition (revised) 1959. (4th Impression 1967.) 14s. Paper 7s. 6d.*

Homans, George C. The Human Group. *Foreword by Bernard DeVoto. Introduction by Robert K. Merton. 526 pp. 1951. (7th Impression 1968.) 35s.*

Social Behaviour: its Elementary Forms. *416 pp. 1961. (3rd Impression 1968.) 35s.*

Klein, Josephine. The Study of Groups. *226 pp. 31 figures. 5 tables. 1956. (5th Impression 1967.) 21s. Paper 9s. 6d.*

Linton, Ralph. The Cultural Background of Personality. *132 pp. 1947. (7th Impression 1968.) 18s.*

Mayo, Elton. The Social Problems of an Industrial Civilization. With an appendix on the Political Problem. *180 pp. 1949. (5th Impression 1966.) 25s.*

Ottaway, A. K. C. Learning Through Group Experience. *176 pp. 1966. (2nd Impression 1968.) 25s.*

Ridder, J. C. de. The Personality of the Urban African in South Africa. A Thematic Apperception Test Study. *196 pp. 12 plates. 1961. 25s.*

Rose, Arnold M. (Ed.). Human Behaviour and Social Processes: an Inter-actionist Approach. *Contributions by Arnold M. Rose, Ralph H. Turner, Anselm Strauss, Everett C. Hughes, E. Franklin Frazier, Howard S. Becker, et al. 696 pp. 1962. (2nd Impression 1968.) 70s.*

Smelser, Neil J. Theory of Collective Behaviour. *448 pp. 1962. (2nd Impression 1967.) 45s.*

Stephenson, Geoffrey M. The Development of Conscience. *128 pp. 1966. 25s.*

Young, Kimball. Handbook of Social Psychology. *658 pp. 16 figures. 10 tables. 2nd edition (revised) 1957. (3rd Impression 1963.) 40s.*

SOCIOLOGY OF THE FAMILY

Banks, J. A. Prosperity and Parenthood: A study of Family Planning among The Victorian Middle Classes. *262 pp. 1954. (3rd Impression 1968.) 28s.*

Bell, Colin R. Middle Class Families: Social and Geographical Mobility. *224 pp. 1969. 35s.*

Burton, Lindy. Vulnerable Children. *272 pp. 1968. 35s.*

Gavron, Hannah. The Captive Wife: Conflicts of Housebound Mothers. *190 pp. 1966. (2nd Impression 1966.) 25s.*

Klein, Josephine. Samples from English Cultures. *1965. (2nd Impression 1967.)*
1. Three Preliminary Studies and Aspects of Adult Life in England. *447 pp. 50s.*
2. Child-Rearing Practices and Index. *247 pp. 35s.*

Klein, Viola. Britain's Married Women Workers. *180 pp. 1965. (2nd Impression 1968.) 28s.*

McWhinnie, Alexina M. Adopted Children. How They Grow Up. *304 pp. 1967. (2nd Impression 1968.) 42s.*

Myrdal, Alva and Klein, Viola. Women's Two Roles: Home and Work. *238 pp. 27 tables. 1956. Revised Edition 1967. 30s. Paper 15s.*

Parsons, Talcott and Bales, Robert F. Family: Socialization and Interaction Process. *In collaboration with James Olds, Morris Zelditch and Philip E. Slater. 456 pp. 50 figures and tables. 1956. (3rd Impression 1968.) 45s.*

Schücking, L. L. The Puritan Family. *Translated from the German by Brian Battershaw. 212 pp. 1969. About 42s.*

7

THE SOCIAL SERVICES

Forder, R. A. (Ed.). Penelope Hall's Social Services of Modern England. *288 pp. 1969. 35s.*

George, Victor. Social Security: Beveridge and After. *258 pp. 1968. 35s.*

Goetschius, George W. Working with Community Groups. *256 pp. 1969. 35s.*

Goetschius, George W. and **Tash, Joan.** Working with Unattached Youth. *416 pp. 1967. (2nd Impression 1968.) 40s.*

Hall, M. P., and **Howes, I. V.** The Church in Social Work. A Study of Moral Welfare Work undertaken by the Church of England. *320 pp. 1965. 35s.*

Heywood, Jean S. Children in Care: the Development of the Service for the Deprived Child. *264 pp. 2nd edition (revised) 1965. (2nd Impression 1966.) 32s.*

An Introduction to Teaching Casework Skills. *190 pp. 1964. 28s.*

Jones, Kathleen. Lunacy, Law and Conscience, 1744-1845: the Social History of the Care of the Insane. *268 pp. 1955. 25s.*

Mental Health and Social Policy, 1845-1959. *264 pp. 1960. (2nd Impression 1967.) 32s.*

Jones, Kathleen and **Sidebotham, Roy.** Mental Hospitals at Work. *220 pp. 1962. 30s.*

Kastell, Jean. Casework in Child Care. *Foreword by M. Brooke Willis. 320 pp. 1962. 35s.*

Morris, Pauline. Put Away: A Sociological Study of Institutions for the Mentally Retarded. *Approx. 288 pp. 1969. About 50s.*

Nokes, P. L. The Professional Task in Welfare Practice. *152 pp. 1967. 28s.*

Rooff, Madeline. Voluntary Societies and Social Policy. *350 pp. 15 tables. 1957. 35s.*

Timms, Noel. Psychiatric Social Work in Great Britain (1939-1962). *280 pp. 1964. 32s.*

Social Casework: Principles and Practice. *256 pp. 1964. (2nd Impression 1966.) 25s. Paper 15s.*

Trasler, Gordon. In Place of Parents: A Study in Foster Care. *272 pp. 1960. (2nd Impression 1966.) 30s.*

Young, A. F., and **Ashton, E. T.** British Social Work in the Nineteenth Century. *288 pp. 1956. (2nd Impression 1963.) 28s.*

Young, A. F. Social Services in British Industry. *272 pp. 1968. 40s.*

SOCIOLOGY OF EDUCATION

Banks, Olive. Parity and Prestige in English Secondary Education: a Study in Educational Sociology. *272 pp. 1955. (2nd Impression 1963.) 32s.*

Bentwich, Joseph. Education in Israel. *224 pp. 8 pp. plates. 1965. 24s.*

Blyth, W. A. L. English Primary Education. A Sociological Description. *1965. Revised edition 1967.*

1. Schools. *232 pp. 30s. Paper 12s. 6d.*
2. Background. *168 pp. 25s. Paper 10s. 6d.*

Collier, K. G. The Social Purposes of Education: Personal and Social Values in Education. *268 pp. 1959. (3rd Impression 1965.) 21s.*

Dale, R. R., and Griffith, S. Down Stream: Failure in the Grammar School. *108 pp. 1965. 20s.*

Dore, R. P. Education in Tokugawa Japan. *356 pp. 9 pp. plates. 1965. 35s.*

Edmonds, E. L. The School Inspector. *Foreword by Sir William Alexander. 214 pp. 1962. 28s.*

Evans, K. M. Sociometry and Education. *158 pp. 1962. (2nd Impression 1966.) 18s.*

Foster, P. J. Education and Social Change in Ghana. *336 pp. 3 maps. 1965. (2nd Impression 1967.) 36s.*

Fraser, W. R. Education and Society in Modern France. *150 pp. 1963. (2nd Impression 1968.) 25s.*

Hans, Nicholas. New Trends in Education in the Eighteenth Century. *278 pp. 19 tables. 1951. (2nd Impression 1966.) 30s.*

Comparative Education: A Study of Educational Factors and Traditions. *360 pp. 3rd (revised) edition 1958. (4th Impression 1967.) 25s. Paper 12s. 6d.*

Hargreaves, David. Social Relations in a Secondary School. *240 pp. 1967. (2nd Impression 1968.) 32s.*

Holmes, Brian. Problems in Education. A Comparative Approach. *336 pp. 1965. (2nd Impression 1967.) 32s.*

Mannheim, Karl and **Stewart, W. A. C.** An Introduction to the Sociology of Education. *206 pp. 1962. (2nd Impression 1965.) 21s.*

Morris, Raymond N. The Sixth Form and College Entrance. *231 pp. 1969. 40s.*

Musgrove, F. Youth and the Social Order. *176 pp. 1964. (2nd Impression 1968.) 25s. Paper 12s.*

Ortega y Gasset, José. Mission of the University. *Translated with an Introduction by Howard Lee Nostrand. 86 pp. 1946. (3rd Impression 1963.) 15s.*

Ottaway, A. K. C. Education and Society: An Introduction to the Sociology of Education. *With an Introduction by W. O. Lester Smith. 212 pp. Second edition (revised). 1962. (5th Impression 1968.) 18s. Paper 10s. 6d.*

Peers, Robert. Adult Education: A Comparative Study. *398 pp. 2nd edition 1959. (2nd Impression 1966.) 42s.*

Pritchard, D. G. Education and the Handicapped: 1760 to 1960. *258 pp. 1963. (2nd Impression 1966.) 35s.*

Richardson, Helen. Adolescent Girls in Approved Schools. *Approx. 360 pp. 1969. About 42s.*

Simon, Brian and **Joan** (Eds.). Educational Psychology in the U.S.S.R. *Introduction by Brian and Joan Simon. Translation by Joan Simon. Papers by D. N. Bogoiavlenski and N. A. Menchinskaia, D. B. Elkonin, E. A. Fleshner, Z. I. Kalmykova, G. S. Kostiuk, V. A. Krutetski, A. N. Leontiev, A. R. Luria, E. A. Milerian, R. G. Natadze, B. M. Teplov, L. S. Vygotski, L. V. Zankov. 296 pp. 1963. 40s.*

9

SOCIOLOGY OF CULTURE

Eppel, E. M., and M. Adolescents and Morality: A Study of some Moral Values and Dilemmas of Working Adolescents in the Context of a changing Climate of Opinion. *Foreword by W. J. H. Sprott. 268 pp. 39 tables. 1966. 30s.*

Fromm, Erich. The Fear of Freedom. *286 pp. 1942. (8th Impression 1960.) 25s. Paper 10s.*
The Sane Society. *400 pp. 1956. (4th Impression 1968.) 28s. Paper 14s.*

Mannheim, Karl. Diagnosis of Our Time: Wartime Essays of a Sociologist. *208 pp. 1943. (8th Impression 1966.) 21s.*
Essays on the Sociology of Culture. *Edited by Ernst Mannheim in co-operation with Paul Kecskemeti. Editorial Note by Adolph Lowe. 280 pp. 1956. (3rd Impression 1967.) 28s.*

Weber, Alfred. Farewell to European History: or The Conquest of Nihilism. *Translated from the German by R. F. C. Hull. 224 pp. 1947. 18s.*

SOCIOLOGY OF RELIGION

Argyle, Michael. Religious Behaviour. *224 pp. 8 figures. 41 tables. 1958. (4th Impression 1968.) 25s.*

Nelson, G. K. Spiritualism and Society. *313 pp. 1969. 42s.*

Stark, Werner. The Sociology of Religion. A Study of Christendom.
Volume I. Established Religion. *248 pp. 1966. 35s.*
Volume II. Sectarian Religion. *368 pp. 1967. 40s.*
Volume III. The Universal Church. *464 pp. 1967. 45s.*

Watt, W. Montgomery. Islam and the Integration of Society. *320 pp. 1961. (3rd Impression 1966.) 35s.*

SOCIOLOGY OF ART AND LITERATURE

Beljame, Alexandre. Men of Letters and the English Public in the Eighteenth Century: 1660-1744, Dryden, Addison, Pope. *Edited with an Introduction and Notes by Bonamy Dobrée. Translated by E. O. Lorimer. 532 pp. 1948. 32s.*

Misch, Georg. A History of Autobiography in Antiquity. *Translated by E. W. Dickes. 2 Volumes. Vol. 1, 364 pp., Vol. 2, 372 pp. 1950. 45s. the set.*

Schücking, L. L. The Sociology of Literary Taste. *112 pp. 2nd (revised) edition 1966. 18s.*

Silbermann, Alphons. The Sociology of Music. *Translated from the German by Corbet Stewart. 222 pp. 1963. 32s.*

SOCIOLOGY OF KNOWLEDGE

Mannheim, Karl. Essays on the Sociology of Knowledge. *Edited by Paul Kecskemeti. Editorial note by Adolph Lowe. 352 pp. 1952. (4th Impression 1967.) 35s.*

Stark, W. America: Ideal and Reality. The United States of 1776 in Contemporary Philosophy. *136 pp. 1947. 12s.*
The Sociology of Knowledge: An Essay in Aid of a Deeper Understanding of the History of Ideas. *384 pp. 1958. (3rd Impression 1967.) 36s.*
Montesquieu: Pioneer of the Sociology of Knowledge. *244 pp. 1960. 25s.*

URBAN SOCIOLOGY

Anderson, Nels. The Urban Community: A World Perspective. *532 pp. 1960. 35s.*

Ashworth, William. The Genesis of Modern British Town Planning: A Study in Economic and Social History of the Nineteenth and Twentieth Centuries. *288 pp. 1954. (3rd Impression 1968.) 32s.*

Bracey, Howard. Neighbours: On New Estates and Subdivisions in England and U.S.A. *220 pp. 1964. 28s.*

Cullingworth, J. B. Housing Needs and Planning Policy: A Restatement of the Problems of Housing Need and "Overspill" in England and Wales. *232 pp. 44 tables. 8 maps. 1960. (2nd Impression 1966.) 28s.*

Dickinson, Robert E. City and Region: A Geographical Interpretation. *608 pp. 125 figures. 1964. (5th Impression 1967.) 60s.*
The West European City: A Geographical Interpretation. *600 pp. 129 maps. 29 plates. 2nd edition 1962. (3rd Impression 1968.) 55s.*
The City Region in Western Europe. *320 pp. Maps. 1967. 30s. Paper 14s.*

Jackson, Brian. Working Class Community: Some General Notions raised by a Series of Studies in Northern England. *192 pp. 1968. (2nd Impression 1968.) 25s.*

Jennings, Hilda. Societies in the Making: a Study of Development and Redevelopment within a County Borough. *Foreword by D. A. Clark. 286 pp. 1962. (2nd Impression 1967.) 32s.*

Kerr, Madeline. The People of Ship Street. *240 pp. 1958. 28s.*

Mann, P. H. An Approach to Urban Sociology. *240 pp. 1965. (2nd Impression 1968.) 30s.*

Morris, R. N., and **Mogey, J.** The Sociology of Housing. Studies at Berinsfield. *232 pp. 4 pp. plates. 1965. 42s.*

Rosser, C., and **Harris, C.** The Family and Social Change. A Study of Family and Kinship in a South Wales Town. *352 pp. 8 maps. 1965. (2nd Impression 1968.) 45s.*

RURAL SOCIOLOGY

Chambers, R. J. H. Settlement Schemes in Africa: A Selective Study. *Approx. 268 pp. 1969. About 50s.*

Haswell, M. R. The Economics of Development in Village India. *120 pp. 1967. 21s.*

Littlejohn, James. Westrigg: the Sociology of a Cheviot Parish. *172 pp. 5 figures. 1963. 25s.*

Williams, W. M. The Country Craftsman: A Study of Some Rural Crafts and the Rural Industries Organization in England. *248 pp. 9 figures. 1958. 25s. (Dartington Hall Studies in Rural Sociology.)*
The Sociology of an English Village: Gosforth. *272 pp. 12 figures. 13 tables. 1956. (3rd Impression 1964.) 25s.*

SOCIOLOGY OF MIGRATION

Humphreys, Alexander J. New Dubliners: Urbanization and the Irish Family. *Foreword by George C. Homans. 304 pp. 1966. 40s.*

SOCIOLOGY OF INDUSTRY AND DISTRIBUTION

Anderson, Nels. Work and Leisure. *280 pp. 1961. 28s.*

Blau, Peter M., and Scott, W. Richard. Formal Organizations: a Comparative approach. *Introduction and Additional Bibliography by J. H. Smith. 326 pp. 1963. (4th Impression 1969.) 35s. Paper 15s.*

Eldridge, J. E. T. Industrial Disputes. Essays in the Sociology of Industrial Relations. *288 pp. 1968. 40s.*

Hollowell, Peter G. The Lorry Driver. *272 pp. 1968. 42s.*

Jefferys, Margot, with the assistance of Winifred Moss. Mobility in the Labour Market: Employment Changes in Battersea and Dagenham. *Preface by Barbara Wootton. 186 pp. 51 tables. 1954. 15s.*

Levy, A. B. Private Corporations and Their Control. *Two Volumes. Vol. 1, 464 pp., Vol. 2, 432 pp. 1950. 80s. the set.*

Liepmann, Kate. Apprenticeship: An Enquiry into its Adequacy under Modern Conditions. *Foreword by H. D. Dickinson. 232 pp. 6 tables. 1960. (2nd Impression 1960.) 23s.*

Millerson, Geoffrey. The Qualifying Associations: a Study in Professionalization. *320 pp. 1964. 42s.*

Smelser, Neil J. Social Change in the Industrial Revolution: An Application of Theory to the Lancashire Cotton Industry, 1770-1840. *468 pp. 12 figures. 14 tables. 1959. (2nd Impression 1960.) 50s.*

Williams, Gertrude. Recruitment to Skilled Trades. *240 pp. 1957. 23s.*

Young, A. F. Industrial Injuries Insurance: an Examination of British Policy. *192 pp. 1964. 30s.*

ANTHROPOLOGY

Ammar, Hamed. Growing up in an Egyptian Village: Silwa, Province of Aswan. *336 pp. 1954. (2nd Impression 1966.) 35s.*

Crook, David and Isabel. Revolution in a Chinese Village: Ten Mile Inn. *230 pp. 8 plates. 1 map. 1959. (2nd Impression 1968.) 21s.*
The First Years of Yangyi Commune. *302 pp. 12 plates. 1966. 42s.*

Dickie-Clark, H. F. The Marginal Situation. A Sociological Study of a Coloured Group. *236 pp. 1966. 40s.*

Dube, S. C. Indian Village. *Foreword by Morris Edward Opler. 276 pp. 4 plates. 1955. (5th Impression 1965.) 25s.*
India's Changing Villages: Human Factors in Community Development. *260 pp. 8 plates. 1 map. 1958. (3rd Impression 1963.) 25s.*

Firth, Raymond. Malay Fishermen. Their Peasant Economy. *420 pp. 17 pp. plates. 2nd edition revised and enlarged 1966. (2nd Impression 1968.) 55s.*

Gulliver, P. H. The Family Herds. A Study of two Pastoral Tribes in East Africa, The Jie and Turkana. *304 pp. 4 plates. 19 figures. 1955. (2nd Impression with new preface and bibliography 1966.) 35s.*
Social Control in an African Society: a Study of the Arusha, Agricultural Masai of Northern Tanganyika. *320 pp. 8 plates. 10 figures. 1963. (2nd Impression 1968.) 42s.*

Ishwaran, K. Shivapur. A South Indian Village. *216 pp. 1968. 35s.*
Tradition and Economy in Village India: An Interactionist Approach. *Foreword by Conrad Arensburg. 176 pp. 1966. (2nd Impression 1968.) 25s.*

Jarvie, Ian C. The Revolution in Anthropology. *268 pp. 1964. (2nd Impression 1967.) 40s.*

Jarvie, Ian C. and **Agassi, Joseph.** Hong Kong. A Society in Transition. *396 pp. Illustrated with plates and maps. 1968. 56s.*

Little, Kenneth L. Mende of Sierra Leone. *308 pp. and folder. 1951. Revised edition 1967. 63s.*

Lowie, Professor Robert H. Social Organization. *494 pp. 1950. (4th Impression 1966.) 50s.*

Mayer, Adrian C. Caste and Kinship in Central India: A Village and its Region. *328 pp. 16 plates. 15 figures. 16 tables. 1960. (2nd Impression 1965.) 35s.*
Peasants in the Pacific: A Study of Fiji Indian Rural Society. *232 pp. 16 plates. 10 figures. 14 tables. 1961. 35s.*

Smith, Raymond T. The Negro Family in British Guiana: Family Structure and Social Status in the Villages. *With a Foreword by Meyer Fortes. 314 pp. 8 plates. 1 figure. 4 maps. 1956. (2nd Impression 1965.) 35s.*

DOCUMENTARY

Meek, Dorothea L. (Ed.). Soviet Youth: Some Achievements and Problems. *Excerpts from the Soviet Press, translated by the editor. 280 pp. 1957. 28s.*

Schlesinger, Rudolf (Ed.). Changing Attitudes in Soviet Russia.
2. The Nationalities Problem and Soviet Administration. Selected Readings on the Development of Soviet Nationalities Policies. *Introduced by the editor. Translated by W. W. Gottlieb. 324 pp. 1956. 30s.*

Reports of the Institute of Community Studies

(Demy 8vo.)

Cartwright, Ann. Human Relations and Hospital Care. *272 pp. 1964. 30s.*

Patients and their Doctors. A Study of General Practice. *304 pp. 1967. 40s.*

Jackson, Brian. Streaming: an Education System in Miniature. *168 pp. 1964. (2nd Impression 1966.) 21s. Paper 10s.*

Jackson, Brian and **Marsden, Dennis.** Education and the Working Class: Some General Themes raised by a Study of 88 Working-class Children in a Northern Industrial City. *268 pp. 2 folders. 1962. (4th Impression 1968.) 32s.*

Marris, Peter. Widows and their Families. *Foreword by Dr. John Bowlby. 184 pp. 18 tables. Statistical Summary. 1958. 18s.*

Family and Social Change in an African City. A Study of Rehousing in Lagos. *196 pp. 1 map. 4 plates. 53 tables. 1961. (2nd Impression 1966.) 30s.*

The Experience of Higher Education. *232 pp. 27 tables. 1964. 25s.*

Marris, Peter and **Rein, Martin.** Dilemmas of Social Reform. Poverty and Community Action in the United States. *256 pp. 1967. 35s.*

Mills, Enid. Living with Mental Illness: a Study in East London. *Foreword by Morris Carstairs. 196 pp. 1962. 28s.*

Runciman, W. G. Relative Deprivation and Social Justice. A Study of Attitudes to Social Inequality in Twentieth Century England. *352 pp. 1966. (2nd Impression 1967.) 40s.*

Townsend, Peter. The Family Life of Old People: An Inquiry in East London. *Foreword by J. H. Sheldon. 300 pp. 3 figures. 63 tables. 1957. (3rd Impression 1967.) 30s.*

Willmott, Peter. Adolescent Boys in East London. *230 pp. 1966. 30s.*

The Evolution of a Community: a study of Dagenham after forty years. *168 pp. 2 maps. 1963. 21s.*

Willmott, Peter and **Young, Michael.** Family and Class in a London Suburb. *202 pp. 47 tables. 1960. (4th Impression 1968.) 25s.*

Young, Michael. Innovation and Research in Education. *192 pp. 1965. 25s. Paper 12s. 6d.*

Young, Michael and **McGeeney, Patrick.** Learning Begins at Home. A Study of a Junior School and its Parents. *About 128 pp. 1968. 21s. Paper 14s.*

Young, Michael and **Willmott, Peter.** Family and Kinship in East London. *Foreword by Richard M. Titmuss. 252 pp. 39 tables. 1957. (3rd Impression 1965.) 28s.*

The British Journal of Sociology. *Edited by Terence P. Morris. Vol. 1, No. 1, March 1950 and Quarterly. Roy. 8vo., £3 annually, 15s. a number, post free. (Vols. 1-18, £8 each. Individual parts £2 10s.*

All prices are net and subject to alteration without notice

1268 H.B.